Distinguished African American Political and Governmental Leaders

by
James Haskins

Foreword by
Eleanor Holmes Norton

Oryx Press
1999

The rare Arabian Oryx is believed to have inspired the myth of the unicorn. This desert antelope became virtually extinct in the early 1960s. At that time, several groups of international conservationists arranged to have nine animals sent to the Phoenix Zoo to be the nucleus of a captive breeding herd. Today, the Oryx population is over 1,000, and over 500 have been returned to the Middle East.

Published by The Oryx Press
4041 North Central at Indian School Road
Phoenix, Arizona 85012-3397

Published simultaneously in Canada
Printed and bound in the United States of America

∞ The paper used in this publication meets the minimum requirements of American National Standard for Information Science—Permanence of Paper for Printed Library Materials, ANSI Z39.48, 1984.

Library of Congress Cataloging-in-Publication Data

Haskins, James, 1941–
Distinguished African American political and governmental leaders / by James Haskins.
p. cm.
Includes bibliographical references and index.
ISBN 1-57356-126-6 (alk. paper)
1. Afro-American politicians—Biography. 2. Afro-Americans—Politics and government. 3. Afro-American leadership. 4. Afro-Americans—Biography. I. Title.
E185.61.H359 1999
973'.0496073'092—dc21 98-55071
[B] CIP

Contents

Foreword

by Congresswoman Eleanor Holmes Norton

Not very long ago, a book titled *Distinguished African American Political and Governmental Leaders* would have been very thin indeed. Denial of opportunity to African Americans translated directly into exclusion from influential positions of all kinds. Nowhere was this discrimination more pronounced and less defensible than in government and politics, the domain of democracy. Private and personal bias is shameful. Official discrimination and systematic exclusion by government itself make a mockery of representative government and preclude democratic participation.

There are many ways to tell the story of race in America—the course of the civil rights movement, the path of court decisions, the heroism of particular Americans, for example. It is also possible to tell the history of the slow but increasingly sure decline of official racism by reading between the lines of the lives of African American elected and appointed officials and political leaders, some of them profiled in this unique volume. By selecting a group among the many African American public officials who have distinguished themselves, James Haskins has offered readers an intriguing way to view black history and the history of our country.

The names and posts of the black officials profiled here come unevenly in larger numbers as time moves toward the present. Their positions ripen with importance. Today, racism in America grasps at straws and demonstrates considerable resilience, but the pull and prominence of black public officials is a powerful response. Government officials are proxies for the state; when they are black, they reverse the historic role of the state in American racism.

That reversal began in earnest hardly 50 years ago with the 1954 Supreme Court decision in *Brown v. Board of Education*, after which sponsored discrimination could not be constitutionally maintained. However, even school segregation, the direct object of the *Brown* decision, did not succumb for years or without "massive resistance."

The struggle against discrimination in government has required a long and varied line of strategies. One of the most successful has been the election and appointment of African Americans to confront directly the problems that result from racial exclusion. Indispensable to the elimination of the stereotypes that perpetuate discrimination is the opportunity for excluded people to hold the same positions as those who have historically excluded them. This compilation begins with the earliest officials, when the numbers were especially low.

Only in recent decades have even ordinary jobs in federal, state, and local government been available to blacks. Leadership positions in government, like those of the African Americans in these pages, were almost always off limits. Extraordinary black pioneers broke through here and there, and their lives and contributions are found in this book. For the most part, however, federal government positions with significant decision-making authority or control of substantial funds were unavailable to blacks until the 1960s. At local and state levels, African Americans were elected as they migrated away from the South, but they could represent only black areas created by segregated housing patterns. State and local appointed officials fared no better and often even worse. Federal appointed officials, such as Justice Thurgood Marshall, who in 1967 became the first African American Supreme Court justice, and Department of Housing and Urban Development secretary Robert Weaver, who in 1966 became the first black cabinet official, made history. Today, it's difficult to imagine the Supreme Court without an African American justice. The new standard for the cabinet and the upper level federal ranks is that they "look like America."

The rise of the African American voter as a national factor in American political life is chiefly responsible for the increasing number of African American elected and appointed officials throughout the country. The direct connection between black voters and black elected officials, especially in the South, of course, is clear. The link between black voters and black *appointed* officials may seem more attenuated. However, black appointed officials, such as those whose contributions are chronicled here, are often directly traceable to the strength of the black vote. White politicians, such as President George Bush, who made Colin Powell the first black chairman of the Joint Chiefs of Staff, and President Bill Clinton, who appointed Ron Brown the first black secretary of commerce, recognize that their own election prospects may be enhanced by acknowledging the importance that African Americans attach to appointments of blacks to leadership positions.

The significance of the black vote to the increasing number of black elected and appointed officials results from the coherence of the vote. The reason for this voter coherence is both strategic and historic. Strategically, a virtual unity among voters on many issues magnifies the African American vote beyond its numbers and makes the vote more valuable in achieving African American goals than otherwise would be the case. One of the most important and persistent goals of the black community has been the elimination of the discrimination that has blocked the election and appointment of government officials who would be most likely to give priority to the problems of African Americans.

Historically, the cause of the coherent African American vote is denial of the vote and discrimination in its exercise. As a result of very long periods of slavery and discrimination, African Americans often perceive issues such as economics and discrimination in the same way because their color has ensured that they would be treated in the same way.

Thus, whether in politics or art, in religion or higher education, black history is woven into the worldview of the African American community. Slavery, which lasted for almost 250 years, and discrimination, which persists until today, have had enduring effects on African Americans and on America. European immigrants, almost all of whom initially experienced harsh discrimination, assimilated into equality, and their original entry into the country is seldom reflected in their voting patterns. Equality has come the hard way for African Americans because of the way they came to the country and because the effects of that entry have resulted in persistent discrimination. Race and racism merged with the culture. Segregating blacks from typical American patterns ensured the development of self-protective responses, none more important than voting patterns. These patterns have been central to increases in the numbers of both elected and appointed officials, such as those who appear in the pages that follow.

In the past few decades, the 1965 Voting Rights Act has been the prime vehicle for the determination of African Americans to increase their leadership in government. This book chronicles 103 of the "firsts"; some from today, others from history, and still others who have distinguished themselves in various ways. Many owe their election or appointment not only to their own qualifications, hard work, and dedication, but also, directly or indirectly, to the Voting Rights Act. Beginning in 1970, when the first statistics are available, there were only 1,469 black elected officials; now there are 8,658. The four states that lead in the number of black elected officials are all in the South—in order of rank: Mississippi, Alabama, Louisiana, and Georgia—unthinkable before the Voting Rights Act. The states in which the most significant increases have occurred and those with the largest numbers of elected officials are directly traceable to the Voting Rights Act. The correlation between the Act and the rising number of appointed officials also is inescapable.

None of us would envy James Haskins the task of choosing 103 African American officials from the long history of so many we have cause to recognize. He has completed a selective but intelligent guide to African American officials. This book will be for some a reference, for others a text, and for still others a good read or a book to thumb through. The volume will serve a wide cross-section of readers and institutions. This much is sure: James Haskins has given us an important new entryway into black history and thus into much of American history that, through efforts like his, only now are rising in visibility.

Preface

The African American historian, poet, and novelist Walter Dean Myers writes,

> What we understand of our history is what we understand of ourselves. If it has come down to us that we are wonderful beings, blessed with all the gifts needed to succeed, then we will naturally seek that success. If we believe that we are fully deserving of the rights to life, liberty, and the pursuit of happiness, then we will fight to retain those rights. (ix)

Distinguished African American Political and Governmental Leaders is a compilation of the lives of many of those men and women who believed that they and all African Americans were and are fully deserving of the rights to life, liberty, and the pursuit of happiness. These are individuals who have fought and who continue to fight within the political arena to strengthen those rights for all.

While there were and are many men and women in politics deserving of recognition for their contributions to black America and to the United States as a whole, the 104 selected for inclusion here were or are leaders who have excelled in their chosen careers in public office and/or marked the path for others to follow. That is, all persons included in this book held either appointed or elected office and either distinguished themselves in office or were the first black persons to be appointed or elected to their positions. **Joseph Hayne Rainey** (1831–1887), for example, was the first black congressman from South Carolina and the first African American to preside over a session of the House of Representatives, demonstrating black leadership in his day. **James Charles Evers** (1922–) was elected the first black mayor of Fayette, Mississippi, in 1969, an event marking the powerful influence of the civil rights movement in the South in the 1960s. Like these two men, the men and women included in this volume did not shy from taking leading roles, but bravely conquered opposition and, at times, overcame violence to achieve their goals.

Arranged alphabetically, *Distinguished African American Political and Governmental Leaders* profiles those from both the past and present, from the early nineteenth century to 1998. Although a few African Americans held minor governmental posts before 1869 when Joseph Rainey was sworn into office—William C. Nell (1816–1874), for instance, was the first black person to hold a federal position (postal clerk in Boston in 1861)—blacks did not become an influential part of government until Reconstruction after the Civil War (Smith 153). African Americans entering the political arena then came from the South and often declared their candidacies at the risk of their own lives to gain a voice in government. Toward the end of the nineteenth century, however, that voice began to fade as southern Reconstruction crumbled and white supremacy reasserted itself. The voice fell completely silent in 1901 when George H. White, a congressman from North Carolina and the last black person in Congress in the nineteenth century, completed his term in office and failed to be reelected. It was not until **Oscar Stanton De Priest** won a seat in Congress from the state of Illinois in 1928 that African Americans regained representation on the federal level. What De Priest began in the early twentieth century gained momentum until today. African Americans are well represented on all levels of government and in every state of the union. Students and scholars of politics and African American history, as well as general readers, will find in *Distinguished African American Political and Governmental Leaders* not only insight into the individual lives of these people but, collectively, a portrait of a struggle for freedom and equality spanning more than a century.

Each of the biographies in this book contains sections on birth, status, education, and positions held, including dates and locations, in easy-to-scan lists. The profiles also cover in more detail leaders' early years, higher education, and career highlights. Specifically, information includes parents' names and backgrounds, schools attended, awards and honors, membership and affiliations, positions and offices held, important actions or achievements, anecdotes and quotes, marriages and spouses' names, children's births and names, and deaths and burials, where applicable. Many of the sources that follow each profile include Web sites for easy access to further information; a general bibliography lists all sources in the book. Four appendixes categorize leaders by birth date, position, state, and party affiliation. In addition, cross-references are provided in bold to lead readers to related profiles in this work.

The biographies included here are drawn from a wide variety of sources, both print and electronic. At times, approximations of dates or other information are given because many of the early records concerning particular African Americans in the United States are fragmentary. Up until the middle of the twentieth century what history African Americans had was frequently dependent upon these fragments and upon memory. Amid the shelves and shelves of histories on the making of America, there seemed to be little room for black America. For the most part, black history lived not in books, but in the remembrances of those who lived it, knew its value, and shared it with others orally.

In the last 50 years, however, a dramatic change has occurred. Historians have sought out the old records, listened to the voices of the past, and documented African American involvement in the making of the United States, pushing aside some of the books on the shelves to make room for the truth. The intent of *Distinguished African American Political and Governmental Leaders* is to build upon that truth, to introduce the past to the readers of today and of tomorrow. Readers are invited to propose additional African American government and political leaders for inclusion in subsequent editions of this book. Please send your nominations to James Haskins; The Oryx Press; 4041 N. Central, Suite 700; Phoenix, Arizona 85012.

Sources

Myers, Walter Dean. *Now Is Your Time! The African-American Struggle for Freedom*. New York: HarperCollins, 1991.

Smith, Jessie Carney, ed. *Black Firsts: 2,000 Years of Extraordinary Achievement*. Detroit, MI: Visible Ink Press, 1994.

Profiles

Benjamin William Arnett

Born: 1838 in Brownsville, Pennsylvania

Status: Died October 9, 1906, in Wilberforce, Ohio; buried in Tarbox Cemetery, Wilberforce, Ohio

Education: Attended a one-room school near Brownsville, Pennsylvania; received a teaching certificate, December 19, 1863; licensed to preach in the African Methodist Episcopal (AME) Church, March 30, 1865

Position: Teacher, Fayette County, Pennsylvania, c. 1863; teacher and principal, Washington, D.C., 1864–1865; teacher, Brownsville, Pennsylvania, 1865–1867; minister, Walnut Hills, Ohio, 1867–1869; ordained deacon in the AME Church, April 30, 1868; ordained an elder in the AME Church, May 12, 1870; minister, St. Paul AME Church, Urbana, Illinois, 1870–1872; minister, AME Church, Columbus, Ohio, 1878–1879; assistant secretary of the Ohio Annual Conference to the General Conference, AME Church, 1876; general secretary of the Ohio Conference to the General Conference, AME Church, 1880; elected to the Ohio legislature, 1886; elected financial secretary of the General Conference of the AME Church, 1880–1888; elected bishop in the AME Church, 1888; bishop to the Seventh Episcopal District, South Carolina, 1888–1892; bishop to the Fourth Episcopal District (Indiana, Illinois, Iowa, and northwestern states), 1892–1900; bishop to the Third Episcopal District of Ohio, California, and Pittsburgh, 1900–1904; bishop, First Episcopal District, 1904–1906

Early Years

Benjamin William Arnett was born in 1838 (exact date unknown) in Brownsville, Pennsylvania. He was "eight parts Negro, six parts Scotch, one part Indian, and one part Irish" (Logan and Winston 17). Arnett's father, Benjamin Arnett, Sr., was a minister in the African Methodist Episcopal (AME) Church and had built the first AME Church in Brownsville.

Arnett's father, being educated himself, wished to see his son similarly schooled. Arnett's uncle, Ephram Arnett, conducted a one-room schoolhouse for black children near Brownsville, and Arnett was sent there at an early age to learn to read and write. He did well, but could see no way that he could continue his education; he had little money, and few colleges took African American students at that time.

Career Highlights

Although educated for the times, Arnett lacked opportunities, and so began his working life doing what many others like him were doing: loading and unloading wagons; working on the steamboats that plied the Ohio and Mississippi Rivers; and waiting on tables in various hotels. But his life was to change drastically.

In March, 1858, Arnett was diagnosed as having a tumor on his leg and, as dictated by the primitive medicine of the day, his leg was amputated. He could no longer do hard labor; he had to find work that would not require two good legs.

That same year, on May 25, 1858, Arnett married Mary Louisa Gordon. Over the years to come, the couple would have seven children—five boys and two girls.

During the 1800s and almost into the twentieth century, teachers did not necessarily have to attend and graduate from a school that taught education. Many communities, after testing a young person who wished to become a teacher, would issue that person a teaching certificate and set him or her to work in the local school. Arnett, unable to do heavy work or to fight in the Civil War that was then raging, was able to obtain such a teaching certificate on December 19, 1863. For a brief period, he taught in Fayette County, Pennsylvania, as the county's first black teacher. From 1864 to 1865, he taught and held the position of principal in a school in Washington, D.C., before returning to his hometown of Brownsville to teach until 1867.

In 1856, Arnett had followed his father into the African Methodist Episcopal Church and, while in Washington, D.C., had become active in the church. On March 30, 1865, while attending the Baltimore Annual Conference of the church in Washington, Arnett was licensed to preach. Upon returning to his home in Pennsylvania, he decided to devote his life to the church, giving up teaching and taking up the ministry full time. He received his first appointment from the church on April 19, 1867, as minister of the Walnut Hill AME Church in Ohio.

In the years that followed, Arnett rose within the church hierarchy from deacon all the way to bishop, the highest office of the AME Church. Arnett traveled from ministry to ministry throughout Ohio and Illinois with his wife and children. Upon assuming the office of bishop, he presided over the Seventh Episcopal District of South Carolina from 1888 to 1892; the Fourth Episcopal District (Indiana, Illinois, Iowa, and northwestern states) from 1892 to 1900; the Third Episcopal District (Ohio, California, and Pittsburgh) from 1900 to 1904; and the First Episcopal District from 1904 to 1906.

During the years of his ministry, Arnett was active both socially and politically. He founded a number of fraternal organizations for African American men and women and spoke eloquently on both religious issues and the political issue of black equality. In 1885, he was elected to the legislature of Ohio by a narrow margin of eight votes, becoming the first black state legislator elected to represent a majority white constituency. During his tenure in office, 1886–1887, he helped legislate against Ohio's "Black Laws," which restricted blacks socially and politically. He also met William McKinley, Jr., who would go on to be elected president. Arnett later presented McKinley with the Bible that was used when McKinley took his oath of office in 1897. During President McKinley's administration (1897–1901), Arnett was said to be the most "powerful individual Negro at the White House" (Logan and Winston 18).

In his later years, Arnett served on a number of religious and educational councils, in addition to overseeing his bishopric. Among other things, he was appointed director of Payne Theological Seminary at Wilberforce, Ohio. He built a home at Wilberforce University that was called "Tawawa Chimney Corner" because it was located near Tawawa Springs, named by early Native Americans. Arnett died there of uremia at the age of 68, on October 9, 1906.

Sources

Kestenbaum, Lawrence. *Political Graveyard: A Database of Historical Cemeteries*, rev. 1/13/98. <http://www.potifos.com/tpg.html>. Accessed: 1/17/98.

Logan, Rayford W., and Michael R. Winston, eds. *Dictionary of American Negro Biography*. New York: W.W. Norton and Co., 1982.

Ploski, Harry A., and James Williams, eds. *The Negro Almanac: A Reference Work on the African American*. Detroit, MI: Gale Research, 1989.

Hannah Diggs Atkins

Born: November 1, 1923, in Winston-Salem, North Carolina

Status: Retired from public office

Education: B.A., 1943, Saint Augustine's College, Raleigh, North Carolina; B.L.S., 1949, University of Chicago, Chicago, Illinois; studied at Oklahoma City University School of Law, Oklahoma City, Oklahoma; M.P.A., 1989, University of Oklahoma, Norman

Position: Reporter, teacher, biochemical researcher, school librarian; law librarian, chief librarian, general reference division, Library of the Oklahoma State Legislature, 1949–1969; state representative, Oklahoma State Legislature, 1969–1980; delegate, 35th Assembly, United Nations, 1980; assistant director of Human Services, State of Oklahoma, 1983–1987; cabinet secretary of human services, State of Oklahoma, 1987–1991; secretary of state of Oklahoma, 1987–1991

Early Years

Hannah Diggs Atkins was born on November 1, 1923, in Winston-Salem, North Carolina, to James Thackeray Diggs and Mabel Kennedy Diggs. Growing up in North Carolina in the 1920s and 1930s was harsh for everyone, with the Depression affecting jobs and life in general during the 1930s, but it was particularly harsh for blacks. Not only was employment nearly nonexistent, but African Americans had difficulty obtaining even basic political rights. In 1927, for example, a case was brought before the Supreme Court, *Nixon v. Herndon* (also known as the "Texas White Primary Case"). In the case, a black resident of El Paso, Texas, sued the state of Texas for refusing to allow him to vote in a Democratic primary. The state had a law on its books that stated "in no event shall a Negro be eligible to participate in a Democratic party primary election held in the state of Texas" (Commager 217). The Supreme Court ruled that the Texas law violated not only the 15th Amendment of the Constitution, but also the 14th.

Texas was not alone in enforcing such laws, and where these laws did not exist, often there were other, more violent means to keep African Americans from exercising their voting rights. As Darlene Hine reports, Hannah Diggs Atkins became interested in politics from "watching her father coming home late at night bloody and beaten for trying to vote during her childhood . . ." (52). Atkins determined at an early age that she would make a difference in how blacks were treated in the United States both politically and generally.

Higher Education

Atkins attended segregated schools in North Carolina and, upon graduation from high school, attended Saint Augustine's College in Raleigh, North Carolina. When she graduated in 1943 with a bachelor of arts degree, she wished to continue her education. However, the United States was in the midst of World War II, and money was tight. Between working and studying, it would be six more years before she would graduate with a bachelor's degree in library science from the University of Chicago. She would later study at Oklahoma City University School of Law, and the University of Oklahoma in Norman, Oklahoma, from which she would receive an M.P.A. in 1989. During the early 1950s she married Charles N. Atkins, and they had three children: Edmund Earl, Charles, and Valerie Ann.

Career Highlights

Atkins and her family did not feel out of place when they moved to Oklahoma, because the state had a significant African American population. During Reconstruction, many blacks had migrated to Kansas and Oklahoma, setting up black communities in an effort to find freedom and opportunity. Although there had been black representation in state government, until Atkins was elected to the Oklahoma State Legislature in 1969, there had never been a black woman elected to the state house of representatives.

During the years before Atkins entered the political arena, she held a number of jobs, including reporter, teacher, and biochemical researcher. Once she received her degree in library science, she worked as a school librarian, law librarian, and then chief librarian of the general reference division of the library of the Oklahoma State Legislature. While working in the latter position, she decided to run for office.

In the 1960s huge strides in civil rights were taking place, and Atkins wanted her voice to be heard. She had worked diligently on the political sidelines in voter registration drives and with the Democratic National Committee. Now it was time, she felt, to jump into the fray. With her election in 1969, her job in the legislature, as she said, was to be a "gadfly to prick the moral conscience of the legislators" (Hine 53). For the next 11 years, until her retirement from the legislature in 1980, Atkins fought for civil rights and improvement in education, mental health, employment, housing, women's rights, and child care for her constituents.

After stepping down from office, Atkins's career did not end. In 1980, President Jimmy Carter named her a delegate to the 35th Assembly of the United Nations. In 1983, she was appointed assistant director of the Oklahoma Department of Human Services, putting into effect much of the legislation she had promoted as a representative. In 1987, she held the joint appointments of Oklahoma secretary of state and cabinet secretary of human resources. With these appointments, she became the first African American to hold a cabinet position in Oklahoma.

Sources

Commager, Henry Steele, ed. *Documents of American History, Volume II: Since 1898*. New York: Appleton-Century-Crofts, 1963.

Hine, Darlene Clark, ed. *Black Women in America: An Historical Encyclopedia*, Vol. I, A–L. Brooklyn, NY: Carlson Publishing Co., 1993.

B

Marion S. Barry, Jr.

Reproduced from AP/WideWorld Photos, by Wilfredo Lee

Born: March 6, 1936, in Itta Bena, Mississippi

Status: Mayor, Washington, D.C.

Education: B.S. in chemistry, LeMoyne College, Memphis, Tennessee; M.S. in chemistry, Fisk University, Nashville, Tennessee; entered the doctoral program in chemistry, University of Tennessee, Knoxville

Position: Cofounder, national chairman, Student Non-Violent Coordinating Committee (SNCC), 1960–1965; director, SNCC, Washington, D.C., 1965–c. 1970; founder, Pride, Inc., Washington, D.C., 1967; board member, president, board of education, Washington, D.C., 1971–1974; member, city council, Washington, D.C., 1974–1978, 1992–1994; mayor, Washington, D.C., 1978–1990, 1994–

Early Years

Marion S. Barry was born on March 6, 1936, in Itta Bena, Mississippi. When Barry was four years old, his father, a Delta sharecropper, died, and his mother, Mattie Cummings, moved the family to Memphis, Tennessee. It was a place, Barry said, where "nobody went anywhere except reform school or jail" (Riley, "A Bright, Broken Promise").

Barry's mother worked as a domestic to support him and his two sisters, but life was hard. Barry, who had ambition and drive at an early age, worked hard in the public schools of Memphis. He also joined the Boy Scouts and devoted himself to moving up in rank to an Eagle Scout. As a teenager, he took various jobs, selling newspapers, waiting on tables, and even picking cotton. The money he earned helped the family a bit, but he used much of it to buy himself "the trappings of status." While in high school he "bought a $50 suit from a store on Memphis's Beale Street" (Riley, "A Bright, Broken Promise"). Barry always desired the good life, an ambition that would cause trouble later in life.

Barry was keenly aware of and angry at the color barrier that existed at that time. According to a profile in *Time Magazine* in 1990, "As a teenager, Barry tossed cups at whites from a movie-theater balcony and sat in the front of the bus" (Riley, "A Bright, Broken Promise"). His desire for equality would plunge him directly into the midst of the civil rights protests in the late 1950s and 1960s.

Higher Education

Barry entered LeMoyne-Owen University in Memphis on a scholarship. It was there that he began to emerge as a leader in civil rights. During his undergraduate years, he and a number of other students tried to desegregate the Memphis buses, lunch counters, and even the county fair (Riley, "A Bright, Broken Promise"). He carried his protests with him to graduate school at Fisk University in Nashville, Tennessee, and later to the University of Tennessee at Knoxville. He was becoming more and more involved in the civil rights protests, however, and left the doctoral program to work on voter registration drives in the South, cofounding and becoming the first national chairman of the Student Nonviolent Coordinating Committee (SNCC).

Career Highlights

During the 1960s, Barry was at the forefront of most of the marches and protests. Yet, even then, some doubted his sincerity to the cause of civil rights. Charlie Cobb, a former SNCC worker said of Barry in 1990, "He's enamored of the perks and privileges of position. I see very little difference between him now and twenty years ago" (Riley, "A Bright, Broken Promise").

In late 1965, Barry moved to Washington, D.C., where he organized a "mancott" of the city bus system and became director of SNCC. In 1967, he founded Pride, Inc., an agency that found jobs for unemployed black youths. Word got out that Barry, in his colorful dashiki, really cared about the poor and the disenfranchised and was one person who worked to make things better.

In 1971, Barry was elected to the Washington, D.C., board of education, serving as its president for three years. In 1974, he left the school board after winning a seat on Washington's first elected city council (previously, Washington was governed by Congress, which also appointed most of the city's officials). On the city council, Barry chaired the Committee on Finance and Revenue, which gave him a clear picture of the city's numerous financial woes.

In 1978, Barry decided to run for mayor. He had the support of the blacks, Hispanics, and white liberals of the city, which enabled him to defeat two other strong contenders for the position. During his first term as mayor, Barry balanced Washington's budget, lured businesses into downtown Washington, and began a successful youth-jobs program that eventually became the Marion Barry, Jr., Youth Leadership Institute. He also pushed for housing for low- and moderate-income families and established day care centers for government employees.

Barry was elected to a second term in office but began to get a reputation for womanizing, and many felt he was more arrogant and less responsive to his contituents. "Allegations of cocaine use began to dog Barry after he made a 1981 visit to a topless club. He claimed he was soliciting campaign contributions" (Riley, "'You Set Me Up!'"). That same year, a drug dealer named Charles Lewis was arrested and sentenced to 15 months in prison; during his trial, Lewis claimed Barry smoked crack with him, an accusation Barry denied.

It was during his third term as mayor, however, that he was propelled into the national spotlight. Again, rumors of womanizing were rampant, accompanied by stories of drug use. He was accused of putting his friends and relatives on the city payrolls. Two of Barry's deputy mayors and 10 other top officials were convicted of corruption. Previously, his second wife had been convicted for misusing federal funds while at Pride, Inc. There were charges that Barry was manipulating the city's minority business contracts. "The contracting process," one city official told *Time* reporter Michael Riley, "is the conduit by which the resources of the city are funneled into a revenue stream that constitutes the lifeblood of Barry's invisible empire. What you've got is a bunch of guys who don't mind wasting a million bucks to make sure one of theirs gets $200,000" (Riley, "A Bright, Broken Promise"). In response to the charges coming from all sides, Barry denied everything, saying, "If all this corruption was going on, I should be in jail" (Riley, "A Bright, Broken Promise").

On January 18, 1990, three days before Barry planned to announce his intention to run for a fourth term as mayor, he was arrested. That evening, Barry attended a ceremony to choose the winners in a homestead auction, then went to room 727 of the Vista International Hotel in Washington with two women: Rasheeda Moore, a model and friend of Barry's who had informed on him to the FBI; and an undercover FBI agent. Unbeknownst to Barry, the room had hidden video cameras, and under the camera's unflinching eye, Moore sold Barry $60 worth of crack cocaine supplied by the Drug Enforcement Administration. "Barry allegedly put the crack in a pipe and smoked it. As soon as he took a few puffs, FBI agents and Washington police made the arrest. According to a police official, Barry shrieked at Moore, 'You set me up!'" (Riley, "'You Set Me Up!'"). Although Barry initially said to the press that he intended to continue fulfilling his mayoral duties, after consulting with his advisors the next day, he turned most of his duties over to city administrator Carol Thompson.

Barry was indicted on six counts of misdemeanor drug offenses in May of 1990, and after his trial the following November, he was convicted of one count of cocaine possession and sentenced to six months in prison, a $5,000 fine, and one year of probation. To many, this appeared to be the end of Marion Barry's career in politics and in Washington.

Those who predicted Barry's political demise, however, had not reckoned with his determination and drive—and his grassroots popularity in the city of Washington. After serving his sentence, Barry ran successfully for city council in 1992, and in 1994 again ran for mayor, defeating city council member John Ray and incumbent mayor **Sharon Pratt Dixon Kelly** in a Democratic primary, garnering 47 percent of the vote. He then went on to defeat Republican Carol Schwartz in the general election.

Barry, in his fourth term in office, confronted problems that had not existed during his earlier terms; the economy had declined, and the city had a large deficit. He began cutting back on some programs, and came up with a plan to privatize 75 percent of the Department of Corrections. Despite financial tourniquets, however, the city and its services to its citizens declined over the next few years. The crime rate was high, and police were ill prepared, with broken or outdated equipment. As *Maclean's* magazine reported in 1997, the public schools "did not open until Sept. 22, three weeks late, because inspectors found 11,000 fire-code violations, including leaky roofs in 43 schools . . . schools are decrepit and students have the lowest test scores of any urban area in the country" (Phillips 33). In the fall of 1997, Barry faced the ignominious position of having the federal government step in and, essentially, take over the city. *Maclean's* reported on October 13, 1997, that "The U.S. federal government has stripped the city's controversial mayor, Marion Barry, of most of his powers and handed them to an appointed control board" (Phillips 32).

Barry raged against the government's intervention in the city, declaring that "Democracy has been raped" (Phillips 32). He tried to rally residents of the city to publicly protest the takeover, but only a few hundred people, most acquaintances of Barry's, came out to demonstrate. There was little that Barry could do.

Many predicted that Barry would not run for an unprecedented fifth term in office, and he has announced that he will not. His own biography on the Washington, D.C., city Internet Web site states, however, that "The new millennium will see a new D.C. as Mayor Barry continues to facilitate downtown development and the full utilization of interactive technology within D.C. government." Many people have predicted the end of Barry's political career over the years, but he has always been the prototypical "come-back kid."

Sources

"Biography of Marion Barry, Jr." Mayor's Page. <http://www.ci.washington.dc.us/MAYOR/mayorbio.htm>. Accessed: 3/13/98.

"Marion Barry Wins D.C. Nomination." *Congressional Quarterly Weekly Report*, 17 September 1994, 2603.

"Mayor Marion S. Barry, Jr." *Congressional Times Journal*. <http://www.usbol.com/cfjournal/>. Accessed: 3/10/98.

"Milestones: Indicted. Marion S. Barry . . ." *Time Magazine*, 21 May 1990. *Time Almanac*, Reference Editon. Fort Lauderdale, FL: Compact Publishing, 1994.

"Milestones: Sentenced. Marion Barry . . ." *Time Magazine*, 5 November 1990. *Time Almanac*, Reference Edition. Fort Lauderdale, FL: Compact Publishing, 1994.

Phillips, Andrew. "A Blight at the Centre of Power." *Maclean's*, 13 October 1997, 32–33.

Riley, Michael. "A Bright, Broken Promise." *Time Magazine*, 26 June 1990. *Time Almanac*, Reference Edition. Fort Lauderdale, FL: Compact Publishing, 1994.

———. "'You Set Me Up!'" *Time Magazine*, 29 January 1990. *Time Almanac*, Reference Edition. Fort Lauderdale, FL: Compact Publishing, 1994.

Mary McLeod Bethune

Reproduced from the Collections of the Library of Congress, by Gordon Parks

Born: July 10, 1875, in Mayesville, South Carolina

Status: Died May 18, 1955

Education: Presbyterian Mission School, Mayesville, South Carolina, 1885–1887; graduate, 1893, Scotia Seminary for Negro Girls, Concord, North Carolina; graduate, 1895, Moody Bible Institute, Chicago, Illinois; the first African American to be awarded an honorary degree from a southern white college, Rollins College in Winter Park, Florida, 1946; awarded 11 honorary degrees from various institutions between 1910 and 1950

Position: Teacher, Haines Institute, Augusta, Georgia, 1895–1896; teacher, Kindell Institute, Sumter, South Carolina, 1897–1898; teacher, Palatka Mission School, Palatka, Florida, 1900–1902; founder, Daytona Normal and Industrial School for Negro Girls (renamed the Daytona Institute; after 1929, it became the Bethune-Cookman College), Daytona Beach, Florida, 1904; president, Bethune-Cookman College,

1904–1942; founder, McLeod Hospital, Daytona Beach, Florida, 1911; founder and president, Southeastern Association of Colored Women, 1920–1925; president, National Association of Colored Women, 1924–1928; appointed to the National Child Welfare Commission; appointed to the Commission on Home Building and Home Ownership; special advisor on minority affairs to President Franklin D. Roosevelt, 1935–1944; director, Division of Negro Affairs, National Youth Administration, 1936–1944; founder and president, National Council of Negro Women, 1935–1949; helped organize the Federal Council on Negro Affairs (the "Black Cabinet"), 1936; consultant to the U.S. secretary of war for selection of female officer candidates, 1942; vice president and consultant to the conference drafting the United Nations Charter, 1945; appointed to the Committee of 12 for National Defense, 1951; director, Afro-American Life Insurance Co.; president, Central Life Insurance Co.; founder and president, Bethune-Volusia Beach, Inc.

Awards and honors: Spingarn Medal, 1935; Frances A. Drexel Award, 1936; Thomas Jefferson Medal, 1942; statue erected in her honor in Lincoln Park, Washington, D.C., 1974; commemorated on a U.S. postage stamp as the first black female educator, March 5, 1985

Early Years

Mary McLeod Bethune was born the 15th of 17 children on June 10, 1875, in Mayesville, South Carolina. Her father and mother and a number of their children had been born into slavery and freed with the end of the Civil War. After the war, her father, Sam McLeod, was able to acquire a small farm of about 35 acres near Mayesville, and it was there that Bethune grew up, chopping cotton and doing other hard work.

Bethune was an intelligent child and her parents wanted her to have the opportunities that the end of the Civil War created for blacks. In 1885, Emma Wilson, a black missionary and educator, began a school in the nearby Trinity Presbyterian Church in Mayesville. Although Bethune was needed on the family farm, her parents decided that she should attend the school. Bethune learned to read and write, showing such aptitude that, in 1887, she received a scholarship to attend Scotia Seminary for Negro Girls in Concord, North Carolina, graduating in 1893.

Higher Education

When Bethune graduated from Scotia Seminary, she hoped to become a missionary and travel to Africa. With that goal in mind, she entered the Bible Institute for Home and Foreign Missions (later renamed the Moody Bible Institute) in Chicago, Illinois, graduating two years later in 1895. When she applied to the Presbyterian Mission Board for an appointment to a mission abroad, however, she was disappointed to learn that they would not accept blacks for missionary positions. Choosing virtually the only other profession open to an educated black woman, Bethune then turned to teaching as a profession.

Career Highlights

Bethune began her teaching career at the Haines Normal and Industrial Institute in Augusta, Georgia, in 1895. There she became close friends with the institute's founder, Lucy Laney, a former slave who had gone to Atlanta University soon after obtaining her freedom, graduating with its first class in 1873. Bethune said later that Laney showed her "Africans in America needed learning and Christ just as much as Negroes in Africa" (Foxworth).

After teaching a year at the Haines Institute, Bethune moved to Sumter, South Carolina, closer to her home, where she taught at the Kindell Institute. While in South Carolina, she met and married Albertus Bethune, a porter, who was five years older than she. The couple moved to Savannah, Georgia, where their son Albert was born. Albertus died in 1918.

In 1900, Bethune and her family moved to Palatka, Florida, where she established a Presbyterian elementary school for black children. In 1904, moving to the east coast of Florida, she founded the Daytona Educational and Industrial Institute with "five little girls, a dollar and a half, and faith in God" (Smith 88).

Bethune was eager to see her school succeed, working constantly to keep it afloat. She held ice cream socials and bake sales to raise money, and solicited donations from the surrounding community. Her major contributors have since become household names: James N. Gamble of Procter and Gamble and Thomas White of White Sewing Machines. By 1922, Bethune's school had become the Daytona Institute, with an enrollment of nearly 300 girls.

In 1923, Bethune's Daytona Institute merged with Cookman Institute (it was renamed Bethune-Cookman College in 1929). With the merger, the institute opened its doors to male students. Bethune was rewarded for its success in 1935, when she was awarded the NAACP's Spingarn Medal.

In addition to teaching, Bethune had become active politically during her years in Daytona. When suffrage was finally granted to women, she urged her female students and friends to take advantage of it and vote, despite threats from the local Ku Klux Klan. She also encouraged women to speak out, founding and assuming the presidency of the Southeastern Association of Colored Women in 1920. Her efforts to involve women in decision making would continue all her life with her participation in such organizations as the National Association of Colored Women, Florida State Federation of Colored Women's Clubs, National Council of Women of the U.S.A., and National Council of Negro Women, many of which she either founded or led as president.

Bethune's sphere of influence expanded beyond Florida and the areas of women's concerns and education. Soon after World War I began, Vice President Thomas Marshall invited her to Washington to solicit her views on the issue of segregation and her aid in enlisting help for the Red Cross. Her acceptance of the invitation was the first step to her involvement in national affairs. In 1930, with the Depression descending over the country, President Herbert Hoover invited Bethune to the White House Conference on Child Health and Protection. She later served on the National Child Welfare Commission and on the Home Building and Home Ownership Commission. And when President Franklin Delano Roosevelt assumed office, he also turned to her for advice. By then, Bethune was a leading spokesperson on black women's concerns and on education. From 1935 until 1944, she was a special advisor to the president on minority affairs and, in 1936, was appointed by Roosevelt as director of the Division of Negro Affairs of the National Youth Administration, making her the first black woman to head a federal office. That same year, she helped organize what was to become known in the press as the "Shadow Cabinet" or "Black Cabinet," a group of prominent African American professionals who helped influence policies regarding federal government programs for blacks.

During this time, Bethune also became close friends with the president's wife, Eleanor Roosevelt. The two women had much in common: both were strong, eloquent, intelligent women with agendas. Both defied the stereotype of a "typical" woman of the times. They were active in life outside the home, and neither fit the profile of attractiveness for a woman of her race. Since the two were close personally and politically, Bethune frequently used her connection with the first lady to promote issues and programs that she considered important.

After Roosevelt's death in 1945, Bethune's voice continued to be heard in Washington. In 1951, President Harry Truman appointed her to the Committee of 12 for National Defense, and she served as an official delegate of the United States to the second inauguration of Liberian president William V.S. Tubman in 1952. The 1950s, however, were not without trouble for Bethune. At the height of Senator Joseph

McCarthy's congressional investigation into Communism in the United States, she was labeled a "subversive." Hundreds of people who had known and admired her came quickly to her defense and protested the charges.

Mary McLeod Bethune had resigned as president of Bethune-Cookman College in 1942 to devote herself more fully to national interests. In 1950, at the age of 75, she finally retired from these tasks also and, five years later on May 18, 1955, died of a heart attack. But her legacy did not end with her death. Her memory has continued in the various memorials to her. Among these was the erection of a statue in her honor in Lincoln Park in Washington, D.C., in 1974, and the issuance, in 1985, of a postage stamp in her honor by the United States Post Office. Perhaps, however, her best memorial lies in the success and achievement of the thousands of children and young people she educated and inspired by her own determination and achievements.

Sources

Asante, Molefi K., and Mark T. Mattson, eds. *The Historical and Cultural Atlas of African Americans.* New York: Macmillan, 1991.

Family Encyclopedia of American History. Pleasantville, NY: The Reader's Digest Assoc., Inc., 1975.

Foxworth, Sharon W. "Mary McLeod Bethune." *Black History Is No Mystery.* 1996. <http://www.bkh.com/bkhallhtmfolder/2powellhtmlfolder/bethune.html>. Accessed: 3/10/98.

"Mary McLeod Bethune." *The African American Almanac,* 7th ed. Detroit, MI: Gale Research, 1997. <http://www.gale.com/gate/bhm/bethune.html>. Accessed: 2/17/98.

"Mary McLeod Bethune." *Mary McLeod Bethune Papers: The Bethune Foundation Collection. University Publications of America.* <http://www.upapubs.com/newtitle/bethune.htm#bethune>. Accessed: 2/18/98.

"Mary McLeod Bethune, Political Leader, Educator, Organizer." *Mary McLeod Bethune Home Page.* <http://www.fas.harvard.edu/-felder/bethune.html>. Accessed: 2/18/98.

"Mary McLeod Bethune." *Women in History.* <http://www.lkwdpl.org/wihohio?beth-mar.htm>. Accessed: 2/18/98.

"Meet Mrs. Bethune." *National Park Service.* <http://www.nps.gov/mamc/bethune/meet/main.htm>. Accessed: 2/18/98.

New Grolier Multimedia Encyclopedia. Novato, CA: The Software Toolworks, Inc./Grolier, Inc., 1993.

Smith, Jessie Carney, ed. *Black Heroes of the 20th Century.* Detroit, MI: Gale Research, 1992.

Lucien E. Blackwell

Reproduced from AP/Wide World Photos, by Pat Rogue

Born: August 1, 1931, in Philadelphia, Pennsylvania

Status: Resident of Philadelphia, Pennsylvania

Education: Attended Philadelphia, Pennsylvania, public schools

Position: Dock worker, foreman, Philadelphia, Pennsylvania, 1940s–1950s; trustee, vice president, business agent, president, Local 1332, International Longshoremen's Association, AFL-CIO, Philadelphia, Pennsylvania, 1960s–1990s; member, Philadelphia City Council, Philadelphia, Pennsylvania, 1974–1991; state representative for two terms, Pennsylvania State Legislature; chairman, Philadelphia Gas Commission, Philadelphia, Pennsylvania, 1980s; commissioner, Delaware River Port Authority, Philadelphia, Pennsylvania, 1980s; U.S. representative from the Second Congressional District of Pennsylvania, 1991–1994

Early Years

Lucien E. Blackwell was born in Philadelphia, Pennsylvania, on August 1, 1931. Growing up in a poor family during the Depression, there were few opportunities for a young black man. Blackwell attended the public schools in Philadelphia and then found a job on the docks of the Philadelphia waterfront.

Career Highlights

Blackwell, although young, knew people and was a persuasive speaker. Although he started out as a laborer, he soon was promoted to foreman. Becoming involved with the union on his job, he soon was elected trustee, vice president, then business agent of Local 1332 of the International Longshoremen's Association, AFL-CIO. At last, he was elected president of the union, a position he held for 18 years until his election to Congress.

As a union official, Blackwell increasingly came into contact with various local and state governmental officials, and eventually decided to enter the political arena himself. Before running for Congress, Blackwell would serve two terms in the Pennsylvania State Legislature and serve for 17 years on the council for the City of Philadelphia; he would also marry fellow council member, who became Jannie L. Blackwell.

During his tenure as a state representative, Blackwell distinguished himself by sponsoring a number of measures. He persuaded the legislature not to lower the drinking age to 18 and sponsored Resolution 67, creating a legislative panel to study Philadelphia's gang problems. The study resulted in the creation of the nationally famous Crisis Intervention Network to combat crime. Blackwell was also successful in persuading the governor to sign a bill forbidding medical experimentation on prisoners.

Because of the length of his tenure as city councilman, Blackwell's accomplishments were even greater than those he achieved in the state legislature. Drawing on his background as an African American who had grown up in Philadelphia, as well as his experience as a union official, Blackwell worked to create jobs and improve housing in the city. He sponsored the city's Human Rights Bill prohibiting discrimination on the basis of age, race, religion, sexual orientation, or national origin, and sponsored bills to support minority businesses. He also stopped the city from misusing federal housing monies by lobbying the Carter administration, and secured funding for the first homeless program in the nation. Once, during his time on the city council, Blackwell fasted for six weeks to protest the lack of police protection and lack of maintenance in the city's public housing projects. By 1990, Blackwell was majority whip and chairman of the Finance Committee of the council.

In 1991, Bill Gray, congressman from the Second Congressional District of Pennsylvania decided to step down from office to accept the job of executive director of the United Negro College Fund. At the suggestion of his supporters, Blackwell resigned his position on the city council, deciding to run in the special election held on November 5, 1991, to fill the vacancy. By then, Blackwell was well known as a man who could get things done, and he easily won the election.

In Congress, Blackwell proved to be as outspoken as he had been on the Philadelphia City Council. He continued to work to improve conditions in his home district and in cities across the country. In Philadelphia, he created the Second Congressional District Drug Think Tank—a coalition of community activists, religious leaders, and public officials—to try to combat the growing drug problems in the city. In Congress, Blackwell sponsored legislation to protect the credit ratings of those who had been laid off as a result of the recession of 1987, and he was appointed by President Bill Clinton and House Speaker Tom Foley to a special task force on homelessness in the United States.

In 1994, Blackwell ran for reelection and, despite his impressive record of action in Congress, was defeated by Chaka Fattah in the Democratic primary; Fattah would go on to win the general election for the Second District. Blackwell returned to Philadelphia where, as of this writing, he resides with his wife in the University City section of the city.

Sources

Clay, William L. *Just Permanent Interests: Black Americans in Congress, 1870–1991*. New York: Amistad Press, 1992.

"Former Black Members of Congress." *Congressional Times Journal*. <http://www.usbol.com/ctjournal/FrBlkCongMemList.html>. Accessed:2/26/98.

Unita Z. Blackwell

Born: March 18, 1933, in Lula, Mississippi

Status: Mayor, Mayersville, Mississippi

Education: M.A. in regional planning, 1983, University of Massachusetts, Amherst; recipient of an honorary doctor of law, University of Massachusetts, 1995

Position: Field-worker, 1950s; organizer, Mississippi Freedom Democratic Party, 1964; mayor, Mayersville, Mississippi, 1976–1993; vice chairwoman, Mississippi Democratic Party, 1976–1980; national president, U.S.-China People's Friendship Association, 1977–1983; appointed to the U.S. National Commission on the International Year of the Child, 1979; president, National Conference of Black Mayors, 1990–1992; Bateman alumna in residence, University of Massachusetts, Amherst, 1990; recipient of the 1992 MacArthur Fellowship, MacArthur Foundation; Mayor, Mayersville, Mississippi, 1997–

Early Years

Unita Blackwell was born in Lula, Mississippi, on March 18, 1933. Much of her childhood was rootless as her parents were poor sharecroppers. The Great Depression had hit the South hard, and the family traveled from place to place throughout the area searching for work. Blackwell would have liked to go to school like other children, but dropped out in the eighth grade because the family needed any money she could earn. The jobs she held, chopping cotton in Mississippi and peeling tomatoes in Florida, were hard labor and paid poorly. The first time Blackwell settled down was when she was 30 years old and a mother. She lived in a three-room shack in Mayersville, Mississippi. Later, she was able to build a large, modern brick house, but she kept the shack, saying, "I'm grateful for this house . . . I kept it because it reminded me of where I came from" (Phelps 11).

Higher Education

Only much later in life was she able to gain the education she wanted. In 1983, she graduated with a master's degree in regional planning from the University of Massachusetts in Amherst, having been admitted to the program despite her lack of formal education, on the basis of her life experiences.

Career Highlights

After settling in Mayersville, Blackwell was drawn into the early civil rights movement in the 1960s. One Sunday, after teaching a Sunday school class, Blackwell met a representative from the Student Nonviolent Coordinating Committee (SNCC), who had come to Mississippi to stage a voter registration drive. Blackwell enthusiastically threw herself into the work, but as a result lost her job chopping cotton. She said, "We had a garden; people would give us a pot of beans . . . SNCC was supposed to send us $11 every two weeks. My husband worked three months of the year for the Army Corps of Engineers, then we'd buy lots of canned goods" (Phelps 17). Somehow, the family survived.

Blackwell's work with SNCC was not without its hazards. One evening, she found a cross burning on her lawn. She and others registering voters were continually harassed. In the process of registering voters and organizing protests and boycotts, Blackwell was arrested and jailed more than 70 times. In 1964, she was one of the organizers of the Mississippi Freedom Democratic Party. The party sent four delegates, Blackwell among them, to the 1964 Democratic National Convention in New Jersey. Although they were unable to unseat any members of the all-white Mississippi delegation, their voices were heard and their opinions were crucial to the passage of the 1964 Civil Rights Act and the Voting Rights Act. In 1965, Blackwell initiated a lawsuit, *Blackwell v. Issaquena County Board of Education*, challenging segregation in Mayersville.

During the 1970s, Blackwell began reaching out to national organizations. Her work with the National Council of Negro Women aided in promoting the construction of low-income housing. She traveled throughout the country promoting this and other programs, emerging as an eloquent speaker and gaining national attention.

In 1976, Blackwell was elected mayor of Mayersville, becoming the first black woman to hold a mayor's office in Mississippi. The task before her was formidable; Mayersville was a town stuck in the 1800s. It had no sidewalks, water system, police force, or street lights. As a first step in dragging the town into the twentieth century, Blackwell worked to have the town incorporated in 1976, thus making it eligible for some federal funding. Over the next 20 years, Blackwell would turn Mayersville around, installing sidewalks and other necessities of modern life.

Over the years, Blackwell had come to the attention of those in the federal government, and in 1977 she was named president of the U.S.-China People's Friendship Association, traveling to China. In 1979, President Jimmy Carter appointed her to the United States National Commission on the International Year of the Child. As she became more prominent, however, she also became acutely aware of her lack of education. In the 1980s, she decided to do something about it.

Applying to the National Rural Fellow Program, she was awarded a scholarship and began working on a master's degree at the University of Massachusetts. The university recognized Blackwell's abilities and her philosophy of life: "to educate by doing and being" (Hine 139). In 1989, Blackwell was elected president of the National Conference of Black Mayors, and in 1992 she was the recipient of the prestigious "Genius Award" given by the MacArthur Foundation. In 1997, she was again elected mayor of Mayersville.

Blackwell's life is one of legend, a tale of the travel from extreme poverty to international success. When she joined the civil rights movement in the 1960s, Blackwell had no idea of the eventual outcome. As she said, "We had no idea we were changing the whole political future of America" (Phelps 11).

Sources

Hine, Darlene Clark, ed. *Black Women in America: An Historical Encyclopedia*, Vol. I, A–L. Brooklyn, NY: Carlson Publishing Co., 1993.

"Honorary Degree Recipients: Unita Z. Blackwell, '83G." *University of Massachusetts*. 1995. <http://www.umass.edu/pubaffs/commencement/95/honord.html>. Accessed: 4/21/98.

Phelps, Shirelle, ed. *Contemporary Black Biography: Profiles from the International Black Community*, Vol. 17. Detroit, MI: Gale Research, 1998.

Julian Bond

Courtesy of NAACP Archives

Born: January 14, 1940, in Nashville, Tennessee

Status: Chairman, National Association for the Advancement of Colored People; professor, Department of History, University of Virginia, Charlottesville

Education: B.A., 1971, Morehouse College, Atlanta, Georgia

Position: Cofounder, Committee on Appeal for Human Rights (COAHR), 1960; cofounder, Student Nonviolent Coordinating Committee (SNCC), 1960; reporter and feature writer, managing editor, *Atlanta Inquirer*, Atlanta, Georgia, 1960s; communications director, SNCC, 1961–1966; state representative, Georgia State Legislature, 1967–1975; president, Atlanta branch, National Association for the Advancement of Colored People (NAACP), 1974–1989; state senator, Georgia State Senate, 1975–1987; television host, "America's Black Forum"; visiting professor, Drexel University, Philadelphia, Pennsylvania, 1988–1989; visiting professor, Harvard University, Cambridge, Massachusetts, 1989; distinguished scholar in residence, American University, Washington, D.C., 1991–1997; professor, University of Virginia, Charlottesville, c. 1989–; chairman, *Crisis Magazine*, NAACP, 1990s; chairman, NAACP, 1998–

Early Years

Although Julian Bond's background was one of comfort and intellectual pursuits rather than a struggle against inequality, in adulthood he would come to represent the civil rights movement after the death of Martin Luther King, Jr., as much as **Jesse Louis Jackson** would. Horace Julian Bond was born on January 14, 1940, in Nashville, Tennessee, one of two sons of Horace Mann Bond, a college administrator and professor, and Julia Washington Bond, a librarian.

Bond's childhood was ideal in many ways. As he writes,

> My family . . . lived for the first five years of my life in rural Georgia on a college campus where my father was president; as a child of the leading figure in that small world, I harbor pleasant childhood memories—a supportive cast of students, college professors and townspeople, lush orchards of juicy peaches, bright cotton fields and warm sunshine. (Bond)

Soon after, Bond's father moved the family to Pennsylvania, where he assumed the presidency of Lincoln University, a black school. Bond admits that he had a sheltered youth, although his father was a key figure in desegregating the local restaurants, schools, and theaters in the area. As he told George R. Metcalf, in an article in *Up From Within: Today's New Black Leaders*, he "never really lived the life of a Southern Negro kid" (Bigelow 22).

Bond attended the local schools that were desegregated by his father and, as a teenager, was enrolled in the George School, a Quaker boarding school in Bucks County, Pennsylvania. Being the only black student in the school did not bother Bond. "The people who say I showed no racial consciousness are probably right . . . The occasion to be a race champion just didn't arise" (Bigelow 23). As a teenager, he integrated the movie theater in nearby Newtown, Pennsylvania, not, he admits, because he had any great sense of racial injustice, but merely because he did not want to sit in the balcony.

Bond was not much interested in his studies, and his grades reflected this. When he graduated from the George School, he was in the bottom quarter of his class. He also had no idea what he really wished to do with his life; it was understood that he would attend college, but the only thing he had decided upon was to attend Morehouse College in Atlanta where, in 1957, his father had accepted the position as dean of Atlanta University's School of Education.

Higher Education

The decision to attend Morehouse was not without its drawbacks for Bond. He had little or no experience in the South or with racial inequality. As he later said,

> That whites held absolute power over Southern blacks was a given to [the other students at Morehouse]. It had only been a distant truth to me. That any white person could strike or kill a black person without fear of retribution became gospel in Atlanta, more real than the distant preachments of black newspapers that had come into my Pennsylvania home. Once we relocated to Atlanta, the far-away horrors they reported took on substance. . . . (Bond)

While at school, Bond rarely went outside the area called "Gate City," where Morehouse College and the other black colleges were located. Gate City seemed to have everything Bond could want—nightclubs and good food and restaurants—and no whites.

Bond still had little motivation for school, although he did show a flair for writing poetry; his work was published in six anthologies while he was a student. As he said, regarding college, "it wasn't a question of being interested in something else and not being interested in college; it just wasn't a big thing" (Smith 74). He also had little interest in activism until approached by fellow students, Lonnie King, Jr., and Joseph Pierce. They were prompted by an article in the *Atlanta Daily World* about a sit-in in Greensboro, North Carolina, in which local college students were protesting an all-white lunch counter. Pierce and King convinced Bond that the students at Morehouse and the other black colleges in the area should stage similar sit-ins in Atlanta. Rounding up others, the students began the *Atlanta Inquirer*, a black newspaper, and formed the Atlanta Committee on Appeal for Human Rights (COAHR).

On March 15, 1960, a group of students, with Bond as their leader, entered the Atlanta City Hall cafeteria and staged a sit-in. This was to be the only time Bond was arrested. After this sit-in and its attendant publicity, the group began to receive advice and support from other civil rights groups and their leaders. Martin Luther King, Jr., and the Southern Christian Leadership Conference (SCLC) invited Bond and other students from black colleges to Shaw University in North Carolina to help them with organization and tactics. It was at this meeting that the Student Nonviolent Coordinating Committee (SNCC) was formed. As he said about the SNCC, "We had nearly $6,000 in the bank, and we had almost 4,000 people picketing in downtown Atlanta, a masterpiece of precision" (Bigelow 24).

Bond's grades were suffering because of the time he was devoting to the various protests in Atlanta and his work on the black, student-run *Atlanta Inquirer*, where he had started as a reporter and moved up to managing editor. He was also dating a student from Spelman College, Alice Clopton. Finally, feeling he could do more by giving all his time to activism, in 1961 Bond dropped out of school, in the middle of his senior year. At the same time, he and Alice married.

Career Highlights

The Atlanta Committee on Appeal for Human Rights had been absorbed by SNCC, and Bond was offered the job of director of communications for the organization. His job involved editing its newspaper, the *Student Voice*, and traveling throughout the South, distributing materials to reporters and radio and television stations. Although he was never attacked, tension was high in the areas in which he was traveling, and occasionally he did encounter tight situations.

By 1964, many who were involved in the civil rights movement were beginning to question its nonviolence; they felt that action, rather than passive resistance, might be more effective. There was also a great deal of political infighting going on in the SNCC itself. Bond had two young children, and he and his wife were expecting a third child; he felt it was perhaps time to move on.

Based on the 1960 census, Georgia had undergone redistricting in 1964, and in 1965 Bond decided to run for the state legislature in one of the new districts. He focused on unemployment, fair housing, and raising the minimum wage and walked away with 82 percent of the vote. However, although he had been duly elected, the Georgia legislature took issue with Bond assuming his seat.

In January of 1966, before Bond was sworn in, SNCC issued a statement condemning the war in Vietnam, and Bond publicly supported the statement, adding that he had great admiration for those who had resisted the draft by burning their draft cards. The legislature accused Bond of treason, and of "giving aid and comfort to the enemies of the United States and the enemies of Georgia" (Smith 75). On January 10, 1966, the Georgia house voted against seating him, 184 to 12, for "disorderly conduct." His case immediately became a national *cause celebre*. Hiring a lawyer, Bond appealed the decision in the federal district court, which upheld the legislature's authority. Bond then appealed to the United States Supreme Court, and on December 5, 1966, the Court ruled that the legislature had "violated Bond's right of free expression under the First Amendment" (Bigelow 25). Although the Georgia legislature had to seat him, they banned Bond from speaking, essentially making him a pariah in the statehouse.

In 1968, Bond again tangled with the Georgia establishment when Governor Lester Maddox appointed only six black delegates out of 107 to the Democratic National Convention. The Georgia Democratic Party Forum, to which Bond belonged, challenged this, and Bond was appointed by them to cochair a rival delegation, which won nearly half of Georgia's delegate votes. Again, national attention focused on Bond, and he received even more attention at the Democratic National Convention, not only for his speeches but for being the Democratic Party's first black candidate for the United States vice presidency. However, he had to decline as the minimum age required for office was 35 and he was only 28 at the time.

The United States was experiencing a turbulent time in 1968. Bond may have been nominated for the vice presidency, but the convention itself was rocked by violence as Chicago mayor Richard J. Daley's police force attacked protesters outside the convention arena, fighting them with clubs and tear gas while the nation, glued to its television sets, watched. As the national election drew near, the nation faced serious issues of contention: the war in Vietnam and the continuing civil rights movement. The civil rights movement had been in upheaval since the assassination of Dr. Martin Luther King, Jr., in April of that year. To many, Bond seemed just the person to take over for King; he was personable, strong-willed, and spoke movingly and with conviction. Reese Cleghorn, writing in the *New York Times Magazine*, quoted SNCC's former chair, John Lewis, as saying, "With the loss of Martin [Luther] King [Jr.] and Senator [Robert F.] Kennedy, I think Julian has real potential to emerge as the symbol that can bring together certain elements within the old civil-rights movement, what we call the peace movement, and the New Politics, and to create a viable political force" (Bigelow 25–26). Bond could have had any number of leadership positions, but with King gone, Nixon in office, the war in Vietnam winding down, and the Watergate scandal in the news, he seemed to have lost motivation to continue as a leader.

In 1971, he returned to Morehouse and completed his college degree while continuing in the Georgia house until 1975, when he ran for the Georgia senate and won a seat in that branch. In 1976, President Jimmy Carter asked Bond to join his new administration, but Bond refused. He lectured a great deal both at colleges and in other forums, and assumed the presidency of the Atlanta branch of the National Association for the Advancement of Colored People (NAACP). Although he continued to be known locally and worked in the Georgia senate to improve conditions for the poorer residents of his district, he faded from national attention; so much so that in 1979, Jacqueline Trescott asked in an article in the *Washington Post*, "What has Julian done lately?" (Bigelow 26).

During the 1980s, Bond seemed to drift. He had a wife and five children, a position in the Georgia senate, and responsibility with the NAACP, but he seemed to lack ambition. During this time, when Bond again ran for reelection, his opponent charged him with inaccessibility and excessive absenteeism. In 1986, he stepped down from the Georgia senate to run for Congress against **John Lewis**, but lost. His family began to suffer from his lack of attention also. In 1987, Alice Bond, his wife, publicly accused him of using cocaine (then recanted). In 1989, she divorced him.

Although his life seemed to be crumbling about him, Bond continued to work, hosting a PBS documentary on the civil rights movement and a syndicated television show, "America's Black Forum," and writing a syndicated newspaper column. In 1988, he taught at Harvard University as a visiting professor, and during the 1990s has been a distinguished scholar in residence at American University in Washington, D.C., and a faculty member in the history department of the University of Virginia in Charlottesville.

In 1990, Bond married Pamela S. Horowitz, an attorney, and on February 21, 1998, was elected chairman of the NAACP when chairwoman Myrlie Evers-Williams stepped down from the position. However, barely two months had passed before Bond was stirring things up with the NAACP with his appointment of James Ghee to a leadership position within the association. Ghee was a convicted embezzler and had been disbarred as an attorney by the Virginia bar. When faced with criticism of Ghee's appointment, Bond said, "I believe in redemption. I believe in giving people second chances" (Shepard 7). Perhaps he felt sympathy for Ghee. In many ways, in assuming the leadership of the NAACP, Bond, too, was given a second chance after the problems he faced during the 1980s.

Sources

Bigelow, Barbara Carlisle, ed. *Contemporary Black Biography: Profiles from the International Black Community*, Vol. 2. Detroit, MI: Gale Research, 1992.

Bond, Julian. "Remembering Another Atlanta: Gate City." *Southern Changes*. Southern Regional Council. <http://www.src.w1.com/bond182nf.htm#Bond>. Accessed: 3/11/98.

"Civil Rights Activist Julian Bond to Deliver Keynote Address during Emory's Martin Luther King Jr. Week." News and Information. *Emory University*. 23 December 1997. <http://www.emory.edu/WELCOME/journcontents/releases/mlkweek.html>. Accessed: 4/20/98.

Dobnik, Verena. "Bond Elected Chairman of NAACP." *The Hartford Courant*, 22 February 1998, A18.

Shepard, Paul. "NAACP Leader's Decisions Stir Up Controversy." *Willimantic Chronicle*, 4 March 1998, 7.

Smith, Jessie Carney. *Black Heroes of the 20th Century*. Detroit, MI: Visible Ink Press, 1998.

Thomas Bradley

Reproduced from AP/Wide World Photos

Born: December 29, 1917, in Calvert, Texas

Status: Died September 29, 1998

Education: Graduate, 1940, University of California at Los Angeles (UCLA); LL.D., c. 1961, Southwestern University, Los Angeles, California; admitted to the California bar in 1961

Position: Police officer, Los Angeles Police Department, Los Angeles, California, 1940–1961; lawyer, 1961–1998; member, Los Angeles City Council, Los Angeles, California, 1963–1973; mayor, City of Los Angeles, California, 1973–1993

Early Years

Thomas Bradley was born on December 29, 1917, in Calvert, Texas, one of five children. His father and mother were sharecroppers and had a hard life. When Bradley was seven, the family moved to Los Angeles hoping to find something better for their children. Bradley attended public school in Los Angeles and, during high school, played football, earning all-city honors and an athletic scholarship to the University of California at Los Angeles (UCLA).

Higher Education

After graduating from UCLA, Bradley joined the Los Angeles Police Department (LAPD). He remained with the force for 21 years, moving up in rank to become the first black person in Los Angeles to be promoted to lieutenant. During his last years with the police, he was also studying for a law degree at Southwestern University's night school, and in 1961, after he had earned his degree in law, he retired from the LAPD to practice law.

Career Highlights

After Bradley graduated and passed the California bar in 1961, he opened his own law practice and, soon after, entered politics. In 1963, he decided to run for Los Angeles City Council. The district in which he was running was only one-third black, but Bradley ran on his thorough knowledge of the city from his time with the police and won, becoming the first African American to hold a position as an elected official in the city. He would hold his seat on the council for the next 10 years, until 1973.

In 1969, Bradley decided to challenge the mayor of Los Angeles, Sam Yorty. Yorty was a colorful character, and popular with voters. In a runoff election, Yorty campaigned on the idea that, if Bradley were elected, the government of Los Angeles would be dominated by black extremists. The rioting in the Watts section of Los Angeles had stirred just such fears in white voters and they—ignoring Bradley's intelligence, moderation, and calm demeanor—gave their votes to Yorty.

Bradley, however, did not let his defeat slow him down. In 1973, he again challenged Yorty. Yorty tried to put a racial slant on the election, but Bradley was prepared this time. He presented strong opinions on non-racial issues that were of importance to Los Angeles voters: safety; the need for more public transport; and assistance for the elderly. When the votes were counted, Bradley had won the election by almost 100,000 votes. Even discounting the votes cast by African Americans, Bradley would have won; he had received 49 percent of the white vote (Joint Center for Political Studies 39). As a result, Bradley became the first black mayor of Los Angeles.

During the 20 years Bradley held this office, he was faced with many challenges. Not only was Los Angeles filled with racial unrest, but the energy crisis of the mid-1970s was hotly debated. Bradley, despite resistance from both voters and the city council, instituted "tough penalties for non-compliance with fuel-saving measures" (Joint Center for Political Studies 39). He also pushed for more public transportation, and was a key figure in negotiating a settlement in a wildcat bus driver strike. Los Angeles, a bastion of conservatism, at last began to trust the liberal Democrat as they saw the kinds of measures he was instituting, and reelected him time and again.

In 1982 and again in 1986, Bradley ran for governor, but he was not successful in his campaigns. In 1992, Bradley decided to step down from the position of mayor (he had had four successful terms), retiring from office in 1993 to return to his law practice and to devote more time to his wife, Ethel, and their two daughters, Lorraine and Phyllis. He died on September 29, 1998.

Sources

"Bradley, Thomas." *Encyclopedia.com.* Electric Library. <http://www.encyclopedia.com/printable/01782-a.html>. Accessed: 2/20/98.

New Grolier Multimedia Encyclopedia. Novato, CA: The Software Toolworks, Inc./Grolier, Inc., 1993.

Estell, Kenneth. *African America: Celebrating 400 Years of Achievement.* Detroit, MI: Visible Ink Press, 1994.

Joint Center for Political Studies. *Profiles of Black Mayors in America.* Washington, DC/Chicago, IL: The Joint Center for Political Studies/Johnson Publishing, 1977.

"Mayor Who Shaped L.A. Dies." *Los Angeles Times,* 30 September 1998, obituary. <http://www.latimes.com>. Accessed: 9/30/98.

Edward William Brooke III

Courtesy of U.S. Senate Historical Office

Born: October 26, 1919, in Washington, D.C.

Status: Lawyer, Washington, D.C.

Education: Graduate, 1936, Dunbar High School, Washington, D.C.; B.S., 1941, Howard University, Washington, D.C.; LL.B., 1948, Boston University Law School, Boston, Massachusetts; LL.M., 1949, Boston University Law School, Boston, Massachusetts; admitted to the bar of Massachusetts, 1949; recipient of more than 30 honorary degrees from various colleges and universities

Position: Second lieutenant, then captain, 366th Combat Infantry Regiment, U.S. Army, 1942–1945; lawyer, Roxbury and Boston, Massachusetts, 1949–1961; second vice president, National Association for the Advancement of Colored People (NAACP), Boston branch, 1950s; chairman, Boston Finance Commission, Boston, Massachusetts, 1961–1962; attorney general of Massachusetts, 1962–1966; U.S. senator from Massachusetts, 1967–1979; appointed to the President's Commission on Civil Disorders, 1967; lawyer, Washington, D.C.

Awards and honors: Spingarn Medal; Charles Evans Hughes Award

Early Years

Edward Brooke was born on October 26, 1919, in Washington, D.C., the second child of a comfortable, middle-class family. His father, Edward Brooke, Jr., was a lawyer with the Veterans Administration. Brooke later said of his childhood, "I was a happy child. I was conscious of being a Negro, yes, but I was not conscious of being underprivileged because of that . . . I grew up segregated, but there was not much feeling of being shut out of anything" (Smith 82).

Although the Depression was being felt across the country, because of his father's job with the government, Brooke did not feel its full impact. He attended the segregated public schools of Washington, D.C., and in 1936 graduated from Dunbar High School at the age of 16.

Higher Education

Brooke entered Howard University in Washington, D.C., in the fall of 1936. He planned to study medicine but found the science courses boring, so he switched to sociology, receiving the bachelor of science degree in 1941.

The United States' active involvement in World War II began with the bombing of Pearl Harbor on December 7, 1941. Brooke had been in the Reserve Officers Training Corps (ROTC) in college, and soon after graduation was drafted into the army at the rank of second lieutenant. He was assigned to the 366th Combat Infantry Regiment, an all-black unit. While he was serving with this regiment, his interest in law began. Brooke was in charge of recreation and discipline for the regiment and often had to defend his men in military court cases while stationed at Fort Devens in Massachusetts. Soon the regiment was called for combat duty overseas, during which Brooke was promoted to the rank of captain. While in the service, Brooke received the Bronze Star and the Distinguished Service Award.

The 366th fought in North Africa and in Italy, among other places. While in Italy, Brooke met Remigia Ferrari-Scacco, who was the daughter of a prominent businessman in Genoa. When Brooke returned to the United States in 1945, he began a correspondence with Remigia that culminated in their marriage on June 7, 1947, in Roxbury, Massachusetts.

After returning from the war, Brooke entered Boston University Law School in September of 1946. During his time there, he served as the editor of the *Boston University Law Review*. He graduated with an LL.B. in law in 1948 and an LL.M. in 1949, and passed the Massachusetts bar examination in 1949 as well.

Career Highlights

Although he had a number of offers from various law firms, Brooke decided he wished to practice alone. He established a law office in Roxbury, where he lived, but soon moved it to downtown Boston. He was increasingly interested in politics and, in 1950, ran in both the Democratic and Republican primaries for a place in the Massachusetts legislature. Although he won the Republican nomination, he lost the election; but this only seemed to whet his appetite for politics.

In 1952, Brooke again ran for the state legislature as a Republican, but lost. At this time, he was still an unknown to voters. Brooke decided to devote his time to his law practice and to community activities. During the 1950s, he became involved with a number of civic groups, and also served as the second vice president of the Boston branch of the National Association for the Advancement of Colored People (NAACP).

By 1960, not only was Edward Brooke much more well known in the commonwealth, but civil rights was becoming an increasingly important issue. That year, he decided to run for Massachusetts secretary of state; his nomination made him the first black to be nominated for a statewide office in Massachusetts. Although he lost in this election, he was more successful when he ran again in 1962 for the office of attorney general of Massachusetts. His election made him the first African American to be elected to a major state office in Massachusetts.

Although his supporters urged him to run for governor, Brooke served as attorney general until 1966, running successfully for reelection in 1964. In 1965, however, Brooke decided to seek higher office and became a candidate for the U.S. Senate from Massachusetts.

The campaign for office was a bitterly fought one. Brooke was running as a Republican in a state that was overwhelmingly Democratic; he was also running against a former Democratic governor, Endicott Peabody. In addition, many criticized his interracial marriage to Remigia. But Brooke had many loyal supporters, including his mother, Helen Brooke, who was a very effective speaker and actively helped him campaign (that same year, 1966, she was named "Mother of the Year" by the National Shriners). When the election returns were counted on November 8, 1966, Brooke had won the election by more than 400,000 votes. Edward Brooke was sworn into office on January 3, 1967, becoming only the third black person to serve in the Senate, after **Hiram Rhodes Revels** and **Blanche Kelso Bruce**; and the first black person to serve in the Senate since 1881. According to U.S. congressman **William Lacy Clay, Sr.**, Brooke said of himself that "he was not just the first Negro this or the highest Negro that, he could likewise be described as a Protestant in a Catholic state and a Republican in a Democratic state" (360).

When Brooke assumed his seat in the Senate, Lyndon B. Johnson was president and Johnson's "Great Society" was still under construction. In 1967, after a number of riots had broken out in major cities across the country, Johnson appointed Brooke to his Commission on Civil Disorders; one outcome of the commission's work was the inclusion in the Civil Rights Act of 1968 of its recommendations against discrimination in housing.

Although he was a Republican, Brooke generally took liberal or moderate positions on issues before the Senate, often putting him at odds with the other Republicans and with President Richard Nixon, who had assumed office in 1969. Unlike many of the Republicans in the Senate, Brooke strenuously fought for affirmative action, low-income housing, an increased minimum wage, job training, and increased Medicare funds. He protested U.S. trade with South Africa and, like a number of other Washington politicians, spoke out against apartheid there. He also opposed the Republicans by voting against three of Nixon's nominees to the Supreme Court: Clement F. Haynesworth, G. Harrold Carswell, and William H. Rehnquist.

In 1972, Brooke ran for reelection against Democrat John J. Droney and won a second term in the Senate. That same year, Richard Nixon was elected to a second term as president. Among his endorsers was Edward Brooke, but Brooke would not give the president his support for long. Even as Nixon was assuming the presidency for a second term, the Watergate scandal was exploding in Washington. In May of 1973, Brooke introduced a resolution before the Senate calling for the appointment of a special prosecutor to investigate the Watergate scandal, and he was the first senator to call for Nixon's resignation when Nixon's involvement in the scandal became apparent.

After Watergate forced Nixon's resignation, Brooke continued his support of public housing and fought for affirmative action under Presidents Gerald Ford and Jimmy Carter. In 1977, he successfully battled against a Health, Education and Welfare Bill amendment that would have kept that department from enforcing quotas to meet affirmative action goals. In 1978, however, when Brooke again ran for reelection, he was defeated by Democrat Paul Tsongas. On his retirement from office, he resumed his law practice.

Over the years, Brooke has been the recipient of numerous awards, most notably the NAACP's Spingarn Medal and the Charles Evans Hughes Award from the National Conference of Christians and Jews for his humanitarianism and work for racial equality. As he himself said, after first being sworn into the Senate in 1967,

> I thought of what my grandmother used to say—"Stay in your place." This advice was given to protect me from injury, because if you didn't follow this advice, you knew what would happen. But this was a statement I never could accept. Your place is anywhere you want to make it. (Smith 85)

Sources

Christopher, Maurine. *America's Black Congressmen.* New York: Thomas Y. Crowell, 1971.

Clay, William L. *Just Permanent Interests: Black Americans in Congress, 1870–1991.* New York: Amistad Press, 1992.

Estell, Kenneth. *African America: Celebrating 400 Years of Achievement.* Detroit, MI: Visible Ink Press, 1994.

"Former Black Members of Congress." *Congressional Times Journal.* <http://www. usbol.com/ctjournal/FrBlkCongMemList.html>. Accessed: 2/26/98.

Smith, Jessie Carney, ed. *Black Heroes of the 20th Century.* Detroit, MI: Visible Ink Press, 1998.

Ronald Harmon Brown

Reproduced from AP/Wide World Photos, by Barry Thumma

Born: August 1, 1941, in Washington, D.C.

Status: Died April 3, 1996, in Croatia; buried at Arlington National Cemetery, Arlington, Virginia

Education: B.A., 1962, Middlebury College, Middlebury, Vermont; J.D., 1970, St. John's University, Jamaica, New York; admitted to the bars of New York, the District of Columbia, and the United States Supreme Court; recipient of a number of honorary degrees from various colleges and universities

Position: Officer, U.S. Army, 1963–1967; lobbyist, staff member, National Urban League, New York, New York, 1968–1972, Washington, D.C., 1973–1979; deputy campaign manager for Senator Edward Kennedy, 1979–1980; chief counsel, U.S. Senate Committee on the Judiciary, 1980; general counsel, staff director for Senator Edward Kennedy, 1981; deputy chairman, chief counsel, Democratic National Committee, 1981–1985; partner, Patton, Boggs and Blow, Washington, D.C., 1985–1989; chairman, Democratic National Committee, 1989–1992; secretary, U.S. Department of Commerce, 1993–1996

Early Years

Ronald Harmon Brown was born on August 1, 1941, in Washington, D.C., where his parents, William H. and Gloria Osborne Brown, were just finishing college at Howard University. Soon after Brown's birth, the family moved to New York City, settling in Harlem, where William Brown managed the Theresa Hotel next to the famous Apollo Theater. Unlike many African American children at the time, Brown's childhood was one filled with famous people, entertainers who were performing next door at the Apollo. He grew up meeting people such as Joe Louis and actor Paul Robeson, and even, in 1952, then vice president Richard Nixon.

Since Brown attended private schools, he rarely encountered the kinds of problems most young people confront on the streets of Harlem or of any large city. He attended Hunter College elementary school on New York's Upper

East Side (he was the only black student in the school), then the Rhodes School, and finally the Walden School, from which he graduated.

Higher Education

In 1958, Brown entered Middlebury College, a private college in Vermont, and was again the only black student in his class. He joined the ROTC to help finance his education and chose a major of political science.

Attending a predominantly white, middle- and upper-class college in rural Vermont gave Brown little opportunity to participate in the kinds of civil rights activism many of his peers were engaged in at that time. The one instance in which he encountered racism came when he was rushed by a white fraternity, Sigma Phi Epsilon. Although the fraternity at Middlebury wished to pledge him—offer him membership—the national organization objected because of a clause in their charter that barred blacks from joining. The local chapter offered Brown house privileges, but without full membership; Brown turned down the offer. As *Time* reported later, "Brown let it be known that he was unwilling to finesse the issue by accepting ..." (Bigelow 32). Finally, the local chapter came to his defense, resulting in the chapter's expulsion from the national organization. This incident led to the college banning all organizations that barred membership based on race or for any other discriminatory reason.

In 1962, Brown graduated from Middlebury and joined the army as a second lieutenant in fulfillment of his ROTC commitment. That year, in August, he also married Alma Arrington; together they would have two children, Tracey Lyn and Michael Arrington.

Brown was sent to West Germany, where he was the only black officer on his base. After he was transferred to Korea, he earned the rank of captain. During this time, according to Brown, he "learned to be comfortable taking charge" (Smith 100).

After completing his service with the army in 1967, Brown returned to the United States and accepted a job in Washington, D.C., with the National Urban League as a caseworker and job training coordinator. He also returned to school, enrolling in the law school of St. John's University in Jamaica, New York. In 1970, he received his law degree from St. John's but continued working for the National Urban League in various capacities, including as a lobbyist, until 1979.

Career Highlights

With an undergraduate major in political science and a degree in law, Brown was well suited for a political career, and in 1971 he made his first run for public office, becoming district leader of the Democratic Party in Mount Vernon, New York. It was not until he moved to Washington, however, that he began to receive national notice. According to the *Washington Post*, Brown said, "Coming to Washington was a way for me to establish my own identity, my own base, my own group of contacts and relationships, putting me into a spokesman role . . . when the Urban League was a very important organization" (Bigelow 32).

In 1979, Senator Edward Kennedy asked Brown to become the deputy manager of his 1979 presidential campaign. Although Kennedy's bid was defeated, Brown gained national attention for his campaign work and, in 1980, was offered the appointment of chief counsel to the Senate Judiciary Committee. In 1981, he became chief counsel of the Democratic National Committee, and in 1982 became deputy chairman. When his term as deputy chair expired in 1985, he joined the Washington law firm of Patton, Boggs and Blow as a corporate attorney.

During 1988, while working as an attorney, Brown also served as campaign manager for **Jesse Louis Jackson** in Jackson's bid for the presidency. A number of times during the campaign, Brown's finely honed negotiating skills were called upon to quell troubled waters, particularly in the conflict between Jackson and Democratic candidate Michael Dukakis, which earned Brown fans from both parties. A Dukakis supporter, Donna Brazile, said, "If Ron was a pop singer, he would have crossover appeal" (Bigelow 33).

Soon after the presidential race ended, Brown ran for the chairmanship of the Democratic National Committee. Here, his skills at organizing and campaigning also helped him, causing his four opponents for the office to drop out of the contest several weeks before the voting. Some critics were leery of Brown because of his support of Jesse Jackson, but the abilities he had shown in negotiating during the Jackson campaign spoke for him. As Harvard professor Martin Kilson said in the *Washington Post*, after Brown's election, "Brown is the new black transethnic politician" (Bigelow 32).

When Brown assumed the position of chairman of the National Democratic Committee, the Democrats had been out of the presidency for nearly 10 years, although they dominated in Congress. As party chairman, Brown faced the challenge of raising funds for the organization and helping elect Democrats to office. During his time as chairman, Brown would see the election of a black governor, **Lawrence Douglas Wilder** in Virginia, and a black mayor, **David Norman Dinkins** in New York City. Brown did come under criticism from African Americans when he backed Democrat Richard M. Daley over Chicago alderman Tim Evans, an African American. But Brown knew that for a Democrat to win the presidency, the party would have to redefine itself, shedding the "tax and spend" image imposed by Republicans.

By the presidential race in 1992, Brown had brought many of the disparate elements of the Democratic Party together to create a unity within that helped Bill Clinton win the nomination at the Democratic National Convention. *The New York Times* quoted former party chairman Paul G. Kirk as saying, "he knew the party had to show it could govern itself before it could hope to govern the country" (Bigelow 35).

With Clinton's election, Brown was offered the position of secretary of the Department of Commerce. Many critics saw this as payback; others charged that Brown was merely a black token in Clinton's cabinet. Still others worried that his past ties as a lobbyist and with Jesse Jackson would influence his decisions. Despite criticism, Brown was confirmed by the Senate on January 14, 1993, and sworn into office on January 22, becoming the first black secretary of commerce.

From its first day in office, the Clinton administration was under a microscope like no other administration had ever been in the past. Every facet of life concerning, it seemed, every employee of the administration came under the scrutiny of the Republicans and the press. Brown was not exempt from this; in May of 1995, he was accused by Republicans of influence-peddling and shady business dealings. That same year, Attorney General Janet Reno appointed an independent counsel to investigate the charges against Brown. Brown, however, continued to conduct the business of his department.

Under Brown's direction, the Department of Commerce became a powerhouse, promoting the United States' exports, technologies, and businesses throughout the world. As an advocate for the department, Brown saw his job, in part, as ensuring economic opportunity for every American and as being the voice of business in the president's cabinet. At the same time, he served on a variety of committees, as well as on the boards of a number of colleges.

In April of 1996, Brown and 36 other federal officials were on a fact-finding trip in Croatia. As their plane attempted to land at Dubrovnik, bad weather caused it to crash into a nearby mountain, killing all aboard. The nation mourned the loss of a compassionate man who had earned the respect and admiration of everyone who knew him. President Clinton said, "Ron Brown was a magnificent life force" (Smith 102).

Sources

Bigelow, Barbara Carlisle, ed. *Contemporary Black Biography: Profiles from the International Black Community,* Vol. 5. Detroit, MI: Gale Research, 1994.

"Brown, Ron." *Biography Online Database.* <http://www.biography.com/find/bioengine.cgi?cmd=1&rec=15916>. Accessed: 4/11/98.

"Ronald H. Brown, 30th U.S. Secretary of Commerce." <http://www.tnp.com/brown/BrownBio.html>. Accessed: 3/18/98.

Smith, Jessie Carney, ed. *Black Heroes of the 20th Century.* Detroit, MI: Visible Ink Press, 1998.

Willie L. Brown, Jr.

Courtesy of the Office of the Mayor, San Francisco, by Dennis DeSilva

Born: March 20, 1934, in Mineola, Texas

Status: Mayor, San Francisco, California

Education: Attended Prairie View A and M College, Prairie View, Texas; B.A., 1955, San Francisco State University, San Francisco, California; J.D., 1958, Hastings College of Law, University of California, Berkeley; admitted to the bar of California, 1959; recipient of five honorary degrees

Position: Attorney, Brown, Dearman and Smith, 1959– ; member, California State Assembly, 1965–1995; speaker of the assembly, California State Assembly, 1980–1995; mayor, San Francisco, California, 1995–

Early Years

Willie L. Brown, Jr., was born in Mineola, Texas, on March 20, 1934. His parents were poor, and as he said in an interview in *Ebony*, "I can remember using cardboard for the bottom of my shoes. I can remember the days of being the fourth person on the list for water for the No. 3 washtub. I remember the outdoor toilets, having to raise half of what I ate, and having meat only once a week" (Bigelow 27).

Brown was not about to let the poverty of his upbringing keep him down, though. He attended schools in Mineola, shining shoes to earn money. Upon graduation from high school, he entered Prairie View A and M College in Prairie View, Texas. However, as he said, "I was invited to leave" (Bigelow 27). He detested the college, its food, and a rule that banned men and women from walking together on the same sidewalk. Instead, he went to San Francisco, California, where an uncle lived, and entered San Francisco State University.

Higher Education

While at San Francisco State University, Brown worked as a janitor, shoe salesman, and playground director to earn money for school. When he graduated in 1955, he entered the Hastings College of Law, not because he had any great desire to be a lawyer but, as he admitted, to avoid the draft. In 1958, he received a J.D. from Hastings and was admitted to the California bar in 1959.

Career Highlights

During his years in college, Brown had begun to take an interest in politics. He had campaigned for Adlai Stevenson in his race for the presidency against Dwight D. Eisenhower, and had joined the National Association for the Advancement of Colored People (NAACP). After graduation, Brown set up a law practice in a San Francisco storefront and, in addition to defending the poor of the city, began fighting against the discrimination that was rampant. In 1962, he entered the race for a seat in the California assembly, but lost. He ran again two years later and was successful.

Brown was a flamboyant and outspoken addition to the California assembly. As one article in *Gentlemen's Quarterly* noted, "Willie was one of those red-hots who wore his dashiki with pride and picketed showrooms in Van Ness because they didn't have black sales personnel" (Bigelow 28). Almost from the moment he entered the assembly, Brown set his sights on the speaker of the assembly position, angering many who felt he was something of an upstart. However, in 1980, he finally achieved his goal, becoming the first black speaker.

Brown also set out to involve more African Americans in California politics. Through his position in the assembly he was able to achieve a number of "firsts" in the appointment of positions: the first African American woman was appointed speaker's chief of staff; the first black chief sergeant at arms was appointed to the legislature, as was the first African American chaplain; the first African American chief clerk was appointed, and the first African American female press secretary to the speaker of the assembly.

Brown's legislative efforts reflected a similar interest in helping the black communities of California. He worked tirelessly to expand business opportunities to minority-owned businesses. In 1977, he pushed through legislation that prohibited state-funded programs from denying benefits or discriminating on the basis of ethnicity, religion, age, sex, color, or physical or mental disability. And as late as 1993, Brown supported a bill that enacted various reforms to prevent insurance discrimination against those with HIV/AIDS or other long-term health problems.

As Brown rose in politics and made more money, he also became known for his flamboyant lifestyle and outspokenness. He bought the finest suits and cars, and dated beautiful women. As he said, "I would not make the sacrifice, for any job, to stop doing what I enjoy doing, whether it's driving my automobiles, owning my horses, going to the Derby, making the Super Bowl, the All-Star Game or the Slam Dunk contest, or wearing the clothing that I wear, or being seen with the dates I'm seen with . . . All of that is just me. And I enjoy every inch of it" (Bigelow 28). The public seemed to enjoy Brown's lifestyle as much as he did, for they elected him again and again to the California assembly.

In addition to pushing legislation that helped minorities, Brown was concerned with other issues. In the 1980s, he spoke out against apartheid in South Africa and, in 1985, designed a plan to ensure that the University of California had no stock in companies doing business with South Africa. In 1986, he coauthored a bill with **Maxine Waters** that required the state to divest itself of any interests in South Africa. Additionally, he supported both Nelson Mandela and Desmond Tutu when they spoke in California, organizing meetings and dinners to provide a forum for them.

In 1992, the California voters approved a bill limiting the terms of legislators, and Brown was faced with a mandated end to his time in the assembly in 1996. But Brown was not ready to retire from the political arena, and in 1995, despite pleas from his supporters to run for governor, he entered the mayoral race in San Francisco. Running on his political record of effective legislation, he easily beat his competitors, assuming office that year. Even today, Brown's goals remain those he enunciated in the 1980s in an interview with *Ebony:* "It's important that I perform well in this position so that successive racial minorities . . . will be judged and treated on merit alone and nothing will be taken away from them or required of them that is not required of any other person holding this office. I'm trying to break the barrier, the assumptions and the stereotypes by performing well" (Bigelow 30).

Sources

Bigelow, Barbara Carlisle, ed. *Contemporary Black Biography: Profiles from the International Black Community*, Vol. 7. Detroit, MI: Gale Research, 1994.

"Biography: Willie L. Brown, Jr." Mayoral Candidates. <http://sf95.election.digital.com/CVF2/BROWN/bio.html>. Accessed: 3/12/98.

Blanche Kelso Bruce

Reproduced from the Library of Congress, courtesy of the U.S. Senate Historical Office

Born: March 1, 1841, in Farmville, Virginia

Status: Died March 17, 1898, in Washington, D.C.; buried in Woodlawn Cemetery, Washington, D.C.

Education: Tutored as a child with the son of his owner; attended Oberlin College, Oberlin, Ohio, late 1850s or early 1860s

Position: Teacher, Lawrence, Kansas, 1861–1864; teacher, Hannibal, Missouri, 1864–1867; porter, steamship *Columbia*,1867; landowner and planter, Floreyville, Bolivar County, Mississippi, 1867–1898; elected sergeant at arms, Mississippi State Senate, 1870; appointed tax assessor, Bolivar County, Mississippi, 1871; elected sheriff and tax collector, Bolivar County, Mississippi, 1872; appointed to the Board of Levee Commissioners of Mississippi, 1872; U.S. senator from Mississippi, 1875–1881; appointed register of the U.S. Treasury Department, 1881–1885, 1897–1898; delegate, nominated for vice president, Republican National Convention, 1880 and 1888; recorder of deeds, District of Columbia, 1889–1893; trustee, District of Columbia public schools, 1893–1897

Early Years

Blanche Kelso Bruce was born into slavery on March 1, 1841, in Farmville, Virginia. In many ways, although a slave, he had fortune on his side. His master, Pettus Perkinson, permitted his son William to tutor Bruce and even allowed Bruce to attend some sessions William had with his own tutor.

Higher Education

Although, like other slaves, Bruce worked hard and was required to do as his master told him, he was apprenticed to a printer as his education increased. Only later, however, was Bruce able to obtain some higher learning, briefly attending Oberlin College in Oberlin, Ohio, sometime in either the late 1850s or the early 1860s.

Career Highlights

A few years before the Civil War began, Perkinson moved himself and his household to Mississippi and then to Missouri. When the war began in 1861, Bruce seized the opportunity to escape his slavery, fleeing with two of his brothers to Hannibal, Missouri, where they tried to enlist with the Union army. Blacks were not being accepted into the Union forces at that time, however, so Bruce then went to Lawrence, Kansas, where, because of his education, he was able to begin the state's first elementary school for black children. In Lawrence, Bruce thought that he would be safe from recapture, but it was there that he nearly lost not only his freedom but his life.

In 1861, William Clarke Quantrill, who was later to be honored by the Confederacy, had formed a proslavery band of terrorists that began raiding and plundering pro-Union settlements in Kansas and other midwestern states. His band was made up of nearly 450 men, including future outlaws Cole Younger and Frank and Jesse James. One member, "Bloody Bill" Anderson, not only murdered Union supporters but scalped them, hanging their scalps from the bridle of his horse.

Lawrence was peaceful under the hot Kansas sun on August 21, 1863, when the quiet was broken by whoops and yells as Quantrill's Raiders galloped over the hills and into the town. Burning, looting, and killing, the band swept the town like a devastating plague. When the dust settled, more than 150 people had been murdered, and the town was ravaged. Blanche Bruce was one of the lucky survivors, but he had had enough. As soon as he could, he moved back to Hannibal, Missouri, where he taught until the end of the war.

About 1867, Bruce obtained a job as a porter on the steamship *Columbia*, traveling the Mississippi River and seeing firsthand the results of the Civil War. In 1869, he left the river and moved to Floreyville, Mississippi, where he was able to buy cheap land and become a successful planter.

Like so many other intelligent, educated black men of the day, Bruce quickly became involved in both state and local politics. In 1870, he was elected sergeant at arms of the Mississippi State Senate, and the following year, 1871, was appointed tax assessor of Bolivar County. In 1872, he was elected to the combined offices of sheriff and tax collector of the same county.

Bruce was becoming widely known in Republican circles. In 1873, he was asked to run for lieutenant governor of the state, but declined, having higher goals in mind. He did, however, strongly support Adelbert Ames and A.K. Davis, who ran for governor and lieutenant governor, respectively. In 1874, this support was rewarded when Governor Ames supported Bruce's nomination for the Senate. Although the election was contentious, Bruce was named the winner on February 3, 1874.

When Blanche Kelso Bruce arrived in Washington, D.C., in March of 1875, he came as the first African American to be elected to a full term of office. (This accomplishment would not be equaled until 1972, nearly 100 years later, when **Edward William Brooke III** would finish his first term as a senator from Massachusetts.) However, before even being sworn in, Bruce received what amounted to a slap in the face.

When a new member of the Senate arrives to be sworn in, it is the tradition of that body for the senior senator from his or her state to escort the new member to his or her seat. Bruce had alienated a number of people in his rapid political climb, among whom was James L. Alcorn, then senior senator from Mississippi. When Bruce was sworn in on March 5, 1875, Alcorn refused to escort him to his seat. Bruce began to walk alone to his seat, pointedly ignoring the slight, but was joined and escorted by Roscoe Conklin, the Republican senator from New York. Conklin not only showed his friendship to Bruce at this time, but guided him through his first days, helping Bruce become elected to the Pensions, Manufacturers, and the Education and Labor Committees. Later, Bruce named his son after Conklin.

During his term in office, Bruce worked unrelentingly for black equality and for the rights of other minorities such as the Chinese and the Native Americans. He also spoke in favor of seating **Pinckney Benton Stewart Pinchback** of Louisiana, whose election to the Senate had been in contention since 1872.

The 1875 election in Mississippi had been a violent one, filled with riot and bloodshed, as the conservative white Democrats seized control of the state. From his position in the Senate, Bruce called upon that body to investigate the election. The Boutwell Committee, formed to look into it, concluded that it was "one of the darkest chapters in American history," and recommended that the new Mississippi State Democratic government not be recognized. Unfortunately, no action was taken on this recommendation, which would affect future elections in the state—they would continue to be violent, discouraging black candidates and voters from participating in the government.

When the Senate reconvened after its recess in 1877, Bruce was a member and temporary chairman of the Mississippi River Improvement Committee. He supported the development of a channel and levee system on the Mississippi to help control flooding and improve commerce by improving the navigation of the river.

On June 24, 1878, Bruce married Josephine Wilson, a schoolteacher. For their honeymoon, the couple toured Europe and were received by a number of American embassies, as William Evarts, then secretary of state, had written ahead introducing the couple. When they returned to Washington, they settled into a five-story brownstone on R Street, entering the social circle of Washington and entertaining. The Bruces were a popular and respected couple.

On February 14, 1879, Bruce presided over the Senate in the absence of Vice President William A. Wheeler, becoming the first African American to do so. The *New York Tribune* wrote the following day,

> This is the first time a colored man ever sat in the seat of the Vice-President of the United States. Senator Bruce is universally respected by his fellow senators and is qualified both in manners and character to preside over the deliberations of the most august body of men in the land. (Christopher 21)

While the *Tribune* praised Bruce, he was having difficulties in the Senate. The 45th Congress reflected the shifts that were occurring in the South, with white conservative Democrats pushing out the Republicans elected during the earlier days of Reconstruction. Bruce now found himself in the minority in a Democratic Congress. As a member of the minority party, he lost his chairmanship of the Mississippi River Committee and found many of his proposals thwarted, particularly those aimed at black and Native American equality.

Although Bruce again presided over the Senate on May 4, 1880, his political career was winding down. Realizing that he no longer had a chance for reelection in Mississippi now that the southern Democrats had reassumed control, instituting Black Codes and suppressing black rights including the right to vote, Bruce and his wife decided to remain in Washington. During the Republican National Convention in 1880, Bruce supported Ohio senator James Garfield in his bid for the presidency (Bruce himself received eight votes for vice president at the same convention). When Bruce's term expired on March 3, 1881, Garfield rewarded his support by appointing him register of the United States Treasury, an office he held from 1881 until 1885.

Bruce was a popular figure in Washington in his later years and was often sought after as a public speaker on race relations. He also spent a great deal of his time writing many articles on this issue for a variety of magazines. In 1885, the Democrats regained the presidency. But when Benjamin Harrison, a Republican, was elected in 1888, he appointed Bruce to the position of recorder of deeds for the District of Columbia. Bruce served in this office from 1889 until 1893 when he became a trustee of public schools for the district. In 1897, he was again appointed by William McKinley to the position of register of the treasury, serving until his death on March 17, 1898, at the age of 57.

Sources

Asante, Molefi K., and Mark T. Mattson, eds. *The Historical and Cultural Atlas of African Americans.* New York: Macmillan, 1991.

"Blanche Kelso Bruce." *Notable Kansans of African Descent.* Kansas State Historical Society. <http:www.ukans.edu/heritage/kshs/people/afampeop.htm>. Accessed: 3/18/98.

Christopher, Maurine. *America's Black Congressmen.* New York: Thomas Y. Crowell, 1971.

Clay, William L. *Just Permanent Interests: Black Americans in Congress, 1870–1991.* New York: Amistad Press, 1992.

Estell, Kenneth. *African America: Celebrating 400 Years of Achievement.* Detroit, MI: Visible Ink Press, 1994.

"Former Black Members of Congress." *Congressional Times Journal.* <http://www.usbol.com/ctjournal/FrBlkCongMemList.html>. Accessed: 2/13/98.

"Quantrill, William C." *New Grolier Multimedia Encyclopedia.* Novato, CA: The Software Toolworks, Inc./ Grolier, Inc., 1993.

Yvonne Braithwaite Burke

Reproduced from AP/Wide World Photos

Born: October 5, 1932, in Los Angeles, California

Status: Attorney, Los Angeles, California

Education: B.A. in political science, 1953, University of California-Los Angeles; J.D., 1956, University of Southern California School of Law, Los Angeles

Position: Attorney, 1956–; deputy corporation commissioner, State of California, 1960s; hearing officer, Los Angeles Police Commission, 1960s; attorney, McCone Commission, Los Angeles, California, 1965; state assemblywoman, California State Assembly, 1966–1972; U.S. representative from the 37th Congressional District of California, 1973–1978; member, Los Angeles County Board of Supervisors, Los Angeles, California, 1979–1980

Early Years

Yvonne Braithwaite Burke was born Perle Yvonne Watson on October 5, 1932, in Los Angeles, California. She grew up attending the public schools in Los Angeles.

Higher Education

After high school, she attended the University of California-Los Angeles, majoring in political science, and graduating in 1953. Burke immediately began law school at the University of Southern California in Los Angeles, receiving her J.D. in 1956.

Career Highlights

After graduation, Burke established a law practice in Los Angeles, but also worked for the City of Los Angeles in varying capacities. She served as deputy corporation commissioner, as a hearing officer for the Los Angeles Police Commission, and as a staff attorney for the McCone Commission that was investigating the Watts riots of 1965.

Burke's work with the city gave her solid political contacts, and in 1966 she decided to run for the California State Assembly. When she was victorious, Burke became the first black woman to be elected to the assembly. During her time as a legislator, Burke fought for the disadvantaged of her city. She cosponsored tenants' rights legislation and child health care bills, and worked for voter education. In 1972, she served as cochair of the Democratic National Convention in Miami. That same year, Burke was also named by Harvard University in Cambridge, Massachusetts, a fellow of its Institute of Politics and the John F. Kennedy

School of Government. In 1975, she taught as Chubb Scholar at Yale University in New Haven, Connecticut.

Burke was well known within her district in California; she had received national recognition for her participation in the Democratic Party, and had fought for legislation that benefited her constituents. In 1972, she decided to make a bid for Congress in the 37th Congressional District. In the primary, she faced four other candidates but was able to defeat them easily. In the general election, she was victorious over Republican Gregg Tia, garnering 64 percent of the vote. During the campaign, she married William A. Burke, a Los Angeles businessman. When Burke took her seat in the House, she became the first African American woman from California to be elected to Congress. In 1973, she became the first member of Congress ever to give birth while in office.

Burke was appointed to the Committee on Interior and Insular Affairs and the Public Works Committee, but immediately began work within the House to help her district. The 37th District of California contained a nearly 50 percent low- and middle-income black population, as well as a 10 percent Latino/Latina and Asian American population. Burke became known in Congress for her attempts to speak out for these people. During her second term of office, she transferred to the Committee on Appropriations, which had more influence than the committees to which she had formerly been assigned. As a member of that committee, Burke proposed an increase in the funding of community nutrition programs and other services for senior citizens. She also supported the Humphrey-Hawkins bill that called for full employment, and was one of several representatives supporting a human rights amendment to the foreign aid bill. In January, 1976, Burke was chosen as the chairperson of the Congressional Black Caucus by unanimous consent, becoming the first woman to chair the caucus. And in 1977, she introduced the Displaced Homemakers Act that provided job training for women entering the job market.

Burke was becoming discouraged, however. She had been unable to get any legislation passed concerning child care, housing, or education. She felt she had little influence over others in Congress, and that the things she felt were important were being ignored. Frustrated, in 1978 she decided to resign her seat in Congress.

Other factors also contributed to her decision. Her husband, William, lived and worked in Los Angeles, and Burke was commuting back and forth between Los Angeles and Washington, trying to maintain a family and a career. Her husband's business was not doing well, either; he had become involved with a bankrupt corporation that was under federal investigation, and many felt this was a liability to Burke's career.

Returning to California, Burke ran for California attorney general, but was defeated by Republican George Deukmejian. After her defeat, she was appointed by Governor Edmund Brown, Jr., to the Los Angeles County Board of Supervisors, serving from 1979 until 1980. Since she stepped down from this post, although she has served on numerous boards of corporations and banks, she has primarily devoted herself to her law practice and her family.

Sources

Clay, William L. *Just Permanent Interests: Black Americans in Congress, 1870–1991*. New York: Amistad Press, 1992.

Estell, Kenneth. *African America: Celebrating 400 Years of Achievement*. Detroit, MI: Visible Ink Press, 1994.

"Former Black Members of Congress." *Congressional Times Journal*. <http://www.usbol.com/ctjournal/FrBlkCongMemList.html>. Accessed: 2/27/98.

Hine, Darlene Clark, ed. *Black Women in America: An Historical Encyclopedia*, Vol. I, A–L. Brooklyn, NY: Carlson Publishing Co., 1993.

"Yvonne Braithwaite Burke." Legislative Biographies. <http://www.glue.umd.edu/~cliswp/Politicians/Leg/Bios/legbiob.htm#burke>. Accessed: 2/27/98.

C

Richard Harvey Cain

Courtesy of the South Caroliniana Library, University of South Carolina, Columbia

Born: April 12, 1825, in Greenbriar County, Virginia

Status: Died January 18, 1887, in Washington, D.C.; buried in Graceland Cemetery, Washington, D.C.

Education: Attended school in Gallipolis, Ohio; ordained a minister in the Methodist Episcopal Church, Hannibal, Missouri, 1844; joined the African Methodist Episcopal (AME) Church, 1848; attended Wilberforce University, Wilberforce, Ohio, 1860; awarded honorary doctor of divinity, Wilberforce University, Wilberforce, Ohio, 1880s

Position: Minister in the midwestern United States, 1844–1860; minister, AME Church, Brooklyn, New York, 1861–1865; minister, Emmanuel Church, Charleston, South Carolina, 1865–c. 1868; participant, Zion Church Colored People's Convention, 1865; editor and publisher, *South Carolina Leader* (renamed the *Missionary Record* in April, 1868), 1866–1872; delegate, South Carolina constitutional convention, 1868; state senator, South Carolina State Senate, 1868–1870; congressman at large for South Carolina, 1873–1875; U.S. representative from the Second Congressional District of South Carolina, 1877–1879; elected bishop in the AME Church, 1880; president, Paul Quinn College, Waco, Texas, 1880–1884; presiding bishop, AME Church, for the New Jersey Conference, 1884–1887

Early Years

Richard Harvey Cain was born on April 12, 1825, in Greenbriar County, Virginia, of free parents. His mother was a Cherokee Indian and his father an African American. When Cain was six years old, he and his family moved to Gallipolis, Ohio, where he received some schooling, probably in Sunday school. After a few years, he and his family moved to Portsmouth, Ohio, and then to Cincinnati.

As a young man, Cain worked on the steamboats that plied the Ohio River, but these jobs were not what he wished to do all his life. Turning to religion, Cain joined the Methodist Episcopal Church of Portsmouth, Ohio. He was ordained a minister in the church in 1844 in Hannibal, Missouri, and then was assigned to various churches in the Midwest.

Cain was not happy in the Methodist Episcopal Church, which practiced segregation within its congregations and in the promotion of its officials. He realized that he could rise only so far in the church hierarchy. As a result, in 1848, Cain left the church, joining the African Methodist Episcopal (AME) Church, and subsequently assuming the ministry of a successive number of churches in the Midwest.

Higher Education

In 1860, Cain was the pastor of the AME Church in Muscatine, Iowa. Keenly aware of his lack of a formal education, Cain enrolled for a year at Wilberforce University in Wilberforce, Ohio, the university that would recognize him later with an honorary doctor of divinity. When the Civil War began the following year, he and a number of other students approached the governor of Ohio to volunteer for the Union army. At that time, however, the army had not begun to recruit black soldiers, so the group was turned down.

Career Highlights

From 1861 to 1865, Cain was assigned the ministry of an AME Church in Brooklyn, New York. At a conference in 1862 in Washington, D.C., he was ordained as an elder in the AME Church.

At the end of the Civil War, many northern churches sent people and goods to the South to aid the freed people. Richard Cain was among them, sent by the AME Church to Charleston, South Carolina, to help the Emmanuel Church there. The church had been closed since 1832, and Cain worked to reestablish it and to open new churches in the state. In 1866, Cain also became editor and publisher of the *South Carolina Leader* (renamed the *Missionary Record* in April of 1868), and entered local politics.

Under Andrew Johnson's guidance, Reconstruction of the South, for the most part, had been left in the hands of white southerners, with the expected results. In South Carolina, a constitutional convention had been called in 1865, but no blacks were in attendance. Instead, the convention was primarily composed of ex-Confederate leaders. After nullifying the Ordinance of Secession and reaffirming loyalty to the federal government, the convention proceeded to enact its infamous "Black Code," a set of laws that denied black suffrage and dictated the terms of employment for blacks—terms little better than the slavery from which they had so recently been freed.

In protest of this all-white convention, black leaders in the state convened the Colored People's Convention at the Zion Church in Charleston in November of 1865, two months after the constitutional convention. One speaker at this convention was Richard Harvey Cain.

The convention sent a message to Congress, asking it to condemn the all-white constitutional convention and to exercise "the strong arm of the law over the entire population of the state," and additionally to abolish the Black Code and permit suffrage for African Americans. Congress responded by refusing to seat the elected delegates (all white) from South Carolina who had been chosen at the constitutional convention.

Congressional Reconstruction then began in South Carolina and, this time, black leaders were included. In 1868, Richard Cain was a delegate to the new state constitutional convention and, in July of that same year, was elected to the South Carolina State Senate. During his two years in the State Senate, Cain was a frequent and forceful speaker, urging the ratification of the 14th Amendment and supporting black equality. The public, impressed by his oratory and his political acumen, elected Cain congressman at large to the House of Representatives in 1872.

Richard Cain took his seat in the House on December 4, 1873. Although he was not the first black man to be seated in the House—that honor belonged to **Joseph Hayne Rainey**, also from South Carolina, who had been seated on December 12, 1870—he was the first black clergyman to hold a congressional seat.

Like so many of his fellow African American congressmen, Cain was not given any important committee assignments. He was appointed to the Committee on Agriculture. From the start of his career in Congress, however, Cain took up the cause of civil rights. Three days after he had been seated, he introduced a bill to supplement the Civil Rights Act of 1866 and later, with other black congressional members, pushed for the passage of a civil rights bill that had been introduced by Senator Charles Sumner in 1870 that was stronger than previous civil rights bills.

Once South Carolina's representatives were accepted by Congress, the state began to reorganize and map out congressional districts; one result was that, with the redistricting, Cain's seat as congressman at large was abolished. In 1874, when his term expired, Cain decided not to run within his district. Two years later, however, he changed his mind and entered the campaign as the Republican candidate for the Second District.

When Cain returned victorious to the 45th Congress in 1877, his seat did not go unchallenged. His Democratic opponent, Michael O'Connor, questioned the validity of Cain's election and his credentials. The House, however, voted in Cain's favor twice, once in October of 1877, and again in May of 1878 when O'Connor tried to unseat him. During this term in office, Cain served on the Committee on Private Claims.

During his second term, Cain again spoke for equality and opportunity for African Americans and other minorities. He introduced two major bills while in office. One was to establish a steamship line to Liberia—the African country established in the early 1800s by the American Colonization Society for free blacks—and the other was to raise funds for education through the sale of public lands. Both bills died in committee.

By the time Cain's term expired in 1879, congressional Reconstruction had ended in the South. Elections were rife with violence, and more and more black voters were being denied their right to the ballot box. In 1878, the South Carolina Republican Party's nominating convention ignored Cain, choosing instead Edmund W.M. Mackey, a white man, to run for the Second District seat. Mackey subsequently lost to Cain's old adversary, Democrat Michael O'Connor.

Cain returned to his ministry and, in 1880, was elected a bishop in the African Methodist Episcopal Church. He was assigned to the territory that included Louisiana and Texas. While in Waco, Texas, Cain helped organize Paul Quinn College and served as its president from 1880 until 1884. In 1884, he and his wife returned to Washington, D.C., where he served as bishop over the New Jersey Conference. It was there that Richard Cain, at the age of 61, died on January 18, 1887.

While Richard Cain, like so many black representatives elected to Congress during this time, was unable to enact many of the programs he promoted for the equality and education of his people, his voice was heard and served as a positive influence for many who were to come after him. One such man, **Robert Brown Elliott**, who worked as associate editor of Cain's newspaper, would follow in Cain's footsteps and be elected to Congress.

Sources

Christopher, Maurine. *America's Black Congressmen.* New York: Thomas Y. Crowell, 1971.

"Former Black Members of Congress." *Congressional Times Journal.* <http://www.usbol.com/ctjournal/FrBlkCongMemList.html>. Accessed: 2/13/98.

Smith, Jessie Carney, ed. *Black Firsts: 2,000 Years of Extraordinary Achievement.* Detroit, MI: Visible Ink Press, 1994.

Henry Plummer Cheatham

Courtesy of the N.C. Division of Archives and History

Born: December 27, 1857, near Henderson, North Carolina

Status: Died November 29, 1935, in Oxford, North Carolina; buried in Harrisburg Cemetery, Oxford, North Carolina

Education: B.A., 1882, Shaw University, Raleigh, North Carolina; honorary master's degree, 1887, Shaw University, Raleigh, North Carolina; studied law

Position: Principal, Plymouth Normal School, Plymouth, North Carolina, 1883–1884; registrar of deeds for Vance County, Henderson, North Carolina, 1884–1888; founder of an orphanage for black children, Oxford, North Carolina, 1887; U.S. representative from the Second Congressional District of North Carolina, 1889–1893; recorder of deeds for the District of Columbia, 1897–1901; superintendent, Oxford Orphanage, Oxford, North Carolina, 1907–1935

Early Years

Henry Plummer Cheatham was born a slave on December 27, 1857, on a plantation near Henderson, North Carolina. His mother was a house slave, and both her and Cheatham's lives were easier than those of the slaves who worked in the fields. At the end of the Civil War in 1865, Cheatham attended public school in Henderson. Because he had had some education as a house slave, he did well once he entered school; and at the age of 18, he entered the normal school of Shaw University in Raleigh, North Carolina.

Higher Education

After three years at normal school, Cheatham began taking college courses at Shaw University. An intelligent young man, he received a bachelor's degree with honors in 1882. Either during or immediately after his years at Shaw, he married his first wife, Louise Cherry.

Career Highlights

Cheatham was able to find a job immediately after his graduation from college. The principal, A.B. Hicks, Jr., of Plymouth Normal School in Plymouth, North Carolina, had died and the school needed a replacement. Cheatham accepted the job, and his wife accepted a position with the school teaching music.

In 1884, Cheatham decided to return to Vance County where he had been born; there he was elected to the position of registrar of deeds for the county. Although during this time he read law with the intention of qualifying for the North Carolina bar, he was too busy to finish. In 1887, his alma mater, Shaw University, awarded him an honorary master's degree in recognition of his accomplishments. That same year he was one of the founders of an orphanage for black children in Oxford, North Carolina.

Although Reconstruction in the South had all but ended by this time, there still existed opportunities for an educated, intelligent African American. Cheatham had become increasingly involved in local and state politics, and his manners and intelligence impressed both black and white political leaders. It was no surprise, then, when in 1888 he was nominated by local Republicans to run for Congress from the Second Congressional District of North Carolina. Although the race was a tight one, Cheatham was able to defeat incumbent Democrat Furnifold McL. Simmons by 653 votes. Simmons, who was white, had a strong record of promoting legislation that strengthened civil rights and was viewed favorably by black voters, but Cheatham was able easily to win the black vote. Allegedly, Cheatham told black voters that President Grover Cleveland and Simmons intended to return them to slavery because it was too expensive to provide them with both work and wages (Logan and Winston 102). Whatever means Cheatham used, they worked; he was seated in the 51st Congress in December of 1889.

When Cheatham assumed his seat in Congress, he was appointed to the Committee on Education and the Committee on Expenditures on Public Buildings. Through these committees, Cheatham tried—unsuccessfully— to have legislation passed that would directly benefit his constituents.

In addition to legislation that would help his voters, during his tenure in Congress Cheatham also introduced a number of broader bills. He introduced legislation for the erection of a public building in Henderson, North Carolina, that could be used as a post office. He also introduced a bill to provide further funds for **Robert Smalls**, who had captured and surrendered to the Union the Confederate ship *Planter* during the Civil War. Many felt that Smalls had been undercompensated for the *Planter*, and Cheatham was one of a number of both black and white representatives who endeavored to increase the monies given Smalls. Cheatham also supported a bill that would have reimbursed the depositors of the Freedmen's Savings and Trust Company, which had failed in 1874. Ever interested in education, he also attempted to push through a bill that called for temporary governmental support for public schools.

In 1890, Cheatham was challenged by Democrat James M. Mewborne and easily won reelection. Other African American members of Congress, however, had not fared so well in their reelection campaigns, and when Cheatham was sworn into the 52nd Congress in 1890, he took his seat as the only black member. He was appointed to the Committee on Agriculture in addition to the committees to which he had previously been assigned. Again, Cheatham introduced a great many bills, but, as in his first term, none was successful.

In 1892, when Cheatham returned to North Carolina to run for reelection, he was faced with a split in voter sympathy. The Populist Party had emerged to challenge both the Republican and Democratic Parties. The split was great enough to cause him to lose the election to Democrat Frederick A. Woodard. Cheatham ran again in 1894 and 1896 but was defeated in both elections. In 1897, Cheatham returned to Washington, D.C., to accept the appointment of recorder of deeds for the District of Columbia, a post offered to him by President William McKinley; he held that office for four years.

In 1907, after his return to North Carolina, he accepted the job of superintendent of the Oxford orphanage that he had cofounded. Cheatham spent the next 28 years at the orphanage, building it into an exemplary institution. He increased the number of acres it held, established a thriving farm, and replaced its wooden buildings with substantial brick ones. Cheatham also served as president of the Negro Association of North Carolina, a position he held for a number of years. He continued his work to help his fellow African Americans until his death in Oxford, North Carolina, on November 29, 1935.

Sources

Christopher, Maurine. *America's Black Congressmen.* New York: Thomas Y. Crowell, 1971.

Clay, William L. *Just Permanent Interests: Black Americans in Congress, 1870–1991.* New York: Amistad Press, 1992.

"Former Black Members of Congress." *Congressional Times Journal.* <http://www.usbol.com/ctjournal/FrBlkCongMemList.html>. Accessed: 4/28/98.

Logan, Rayford W., and Michael R. Winston, eds. *Dictionary of American Negro Biography.* New York: W.W. Norton and Co., 1982.

Shirley Anita St. Hill Chisholm

Reproduced from AP/Wide World Photos

Born: November 30, 1924, in Brooklyn, New York

Status: Retired

Education: Graduate, 1942, Girls' High School, Brooklyn, New York; B.A. cum laude in sociology, 1946, Brooklyn College, Brooklyn, New York; M.A., 1952, Columbia University, New York, New York

Position: Teacher's aide, then teacher, Mount Calvary Child Care Center, New York, New York, 1946–1952; director, Friend in Need Nursery School, Brooklyn, New York, 1952; director, Hamilton-Madison Child Care Center, New York, New York, 1953–1959; educational consultant, Division of Day Care, Department of Social Services, New York, New York, c. 1960–c. 1964; representative from the 55th District, New York State Legislature, 1964–1968; U.S. representative from the 12th Congressional District of New York, 1969–1982; candidate for the Democratic nomination for president, 1972; professor, Mount Holyoke College, Holyoke, Massachusetts, 1983–1985

Early Years

Shirley Anita St. Hill Chisholm was born on November 30, 1924, in Brooklyn, New York. Both her father and mother, Charles St. Hill and Ruby Seale St. Hill, were born and grew up in the Caribbean, then moved to the United States in the early 1920s. Chisholm was the eldest of the family's children; her sister Odessa was born a year after her, and Muriel two years later.

At the time of Chisholm's birth, her father, being unskilled, worked as a baker's helper and, later, as a factory hand. Her mother worked as a seamstress. But city life was not what they wished for their children, so, in 1928, Chisholm, along with her mother and two sisters, traveled back to her mother's home in Barbados. Ruby St. Hill left her children in her mother's care, returning to Brooklyn to earn money for the family. The little girls had no chance to be lonely, as Chisholm would later write,

> We children had each other, Grandmother, Mother's younger brother Lincoln and younger sister Myrtle, and no fewer than four cousins for company . . . We seven children ranged up to nine years old. There was a lot for us to explore, even though it was a small farm and a small village. (Chisholm 19)

When she was four, Chisholm started school in the village. The school was a strict,

British-style school, stressing reading and writing. She then attended Vauxhall Coeducational School in Barbados. Chisholm later credited her ease in writing and speaking to this early start in education and to the emphasis placed on communication skills in the island schools.

In 1934, when Chisholm was 10 years old, she and her sisters returned to Brooklyn to be with their parents. Existence there was far different than on the open, airy farm in Barbados. The Depression made things hard for everyone. Chisholm's father had experienced a cutback in the hours he could work at the factory and her mother worked as a domestic to help make ends meet, but still they could afford only a squalid apartment; with no heat or hot water, in the Brownsville section of Brooklyn.

School, too, was not like those on the island, and Chisholm had some difficulty. Because of this, the school officials placed her in the third grade; on the islands, she would have been in the sixth. As a result of boredom, she said, "I became a discipline problem . . . Luckily someone diagnosed the trouble and did something about it. The school provided me with a tutor in American geography and history for a year and a half, until I caught up with and passed my age-grade level" (Chisholm 28). Once she caught up with her peers, Chisholm did well in Girls' High School in Brooklyn, graduating in 1942 with several scholarship offers for college.

Higher Education

Although Chisholm wanted to accept the scholarship offered by either Oberlin College in Ohio or Vassar in Pennsylvania, her parents could not afford the cost of room and board if she lived away from home; so Chisholm chose to go to nearby Brooklyn College for her undergraduate studies.

Chisholm's father was a voracious reader and a follower of Marcus Garvey, and Chisholm spent her youth listening to her father detail the inequities caused by racial discrimination. However, she did not become involved in politics until she entered college. At Brooklyn College, she joined with other black students in discussions of discrimination and, in her senior year, met a man, Wesley McD. Holder, who would steer her into activism. He was, according to Chisholm, "a black man from Guiana who had been upsetting white politicians as far back as the 1930s" (Chisholm 43). Although Holder himself did not wish to run for office, he felt there should be more black candidates and black office holders.

Holder became a mentor to Chisholm. After her graduation cum laude in 1946, she continued working with him in various political organizations in Brooklyn, pushing for black candidates and for the discussion of black issues by elected officials. Holder organized the Bedford-Stuyvesant Political League (BSPL) to offer a choice to voters. The BSPL ran a slate of black candidates against the regular Democrats. While unsuccessful, the slate served to warn the white political machine that they had to begin considering African American candidates and issues.

At the same time she was working with the BSPL, Chisholm was working on her master's degree in early childhood education at Columbia University, and beginning a family. Chisholm had met a young man, Conrad Chisholm, while studying at Columbia. Initially, she was not taken with him, but he persisted in courting her, and in 1949 they were married.

Career Highlights

After she had received a bachelor of arts degree from Brooklyn College, Chisholm began working at the Mount Calvary Child Care Center in New York where she was soon promoted to teacher. Upon receiving her master's degree from Columbia, Chisholm accepted the position of director of the Friend in Need Nursery School in Brooklyn; in 1953, she became director of the Hamilton-Madison Child Care Center in New York. In 1959, she said,

> my last and biggest job in education came to me. In 1959, I left the Hamilton-Madi-

> son Center to become a consultant to the City Division of Day Care. There I was responsible for general supervision of ten day care centers with ten directors, seventy-eight teachers, thirty-eight other employees, and a budget of $397,000. (Chisholm 59)

During the 1950s, Chisholm was busy with her family and job, but in 1960 she again became actively involved in politics. With six others, she formed a new organization, the Unity Democratic Club. Its goals were similar to those held by the BSPL earlier—to elect black candidates and promote black interests. In the next campaign, the Unity Club was successful in promoting its candidate, Tom Jones, for the New York assembly. In 1964, however, Jones stepped down to take a position on the bench, and Chisholm was urged to run for his vacant seat.

Chisholm met hostility from all quarters while running for office. Some were against a black candidate; others objected to a woman running. As she later said, however,

> Men always underestimate women. They underestimated me, and they underestimated women like me. If they had thought about it, they would have realized that many of the homes in black neighborhoods are headed by women . . . The women are always organizing something . . . they are the backbone of the social groups and the civic clubs, more than the men. So the organization was already there. All I had to do was get its help. I went to the presidents and leaders and asked, Can you help me? ("Will Women Vote for Women?")

Chisholm rallied her support from the various women's groups and, through her speaking engagements, managed to win over a great many of the male voters. When the votes were tallied, she had won by a significant margin over two other candidates.

Chisholm's tenure in the New York State Assembly was marked by individuality. She quickly established the fact that she was not part of an inbred political machine. She was warned when she took an unpopular (nonparty) stance that she was committing political suicide; but as she kept repeating, she was only fighting for what she believed in. During her time in office, Chisholm managed to get 50 bills introduced into the legislature, and eight of them passed—a very high proportion. She was especially pleased with two. One created a program called SEEK, which provided educational assistance to disadvantaged young people so they could continue their education. The other set up the state's first unemployment insurance coverage for personal and domestic employees.

In 1968, Chisholm was asked to run for Congress from New York's 12th District. In many ways, her campaign for Congress was a repeat of her earlier run for the state legislature. Again, as the only female candidate, she was attacked for her gender and race, and again she rallied the votes. This time, however, she had her record in the New York State Assembly to speak for her. Running under the slogan "Fighting Shirley Chisholm—Unbought and Unbossed," she went door-to-door, stood on street corners, and spoke at every opportunity in meetings and gatherings. The primary saw a small turnout of voters, but it was enough; Chisholm had won by about 1,000 votes. Then she had to face the Republicans.

In the middle of all this, Chisholm was diagnosed with a tumor and had to undergo surgery for its removal. Despite the fact that she was still recovering, Chisholm continued to campaign. At election time, she defeated both James Farmer, a Republican, and Ralph J. Carrano of the Conservative Party, becoming the first black woman to be elected to Congress.

When Chisholm was sworn into the 91st Congress, she was assigned to the Ways and Means Committee and the Committee on Agriculture, as well as its Subcommittee on Rural Development and Forestry. Despite the fact that she was a freshman representative without much leverage, Chisholm protested the assignment to the Agriculture Committee, asking the party caucus for an assignment more appropriate for a representative from an innercity district. Eventually, she was transferred to the Veterans Affairs Committee. In later years, she would also serve on the Committee on Education and Labor and the influential Rules Committee, as well as the Committee on Organization Study and Review.

During her time in Congress, Chisholm was an outspoken advocate for the establishment of social programs and increased funding for day care, education, and other services to the public. She fought for a decrease in military spending and against apartheid in South Africa. During the terms of Richard Nixon, Gerald Ford, and Ronald Reagan, Chisholm battled against cuts in the funding of the very social programs she had championed that were now under attack by Republicans. And, as always, she spoke her mind energetically and honestly.

In 1972, Chisholm surprised everyone by declaring her candidacy for the Democratic presidential nomination, becoming the first black woman to be a candidate for this office. Traveling throughout the country, she entered primaries in key states and waged a vocal campaign. Even though she had garnered the admiration and affection of millions of Americans, she received only 152 votes on the first ballot at the Democratic National Convention in Miami; the time had not yet come for a female presidential candidate.

After being reelected time and again, in 1982 she announced her retirement from office. She said that the increasingly conservative atmosphere of Congress created more difficulties than she could face in effecting change for her constituents, and that she wished to return to private life. Although she retired from Congress, she did not retire from her many activities. For a time she taught at Mount Holyoke College in South Hadley, Massachusetts, and, in 1992, was offered the post of United States ambassador to Jamaica. During her political career, Chisholm not only broke the gender barrier in Congress but was effective through her commitment and energy.

Sources

Chisholm, Shirley. *Unbought and Unbossed.* New York: Avon, 1970.

Christopher, Maurine. *America's Black Congressmen.* New York: Thomas Y. Crowell, 1971.

Clay, William L. *Just Permanent Interests: Black Americans in Congress, 1870–1991.* New York: Amistad Press, 1992.

New Grolier Multimedia Encyclopedia. Novato, CA: The Software Toolworks, Inc./Grolier, Inc., 1993.

"Shirley Anita Chisholm." Legislative Biographies. <http://www.glue.umed.edu/~cliswp/Politicians/Leg/Bios/legbioc.htm>. Accessed: 2/27/98.

"Shirley Chisholm." *African-American Pioneers.* <http://www.kaiwan.com/~mcivr/chisholm.html>. Accessed: 2/20/98.

Smith, Jessie Carney, ed. *Black Heroes of the 20th Century.* Detroit, MI: Visible Ink Press, 1998.

Telephone interview with staff at Mount Holyoke College, Department of Sociology, 4 January 1999.

Telephone interview with staff at U.S. Embassy of Jamaica, 4 January 1999.

"Will Women Vote for Women?" <http://www.glue.umed.edu/~cliswp/Politicians/Issues/womvote.html>. Accessed: 2/27/98.

William Lacy Clay, Sr.

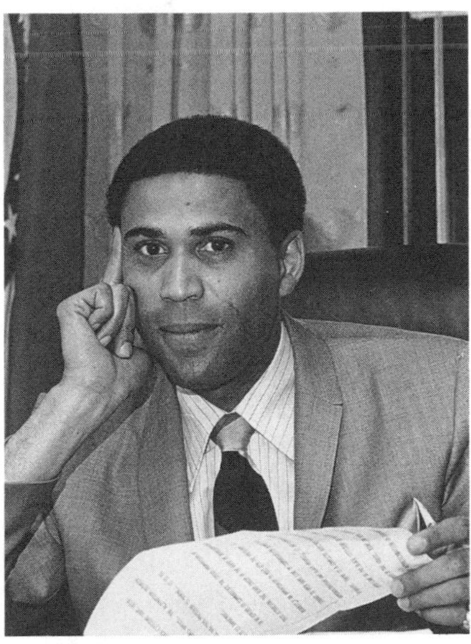

Reproduced from UPI/Corbis-Bettmann

Born: April 30, 1931, in St. Louis, Missouri

Status: U.S. representative from the First Congressional District of Missouri

Education: B.S. in history and political science, 1953, St. Louis University, St. Louis, Missouri; recipient of numerous honorary degrees from various colleges and universities

Position: U.S. Army, 1953–1955; alderman from the 26th Ward, St. Louis Board of Aldermen, 1959–1964; committeeman of the 26th Ward, St. Louis, Missouri, 1964–c. 1969; business representative, State, County and Municipal Workers' Union, 1961–1964; education coordinator, Pipefitters' Local 562, 1966–1969; U.S. representative from the First Congressional District of Missouri, 1969–

Early Years

William Lacy Clay, Sr., was born in St. Louis, Missouri, on April 30, 1931, one of nine children. His father, Irvin Clay, worked as a welder while his mother, Luella, stayed home with the children. During the Depression, the Clays lived in a tenement in the black section of St. Louis with no indoor plumbing or hot water.

Clay attended the public schools of St. Louis, and started working as a teenager. When he was 13, he got a job as a janitor. After his sister taught him to sew, he worked as a tailor, then a salesman in a St. Louis clothing store. By the time he had graduated from high school, he had earned and saved enough money to go to college, and he enrolled in St. Louis University.

Higher Education

At St. Louis University, Clay majored in history and political science. He was intelligent and did well, but school was a different experience for him. St. Louis University was predominantly white; there were only four other black students in the university, and Clay was keenly aware of the differences between himself and the white students. This and other experiences were to shape Clay's strong stance on civil rights. In 1953, Clay graduated and, the day after graduation exercises, entered the army.

Career Highlights

The army only bolstered Clay's attitudes toward inequality. Stationed at Fort McClellan near Anniston, Alabama, Clay encountered the full force of the Jim Crow rules of the South. Despite rulings that forbade discrimination in the armed services, segregation was alive and well at Fort McClellan. At the fort, which was nominally desegregated, black soldiers were barred from many activities. They could not swim in the base pool or attend the dances held weekly at the noncommissioned officers' club. They also could not get haircuts at the base barbershop, except on Saturdays when a black barber was brought in specifically to cut the black soldiers' hair.

Never one to sit back and watch, Clay organized a protest of the Jim Crow rules. Clay and a number of other soldiers boycotted the black barber, refusing to get their hair cut. When the base colonel ordered Clay to have his hair cut, he later said, "I didn't refuse the order. I merely refused to have a haircut on Saturdays. I went to the barber shop Monday through Friday each day. The colonel, after about a week of this, was more adamant about his intention to court-martial me. At this point I decided to give real grounds for such action" (Christopher 250).

Clay, his family, and a group of other soldiers descended upon the base pool and went swimming. They blocked the doors of the NCO club, preventing the white soldiers from entering. When the black press got word of the protest occurring on the base, the story became generally known. The colonel did not court-martial Clay; instead, he transferred Clay to another base. But Clay had appealed to Congressman **Charles Coles Diggs, Jr.,** for an investigation into the discriminatory practices of the base. The other soldiers continued to protest after Clay's transfer, and Diggs launched an investigation that eventually did away with the Jim Crow rules at the fort.

After Clay was discharged from the army, he worked in a number of jobs but also became involved in the budding civil rights movement of the late 1950s and early 1960s. Through his participation in various civil rights organizations, Clay became more interested in politics and, in 1959, entered the race for alderman on the St. Louis City Council. The incumbent was a white man, but the 26th Ward of St. Louis was almost entirely black and Clay had no difficulty defeating him. Clay also accepted the position of business representative for the State, County and Municipal Workers' Union in St. Louis during this time. In this position, Clay revealed the racial bias exercised in hiring among the businesses of the city, and opened up jobs for blacks.

In 1963, Clay and a number of other protesters were fined and jailed for protesting the hiring policies of the Jefferson Bank and Trust Company in the city. Clay was in jail for 112 days and fined $1,000 plus court costs, but the bank did change its policies and increased the number of African Americans hired (Christopher 251). Other businesses, seeing the results of the protests, also began to increase their minority hiring. Clay, in his role as alderman, introduced and obtained passage of the city's first Fair Employment Act. In 1964, Clay resigned his position as alderman after being elected committeeman of the 26th Ward of St. Louis; and in 1966 he accepted a job as education coordinator of Pipefitters' Local 562 and held it until 1969.

In 1968, the courts had ordered the redistricting of Missouri. As a result, the First Congressional District included most of St. Louis's black population. The incumbent congressman, Frank Karsten, who was white, announced that he would not run for reelection, feeling he had little chance of winning. With that, Clay threw his own hat into the ring.

Clay was well known in his district as a union official, as someone who worked for job opportunities, and as a man who was not afraid to put himself on the line for civil rights. In the August primary, Clay faced five challengers from within the Democratic Party and easily beat them. In the general election, he faced Curtis Crawford, a Republican lawyer. Crawford was calling for cuts in federal spending. In the poverty-ridden First District, which was sorely in need of the kinds of spending and social programs that had been instituted under President Lyndon Johnson, this stance was highly unpopular. Clay campaigned on welfare reform, increased housing and job opportunities, and better schools. In the election, Clay walked away with the victory, defeating Crawford by nearly 35,000 votes.

When Clay was sworn into the 91st Congress in January of 1969, he was assigned to the Education and Labor Committee and began work on the legislative agenda of "workers' rights" that he continues to pursue today. When students protested the war in Vietnam, he spoke in their support:

> The black man has been told to obey the law, but not to expect equal rights under the law. The student has been taught to respect the truth of democracy and the rights of man—but not to question war or discrimination or poverty or hunger. If there is truly an alliance of black people and youth today—it is obvious why. They share an equal disgust for the double standard and hypocrisy which exist. (Christopher 253)

During his first term in Congress, Clay pushed to strengthen existing civil rights laws, although he was unsuccessful. He was more successful in calling for the black members of Congress to form a united front. "On New Year's Eve 1970, I drafted a memo and circulated it to all members of the Democratic Select Committee, warning, 'Without adequate programming and planning, we . . . might well degenerate into a Kongressional Koffee Klatch Klub'" (Clay 117). In the face of President Nixon's increasing pressure to cut social programs, the African Americans in Congress, Clay and others felt, needed to unify to push legislation that benefited minorities. Soon after Clay's memo went out, the majority of black members of Congress formed the Congressional Black Caucus for this purpose and named Charles Coles Diggs, Jr., its chairman.

In February of that same year, Clay requested an appointment with President Richard Nixon to lay before him the concerns of minorities in the United States. Again and again, Nixon refused to meet with Clay. Finally, in May, Clay went public with the snub:

> There is no question about where Mr. Nixon has placed his priorities. He has traveled more than 35,000 miles in foreign countries. He has entertained hundreds of foreign dignitaries but refuses to meet with the elected representatives of the black "nation" within this country. (Christopher 249)

Clay was joined in his protest by Charles Diggs and other congressmen, and later that year, in July, Clay united with **Louis Stokes** and **John Conyers, Jr.**, to criticize Nixon's stance on civil rights. During Nixon's term in office, his administration had cut back on the Job Corps program and reduced the education and poverty budgets, acts that keenly affected Clay's constituents.

Over the years, reelected time and again to his seat in Congress, Clay has continued to work for minority and workers' rights. In 1993, he was the key sponsor of the Family and Medical Leave Act that was signed into law by President Bill Clinton. He also successfully pushed legislation that requires mandatory notification to workers of plant closings, and for the protection of striking workers. He has been the recipient of numerous honorary degrees from various colleges and universities and has published two books, *To Kill or Not to Kill* (1990) and *Just Permanent Interests* (1992).

Sources

"Biography: Honorable William L. Clay." *U.S. House of Representatives*. <http://www.house.gov/clay/bio.htm>. Accessed: 3/6/98.

Christopher, Maurine. *America's Black Congressmen.* New York: Thomas Y. Crowell, 1971.

Clay, William L. *Just Permanent Interests: Black Americans in Congress, 1870–1991.* New York: Amistad Press, 1992.

Eva M. Clayton

Reproduced from AP/Wide World Photos, by Bob Jordan

Born: September 16, 1934, in Savannah, Georgia

Status: U.S. representative from the First District of North Carolina

Education: B.S., 1956, Johnson C. Smith University, Charlotte, North Carolina; M.S., North Carolina Central University, Durham; attended law school, University of North Carolina, Chapel Hill, and North Carolina Central University, Durham

Position: Founder and owner, Technical Resources International, 1981; member Warren County Board of Commissioners, Warren County, North Carolina, 1982–1990; U.S. representative from the First District of North Carolina, 1993– ; executive director, Soul City Foundation; director, North Carolina Health Manpower Development Program, University of North Carolina, Chapel Hill, North Carolina; named "Outstanding North Carolina County Commissioner," 1990

Early Years

Eva M. Clayton was born in Savannah, Georgia, on September 16, 1934. Growing up, she did well in school and was active in the local Presbyterian Church, an avocation that would continue into her adult life. In 1991, she traveled to Switzerland to participate in an Ecumenical Consultation on the Environment.

Higher Education

After graduating from high school, Clayton continued her education at Johnson C. Smith University at Charlotte, North Carolina, graduating in 1956. Later, she would receive a master's degree from North Carolina Central University in Durham, and would work toward a law degree at the University of North Carolina and North Carolina Central University. Soon after graduating from college, she married Theaoseus T. Clayton, Sr.; the couple would have four children: Theaoseus, Jr., Martin, Reuben, and Joanne.

Career Highlights

Clayton did not enter politics until the 1980s, although she was active in her community. She founded Technical Resources International (TRI), a firm specializing in economic development, in 1981. In 1982, she was elected to a position on the Warren County Board of Commissioners, which she held until 1990. That year, she was named "Outstanding North Carolina County Commissioner" by her fellow commissioners of North Carolina ("Biography . . .").

In addition to her position on the board of commissioners, Clayton served in a number of other positions. She was executive director of the Soul City Foundation and director of the North Carolina Health Manpower Development Program of the University of North Carolina at Chapel Hill. She served on numerous other local and state boards, as well.

In 1992, Clayton entered the race for a congressional seat from the First Congressional District of North Carolina to finish the term of Congressman Walter B. Jones, Sr., who had died in office. Through her many activities, she was a well-known figure in the area, and she was easily elected, becoming the first African American woman to be elected from North Carolina.

When she took her seat in the 103rd Congress in 1993, although a freshman in the House, Clayton automatically gained seniority and a visible presence as she was finishing Jones's term. She was assigned to the House Speaker's Committee on Policy Development and the Presidential Entitlement Committee, and she was elected co-president of the Democratic Freshman Class for that year, the first woman to hold this position. During her first term in Congress, she was active in coauthoring legislation saving the Section 515 Housing Program that provides affordable housing. For her work on this, Clayton was presented an award by the Housing Assistance Council.

In the 104th Congress, Clayton served as vice chair of the Democratic Policy Committee on Research, and on the Agricultural Committee, among other assignments. Her work in the field of legislation on agriculture earned her awards from the Food Research Action Committee.

Clayton continues to be a strong force in Congress, promoting education, economic development, rural health care, and an increased minimum wage. As of 1998, she has served as co–vice chair of the House Congressional Advisory Board to the National Campaign to Prevent Teenage Pregnancy.

Sources

"Biographical Sketch of Congresswoman Eva M. Clayton." *U.S. House of Representatives.* <http://www.house.gov/clayton/bio.htm>. Accessed: 4/28/98.

"Biography of Congresswoman Eva Clayton, Vice Chair for Policy." Who Are the Democratic Leaders? *U.S. House of Representatives.* <http://www.house.gov/democrats/bio_eva_clayton.html>. Accessed: 4/28/98.

James Enos Clyburn

Reproduced from AP/Wide World Photos, by Doug Mills

Born: July 21, 1940, in Sumter, South Carolina

Status: U.S. representative from the Sixth Congressional District of South Carolina

Education: B.S., 1962, South Carolina State University, Orangeburg, South Carolina; recipient of honorary degrees from Winthrop University, The Medical University of South Carolina, the College of Charleston, and Saint Augustine's College

Position: Teacher, employment counselor, then director of two youth and community development projects, 1962–1971; staff member to Governor John West of South Carolina, 1971–1973; commissioner, South Carolina Human Affairs Commission, 1974–1992; U.S. representative from the Sixth Congressional District of South Carolina, 1993–

Early Years

James Enos Clyburn was born on July 21, 1940, in Sumter, South Carolina, where he spent most of his youth. During his early adult years, he lived in Charleston, South Carolina, then moved to Columbia.

Higher Education

After graduating from high school in 1958, Clyburn entered South Carolina State College (now, University). At South Carolina State, Clyburn gained a reputation as an activist, joining with other students in the early civil rights movement, organizing and protesting against the discrimination that was so blatant at the time.

Career Highlights

After Clyburn graduated from South Carolina State in 1962, he took a number of jobs; he was a teacher, an employment counselor, and a director of two youth and community development projects. Throughout his youth, his ambition was to follow one day in the footsteps of his great-uncle who, nearly 100 years before, had served in Congress during the Reconstruction. And, as Clyburn later said, "If conditions were different I would have done it at 32, rather than at 52" ("Biography . . ."). However, in the 1960s, the opportunity for a black man to serve in the Congress was an impossible dream. Although advances had been made in civil rights nationally, South Carolina was slow to adjust.

In 1971, Clyburn obtained his first opportunity to move into a political arena. He was offered a position on South Carolina governor John West's staff; and in 1974 Governor West appointed Clyburn commissioner of the South Carolina Human Affairs Commission, a post he held until 1992.

In 1992, Clyburn stepped down from his position as commissioner to run for Congress from the Sixth Congressional District of South Carolina. The Sixth District contains a wide variety of people. It runs from near the North Carolina border, including tobacco farming areas, to the Atlantic coast, reaching, on the south, nearly to the Georgia border. It is a mix of rural and urban areas and is one of South Carolina's poorest districts, with 23 percent of its population living below the poverty level ("Biography . . .").

Clyburn, with his strong record of working for human rights and helping the poor, had little trouble winning the election. In 1993, he was sworn into the 103rd Congress, becoming the first black member of the House of Representatives from South Carolina since his great-uncle ("Biography . . .").

Once in Congress, Clyburn was assigned to the Transportation and Infrastructure Committee and, later, the Committee on Veterans Affairs. During his first term in Congress he was elected co-president with North Carolina Representative **Eva M. Clayton** of the Freshman Democratic Caucus.

Concerned about the poverty levels in his own district and the effects that military base closures had had on it during the previous decade, Clyburn introduced his first bill on the floor, which included a plan to create Enterprise Communities in these areas. Although the bill itself met with defeat, Clyburn was successful in having the language included in the Omnibus Budget Reconciliation Bill of 1993. Clyburn also aided his district by obtaining increased federal funds and attracting new businesses to the area.

From the start, Clyburn's agenda included protecting human rights and fighting for equality on all fronts. When there was a move during the 104th Congress to eliminate affirmative action, Clyburn campaigned against this, arguing,

> the stage is being set for an all out assault on affirmative action—an assault that is based, not on any true assessment of the merits of these programs, but rather on thinly disguised political tactics created to further incite rage and anger in an electorate already anxious over economic uncertainties. ("Biography . . .")

Clyburn supported President Bill Clinton's stance of "mend it, don't end it." Clyburn also campaigned to raise the minimum wage by 2000, introducing legislation to that effect, and supported the Livable Wage Act of 1995.

Because his district includes a great many tobacco farms, Clyburn has fought against both President Clinton and congressional attempts to raise excise taxes on cigarettes. As he said, "Until viable alternative crops are developed, I feel compelled to advocate fair treatment for the industry and the affected families, many of whom have little hope for a decent living otherwise" ("Biography . . .").

Clyburn has worked long and hard to bring equality to his district and the nation through various legislative means. His constituents have shown their appreciation of his efforts by re-electing him for four terms. Most recently, in the fall of 1998, Clyburn was chosen to chair the Congressional Black Caucus.

Sources

"Biography of Congressman James E. Clyburn." *U.S. House of Representatives.* <http://www.house.gov./clyburn/bio.html>. Accessed: 3/11/98.

"Rep. Clyburn of S. Carolina Will Chair Black Caucus." *The Washington Post,* 18 November 1998, A04. <http://search.washingtonpost.com/wp-srv/WPlate/1998-11/18/0471-111898-idx.html>. Accessed: 11/19/98.

"US Representative James Clyburn." South Carolina Politics. 1997. <http://www.ricommunity.com/scenic/politics/clyburn.htm>. Accessed: 2/26/98.

Barbara-Rose Collins

Reproduced from AP/Wide World Photos, by Richard Sheinwald

Born: April 13, 1939, in Detroit, Michigan

Status: Resident of Detroit, Michigan

Education: Attended Wayne State University, Detroit, Michigan

Position: Business manager, Wayne State University, Detroit, Michigan; member, Detroit School Board, Region One, Detroit, Michigan, 1970–1973; state representative, Michigan State Legislature, 1975–1982; member, Detroit City Council, Detroit, Michigan, 1982–1991; U.S. representative replacing retiring congressman George W. Crockett, Jr., 13th Congressional District of Michigan, 1991; U.S. representative from the 15th Congressional District of Michigan, 1992–1997

Early Years

Barbara-Rose Collins was born in Detroit, Michigan, on April 13, 1939, the daughter of Versa Richardson. Growing up in Detroit and attending its public schools, Collins saw the city slowly crumble from the economic prosperity of World War II, when its industries were geared up for the war effort, to become a city burdened by crime, homelessness, and drugs. It was all but abandoned by white businesses that fled its downtown area over the years.

Higher Education

After graduation from high school, Collins attended Wayne State University in Detroit, majoring in anthropology and political science, although she never finished her degree. For a time, she worked as a business manager at the university while attending to her family, which includes two children, Cynthia and Christopher.

Career Highlights

Collins's first step into politics came with her election to the Detroit School Board, Region One, in 1970. She was concerned about the deterioration of the city's schools and their educational quality. This concern, as well as her concern for the city as a whole, spurred her to run for the Michigan house of representatives in 1975 as a delegate from the 21st District of Detroit.

In the legislature, Collins became chairperson of the House Standing Committee on Urban Affairs, as well as chair and founding member of the Michigan Legislative Black Caucus. Her membership on the Committee on Urban Affairs gave her a forum from which to express her viewpoint on Detroit's deterioration. As she was later to say while in Congress, "What you see happening in Detroit, you will eventually see everywhere. Our problems are like a malignancy—it spreads . . . It is in the interest of the nation to solve these problems" (Bigelow 43).

In 1982, Collins left the legislature for a position on the Detroit City Council, where she would serve for eight years. During her tenure on the city council, Collins initiated ordinances on toxic waste cleanup and single-room occupancy housing for the homeless, and served as chair of both the Task Force on Litter and Cleanup and the Task Force on Teenage Violence and Juvenile Crime. This latter task force held personal meaning for her because her son, Christopher, had served a prison term for armed robbery.

In 1988, Collins unsuccessfully sought the Democratic nomination to the House of Representatives. But in 1991, when incumbent representative George W. Crockett, Jr., announced he was retiring from office, she was elected to fill his seat for the remainder of his term of office. When Collins took office, she went to Congress from the 13th Congressional District of Michigan. Yet, due to redistricting, when Collins ran for a full term in office, she was running from the new 15th Congressional District of Michigan. She had little opposition and received 87 percent of the vote in November, 1992.

Collins was appointed to the Post Office and Civil Service Committee and the Public Works and Transportation Committee, and during the 103rd Congress, she was appointed majority whip at large. However, her focus, as it always had been, was on the plight of

America's cities, an issue she felt was all but ignored in many quarters. Before taking her place in the House, Collins had enrolled in an orientation seminar for freshmen congressmen and congresswomen given by Harvard's Kennedy School of Government. Collins said, "We spoke with some of the greatest minds of the nation, and none of them dealt with the bread-and-butter problems of the cities" (Bigelow 42).

During her third full term in office, Collins began to come under criticism for some of the actions she had taken while in office. *The Detroit News* reported in April of 1996 that Collins had come under investigation by the U.S. Department of Justice for financial irregularities in her campaign and office accounts. She was criticized for her poor voting record; Collins had missed 25 percent of the House votes in 1995, pleading ill health. Perhaps the most controversial move she had made during this time was the firing of a staff member who was gay. As *The Detroit News* reported,

> He filed a complaint with Congress' internal grievance system alleging he was fired because Collins thought he might be HIV-infected and could be absent frequently. He won, and it was the first time a person won a grievance against a congressman. ("Collins' Backers . . .")

Collins's supporters said there was a conspiracy to remove her from office, and she herself "maintained that much of the criticism of her is racially motivated" (Bigelow 42).

Unfortunately, the controversy paid off for Collins's opponents. In the election held in the fall of 1996, Collins lost the primary to Carolyn Cheeks Kilpatrick. Kilpatrick then went on to win the election by a 9 to 1 margin; Collins stepped down from the House of Representatives in January of 1997.

Sources

"Barbara-Rose Collins." <http://www.inform.umd.edu/EdRes/Top...graphics/House/collins-barbara-rose>. Accessed: 2/26/98.

Bigelow, Barbara Carlisle, ed. *Contemporary Black Biography: Profiles from the International Black Community*, Vol. 7. Detroit, MI: Gale Research, 1994.

"Collins' Backers Stay Loyal Despite Allegations." *The Detroit News*, 3 April 1996. <http://www.detnews.com/menu/stories/42365.htm>. Accessed: 5/12/98.

Congressional Black Caucus '93–'94 Guide. <http://www.sas.upenn.edu/African_Studies/Govern_Political/CBC_Guide.html>. Accessed: 3/5/98.

"Representative Barbara-Rose Collins." *Project Vote Smart*. <http://www.vote-smart.org/congress/104/mi/mi-15-a/mi-15-ab.html>. Accessed: 2/26/98.

Cardiss Robertson Collins

Born: September 24, 1931, in St. Louis, Missouri

Status: Retired from Congress in 1996

Education: Attended Northwestern University, Evanston, Illinois; recipient of honorary degrees from Barber-Scotia College, Spelman College, and Winston-Salem State University

Position: Secretary, Illinois Department of Labor, early 1950s; secretary, accountant, revenue auditor, Illinois Department of Revenue, Chicago, Illinois, 1950s–c. 1970s; elected committeewoman, 24th Ward, Chicago, Illinois, c. 1969; U.S. representative from the Seventh Congressional District of Illinois, 1973–1996

Early Years

Cardiss Robertson Collins was born in St. Louis, Missouri, on September 24, 1931. She was the only child of Finley Robertson, a laborer, and Rosia Mae Cardiss Robertson, a nurse. When Collins was 10 years old, the family moved to Detroit, Michigan, where she attended public school. In 1949, after graduating from Detroit High School of Commerce, Collins moved to Chicago and tied mattresses at a mattress factory; she also worked as a stenographer at a carnival equipment company (Hine 264).

Higher Education

Collins realized that unless she got more education, she would remain at a low-level job, so she began attending evening classes at Northwestern University in nearby Evanston, Illinois. She also got a new job, this one as a stenographer with the Illinois Department of Labor. In time, the classes at Northwestern paid off for Collins, earning her a transfer to the Illinois Department of Revenue. She was then promoted to accountant and, finally, to revenue auditor.

Career Highlights

In the late 1950s, Collins met her husband, George W. Collins. He also had gone to Northwestern, earning a degree in business while working for the Chicago Municipal Court. The two were married in 1958, and soon had a son.

In 1964, George Collins decided to run for the Chicago Board of Aldermen from the 24th Ward of Chicago. Cardiss Collins became actively involved in her husband's political career, campaigning for him and serving as a Democratic committeewoman of Chicago's 24th Ward. In 1969, George Collins successfully ran for Congress, winning a seat from the Seventh Congressional District of Illinois. His wife and family remained in Chicago while he attended Congress, but almost every weekend, he flew home to Chicago to see them and to work with his constituents.

At Christmastime in 1972, George Collins was flying home to be with his family for the holidays. As his plane neared Midway Airport in Chicago, it suddenly went out of control, crashing into a house on Chicago's South Side. George Collins was killed, along with 43 other people. Cardiss Collins was left alone to support and raise a young son.

Almost immediately, Mayor Richard Daley of Chicago suggested that Collins make a bid for her husband's vacant seat in Congress. After a special election that Collins easily won, she took her seat in Congress on June 5, 1973, the first African American woman to represent a congressional district in the Midwest. Two years after her election, in 1975, she became the first woman to be appointed whip at large for the Democrats in Congress. During the 1970s, Collins also became the first African American and the first woman to chair the House Government Operations Subcommittee on Manpower and Housing and, in 1979, was elected chair of the Congressional Black Caucus. In 1991, she became the first woman and the first African American to chair a subcommittee of the Committee on Energy and Commerce.

Because of her husband's accident, over the years Collins took a leading position in the investigations into airport security and air safety practices. In 1987, she launched an investigation into the charges that Eastern Airlines had failed to repair critical equipment on their planes. The investigation led to charges against Eastern Airlines and nine of its managers.

One theme that has characterized much of the legislation generated by Collins is women's rights. In 1990, Collins wrote the law expanding Medicare coverage to mammography screening, as well as to PAP smears for the early detection of cervical and uterine cancer. She supported the establishment of day care centers, and authored the Child Safety Protection Act of 1993 that requires warning labels on dangerous toys and established federal safety standards for bicycle helmets. Additionally, she supported universal health care coverage, cosponsoring the Universal Health Care Act of 1991 and the Family and Medical Leave Act of 1991.

For 23 years, Collins was reelected time and again with little or no challenge, usually receiving more than 80 percent of the vote. In 1996, however, she decided to relinquish her seat. She had been in office longer than most and felt it was time to retire and return to her home in Illinois, where she presently resides.

Sources

"Biography of Congresswoman Cardiss Collins." <http://www.inform.umd.edu/EdRes/Top...s/Biographies/House/collins-cardiss>. Accessed: 2/27/98.

"Cardiss Collins." Legislative Biographies. <http://www.glue.umd.edu/~cliswp/Politicians/Leg/Bios/legbioc.htm>. Accessed: 2/27/98.

Clay, William L. *Just Permanent Interests: Black Americans in Congress, 1870–1991*. New York: Amistad Press, 1992.

Congressional Black Caucus '93–'94 Guide. <http://www.sas.upenn.edu/African_Studies/Govern_Political/CBC_Guide.html>. Accessed: 3/10/98.

Estell, Kenneth. *African America: Celebrating 400 years of Achievement*. Detroit, MI: Visible Ink Press, 1994.

Hine, Darlene Clark, ed. *Black Women in America, An Historical Encyclopedia*. Vol. I, A–L. Brooklyn, NY: Carlson Publishing Co., 1993.

George Washington Collins

Reproduced from AP/Wide World Photos

Born: March 5, 1925, in Chicago, Illinois

Status: Died December 8, 1972; buried at Burr Oak Cemetery, Chicago, Illinois

Education: Graduate, 1943, Waller High School, Chicago, Illinois; graduate, 1954, Central YMCA College, Chicago, Illinois; degree in business law, 1957, Northwestern University, Evanston, Illinois

Position: Private, sergeant, Army Corps of Engineers, 1943–1946; clerk, Chicago Municipal Court, Chicago, Illinois, 1954–1957; deputy sheriff, Cook County, Illinois, 1958–1961; secretary to Alderman Benjamin Lewis, 24th Ward, Chicago, Illinois, 1958–1961; administrative assistant, Chicago Board of Health, Chicago, Illinois, 1958–1961, alderman from the 24th Ward, Chicago Board of Aldermen, Chicago, Illinois, 1963–1969; U.S. representative from the Sixth Congressional District of Illinois, 1970–1972

Early Years

George Washington Collins was born on March 5, 1925, in Chicago, Illinois. Collins attended Chicago's public schools and in 1943 graduated from Waller High School. When he graduated, the United States was deeply involved in World War II, and he entered the army as a private. Assigned to the Corps of Engineers, he served in the South Pacific, moving up in rank to sergeant by the time of his discharge in 1946.

Higher Education

As it did for so many other former soldiers, the passage of the G.I. Bill after the war opened doors for Collins. Under the G.I. Bill, he could afford to attend college and, upon his return to Chicago, he enrolled in Central YMCA College, from which he graduated in 1954.

Always interested in law, Collins continued his education at Northwestern University in Evanston, Illinois. While he attended school, he also worked as a clerk in the Chicago Municipal Court. He graduated with a degree in business law from Northwestern in 1957.

Career Highlights

Unlike other places in the United States, Chicago politics were dominated by a "political machine" that dictated how things would be done and who would be elected. Early in his career, Collins began working in the machine. He worked hard to garner African American votes for various candidates and, from 1958 to 1961, served as secretary to Chicago Alderman Benjamin Lewis of the 24th Ward. In addition to his political activities, Collins was employed as a deputy sheriff for Cook County and as an administrative assistant for the Chicago Board of Health. In 1963, Collins's devotion to the machine paid off. When Benjamin Lewis died, Collins took his place as alderman, a position he would hold until his election to Congress.

In August of 1969, Representative Daniel J. Ronan died, leaving the Sixth Congressional District seat vacant. Ronan had been running for reelection, but died before the election could be held. A special primary was called to fill the vacancy, and two candidates were nominated: Brenetta M. Howell and George Collins.

Because of his past political activities, Collins was a well-known and well-liked figure in the Sixth District. It was no surprise, then, when Collins defeated Howell by a landslide, 36,350 to 5,940 (Clay 120). In the general election, Collins faced Republican Alex J. Zabrosky. Chicago was a Democratic town and Collins had the backing of Mayor Daley's constituency. Because of this, Collins was able to get support in white areas of his district that otherwise might have ignored him. As in the primary, Collins ran away with the election, gathering 68,182 votes to Zabrosky's 14,942 (Clay 120). Collins was elected to fill out Ronan's unexpired term in the 91st Congress, and then was elected to a full term in the 92nd Congress.

Collins began his first term in Congress on November 3, 1970. He was assigned to the Public Works and Government Operations Committees. Although a Democrat, Collins supported President Richard Nixon's proposals to allow a minimum federal payment to low-income families with children, and to share federal tax revenues with state and local governments. He was, however, against the levels of funding proposed, feeling they were too low. During his time in office, Collins also sought increased funding for education and mass transit programs, and for help for residents of cities who had been dislocated from their neighborhoods by road construction.

In 1970, Collins joined with other black members of Congress at a meeting called by **Charles Coles Diggs, Jr.**, the representative from Michigan. The purpose of the meeting was to discuss joining together to support minority interests in Congress. They felt some sort of unity was needed to pressure President Nixon and Congress in general in the enforcement of civil rights and passage of other legislation of interest to minorities. It was agreed by those attending that some sort of formal organization among black members of the House was needed. Throughout the coming year, discussions were held. Finally, on February 2, 1971, at a meeting of the Democratic Select Committee, they reached an agreement. The minutes read, "... at this point it was unanimously agreed that the Caucus be composed of only black members and that the word 'black' remain in the name," and the Congressional Black Caucus was born (Clay 121).

Collins worked hard for the Congressional Black Caucus and for his constituents throughout the following year. He was entering the last half of his first full term in Congress and looking ahead to reelection. He introduced a bill that would have, had it been passed, provided free preparation of income tax forms for low- and moderate income taxpayers. He also joined with others in an effort to reform the Federal Housing Administration after it had been revealed by an investigating committee that low-income homeowners were being defrauded by real estate brokers and other agencies.

A month after his successful reelection to Congress, on December 8, 1972, Collins was flying back to Chicago from Washington. He was returning for Christmas, planning to buy toys for the children of his ward's annual Christmas party. As his United Airlines plane circled Midway Airport for landing, the plane plummeted, crashing into a house on Chicago's South Side. Forty-four people, including George Collins, died in the crash.

Sources

Clay, William L. *Just Permanent Interests: Black Americans in Congress, 1870–1991.* New York: Amistad Press, 1992.

"Former Black Members of Congress. *Congressional Times Journal.* <http://www.usbol.com/ctjournal/FrBlkCongMemList.html>. Accessed: 2/21/98.

John Conyers, Jr.

Reproduced from AP/Wide World Photos, by Dennis Cook

Born: May 16, 1929, in Detroit, Michigan

Status: U.S. representative from the 14th Congressional District of Michigan

Education: B.A., 1957, Wayne State University, Detroit, Michigan; J.D., 1958, Wayne State University, Detroit, Michigan; recipient of numerous honorary degrees from various colleges and universities

Position: U.S. Army Corps of Engineers, 1948–1957; legislative assistant to Michigan State representative John Dingell, 1959–1961; senior partner and attorney, Conyers, Bell, and Townsend, Detroit, Michigan, 1959–1961; referee, Michigan Workman's Compensation Department, 1961–1964; U.S. representative from the First (later, the 14th) Congressional District of Michigan, 1965–; awarded the Rosa Parks Award, 1967, by the Southern Christian Leadership Conference

Early Years

John Conyers, Jr., was born on May 16, 1929, in Detroit, Michigan, to John and Lucille Conyers. His father worked on the Chrysler Corporation assembly line and was a strong union man, serving on the board of the United Automobile Workers (UAW) union. Conyers attended public schools in Detroit and, as did so many young men there, began working on the Lincoln-Mercury assembly line when he graduated from high school. He himself joined the union and was named education director of UAW Local 900.

Higher Education

Conyers did not wish to spend his life on the assembly line, though, and when he was 21, he enrolled at Wayne State University in Detroit. However, in August of 1950, his National Guard unit, which he had joined in 1948, was called to active duty and Conyers had to leave school. During his four years with the Guard, he attended officer training school and attained the rank of second lieutenant, serving a year in Korea during the Korean War.

When he was discharged from active duty in the army in 1954, he continued in the National Guard until 1957 but also returned to school at Wayne State University, graduating in 1957 and immediately entering Wayne State's law school. When he received his law degree the following year, Conyers began practicing in his own firm, Conyers, Bell and Townsend.

Career Highlights

Although he was busy with his law practice, Conyers was also becoming interested in politics and accepted the position of legislative assistant to John Dingell, who was then a state representative in Michigan (Dingell would later go on to be elected to the U.S. Congress). Following in his father's footsteps, Conyers served as general counsel for the Detroit Trade Union Leadership Council. In 1961, after leaving his position with Dingell, he was appointed a referee with the Michigan Workmen's Compensation Department. In 1963, he was appointed by President John F. Kennedy to the National Lawyers Committee for Civil Rights.

In 1964, Conyers decided to run for Congress in Michigan's First Congressional District. He drew upon his union contacts and the political base he had been building to challenge a crowded field of contenders in the Democratic primary, eking out a victory by 45 votes over his nearest competitor. In the general election, he faced Republican Robert Blackwell in a predominantly Democratic district, winning by a wide margin and becoming the youngest member of the U.S. House of Representatives.

When Conyers was sworn into Congress in 1965, the civil rights movement was at its height. Backed by the National Association for the Advancement of Colored People (NAACP), as well as by lobbyists with an interest in minority rights, Conyers was able to obtain an appointment on the powerful House Judiciary Committee.

From the start, Conyers made no bones about his positions on issues. Although President Lyndon Johnson was pursuing the war in Vietnam with congressional approval, Conyers spoke out against it and for peace. A vocal supporter of civil rights, Conyers cosponsored the 1965 Voting Rights Bill, as well as Johnson's Medicare program. With this kind of record in the House, Conyers had no difficulty winning reelection in 1966.

During his second term, Conyers was named the sole black person on the investigating committee looking into the activities of **Adam Clayton Powell, Jr.** While others spoke of ousting Powell from his seat in the House entirely, Conyers spoke in his favor. Conyers felt that the harsh censure of Powell passed by the House was a blow against African Americans. He again defended Powell in 1969, although Powell had called him a "black Judas" for serving on the original investigating committee in 1967.

Throughout his career in Congress, Conyers has tenaciously fought for civil rights and for various social programs that would help minorities and the disadvantaged. He has actively shaped public policy, writing legislation such as the Racial Justice Act, Voter Registration Reform Act, Martin Luther King, Jr., Holiday Bill, and Public Safety Officers Benefits Bill. And in 1970, he was one of the founding members of the Congressional Black Caucus, formed to promote minority interests in Congress. Columnist Jack Anderson said of Conyers in 1994 that he "is a serious player and a junkyard dog investigator, watching out for the taxpayers' wallets by rooting out fraud, waste, and abuse in every corner of the bureaucracy . . . His only special interest appears to be his constituents in Detroit" ("Biography ..."). With his reelection in 1994, he became the first African American to serve as the Democratic leader of the House Committee on the Judiciary, where, in 1998, he was a leading voice against the impeachment of President Bill Clinton.

Earlier in his career, Conyers said,

> Some see the black American's choice as between withdrawing from their "hopeless" government or overthrowing the entire system. I see our choice as between political involvement or political apathy. America is the black man's battleground. It is here where it will be decided whether or not we will make America what it says it is. . . . (Christopher 242)

Conyers has spent his life trying to make America "what it says it is," and continues to do so to this day.

Sources

Bigelow, Barbara Carlisle, ed. *Contemporary Black Biography: Profiles from the International Black Community*, Vol. 4. Detroit, MI: Gale Research, 1993.

"Biography of Congressman John Conyers, Jr." *U.S. House of Representatives*. 1995. <http://

www.house.gov/conyers/bio_john_conyers.html>. Accessed: 3/6/98.

Christopher, Maurine. *America's Black Congressmen.* New York: Thomas Y. Crowell, 1971.

Clay, William L. *Just Permanent Interests: Black Americans in Congress, 1870–1991.* New York: Amistad Press, 1992.

Estell, Kenneth. *African America: Celebrating 400 years of Achievement.* Detroit, MI: Visible Ink Press, 1994.

"John Conyers, Jr." Michigan Democratic Party. <http://www.hven.org/info/mdp/Congress/Conyers.htm>. Accessed: 2/26/98.

O'Brien, Catherine. "Millions Await Conyers, Other Long-Serving Pols in Retirement." *The Detroit News,* 12 May 1996. <http://www.detnews.com/menu/stories.47505.htm>. Accessed: 5/7/98.

D

William Levi Dawson

Reproduced from the Collections of the Library of Congress

Born: April 26, 1886, in Albany, Georgia

Status: Died November 9, 1970, in Chicago, Illinois

Education: B.A. magna cum laude, 1909, Fisk University, Nashville, Tennessee; attended Kent College Law School, Chicago, Illinois; law degree, Northwestern University law school, Evanston, Illinois; admitted to the Illinois bar, 1920

Position: First lieutenant, U.S. Army (WWI), 1917–1919; established law practice, 1920; elected Republican state committeeman, Chicago, Illinois, 1932; member, Chicago City Council, Chicago, Illinois, 1933–1939; elected committeeman of the Second Ward, Chicago, Illinois, 1940; appointed assistant chairman, Democratic National Committee, 1944; elected vice chairman, Democratic National Committee; U.S. representative from the First Congressional District of Illinois, 1943–1970

Early Years

William Levi Dawson was born on April 26, 1886, in Albany, Georgia. His father, Levi Dawson, a barber, died when Dawson was just a child. Dawson's family was financially comfortable for the times. His mother, Rebecca Kendrick Dawson, worked hard to instill in Dawson and his siblings the value of a good education. Dawson was a bright child and did well in the schools in Georgia; upon graduation from high school, he enrolled at Fisk University in Nashville, Tennessee.

Higher Education

Dawson worked his way through Fisk University, graduating magna cum laude in 1909. He then began studying law at Kent College in Chicago, Illinois. He had intended to study medicine, but decided to change to law when he realized that becoming a doctor would take many years. He wanted to finish in as little time as possible to start working and earning money to help his mother put his brothers and sisters through college.

Dawson had transferred to Northwestern University School of Law and was working and studying in Evanston, Illinois, when the United States entered World War I. He joined the army and was commissioned as an officer in the U.S. Expeditionary Forces. While distinguishing himself in battle, he also suffered injuries. He was overcome by poison gas, then received a wound to his leg that shattered the bone and left him with a permanent limp.

After returning home at the end of the war, Dawson resumed his education. He graduated from the Northwestern school of law and established a practice in Chicago after passing the Illinois bar examination in 1920. That same year, on December 20, he married Nellie Brown, the daughter of a Washington minister.

Career Highlights

Like most African Americans at that time, Dawson was a Republican, the party that had championed Radical Reconstruction and equal rights for blacks during the previous century. In 1928, he decided to become actively involved in politics, challenging the incumbent white congressman from the First District of Illinois, a predominantly black district. Although he lost, he caught the attention of party leaders and demonstrated the importance of race in the political arena. In 1932, he was elected a Republican state committeeman and, the following year, won a seat on the Chicago City Council.

In 1938, Dawson again ran for Congress, this time challenging Democrat **Arthur Wergs Mitchell**. Dawson was at a disadvantage, however. The Great Depression was devastating Illinois as well as the rest of the country, and the Republicans were falling out of favor, particularly among black voters, because of their opposition to Franklin Roosevelt's New Deal policies that helped the poor. During the Depression, blacks were hit the hardest economically. Jobs that traditionally had been held by blacks were now seen as the province of whites seeking employment. As a result, black unemployment skyrocketed; many were teetering on the brink of starvation and saw Roosevelt's New Deal as their salvation. But Republicans fought bitterly against the programs Roosevelt proposed, and the Republican Party was no longer seen as the salvation of African Americans. Dawson was keenly aware of this development, and after a number of discussions with Chicago's Democratic mayor, Edward J. Kelly, decided to change parties. The Democrats sought to help the disadvantaged, both black and white, and Dawson could see the beneficial effects of New Deal programs in his own city. Having switched parties, Dawson was elected Democratic committeeman of the Second Ward of Chicago and set to work to establish himself within that party.

By 1942, Dawson had gained the political influence necessary to mount a challenge for Arthur Mitchell's congressional seat; Mitchell, who had served four terms in Congress, had decided to retire, saying that he was tired of Congress. Dawson ran a successful campaign against former Republican state senator William King, defeating him by nearly 3,000 votes.

When William Dawson took his seat in Congress in 1943, there were few other black representatives. A quiet, thoughtful man who knew the ins and outs of the political system and staunchly defended the rights of blacks, Dawson called for an end to discrimination against blacks within the defense industries and the armed forces and testified against poll taxes before the House Judiciary Committee. He also devoted time to building the Democratic Party itself. In 1944, he was appointed assistant chairman of the Democratic National Committee and was soon elected its vice chairman, the first black person to be elected to this office.

In 1949, Dawson was named chairman of the House Committee on Expenditures in Executive Departments (later renamed the Committee on Government Operations). In assuming this position, he became the first black member of Congress to chair a standing committee.

Throughout his career in Congress, Dawson championed black rights, although in the 1950s, because of his quiet demeanor, he was often unjustly compared to the showier **Adam Clayton Powell, Jr.**, congressman from New York. As one article in the *Washington North Star* noted, "Dawson presented a sharp contrast to his soon-to-be ally Adam Clayton Powell, Jr., who loudly blasted discrimination wherever he found it . . ." (Clay 78). Although Powell and Dawson would work together to support the civil rights issues of the 1950s and 1960s, Powell was the more noticeable man. But while Powell was shouting and grandstanding, Dawson was quietly working to do away with discrimination, supporting efforts to increase voter registration among blacks in the South and working to support school integration. Dawson himself said that, unlike Powell, he utilized "speeches only as the artisan does his stone, to build something" (Christopher 188).

In December of 1960, President-elect John F. Kennedy offered William Dawson the office of postmaster general in his new administration. Dawson had worked tirelessly to deliver Illinois votes to the Democratic ticket in the 1960 presidential campaign. Although honored by the offer, Dawson declined. As Kennedy said, Dawson, "after some reflection . . . declined on the grounds that he could best serve his country, his party, and Illinois in Congress" (Christopher 189).

Dawson's service to his district in Illinois did not go unrewarded throughout the years; he was reelected to Congress time and again, even during the years when his quiet demeanor had earned him the pejorative label of "Uncle Tom" from some of the more radical elements in black society. By 1969, age and ill health were having their effect upon him. When he took his seat in Congress that year after winning reelection yet again, he was the oldest chairperson of a standing committee. In the middle of his term, his 14th in Congress, he announced that the time had come to retire. It is indicative of the respect and power he commanded that he was able to name a successor to his seat who was elected and accepted by his constituency. He chose as his successor a young man named Ralph H. Metcalfe, then an alderman in the Chicago City Council, who assumed Dawson's seat after a special election in November, 1970. A few days later, on November 9, 1970, Dawson passed away from cancer in Chicago, Illinois.

When William Dawson retired, he had served in the United States Congress longer than any other black man. Although often harshly, and unfairly, criticized during his time in office, which lasted 27 years, his steady, quiet battle for black equality left its indelible mark on both his own city, Chicago, and on the country as a whole.

Sources

Christopher, Maurine. *America's Black Congressmen*. New York: Thomas Y. Crowell, 1971.

Clay, William L. *Just Permanent Interests: Black Americans in Congress, 1870–1991*. New York: Amistad Press, 1992.

Robert Carlos DeLarge

Reproduced from the Collections of the Library of Congress

Born: March 15, 1842, in Aiken, South Carolina

Status: Died February 14, 1874, in Charleston, South Carolina; buried at Brown Fellowship Graveyard in Charleston, South Carolina

Education: Attended Wood High School, Charleston, South Carolina

Position: Farmer; tailor; agent for hire, Freedmen's Bureau, c. 1865–c. 1868; organizer, South Carolina Republican Party, 1860s; chairman, credentials committee, Republican State Convention, 1867; member, Committee on Franchise and Elections, South Carolina constitutional convention, 1868; state representative, South Carolina State Legislature, 1868–1870; land commissioner, 1870; U.S. representative from the Second Congressional District of South Carolina, 1871–1873; magistrate, Charleston, South Carolina, 1873–1874

Early Years

Robert Carlos DeLarge was born a slave on March 15, 1842, in Aiken, South Carolina. Little is known about his childhood, but it is known that he did get an education at Wood High School in Charleston, South Carolina, probably during or just after the Civil War. After being freed, DeLarge worked as a farmer and a tailor, and as an agent for the Freedmen's Bureau, then became involved in politics, working as an organizer for South Carolina's Republican Party.

Career Highlights

In 1865, the newly freed African Americans held their own convention, the Colored People's Convention, after no black was included in the first South Carolina state constitutional convention. DeLarge, as an intimate member of the Republican Party in the state, chaired the credentials committee; later he would chair the platform committee of the 1867 Republican State Convention. At the 1868 South Carolina State Constitutional Convention, to which blacks were finally invited, DeLarge served on the Committee on Franchise and Elections. That same year, he was elected to the South Carolina legislature, and was named chairman of its Ways and Means Committee. When he stepped down from office in 1870, the legislature appointed DeLarge land commissioner in charge of the sale and transfer of 2,000 tracts of land to homeowners who then had eight years to pay for the land.

DeLarge was an intense man, scrupulously honest and constantly looking for ways to promote equality. In the summer of 1870, he was nominated to run as the Republican candidate for the seat in the House from the Second Congressional District of South Carolina. His only other challenger was a fellow Republican, Christopher C. Bowen. The race was tight, but DeLarge was declared the winner by 986 votes. However, Bowen immediately challenged the results on the basis of voter fraud. Despite the challenge, DeLarge was sworn into the 42nd Congress on March 4, 1871, and assigned to the Committee on Manufactures.

Although his seat in the House was in question, DeLarge represented his state as if there were no challenge. In 1871, he added an amendment to an appropriations bill to provide $20,000 for the rebuilding of a Charleston orphanage destroyed during the war. He also fought to maintain federal troops in the South, and for the government to enforce the 14th Amendment to prevent the intimidation of blacks by various white terrorist groups.

In December of 1871, the House Committee on Elections at last began deliberation on Bowen's charges against DeLarge and the election results of 1870. DeLarge's health was poor, yet, despite that, he undertook the task of preparing a case defending himself and the election results. The House Committee on Elections looked into numerous instances of voter fraud in connection with the election and, finally, on January 18, 1873, declared that the election had so many instances of abuse and so many irregularities that there was no way to determine a winner. It stated that neither Bowen nor DeLarge was the winner; the seat was vacant.

In ill health, DeLarge declined to run in 1872, and Alonzo J. Ransier, another black Republican, won the election. DeLarge remained in Columbia, South Carolina, for a short period, then returned to his home in Charleston, where he was appointed magistrate of that city by the governor. Shortly thereafter, on February 14, 1874, DeLarge died of consumption at the age of 31. A quiet, dignified, and intelligent man, he had made his mark on history despite the bad luck that seemed to plague him in life.

Sources

Christopher, Maurine. *America's Black Congressmen.* New York: Thomas Y. Crowell, 1971.

Clay, William L. *Just Permanent Interests: Black Americans In Congress, 1870–1991.* New York: Amistad Press, 1992.

"Former Black Members of Congress." *Congressional Times Journal.* <http://www.usbol.com/ctjournal/FrBlkCongMemList.html>. Accessed: 4/2/98.

Lamson, Peggy. *The Glorious Failure: Black Congressman Robert Brown Elliott and the Reconstruction in South Carolina.* New York: W.W. Norton and Co., 1973.

Ronald Vernie Dellums

Reproduced from AP/Wide World Photos, by John Duricka

Born: November 24, 1935, in Oakland, California

Status: Retired

Education: A.A., 1958, Oakland City College, Oakland, California; B.A., 1960, San Francisco State College, San Francisco, California; M.S.W., 1962, University of California at Berkeley, California; recipient of an honorary doctor of law degree from Wilberforce University, 1975

Position: U.S. Marine Corps, 1954–1956; social worker, California Department of Mental Hygiene, 1962–1964; program director, Bayview Community Center, San Francisco, California, 1964–1965; associate director, then director, Hunters Point Youth Opportunity Center, San Francisco, California, 1965–1966; planning consultant, Bay Area Social Planning Council, San Francisco, California, 1966–1967; director, Concentrated Employment Program, San Francisco Economic Opportunity Council, San Francisco, California, 1967–1968; senior consultant, Social Dynamics, Inc., 1968–1970; lecturer, San Francisco State College, San Francisco, and the School of Social Work, University of California at Berkeley, 1968–1970; member, Berkeley City Council, Berkeley, California, 1967–1970; U.S. representative from the Eighth (later, the Ninth) Congressional District of California, 1970–1998

Early Years

Ronald Vernie Dellums was born on November 24, 1935, in Oakland, California. He was not a motivated student and, after graduation from high school in 1954, joined the U.S. Marine Corps.

Higher Education

When he was discharged from the Marines, Dellums decided to continue his education and enrolled at Oakland City College, receiving an associate's degree in 1958.

His own experiences in the ghetto while he was growing up determined his career choice. He studied social work, hoping to help others in poverty. In 1960, he received a bachelor's degree from San Francisco State College and, in 1962, a master's of social work degree from the University of California at Berkeley.

Career Highlights

Dellums's first job was as a social worker with the California Department of Mental Hygiene and, over the years, as with his first job, the positions he accepted were geared toward helping others. As Edward Glynn wrote of Dellums in *America*, "He truly desires to bring people from various racial, ethnic, and social backgrounds together to work at solving the human problems of war, poverty, racism, nationalism, hunger, employment, and oppression that afflict all peoples" (Bigelow 55).

Berkeley in the 1960s was a place where Dellums could find support in these goals. The home of the student protest, free love, and the hippy movements fostered liberal ideas and encouraged Dellums. In 1967, he won a place on the Berkeley City Council, but in 1970 he decided to run for Congress in an effort to better effect change. He was endorsed in his campaign by Coretta Scott King, the wife of slain civil rights leader Martin Luther King, Jr., and by César Chavez. One thing that bolstered his campaign was a remark by President Richard Nixon's vice president, Spiro Agnew. While campaigning in the area, Agnew called Dellums an "out-and-out radical" (Bigelow 55). For the residents of Berkeley, there could be no higher endorsement. Dellums defeated incumbent Jeffrey Cohelan in the primary election with 57 percent of the vote, and easily won the election.

When Dellums took his seat in Congress, his liberal views outraged many. He had no fear about attacking some of the United States' most cherished institutions and went after corporations and the military alike. As he said early in his congressional career, "We've always subsidized major corporations. We've subsidized electronics firms. We've subsidized oil millionaires with oil depletion allowances . . . I'd like to have a bill passed that gave the poor a brand new industry and then have the government subsidize it" (Bigelow 55). Dellums was also an outspoken opponent of the Vietnam War, in which the United States was involved at the time, and a fierce advocate of civil rights. When he was named to the Armed Services Committee in 1973, many thought he might have changed his stance on the war and the military, but he said,

> I did not join the Armed Services Committee to learn about missiles, planes, and ships; I joined because I knew I would need to become an expert in this field in order to argue successfully for military spending reductions that would free-up resources for the desperate human needs that I see every day in my community. ("A Biography" 1)

Dellums's positions on issues did not endear him to a great many in Congress, and created many opponents who, over the years, tried unsuccessfully to discredit him. At one time, a reporter for the *National Review* claimed Dellums had ties to Communists. Despite criticism, Dellums continued to fight for reduced military spending, civil rights, education, and increased opportunities for minorities.

In 1971, Dellums was the first congressman to call for economic sanctions against the apartheid government of South Africa, introducing a bill to that effect and joining in protest marches on the South African Embassy. Fifteen years later, the bill was finally passed by Congress, with modifications, over President Ronald Reagan's veto.

Throughout his career, Dellums fought against the erosion of the gains in civil rights that had occurred during the 1970s and 1980s. In 1991, he was a vocal supporter of the 1991 Civil Rights Restoration Act, and for the reauthorization of the 1967 Voting Rights Act. But Dellums's *béte noire* during his tenure in Congress has and continues to be military spending and the United States' nuclear arms policies. In 1983, he published *Defense Sense: The Search for a Rational Military Policy* (Cambridge, MA: Ballinger Publishing). The book grew out of a series of hearings Dellums conducted on "The Full Implications of the Military Budget." In it, he detailed the social and economic impacts of U.S. military stockpiling and the threat of the weapons' eventual use.

Despite his liberal stances and his boldness, Dellums continued to be popular until his retirement on February 6, 1998. In 1997, he had won reelection with 154,806 votes to his Republican challenger's 37,126 votes. Throughout his political career he spoke up for and advocated what he believed. As he said in an interview in *Mother Jones*, "Democracy is not about being a damn spectator against the backdrop of tap-dancing politicians swinging in the winds of expediency" (Bigelow 54).

Sources

Bigelow, Barbara Carlisle, ed. *Contemporary Black Biography: Profiles from the International Black Community*, Vol. 2. Detroit, MI: Gale Research, 1992.

"A Biography." *U.S. House of Representatives*. <http://www.house.gov/dellums/dellums_bio.html>. Accessed: 3/6/98.

Oscar Stanton De Priest

Reproduced from the Collections of the Library of Congress

Born: March 9, 1871, in Florence, Alabama

Status: Died May 12, 1951, in Chicago, Illinois; buried in Graceland Cemetery, Chicago, Illinois

Education: Graduated elementary school, Salina, Kansas; studied bookkeeping, Salina Normal School, Salina, Kansas

Position: Real estate broker, Chicago, Illinois; elected to Cook County Board of Commissioners, Chicago, Illinois, 1904; alderman, Chicago City Council, Chicago, Illinois, 1915–1917, 1943–1947; elected Third Ward committeeman, Chicago, Illinois, 1924; U.S. representative from the First Congressional District of Illinois, 1929–1935; delegate, Republican National Convention, 1936

Early Years

Oscar Stanton De Priest was born in Florence, Alabama, on March 9, 1871, just as Reconstruction was permitting blacks to gain political leadership in the South. As he was growing up, however, De Priest would see that leadership evaporate to a trickle and then finally dry up as southern white conservatives regained their hold over politics. De Priest himself would break that hold in 1928, becoming the first black congressman to be elected in the twentieth century and the first black congressman to be elected from a northern state.

De Priest's childhood was relatively uneventful. In 1878, when he was seven years old, De Priest's family moved from Alabama to Salina, Kansas, seeking greater opportunity. De Priest graduated from elementary school in Salina and continued his education at the Salina Normal School, studying bookkeeping.

About the age of 18, De Priest left home with two friends for Dayton, Ohio, then moved to Chicago, working for a time as a painter, plasterer, and decorator. His training in bookkeeping and knowledge of finances helped him during these years. He saw the opportunity to make money in real estate and began investing in land, starting a real estate business and speculating in the stock market.

Career Highlights

By the turn of the century, De Priest had amassed enough wealth to be an influential voice in local politics and, in 1904, he actively entered the political arena, running successfully for Cook County commissioner. In 1908, he attended the Republican National Convention as an alternate delegate and, in 1915, he was elected alderman to the Chicago City Council, the first black man to be elected to the city council.

Chicago politics was a rough arena, and graft and corruption were rampant. In 1917, De Priest experienced firsthand the "machine" that was Chicago politics. He was charged with accepting protection money from gamblers and, facing a lengthy trial, resigned from his position as alderman. Fortunately, he was defended by the great Clarence Darrow who proved that the charges were trumped up by De Priest's political enemies, and he was acquitted.

During the years following his trial, De Priest attempted to regain his city council seat a number of times but was unsuccessful. Finally, in 1924, after regaining some of the influence he had lost because of the accusations against him, he was elected committeeman of the Third Ward. When First District congressman Martin Madden died in April, 1928, De Priest was nominated to fill his seat, and the following November, despite charges (again) of accepting bribes, he was elected the first black congressman in nearly 30 years.

When De Priest entered Congress on April 15, 1929, southerners in Congress considered challenging his seating. Then speaker of the House Nicholas Longworth devised a strategy to defeat any challenge to De Priest's assumption of his seat. Instead of swearing each member in individually, as was usual, he took the bold step of swearing in all the new congressmen at once so that those who might have been sworn in before De Priest, and who would have been able to protest his seating, could not object.

For many African Americans at that time, De Priest represented their lone voice in government. De Priest was appointed to the Committee on Enrolled Bills, the Committee on Indian Affairs, and the Committee on Invalid Pensions. He and his wife also went to social affairs for congressmen held in the Capitol. Their presence, unlike that of their white counterparts, sometimes caused political fallout. In an August 17, 1936, *Time Magazine* article,

"Black Game," a writer noted how socializing with blacks hurt one presidential contender:

> In 1928 Herbert Hoover won four Southern states but lost them the next year when Mrs. Hoover invited Mrs. Oscar De Priest, wife of Chicago's Negro Representative, to the White House for tea. ("Black Game")

After his reelection in 1930, De Priest took up the cause of black equality, both within government and in society. He proposed a bill that would have allowed Congress to reduce the number of seats held by states that actively tried to prevent black voters from voting, and a bill providing for a pension to be paid to ex-slaves over the age of 75. Both proposals were unsuccessful. De Priest also proposed that Abraham Lincoln's birthday be made a public holiday.

In January, 1934, black equality became a more personal issue for De Priest. Democrat Lindsay C. Warren, congressman from North Carolina and chairman of the House Committee on Accounts, ordered that De Priest's secretary, Morris W. Lewis, and Lewis's son not be admitted to a "whites only" public House restaurant. Although De Priest circulated a petition calling for an investigation and obtained 145 signatures, a House special committee appointed to this task refused to change the policy. The treatment of his staff was to be cause for battle for De Priest during his entire tenure in office. Although he himself was able to receive service in many of the government-run restaurants, his staff was continually refused even admittance.

After his reelection in 1932, De Priest joined with the rest of Congress to tackle the ravages the Depression was wreaking on the country. President Franklin Delano Roosevelt was beginning to institute many of his relief programs, and De Priest was concerned that these programs would be offered only to whites. Seeking to ensure that they be made available to unemployed blacks also, on March 29, 1933, De Priest added an amendment to the Civilian Conservation Corps (CCC) Bill that would bar discrimination in the corps because of race, color, or creed. The bill, including the amendment, passed both the House and Senate and was signed into law by President Roosevelt.

Although De Priest supported the CCC Bill, he did not favor many of Roosevelt's other relief proposals, much to the dismay of the voters in his district. In the election of 1934, this stance was his downfall. He was defeated by Democrat **Arthur Wergs Mitchell**, who actively supported Roosevelt's New Deal. Mitchell became the first black Democrat elected to Congress.

De Priest returned to Chicago and to his real estate business, but he kept his hand in politics. In 1943, he was again elected an alderman to the Chicago City Council from the Third Ward, serving until 1947, when he was defeated in his reelection bid.

During his last years, De Priest managed his real estate business with his son Oscar De Priest, Jr. The Republicans in Chicago had lost their control of city politics, and there was little chance of a successful challenge to the Democrats. De Priest retired from the political arena, but not without having left his mark upon it. At the age of 80, Oscar Stanton De Priest died of kidney failure on May 12, 1951.

Sources

"Black Game." *Time Magazine*, 17 August 1936. *Time Almanac*, Reference Edition. Fort Lauderdale, Fl: Compact Publishing, 1994.

Christopher, Maurine. *America's Black Congressmen*. New York: Thomas Y. Crowell, 1971.

Clay, William L. *Just Permanent Interests: Black Americans in Congress, 1870–1991*. New York: Amistad Press, 1992.

"Former Black Members of Congress." *Congressional Times Journal*. <http://www.usbol.com/ctjournal/FrBlkcongMemList.html>. Accessed: 2/13/98.

Charles Coles Diggs, Jr.

Reproduced from AP/Wide World Photos

Born: December 2, 1922, in Detroit, Michigan

Status: Died August 24, 1998, in Hillcrest Heights, Maryland

Education: Graduate, 1940, Miller High School, Detroit, Michigan; attended the University of Michigan, Ann Arbor, Michigan, 1940–1942; attended Fisk University, Nashville, Tennessee, 1942; graduate, 1946, Wayne College of Mortuary Science, Detroit, Michigan; law degree, 1951, Detroit College of Law, Detroit, Michigan

Position: Private, then second lieutenant, U.S. Army Air Corps, 1943–1945; mortician, board chairman, House of Diggs, Inc., Detroit, Michigan, 1946–1955; senator, Michigan State Senate, 1951–1954; U.S. representative from the 13th Congressional District of Michigan, 1955–1980

Early Years

Charles Coles Diggs, Jr., was born on December 2, 1922, in Detroit, Michigan, to Charles and Mayme Jones Diggs. His father was a busy and prosperous man. He was the owner of mortuary, insurance, and ambulance businesses, and had served as a Michigan state senator.

Diggs grew up in Detroit, attending Detroit's public schools, in which he won awards in debating. He spent his free time working in his father's various businesses and, in 1940, graduated from Miller High School in Detroit.

Higher Education

The fall after his graduation from Miller, Diggs entered the University of Michigan in Ann Arbor, Michigan, where he studied for two years. In the fall of 1942, he transferred to Fisk University in Nashville, Tennessee, but in 1943 his education was interrupted when he was drafted into the army.

Diggs entered the U.S. Army Air Corps as a private, but soon earned promotion to the rank of second lieutenant. When the end of the war came in 1945, he was stationed at the Tuskegee Air Field in Alabama. He received his discharge on June 1 of that year.

Returning to Michigan, Diggs enrolled in the Wayne College of Mortuary Science in Detroit, graduating the following year, 1946, in June. He then joined his father in his mortuary business, House of Diggs, Inc., as a licensed mortician, soon becoming chairman of the board of the mortuary.

Career Highlights

One reason for Diggs's promotion to chairman was the arrest and imprisonment of his father. Charles Diggs, Sr., had first been elected to the Michigan State Senate in 1937. During the late 1940s, he was charged with "legislative bribe conspiracies" and sentenced to two concurrent terms of three to five and four to five years in prison. In 1950, the elder Diggs was paroled after serving 15 months in prison and, astonishingly, was reelected to the state senate. His election was challenged in the state senate, however, which voted not to reseat him.

Charles Diggs, Jr., was in law school at the time his father lost his seat in the state senate. A special Democratic primary was called to fill the elder Diggs's vacant seat as well as that of Anthony Wilkowski, who had also been refused a seat because of a term in prison. Diggs decided to run for his father's seat in the state senate and, at the same time, defend his father's record. Diggs won the primary and went on to soundly defeat his Republican opponent, Robert Ward, assuming his seat in the Michigan State Senate in 1951.

Although quiet and self-effacing, Diggs had a great deal of political ambition and, in 1953, ran for the Detroit City Council. While he was defeated, remaining in the state legislature, his face was becoming known as were his pro-labor positions.

In 1954, Diggs decided to challenge incumbent congressman George O'Brien in the Democratic primary. Many thought Diggs was being foolish; O'Brien had been in office for many years, and Diggs had been in political office only four years. Diggs campaigned under the slogan "Make Democracy Live," and spoke wherever he could find an audience. O'Brien, on the other hand, felt that Diggs's challenge was so minimal that he did not even return home from Washington to campaign until it was nearly time for the primary in August. It was a complete surprise to O'Brien when Diggs won the primary.

Diggs faced Republican Landon Knight in the election. Knight was the son of the owner of the *Detroit Free Press*, and many felt that because of this connection, he stood a better chance than Diggs, particularly since Diggs was running in a district that was 55 percent white. When Diggs unexpectedly carried the election, he said his victory was "a victory for all the people . . . This is a great victory for the Democratic party, and it also settles the deeper issues—the racial issue. This is proof that the voters of the 13th District have reached maturity" (Christopher 210). With his election, Diggs became Michigan's first black member of Congress.

Charles Diggs was sworn into the House of Representatives on January 3, 1955, and named to the Committee on Interior and Insular Affairs and the Veterans Affairs Committee. He immediately plunged into the issues of the day concerning civil rights, often becoming actively involved. In addition to joining New York's **Adam Clayton Powell, Jr.**, in seeking civil rights legislation and adamantly fighting for the Civil Rights Act of 1957, during the next 10 years Diggs often went to areas where the actual battles for equality were taking place. He traveled to Mississippi, urging blacks to register to vote. And he was a guest at the home of Aaron Henry, president of the Mississippi chapter of the National Association for the Advancement of Colored People (NAACP), when a bomb destroyed Henry's house.

In addition to fighting for civil rights, Diggs also spoke out about the importance of black Africa's emerging countries, earning the title given him by former congressman **William Lacy Clay, Sr.**, of the "Father of African-American Foreign Relations" (Clay 86). In 1957, Diggs accompanied then vice president Richard Nixon on a tour of African nations and, in 1959, was appointed to the Committee on Foreign Affairs, becoming, a decade later, the chairman of the Subcommittee on Africa.

During the 1960s, Diggs came to the defense of Adam Clayton Powell, Jr., when the House refused to seat him. He urged the House to reseat Powell and give him the salary that had been withheld during the time he had been unseated, but the House refused to consider his motions.

In 1972, when Powell died, Diggs became the senior black member of Congress at the age of 50; a year earlier he had been one of the founders and served as chairman of the first Congressional Black Caucus, a group that continues today. Diggs's efforts on behalf of black African nations also continued. He traveled frequently to various African countries and worked diligently on their behalf. Diggs had been appointed to the United States delegation to the United Nations, but resigned and walked out of a session of the United Nations in protest of American sales of arms and planes to Portuguese and South African forces for the purpose of fighting black Africans. In 1973, he was chairman of a coalition that lobbied the government for $30 million in famine relief for the Sahel region of Africa. So great an advocate was Diggs that, in 1975, on yet another trip to Africa, the South African government refused him entry into that country. Diggs was the champion in the United States of black rights in Africa.

Charles Diggs's illustrious career in Congress came to an abrupt end in 1978, however, when, after a lengthy investigation, he was convicted of federal income tax evasion and misuse of public funds. After an investigation by the House Committee on Standards of Official Conduct, Diggs was officially censured on July 31, 1979.

Diggs had appealed his conviction to the Supreme Court, but the Court refused to review his case. So, on June 3, 1980, Diggs resigned his seat in the 96th Congress, going from one of the highest offices in the country to a prison cell. Former representative William L. Clay notes that, "even more tragic is that after Diggs suffered his personal humiliation and served his time in prison, not one African nation offered him a contract to represent their interests here in the United States" (89). After Diggs's release from prison, he ran a funeral home business in Hillcrest Heights, Maryland, until his death on August 24, 1998.

Sources

Christopher, Maurine. *America's Black Congressmen.* New York: Thomas Y. Crowell, 1971.

Clay, William L. *Just Permanent Interests: Black Americans in Congress, 1870–1991.* New York: Amistad Press, 1992.

"Former Black Members of Congress." *Congressional Times Journal.* <http://www.usbol.com/ctjournal/FrBlkCongMemList.html>. Accessed: 3/6/98.

Gunzburger, Ron, ed. "Politics 1: The Last Hurrah (Deaths, Scandals and Other Milestones." *Politics 1.* <http://www.politics1.com/hurrah.htm>. Accessed: 1/7/99.

David Norman Dinkins

Reproduced from AP/Wide World Photos, by Ed Bailey

Born: July 10, 1927, in Trenton, New Jersey

Status: Professor in the practice of public affairs, Barnard-Columbia Center for Leadership in Urban Public Policy, New York, New York

Education: B.S. magna cum laude in mathematics, 1950, Howard University, Washington, D.C.; attended Rutgers University, New Jersey, 1950; LL.B., 1956, Brooklyn Law School, Brooklyn, New York

Position: U.S. Marines, 1945–1946; attorney and partner, Dyett, Alexander, Dinkins, Paterson, Michael, Dinkins, and Jones, 1956–1975; state representative, New York assembly, 1965–1966; president, Carver Democratic Club, Harlem, New York, 1967–c. 1997; president, New York City Board of Elections, New York, New York, 1972–1973; New York City clerk, New York, New York, 1975–1985; president, Borough of Manhattan, New York, New York, 1986–1989; mayor, New York, New York, 1990–1993; visiting Chubb fellow, Yale University, New Haven, Connecticut, 1993; professor, practice of public affairs, Bernard-Columbia Center for Leadership in Urban Public Policy, New York, New York, 1994–

Awards and honors: Named pioneer of excellence, World Institute of Black Communications; Righteous Man Award, New York Board of Rabbis; Distinguished Service Award, Federation of Negro Civil Service Organizations

Early Years

David Norman Dinkins, the oldest son of William H. and Sally Dinkins, was born in Trenton, New Jersey, on July 10, 1927. The year before his birth, his parents had moved from Newport News, Virginia, to New Jersey. His father, a barber, became a real estate agent in 1962.

In 1933, Dinkins's parents divorced, his mother moving to Harlem in New York City. For a while, he and his younger sister, Joyce, lived with his mother. But during most of his childhood, Dinkins and his sister lived with his father and stepmother, Lottie Hartgell Dinkins, in New Jersey, attending the public schools there.

The elementary and junior high schools Dinkins attended in Trenton were segregated, but the high school nominally was not. Although it admitted black students, there were restrictions placed upon them that were not placed upon the white students. Dinkins, or "Dink" as his friends called him, and the few other black students in the predominantly white school, among other things, were not permitted to use the school swimming pool. Despite the restrictions placed upon him, Dinkins won over the other students with his quiet charm and was elected president of his homeroom in 1943.

When Dinkins graduated in 1945, he tried to join the marines but was turned down as the marines' "Negro quota" had been met at that time. He was drafted into the army, later transferring to the marines and was stationed at Camp Lejeune, North Carolina, for most of his time in the service. When he was discharged in 1946, he took advantage of the G.I. Bill and enrolled at Howard University in Washington, D.C.

Higher Education

Howard University was a black university, and Dinkins was popular on campus; he joined a fraternity and did well in his studies in mathematics. While at Howard, Dinkins met his future wife, Joyce Burrows, and they became engaged.

When Dinkins graduated magna cum laude in 1950, he received a fellowship to attend Rutgers University but, restless, he dropped out after only a semester and got a job selling insurance. Again, because of his affable manner, he soon became one of the insurance agency's top salesmen. In 1953, he quit his job and began studying at Brooklyn Law School. That same year, on August 30, he married his college sweetheart, Joyce; the Dinkins would have two children, David, Jr., and Donna Hoggerd. In 1956, he received his degree in law and joined the law firm of Dyett and Phipps (later, Dyett, Alexander, Dinkins, Paterson, Michael, Dinkins, and Jones).

Career Highlights

Dinkins's father-in-law, who owned a liquor store in Harlem, was actively involved in New York politics. He was a former assemblyman and district leader, and he encouraged Dinkins to become similarly involved. Basil Paterson, a partner of the firm in which Dinkins practiced law, was then the vice chairman of the Democratic National Committee, and he, too, encouraged Dinkins. Dinkins and his wife were living in Harlem, and her father introduced Dinkins to the Carver Democratic Club, something of a political "machine" in Harlem. Anyone who had political aspirations in Harlem relied on the club's support.

Dinkins devoted a great deal of time to the Carver Club, working on voter registration drives, putting up posters, and generally "paying his dues." His charm and affability stood him in good stead with the other members, many of whom, like Dinkins, would eventually hold positions of power—Basil Paterson,

Charles Bernard Rangel, and Percy Sutton. He also began making contacts outside the club, among the city's white politicians.

In 1965, Dinkins successfully ran for the New York State Assembly and, in 1967, became district leader of the Carver Democratic Club. During his time in the New York assembly, however, the lines on his district had been redefined, and Dinkins decided not to run for reelection, feeling that he had lost much of his base of support. Mayor Abraham Beame offered him the post of deputy mayor of the city, but Dinkins declined, accepting instead the post of New York City clerk, a position he held until 1985.

Dinkins continued working politically for the Carver Club and the candidates it promoted, as well as practicing law and building his own political base. During the 1970s, he headed the Coalition of Black Elected Democrats and, in 1984, supported **Jesse Louis Jackson** for president over Democratic candidate Walter Mondale, a decision that would later haunt him.

In 1985, Dinkins was elected president of the borough of Manhattan, a position that gained him political power because, as president, he was an ex-officio member of the Board of Estimates, the board that reviewed New York City's budget and major contracts. During his time as president, Dinkins held to a moderate position on most issues, although he did support AIDS services in the community. Because of his deliberation and moderation, many called him a procrastinator; others saw him as reasonable and sensible.

In 1989, Dinkins's supporters urged him to challenge incumbent mayor Ed Koch. Koch had alienated many black voters because of budget cuts that affected low-income and minority neighborhoods. Black leaders felt Koch had become indifferent to their concerns. Drawing on the political base he had spent years building, Dinkins was able to narrowly defeat Koch in the Democratic primary and to win over Republican Rudolph Giuliani, who was a district attorney. With the victory, Dinkins became New York City's first black mayor.

During the election, his earlier alliance with Jesse Jackson came back to haunt Dinkins; while campaigning for president, Jackson had referred to New York as "Hymietown," alienating Jewish voters who saw Dinkins's support of Jackson as support for anti-Semitism. Dinkins was hard put to distance himself from Jackson's remarks. Dinkins's finances also were a stumbling block in the campaign. He had failed to pay income taxes from 1969 to 1972 and was accused of underreporting the value of his stock portfolio, which he had turned over to his son when he declared his candidacy for mayor. Dinkins later paid his back taxes, and an investigation revealed no wrongdoing concerning his portfolio, but at the time of the election, the charges cast a shadow over his campaign. New York City, however, was facing numerous problems, and Dinkins seemed to be the candidate who might have solutions. As *The New York Times* reported,

> David Dinkins comes to the office of mayor after three decades of loyal, quiet service to the Democratic party—making him a man who is a groundbreaker and very much bound by tradition. In a race against two high-profile opponents, Mr. Dinkins was the candidate of moderation, a middle-of-the-road choice for a city that seemed eager to lower its own decibel level. His strategy was to soothe, not excite—and it worked. (Bigelow 65)

The job that Dinkins had undertaken was not an easy one; the city was facing a massive deficit, racial unrest, a national recession, and rising crime rates. Rather than pandering to popularity, Dinkins did what had to be done, cutting departmental budgets, including social programs, and laying off city workers to reduce the deficit. And, in fact, the city showed a budget surplus in 1992.

When protests erupted in 1991 after a car driven by a Jewish leader in Brooklyn killed a young black man in Queens, Dinkins's quiet style quelled the upheaval. He was similarly put to the test in 1992, after the verdict against Rodney King, who had been brutalized by police in California, threatened to cause racial riots in cities across the country. John A. Marino, Democratic chairman, said in *The New York Times*, "This was a defining moment for him. He showed why he was elected" (Bigelow 68).

As the election of 1993 approached, however, many of the good things Dinkins had done for the city were forgotten. Critics attacked him for appointing incompetent people to posts in the city, a lack of strong leadership, his budget cuts that had laid off so many, and, again, procrastination. In the election, Dinkins was defeated by Republican Rudolph Giuliani.

After stepping down from the position of mayor, Dinkins first accepted a teaching position for a year at Yale University as a Chubb fellow, then became a professor with the Barnard-Columbia Center for Leadership in Urban Public Policy where he continues to teach. In August of 1995, he underwent quadruple bypass surgery, but returned to his teaching in New York in September of that same year.

Sources

Bigelow, Barbara Carlisle, ed. *Contemporary Black Biography: Profiles from the International Black Community*, Vol. 4. Detroit, MI: Gale Research, 1993.

"David Dinkins Returns to the Classroom." *Columbia University Record*, 29 September 1995. <http://www.columbia.edu/cu/record21/record2104.32.html>. Accessed: 5/5/98.

"David Norman Dinkins." SIPA Faculty Bio. *Columbia University*. <http://www.columbia.edu/cu/sipa/RESEARCH/DDinkins.html>. Accessed: 3/1/98.

Estell, Kenneth. *African America: Celebrating 400 Years of Achievement*. Detroit, MI: Visible Ink Press, 1994.

Smith, Jessie Carney, ed. *Black Heroes of the 20th Century*. Detroit, MI: Visible Ink Press, 1998.

Julian Carey Dixon

Reproduced from AP/Wide World Photos, by John Duricka

Born: August 8, 1934, in Washington, D.C.

Status: U.S. representative from the 32nd Congressional District of California

Education: B.S., 1962, California State University, Los Angeles; LL.B., 1967, Southwestern University, Los Angeles, California

Position: U.S. Army, 1957–1960; attorney, 1967– ; legislative aide to California state senator Mervyn Dymally, c. 1970–1971; assemblyman, California State Assembly, 1972–1978; U.S. representative from the 28th (later, the 32nd) Congressional District of California, 1979–

Early Years

Julian Carey Dixon was born August 8, 1934, in Washington, D.C.

Higher Education

With his graduation from California State University in Los Angeles in 1962, Dixon entered graduate school, receiving an LL.B. in 1967 from Southwestern University in Los Angeles.

Career Highlights

After practicing a few years as an attorney, Dixon was offered the position of legislative aide to California state senator **Mervyn Malcolm Dymally** (who would himself be elected to Congress in 1981). But, as **William Lacy Clay, Sr.**, points out, "his rise in politics was not tied to Dymally's star. It was, rather, the result of a series of vacancies created by **Yvonne Braithwaite Burke**" (261). Burke stepped down from her seat in the California State Assembly to run for Congress in 1972, and Dixon was elected to the vacant seat.

During his time in the California State Assembly, 1972–1978, Dixon worked on legislation dealing with criminal justice, education, and fair employment practices, making a name for himself as a fair, nonpartisan legislator who was interested in minority rights and opportunities. In 1978, Yvonne Burke again provided an opportunity to Dixon when she left her seat in Congress from the 28th Congressional District of California to run for the office of attorney general of California.

The race for Congress was not as smooth as the one for the California assembly had been, however. Dixon was faced with eight other contenders for the seat. In the primary, the major candidates were Dixon, Los Angeles city councilman David S. Cunningham, and State Senator Nate Holden. The one advantage Dixon had over these two was the size of his campaign funds. He was supported by State Assemblyman Howard L. Berman and U.S. Representative Henry Waxman, who were skilled fundraisers. While Cunningham and Holden were having trouble financing adequate radio and television spots, as well as other means of promotion, Dixon was easily able to publicize his campaign. Funding, combined with his legislative record, garnered the primary election for Dixon; he was able to defeat his closest rival, Holden, by 48 percent (Clay 261).

Since his initial election to Congress in 1978, Dixon has served nine consecutive terms, initially representing the 28th District, which, following a redistricting in California, became the 32nd. Steadily over the years, he has worked for civil rights. In 1983, he authored the first law calling for economic sanctions against South Africa and, four years later, the legislation providing humanitarian aid to southern Africa. He pushed for restrictions on the funding to the U.S. Civil Rights Commission after there were attempts made to thwart its mission. Dixon has also been a strong supporter of low- and moderate-income housing, education, job opportunities, and expanded health care. In championing his own state, Dixon has also met with success. He supported a Los Angeles subway project, now under construction, and worked for funds to help communities hurt by defense spending cuts.

During his tenure in office, Dixon became the first African American to chair an appropriations subcommittee on the District of Columbia and, in 1984, the first African American to serve as chairman of the Standing Committee on Rules for the Democratic National Committee. Dixon has chaired the Congressional Black Caucus and, from 1986 to 1990, served as president of the Congressional Black Caucus Foundation, which encourages minority participation in the legislative process.

Named one of the 12 "Unsung Heroes in Congress" by *Politics in America*, Dixon continues to work quietly, yet effectively, for civil rights and other issues in Congress. During his years in office, he has faced no difficult challenge to his reelection.

Sources

Clay, William L. *Just Permanent Interests: Black Americans in Congress, 1870–1991*. New York: Amistad Press, 1992.

Congressional Black Caucus '93–'94 Guide. <http://www.sas.upenn.edu/African_Studies/Govern_Political/CBC_Guide.html>. Accessed: 3/10/98.

"Incumbent Tremors in Illinois." *Congressional Quarterly Weekly Report*, 21 March 1992, 739–44.

Telephone interview with staff at Congressman Dixon's Washington, D.C., office, 26 May 1998.

Mervyn Malcolm Dymally

Reproduced from AP/Wide World Photos

Born: May 12, 1926, in Cedros, Trinidad, British West Indies

Status: Retired from Congress, 1992

Education: B.A. in education, 1954, California State University, Los Angeles; M.A. in government, 1969, California State University, Sacramento; Ph.D. in human behavior, 1978, United States International University, San Diego, California

Position: Teacher of exceptional children, Los Angeles Public Schools, Los Angeles, California, 1956–1963; state representative, California assembly, 1963–1966; state senator, California State Senate, 1967–1975; lieutenant governor of California, 1975–1979; U. S. representative from the 31st Congressional District of California, 1981–1992

Early Years

Mervyn Malcolm Dymally was born in Cedros, Trinidad, in the British West Indies on May 12, 1926. After attending Cedros Government School and St. Benedict and Naparima secondary schools in San Fernando, Trinidad, Dymally came to the United States in 1946 to continue his education.

Higher Education

Once in the United States, Dymally began studies at Lincoln University in Jefferson City, Missouri, but soon transferred to California State University at Los Angeles. There he majored in education and, in particular, special education, graduating with a bachelor's degree in 1954. Later, Dymally attended school while also pursuing his legislative career, earning a master's degree in government from California State University in Sacramento in 1969, and a Ph.D. in human behavior from the United States International University in San Diego, California, in 1978.

Career Highlights

After graduating from college, Dymally began teaching exceptional children in Los Angeles and also became involved in California politics. In 1963, he was elected as a representative to the California State Assembly, becoming the first black person ever to serve in the California legislature and, from 1967 to 1975, served in the California State Senate. Throughout his career in the California legislature, Dymally worked on improving education and increasing opportunities for minorities. While in the state senate, among other things, he chaired a committee on social welfare.

On November 5, 1974, Dymally was elected lieutenant governor of California, the first African American to be elected to this post in California. At the same time, he headed the State Commission for Economic Development and the Commission of the Californias. He successfully ran for reelection to the position of lieutenant governor in 1978.

In 1980, Dymally decided to move from the state to the federal level, running for Congress in the 31st District of California against incumbent representative Charles H. Wilson and three other candidates in a June primary. Because of his sound record of social service, Dymally was easily able to defeat all three and go on to win the general election in November of 1980, taking his seat in Congress in 1981.

During his 11-year career in the House of Representatives, Dymally served on a variety of committees: the House Foreign Affairs Committee, the Post Office and Civil Service Committee, and the District of Columbia Committee, among others. He also chaired the Congressional Black Caucus from 1987 to 1989. Dymally quietly worked for civil rights throughout his career. He focused on increasing funding for education and pushed support for minority-owned and -operated energy firms. Because of his background, he devoted a great deal of time to United States policies toward the various countries in the Caribbean.

In 1992, Mervyn Dymally announced his retirement from Congress. He had served for more than a decade, meeting and defeating a number of challenges for his seat, and at the age of 66 he stepped down. Dymally left Congress with a solid record of support for human rights and equality.

Sources

Clay, William L. *Just Permanent Interests: Black Americans in Congress, 1870–1991.* New York: Amistad Press, 1992.

"Former Black Members of Congress." *Congressional Times Journal.* <http://www.usbol.com/ctjournal/FrBlkcongMemList.html>. Accessed: 2/21/98.

E

Joycelyn Elders

Reproduced from AP/Wide World Photos, by Wilfredo Lee

Born: August 13, 1933, in Schaal, Arkansas

Status: Professor of pediatrics, University of Arkansas Medical School, Little Rock, Arkansas

Education: B.A., 1952, Philander Smith College, Little Rock, Arkansas; M.D., 1960, University of Arkansas School of Medicine, Little Rock, Arkansas; certified pediatric endocrinologist, 1978

Position: Pediatric intern, University of Minnesota, 1960–1961; pediatric resident, 1961–1963, chief pediatric resident, 1963–1964, pediatric research fellow, 1964–1967, assistant professor, 1967–1971, associate professor, 1971–1976, professor of pediatrics, 1976–1987, 1994–, University of Arkansas Medical Center, Little Rock; director, Arkansas Department of Health, 1987–1993; United States surgeon general, 1993–1994

Early Years

Joycelyn Minnie Elders was born Minnie Lee Jones on August 13, 1933, in Schaal, Arkansas, the eldest of eight children. Her parents, Curtis and Haller Jones, were sharecroppers and, while growing up, Elders worked in the fields with her parents and siblings. The sharecropper's house in which they lived had no electricity or indoor plumbing, and the children had to walk five miles to catch the school bus that would then take them 13 miles to the nearest school. But Elders enjoyed learning and did well, encouraged by her grandmother, who also lived with the family.

By the time Elders graduated from high school at the age of 15, she excelled enough to obtain a scholarship to Philander Smith College, a black college in Little Rock, Arkansas. She was starting a new life with college and decided she needed a new name, so she changed her first name to Joycelyn; she had seen the name on a piece of peppermint candy and liked it (Smith, *Black Heroes*, 218).

Higher Education

Elders discovered that she enjoyed science—biology and chemistry—and initially decided to become a laboratory technician. But while at Philander Smith she heard a speech by Edith Irby Jones, the first black woman to study medicine at the University of Arkansas, and raised her sights. She would aim for a career as a doctor.

After graduating in 1952 from Philander Smith, Elders joined the army and trained as a physical therapist. By serving in the army, Elders would be able to go to graduate school under the G.I. Bill and train to become a doctor. In 1956, after her discharge, she entered the University of Arkansas School of Medicine as the only black woman in her class.

Being the only female and one of three African Americans in the class was difficult for Elders. She was the target of derision from the white male class members and, being African American, faced a wall of discrimination. The black students were forced to eat in the dining room reserved for the school's cleaning staff as they were not permitted in the university dining room. Elders, however, ignored the slights and jabs from other students and the discrimination with which she had grown up, keeping her eyes on her goal of becoming a physician.

While in school, she met Oliver Elders, a basketball coach in a nearby high school. She had been giving physicals at the high school as a means of earning extra money. The two were married in 1960. Although Elders's career consumed much of her time in later years, she felt family was of equal importance and came to as many games as possible played by the teams her husband coached.

The same year she married Oliver Elders, Joycelyn Elders graduated with her medical degree from the University of Arkansas. After interning at the University of Minnesota, she returned to Arkansas, assuming a residency at the University of Arkansas Medical Center. Elders was quickly promoted to chief pediatric resident, and then named a pediatric research fellow, specializing in pediatric endocrinology.

Career Highlights

Much of her research and work in pediatric endocrinology dealt with young people suffering from insulin-dependent diabetes. In the course of treating these young people, Elders began to advocate the stance that would cause her problems in the future. She realized that pregnancy was a great risk for diabetic females, particularly when they were young. She began to advise her young diabetic patients about the dangers of pregnancy. As she said, "If I wanted to keep those kids healthy, I decided I had no choice but to take command of their sexuality at the first sign of puberty" (Bigelow 84).

Elders's work was becoming better known. She had published a great many papers in her field. In 1987, Bill Clinton, who was then governor of Arkansas, appointed her the head of the Department of Health in Arkansas. Elders saw the appointment as an opportunity to help even more young people than she had before. As she had been in her practice, she was concerned about the increasing rate of teenage pregnancies. Although the national pregnancy rate among teens nationally was 13 percent, in Arkansas it was 20 percent (Bigelow 84–85). Elders realized that the cost to the public for these children was enormous. She also realized something had to be done about the spread of AIDS and other sexually transmitted diseases.

Elders began speaking out about the necessity of contraception for teenagers, advocating statewide sex education classes and the distribution of condoms in the schools. She also set up a number of health clinics in various schools to advise students on contraception and sexually transmitted diseases. Although she discouraged abortion, advocating prevention, she was also pro-choice.

The reaction to Elders's programs from some quarters was vitriolic. Although the number of teenage pregnancies had fallen in the state in proportion to the national average, she had many opponents. Many charged that the clinics she had set up were merely teaching the young people how to have sex, others claimed that her efforts infringed upon individual rights, and still others objected on religious grounds. Right-to-life groups jumped on her pro-choice stance.

Elders faced her opponents with equanimity. She knew she also had her supporters and that the facts spoke for themselves. She accused the anti-abortion groups of having "a love affair with the fetus." Never one to mince words, she said in an interview in *USA Today*, "Abortion foes are part of a celibate, male-dominated church, a male-dominated legislature and a male-dominated medical profession" (Smith, *Black Heroes*, 218).

In 1993, when Bill Clinton was elected president, he nominated Elders for the office of surgeon general of the United States, and the criticism she had endured in Arkansas became national. Although she was recommended by C. Everett Koop, the previous surgeon general, her stances on abortion, contraceptives, and teenage pregnancy were examined and debated during the confirmation hearings. Every aspect of her life came under scrutiny. She had been on the board of the National Bank of Arkansas, which was sued for allegedly authorizing $1.5 million in bad loans. The suit had been settled, but that did not mean the Senate dismissed it. There was also criticism that her husband did not pay social security taxes to a caregiver for his mother who had Alzheimer's disease.

Through all the criticism, Elders continued to hold her ground. A group of Republicans managed to delay the confirmation vote but, finally, on September 7, 1993, she was confirmed as surgeon general, the first black woman to be appointed to this position in the United States.

In discussing her nomination, *Time Magazine* said, "If Elders gets to don the gold-braided uniform of the nation's No. 1 doctor, she may end up . . . infuriating her supporters and amazing her detractors" (Carlson). All too soon, this prediction came true. As she had all her life, she voiced her opinions bluntly and unequivocally. In December, 1993, after stating her support for the legalization of drugs to reduce the nation's crime rate, the Clinton administration hastily issued a statement denying that this view was shared by the president. Elders also continued to advocate sex education and abortion rights in the schools. While many applauded her outspokenness, others were outraged.

Finally, in December, 1994, Elders went beyond the limit deemed acceptable by the Clinton administration. In a speech on World AIDS Day at the United Nations, when asked if she advocated masturbation as a means of curbing sexual activity among children, she stated, "With regard to masturbation, I think that is something that is part of human sexuality and a part of something that perhaps should be taught" (Smith, *Black Heroes*, 220). Although she later stated that she meant that all issues dealing with sexuality should be taught, and not that school children should be taught how to masturbate, the damage was done. The day after her speech, President Clinton demanded and received her resignation from office.

Outspoken, with strong views, Joycelyn Elders made her mark upon the Clinton administration when she voiced her opinions on sex education, contraception, and legalizing drugs all to ebb the rising tide of AIDS. Even before her confirmation by Congress, she was labeled by *Time* as a "verbal bomb thrower" (Carlson). After resigning, Elders returned to her position at the University of Arkansas Medical Center, continuing her work in pediatric endocrinology. In 1996, she published her autobiography, *Elders, M.D.: From a Sharecropper's Daughter to Surgeon General* (New York: Morrow). Although she has retired from the very public forum in which she spoke as surgeon general, she continues to candidly and frankly express her views.

Sources

Bigelow, Barbara Carlisle, ed. *Contemporary Black Biography: Profiles form the International Black Community*, Vol. 6. Detroit, MI: Gale Research, 1994.

Carlson, Margaret, et al. "Prognosis: Controversy." *Time Magazine*, 19 July 1993. *Time Almanac*, Reference Edition. Fort Lauderdale, FL: Compact Publishing, 1994.

"Elders, M. (Minnie) Joycelyn." *Biography Online Database*. 1995. <http://www.biography.com/find/bioengine.cgi?cmd+1&rec+17292>. Accessed: 4/11/98.

Smith, Jessie Carney, ed. *Black Heroes of the 20th Century.* Detroit, MI: Visible Ink Press, 1998.

———. *Notable Black American Women*, Vol. II. Detroit, MI: Gale Research, 1992.

Robert Brown Elliott

Courtesy of the South Caroliniana Library, University of South Carolina, Columbia

Born: August 11, 1842, perhaps in Liverpool, England

Status: Died August 9, 1884, in New Orleans, Louisiana; buried in St. Louis Cemetery No. 2, New Orleans, Louisiana

Education: Unknown; admitted to the bar of South Carolina, September 23, 1868

Position: Associate editor, *South Carolina Leader*, Charleston, South Carolina, 1867–c. 1871; law partner, Whipper, Elliott and Allen, Charleston, South Carolina, 1868–c. 1871; member, South Carolina State Constitutional Convention, 1868; appointed assistant adjutant general of the State of South Carolina, 1869; representative, South Carolina State Legislature, 1868–1869, 1874–1876; U.S. representative from the Third Congressional District of South Carolina, 1871–1872, 1873–1874; attorney general, State of South Carolina, 1876–1877; special customs inspector, Charleston, South Carolina, 1879–1881; lawyer, New Orleans, Louisiana, 1882–1884

Early Years

The Civil War afforded the opportunity to many to reshape their lives, and it seems that Robert Brown Elliott was one who seized this opportunity. There are a variety of accounts of Elliott's early life, but very little documentation to support any of these. One account places his birth in Boston, Massachusetts, and another in Liverpool, England. Neither account can be verified. At that time, record keeping was haphazard, particularly for "people of color" in both England and New England. His parents may have been of West Indian origin, but it is equally likely that he was born into slavery in South Carolina. The one thing each version of his story does agree upon is that he was born on August 11, 1842.

As with the origins of his birth, Robert Elliott's education is similarly clouded. One account, which biographer Peggy Lamson conjectures was gleaned from the *Congressional Directory* and probably written by Elliott himself, claims that he was privately educated in Boston where he was born, then sent to an uncle in Jamaica for more schooling, and finally sent to England to complete his education in 1853.

Higher Education

In England, he supposedly attended High Holborn Academy and, in 1855, entered Eton College, from which he graduated with honors in 1859. Then he is said to have read law with a Sergeant Fitzherbert in London and to have returned to the United States in 1861.

No documentation exists to support this story. In investigating Elliott's background for her biography, *The Glorious Failure: Black Congressman Robert Brown Elliott and the Reconstruction of the South*, Peggy Lamson found no evidence that an academy named High Holborn ever existed in England. Similarly, "at Eton College, the authorities there categorically state that no Robert Brown Elliott ever attended Eton, nor is it possible that he enrolled under a different name, for there was no one who could have fit his description at the school during the years 1853 to 1859" (24). There is also no evidence that Robert Elliott ever read law with a Sergeant Fitzherbert in London in 1860, or that a Sergeant Fitzherbert even existed.

If Elliott was educated—and contemporary records indicate he must have been as he was said to be an intelligent, polished speaker and writer—the sources of that education are unknown. His legal studies may merely have consisted, as John Cromwell suggests in his book *The Negro in American History* (1914), of "six months close study of the South Carolina Code" to be admitted to the bar (Lamson 179).

Career Highlights

The first verifiable mention of Robert Brown Elliott comes with his appearance in 1867 in Charleston, South Carolina, where he was employed as associate editor at Richard H. Cain's newspaper, the *South Carolina Leader.* Like Cain, and probably encouraged by him, Elliott immediately became involved in Reconstruction politics and, from the start, emerged as a natural leader. In 1868, he attended the South Carolina state constitutional convention where he helped shape the state's new constitution and obtain its passage. He also pushed for compulsory public education and fought against former slaveholders being paid for the loss of their slaves. That same year, Elliott was elected to the South Carolina house of representatives.

On March 25, 1869, when Elliott's term in the legislature expired, Governor Robert K. Scott named him assistant adjutant general of the State of South Carolina. His duties included organizing a militia to protect citizens from such terrorist groups as the Ku Klux Klan. Elliott resigned this position in December of 1870, suspecting that Scott wished to use the militia for his own political purposes.

In 1868, Elliott had been admitted to the South Carolina bar and joined two other lawyers in the Charleston firm of Whipper, Elliott, and Allen, the first of a number of law firms with which he would ally himself over the years. According to Peggy Lamson, Macon B. Allen, the third partner of the firm, was the first African American in the United States to be admitted officially to the bar, on May 3, 1845, in Massachusetts.

Elliott, while successful in his law practice, had higher ambitions and was aiming for a seat in Congress. In 1870, he was nominated for Congress in South Carolina's Third District and, later that year, defeated Democrat John E. Bacon. In March of 1871, Elliott fulfilled his ambition of becoming a congressman and was named to the Committee on Education and Labor. With the assumption of his seat in the 42nd Congress, Elliott became the first full-blooded black man to be elected to Congress.

At some point during 1870, Robert Elliott apparently married Grace Lee Elliott, although, as with the stories of his education, there is some confusion. According to various land deeds, letters, and other records dating from 1870 and 1871, Elliott regarded Grace Lee Elliott as his wife. An 1874 account in *The New York Herald*, however, has Elliott married to a "pretty rose-tinted light mulatto" named Nancy Fat (Lamson 32). There is little doubt, though, that Grace Lee Elliott considered herself Elliott's wife at the time of his death. When his will was probated, she produced letters from him addressing her as "my dear wife" as evidence of the relationship. Nancy Fat and her relationship to Elliott remain a mystery.

During his term in Congress, Elliott vehemently spoke against the restoration of rights to ex-Confederates and against the terrorist activities of the Ku Klux Klan in South Carolina and throughout the South. His eloquence on the latter issue was rewarded with the April 20, 1871, passage of the "KKK" Act meant to protect against terrorist groups; however, within 12 years, the Supreme Court had declared it unconstitutional.

Returning to South Carolina to run for reelection in August of 1872, Elliott faced charges by his opponent that he had accepted bribes. Despite these, he easily won reelection and returned to Congress. Again, however, he wanted to aim higher. **Hiram Rhodes Revels** had been elected to complete the unexpired term of Jefferson Davis in the Senate in 1870, and Elliott hoped to become the first black man to be elected to a full term in the Senate (an honor that would go to **Blanche Kelso Bruce** in 1875). Accordingly, in the fall of 1872, Elliott ran for a seat in the Senate against John J. Patterson. Surprisingly, Elliott did not gain the support of the black members of the South Carolina legislature and, lacking this critical support, was defeated. He returned to the House of Representatives to finish the session ending on March 3, 1873.

When Elliott again took his seat in Congress on December of 1873, he did not know he would soon be in the national spotlight. In January of 1874, civil rights legislation came before the House banning discrimination against African Americans in public inns, public transportation, and other public areas. Alexander H. Stephens of Georgia, the former vice president of the Confederacy, spoke against the bill, and Robert Brown Elliott was chosen to speak in its favor. *The New York Tribune* reported on his eloquence, noting that "The African love of melody was noticeable in the harmony of his delivery" (Lamson 175). Although Elliott had made a dramatic positive impression on both Congress and the nation, he would not be in Congress to see the bill's passage in February of 1875.

On November 1, 1874, Elliott resigned his House seat and returned to South Carolina. As in so many southern states at this time, Reconstruction Republicans were battling against conservative Democrats who wished to regain political control and do away with much of the progress toward equality that had been made between blacks and whites since the Civil War. Elliott felt he was needed at home to help in this battle and, returning from Washington, again won a seat in the South Carolina legislature.

Yet Elliott's endeavors were too little, too late; the Republicans were split and in disarray, and the Democrats were gaining power. In 1876, Elliott was elected state attorney general but was forced out of office in 1877.

Through his political connections, Elliott obtained an appointment as a special customs inspector for the Treasury Department, based in Charleston, in 1879. On an inspection to Florida, however, he contracted malaria for which there was no available cure at that time, weakening his health and plaguing him the rest of his life.

Elliott's fortunes as well as his health were declining. A house in Columbia, South Carolina, that he and his wife owned was sold through foreclosure. Grace Elliott was also suffering from ill health. Then, in May of 1881, the Treasury Department, with little notice, transferred Elliott to New Orleans, Louisiana. Once there, he ran afoul of local politics and was dismissed from his position in August 1882. Although Elliott tried to establish a law practice in New Orleans, it failed because Elliott did not have the influence or connections he had possessed in South Carolina. When he died of a final bout of malaria on August 9, 1884, he was virtually penniless. After his death, however, he was praised by no less a figure than Frederick Douglass, who wrote of him:

> To all outward seeming, he might have been an ordinary Negro . . . Yet from un-

> der that dark brow there blazed an intellect and a soul that made him aim for high places among the ablest white men of the age . . . (Lamson 289)

Sources

Christopher, Maurine. *America's Black Congressmen.* New York: Thomas Y. Crowell, 1971.

Clay, William L. *Just Permanent Interests: Black Americans in Congress, 1870–1991.* New York: Amistad Press, 1992.

Cromwell, John W. *The Negro in American History.* Washington, DC: American Negro Academy, 1914.

"Former Black Members of Congress." *Congressional Times Journal.* <http:www.usbol.com/ctjournal/FrBlkCongMemList.html>. Accessed: 2/13/98.

Lamson, Peggy. *The Glorious Failure: Black Congressman Robert Brown Elliott and the Reconstruction in South Carolina.* New York: W.W. Norton and Co., 1973.

A. Michael "Mike" Espy

Reproduced from AP/Wide World Photos, by Barry Thumma

Born: November 30, 1953, in Yazoo City, Mississippi

Status: Attorney, Crosthwait Terney, TLLC Professional Limited Liability Co., Jackson, Mississippi

Education: B.A., 1975, Howard University, Washington, D.C.; J.D., 1978, University of Santa Clara School of Law, Santa Clara, California

Position: Attorney and manager, Central Mississippi Legal Services, Yazoo, Mississippi, 1978–1980; director of public lands and elections, Mississippi Secretary of State's Office, 1980–1984; assistant attorney general of consumer protection, Office of the Mississippi Attorney General, 1984–1985; U.S. representative from the Second Congressional District of Mississippi, 1987–1993; U.S. secretary of agriculture, 1993–1994; attorney, Crosthwait Terney, TLLC Professional Limited Liability Co., Jackson, Mississippi, 1996–

Early Years

Alphonso Michael "Mike" Espy was born on November 30, 1953, in Yazoo City, Mississippi. His family, which had lived in the Delta region of Mississippi for generations, owned a funeral business and was economically comfortable. Espy attended segregated public school in the state, graduating from high school in 1971 and entering Howard University in Washington, D.C.

Higher Education

After receiving a bachelor's degree at Howard, Espy continued his studies at the University of Santa Clara, from which he graduated in 1978 with a degree in law.

Career Highlights

Upon graduation, Espy returned to his hometown of Yazoo City, Mississippi, and established a law practice. At the same time, he also became involved in local politics, utilizing many of the ties his family had in the region and serving as assistant secretary of state for Central Mississippi Legal Services.

In 1980, Espy was appointed assistant secretary of state of the public lands division, and, in 1984, served as assistant state attorney of the consumer protection division, Office of the Mississippi Attorney General. Although there was talk about Espy running as Mississippi's first black governor, in 1985 he decided to run for Congress.

The race was a close one, but again Espy's ties to the region, as well as his solid record with the Mississippi government, gave him the edge he needed. The Second Congressional District was predominantly black, which also helped Espy's chances. In 1987, he was sworn into the 100th Congress as Mississippi's first black congressman since **John R. Lynch** stepped down from his seat in Congress in 1883. Espy was appointed to the Agriculture and Budget Committees, and the Select Committee on Hunger.

From the start, Espy made a mark on the House. Although still a freshman, he managed to get a major piece of legislation passed: the Lower Mississippi River Valley Delta Development Act, a "blueprint for economic development in a seven-state area" (Clay 371). Then, in 1992, President-elect Bill Clinton asked Espy if he would serve as secretary of the Department of Agriculture.

In 1993, Espy resigned his seat in Congress and was sworn in, becoming the first black secretary of agriculture. Almost from the start, however, Espy ran into trouble. President Bill Clinton and practically every member of his staff and cabinet were under the scrutiny of both the Republicans and the press almost from the moment Clinton took office. Between 1993 and 1994, charges began to surface that Espy had accepted favors and gifts from government-regulated businesses and then tried to cover them up. By 1997, when Espy was indicted by a grand jury, the charges included accepting more than $35,000 in gifts. Among other things he was alleged to have accepted were football playoff tickets, plane trips, and limousine rides from Tyson Foods, and luggage and U.S. Open Tennis tickets from Sun-Diamond Growers (Novak). In 1994, the criticisms of Espy had become so harsh that President Clinton asked him to resign.

After stepping down from office, Espy returned to Mississippi, joining Crosthwait Terney, TLLC Professional Limited Liability Company, in Jackson, Mississippi. Although he was no longer with the government, the investigation against him continued, led by independent counsel Donald Smaltz. In August of 1997, Smaltz met before a grand jury, receiving an indictment against Espy of 39 criminal counts of accepting gifts. As *Time* reported, the indictment claimed that

> As the transgressions came to light . . . Espy scrambled to conceal them or to make belated reimbursement. He may be most vulnerable to the charge that he had a clerk alter an itinerary for a January 1994 Dallas Cowboys football game to delete references to Tyson [Foods] before giving the document to investigators . . . Espy's lawyer Raid Weingarten did not deny any of the charges but accused Smaltz of distorting "trivial, personal and entirely benign activities" into criminal wrongdoing. (Novak)

During the following months, Espy and his lawyers fought the charges through various motions and, in the process, were able to reduce the charge by four counts. Arkansas-based Tyson Foods, Inc., received a $6 million assessment against it for giving out nearly $12,000 in gratuities ("Mike Espy Trial . . ."). In February of 1998, U.S. District Judge Ricardo Urbina postponed the trial against Espy "to await the outcome of two appeals related to his case" ("Mike Espy Trial . . ."). In December of 1998, Espy was fully acquitted after a seven-week trial and a four-year independent counsel probe.

Sources

Clay, William L. *Just Permanent Interests: Black Americans in Congress, 1870–1991*. New York: Amistad Press, 1992.

"Espy Acquitted in Gifts Case." *The Washington Post*, 3 December 1998, A01. <http://www.washingtonpost.com/wp-srv/politics/special/counsels/stories/espy120398.htm>. Accessed: 12/3/98.

Estell, Kenneth. *African America: Celebrating 400 Years of Achievement.* Detroit, MI: Visible Ink Press, 1994.
"Mike Espy." *Congressional Times Journal.* <http://www.usbol.com/ctjournal/MEspybio.html>. Accessed: 2/26/98.
"Mike Espy Joins Mississippi Law Firm." *Jet*, 29 January 1996, 40.
"Mike Espy Trial Is Postponed." *Nation's Restaurant News*, 30 March 1998, 68.
Novak, Viveca. "Chasing Good-Time Charlie." *Time Magazine*, 8 September 1997. <http://www.pathfinder.com/time/magazine/1997/dom/970908/nation.chasing.godti.html>. Accessed: 3/10/98.

Melvin Herbert Evans

Born: August 7, 1917, Christiansted, St. Croix, Virgin Islands

Status: Died November 27, 1984, in Christiansted, St. Croix, Virgin Islands

Education: B.S., 1940, Howard University, Washington, D.C.; M.D., 1944, Howard University College of Medicine, Washington, D.C.

Position: Health commissioner, Virgin Islands, 1959–1967; governor, U.S. Virgin Islands, 1969–1975; elected vice chairman, Southern Governor's Conference, 1972; named member, board of trustees, College of the Virgin Islands, c. 1975; delegate to Congress from the U.S. Virgin Islands, 1979–1980; ambassador to Trinidad and Tobago, 1981–1984

Early Years

In 1917, the United States purchased the Danish Virgin Islands for $25 million. That same year, shortly after the purchase, Melvin Herbert Evans was born on August 7 in Christiansted, St. Croix. After he was grown, he would become an important part of United States-Virgin Islands' history by becoming the first elected governor of the islands.

Higher Education

Evans graduated from high school on St. Thomas Island and decided to attend college on the U.S. mainland, enrolling in Howard University in Washington, D.C. After receiving his B.S. in 1940, he went on to study medicine and received an M.D. from Howard University's college of medicine in 1944. For the next decade and a half, Evans practiced medicine, first as a resident in the United States, then in private practice and in various public health posts in the Virgin Islands.

Career Highlights

In 1959, Evans was appointed the Virgin Islands' health commissioner. This marked his first step into the political arena. Although his earlier stints in public health had given him contacts with many politicians, this appointment brought him into the public eye, and in 1969, after returning to private practice for two years, he was appointed governor of the Virgin Islands by President Richard Nixon.

The year before, in 1968, the Virgin Islands' Elective Governor Act had been passed by Congress. It provided for the election of a governor by the residents of the U.S. Virgin Islands; previous to the passage of this act, governors had been appointed. Evans was appointed governor until an election could be held and, in 1970, he ran for the office and was elected. He remained in the governor's office until 1975, filling out the remainder of his term after he was defeated in a bid for reelection in 1974.

Although he had failed in his reelection campaign, Evans remained active politically. He served as the Republican national committeeman from the Virgin Islands, representing his territory at the Republican National Convention. During this time, he also was appointed a trustee on the board of the College of the Virgin Islands.

Congress had provided a nonvoting seat to the Virgin Islands since the purchase of the Islands in 1917, and three years after stepping down as governor, Evans ran for Congress as the delegate from the Islands. He campaigned successfully against Democrat Janet Watlington and was sworn into the 96th Congress on January 3, 1979.

Evans was appointed to the Armed Services, Interior and Insular Affairs, and Merchant Marine and Fisheries Committees, and, although his position was a nonvoting one, he championed his constituents' interests. In Congress, he was able to obtain additional funding for public education in the Virgin Islands and improve health care by pushing legislation that allowed foreign doctors to practice there. One of his major accomplishments was to have the Islands redefined as a "state" so that full law enforcement funding would become available to them. Evans also joined other black legislators in support of a bill by Representative **John Conyers, Jr.**, to make the birthday of Martin Luther King, Jr., a holiday, a bill Conyers had been fighting for since 1968. Although unsuccessful at this time, it was later passed into law.

In 1980, Evans again ran for reelection but was defeated by Ron de Lugo. After stepping down from his congressional seat, Evans was appointed ambassador to Trinidad and Tobago by President Ronald Reagan. He remained in that office until his death on November 27, 1984.

Sources

Clay, William L. *Just Permanent Interests: Black Americans in Congress, 1870–1991*. New York: Amistad Press, 1992.

"Former Black Members of Congress." *Congressional Times Journal*. <http://www.usbol.com/ctjournal/FrBlkCongMemList.html>. Accessed: 2/18/98.

James Charles Evers

Reproduced from AP/Wide World Photos

Born: September 4, 1922, in Decatur, Mississippi

Status: Businessman and restaurant owner, Fayette, Mississippi

Education: Graduate in social sciences, 1951, Alcorn Agricultural and Mechanical College (now Alcorn State University), Lorman, Mississippi

Position: U.S. Army, 1941–1945; funeral home, hotel, and taxi company owner, Philadelphia, Mississippi, 1952–1956; first black disc jockey in Mississippi, 1956; meat packer, Chicago, Illinois, 1956–1959; liquor store, tavern, and apartment building owner, Chicago, Illinois, 1959–1963; field director, Mississippi NAACP, 1963–1969; co-organizer, Mississippi Freedom Democratic Party, 1964; mayor, Fayette, Mississippi, 1969–1989; business owner, Fayette, Mississippi, 1988–

Early Years

"My mama was Jessie Wright Evers," Charles Evers wrote in his autobiography, *Have No Fear.* "My daddy was Jim Evers. Both were strong people. Daddy taught me to fear no one. Mama taught me religion" (Evers and Szanton 11). With two strong parents, James Charles Evers felt he could achieve anything as a boy despite the fact that he was a black child in Mississippi, a place where, at the time of his birth, a black child had few opportunities.

James Charles Evers was born on September 4, 1922, in Decatur, Mississippi. His mother, Jessie, had three children from an earlier marriage: Eddie, Eva Lee, and Gene. After she married Jim Evers, they had four more children: James Charles, Medgar, Liz, and Mary Ruth. Religion, hard work, and education ruled the Evers household. While Jim Evers was working at the local sawmill or railroad, or doing repairs on the two small houses he rented out, Jessie Evers was busy caring for her children and cleaning and laundering for white families.

Just as Jessie and Jim Evers stressed religion and hard work, they also emphasized the value of education. "Mama knew the time was coming," Charles Evers said, "when Negroes would need education. She pounded that into our heads" (Evers and Szanton 11). Although the other children stopped at a high school education, Charles and his brother, Medgar, would go on to college, something few blacks were able to do at that time.

The most graphic lessons the two boys learned, however, came from the white people in Decatur, Mississippi. As children, they encountered instances of discrimination and even outright brutality almost daily. For a time, when Charles and Medgar were teenagers, they plotted to kill whites, but when their mother found out, she soon put a stop to such thoughts.

While in high school, Charles and Medgar began a lucrative bootlegging operation. With the start of World War II, the brothers decided to join the army, which for Charles provided more opportunity to make some easy money. Because of a knee injury, he was assigned an office job in the Philippines. Evers established a prostitution business, providing prostitutes to the G.I.s stationed there, but, ultimately, the end of the war brought an end to his "business."

Higher Education

When Evers returned to Mississippi, he finished high school and, in 1946, entered Alcorn Agricultural and Mechanical College (now Alcorn State University), a black college in Lorman, Mississippi. Medgar soon followed him there. The two young men joined the National Association for the Advancement of Colored People (NAACP) and began to work to combat discrimination.

During his senior year in college, Evers married Manie (Nan) Laura McGee from Mount Olive, Mississippi. He had expected to finish his education quickly and begin his married life with Manie, but his army reserve unit was called to active duty for a time, and Evers graduated with a degree in social sciences from Alcorn in 1951 rather than in 1950.

Career Highlights

"In '51, Nan and I moved to a room in Philadelphia, Mississippi, over the funeral parlor of my great-uncle Mark Thomas. I managed the funeral parlor for Mark and picked up nineteen dollars a month teaching history and coaching football in Noxapater, Mississippi, north of town," Evers writes. "Between teaching, bootlegging, and undertaking, I cleared a hundred dollars a month" (Evers and Szanton 71). Evers was arrested in Philadelphia not for bootlegging, but for protesting when the principal of the Noxapater school where he taught refused to accept Evers's daughter, Pat, as a student. The family did not live in the Noxapater school district, but Evers wished to have his daughter there as it was a better school than those in Philadelphia.

Evers was jailed for only a short time, but his experience caused him to leave teaching and run his uncle's funeral home full time. Later, he bought the funeral home, established the first black taxi company in Philadelphia, and built a hotel for blacks there. During the same period, Medgar moved to Philadelphia and, with Charles, began doing civil rights work for the NAACP. In 1954, Medgar was appointed Mississippi field director for the NAACP.

Charles Evers, meanwhile, in addition to running his various businesses, became the first black disc jockey in Mississippi, working at a Philadelphia radio station. When he began urging blacks to vote, however, he was fired for "stirring up" the local black population, and a number of lawsuits were instituted against him based on false charges and old blue laws. He was forced to sell his businesses to pay the costs of the suits, and the court even auctioned off his house. While his wife, Nan, and their children went to stay with her mother, at the suggestion of Medgar, Charles traveled to Chicago to find work.

Initially, he got a job as a meat packer in Chicago, but soon his flair for business exerted itself again. He bought a building in the city and opened a liquor store and tavern. He also bought an apartment building jointly with Medgar, who was still in Mississippi working for the NAACP.

On the evening of June 12, 1963, Medgar Evers was returning home from a meeting in Jackson, Mississippi. As he neared his house, a shot rang out, hitting him in the back. He managed to drag himself to his house, but died within the hour.

When Charles Evers heard of the death of his brother, he was galvanized to action. As he later said, "The only thing I have never been able to accept is Medgar's death. I still can't accept that" (Haskins 104). Returning to Mississippi, Evers took over where his brother had left off, assuming Medgar's position as Mississippi field director for the NAACP.

The civil rights movement was coming to a head; Medgar Evers's death became an emblem of the violence and discrimination rampant at the time against blacks. When Charles Evers took over in 1963, he and other civil rights workers faced a time of extreme challenge. Many were arrested, beaten, and jailed during voter registration drives and marches. The passage of the Civil Rights Act of 1964 and the Voting Rights Act of 1965 eased some of the tension, although it would be a long time before Mississippi and other southern states fully complied with those federal laws.

In 1964, Evers helped organize the Mississippi Freedom Democratic Party, which tried unsuccessfully to unseat the all-white Mississippi delegation to the 1964 Democratic National Convention. Locally, Evers worked to have black candidates placed on the ballots and to register black voters.

Evers was becoming more and more well known and, in 1968, he was asked to run for the United States Congress. In January, 1968, Representative John Bell Williams stepped down from his seat to assume the governorship of Mississippi. A special election was called to fill the vacancy, and Evers's supporters urged him to run for the seat. Initially he refused but, after more urging, decided to run. Because there were a number of Democratic candidates—seven in all—even though Evers received the majority of the votes in a primary, he was faced with a runoff with the runner-up, Charlie Griffin, a white candidate. Evers lost the election, but he and his supporters celebrated because of the large turnout of black voters who had never before voted in an election.

The following year, buoyed by the support he had received in his run for Congress, Evers ran for mayor of Fayette, Mississippi. In a tight race, he defeated the incumbent, R.J. "Turnip Green" Allen by 128 votes becoming the city's first black mayor.

Evers was determined to succeed as mayor. As he writes, "Fayette was a pioneer black-run town. The eyes of the nation were upon us. I told my friends, 'Fayette has got to succeed. *Fayette is our Israel.* If we fail here, civil rights in America will suffer" (Evers and Szanton 255). With this motivation, Evers decided to "clean up his act." He had earlier ceased all his illegal activities, such as bootlegging, but he had been unfaithful to Nan, his wife, numerous times. He decided to make a clean break and divorce her.

For the next 20 years, Evers led the city of Fayette, Mississippi, on the path of equal opportunity for all races, and inspired blacks across the state and the South to seek elective office. As he said when sworn into office in 1968, "I hope white people and black people, particularly in Mississippi, understand that we've only done the thing that God wanted us to do—to take part in our government and make it work for everybody" (Haskins 117).

Evers also rescued Fayette from a slow death in the Mississippi dust. When Evers became mayor, the small town had few businesses that were doing well. Evers set out on a campaign to clean up the city, raise money, and bring in jobs.

With his success in Fayette, Evers decided to run for governor in 1971. He ran as a candidate for the "Loyalists" Democratic Party, but despite support from various national figures, such as Coretta Scott King, he was defeated.

In May of 1989, Evers decided to switch parties and become a Republican, much to the dismay of his Democratic friends and supporters. He worked to bring more African Americans into the Republican Party but, in 1989, when he again ran for mayor of Fayette, he found he no longer had the support he had enjoyed as a Democrat. On May 4, 1989, Fayette elected Kennie Middleton to replace Evers as its mayor.

Evers continues to be involved in business and politics in Mississippi. As he wrote, "To all people I say, it's not enough to live. You must make your life mean something. You can't let fear hold you back from reaching out to strangers. . . And if you haven't made this world better yet, then start today" (Evers and Szanton 312).

Sources

Evers, Charles, and Andrew Szanton. *Have No Fear: The Charles Evers Story.* New York: John Wiley and Sons, 1997.

Haskins, James. *A Piece of the Power: Four Black Mayors.* New York: Dial, 1972.

Joint Center for Political Studies. *Profiles of Black Mayors in America.* Washington, DC/Chicago, IL: The Joint Center for Political Studies/Johnson Publishing, 1977.

New Grolier Multimedia Encyclopedia. Novato, CA: The Software Toolworks, Inc./Grolier, Inc., 1993.

F

Walter Edward Fauntroy

Copyright Washington Post, *reprinted by permission of D.C. Public Library*

Born: February 6, 1933, in Washington, D.C.

Status: Pastor, New Bethel Baptist Church, Washington, D.C.; president, Walter E. Fauntroy and Associates, Washington, D.C.

Education: B.A. cum laude, 1955, Virginia Union University, Richmond, Virginia; B.D., 1958, Yale University Divinity School, New Haven, Connecticut

Position: Pastor, New Bethel Baptist Church, Washington, D.C., 1959–; vice chairperson, city council of Washington, D.C., 1967–1969; delegate from the District of Columbia to Congress, 1971–1990; president, Walter E. Fauntroy and Associates, Washington, D.C., 1990–

Early Years

Walter Edward Fauntroy was born the fourth of seven children on February 6, 1933, in Washington, D.C. His father worked as a clerk in the United States Patent Office, and between the Depression and the number of children in the family, money was tight. Fauntroy grew up in the Shaw community in Washington, D.C., an area plagued then as now with poverty and drugs. As Fauntroy himself said, although he didn't realize it as a child, the ghetto was like a plantation, with "the dope, the bootleg liquor, the payoffs to the cops, the general fear of the white man" (Mabunda and Phelps 78).

Fauntroy attended Washington's segregated schools and grew up in a neighborhood rife with crime, but he found a quiet place to play on the grounds of the New Bethel Baptist Church near his home. It wasn't until he was in high school, however, that he felt called to become a minister. When he graduated from Dunbar High School, his church held fund-raisers to get him money for college, and raised enough to pay the tuition for his freshman year at Virginia Union University in Richmond, Virginia.

Higher Education

Fauntroy did well at Virginia Union and also became involved in the civil rights movement. He met a young man named Martin Luther King, Jr., who, at 22, was already a minister and who had ideas Fauntroy had never heard before. The two became good friends and Fauntroy later joined the Southern Christian Leadership Conference (SCLC) founded by King and, in the 1960s, worked as a lobbyist in Congress for civil rights issues.

Graduating with honors from Virginia Union, Fauntroy went to New Haven, Connecticut, where he earned a bachelor's degree in divinity at the Yale University School of Divinity. He then returned home to Washington, D.C., and became the pastor of the New Bethel Baptist Church.

Career Highlights

Fauntroy did not believe that brotherhood was something to be practiced only on Sundays. Religion was the keystone of everyday life and Fauntroy practiced his religion in church as well as in civil rights marches, sit-ins, and meetings. Eventually, he became the chairman of the board of King's Southern Christian Leadership Conference and worked for civil rights in Washington and across America. He was coordinator of the 1965 march from Selma to Montgomery, Alabama, and also of the 1968 Poor People's Campaign. One program he helped to institute in his own city was the Model Inner City Community Organization (MICCO), which he headed in 1971. The organization, with the help of federal grants, was formed to help clean up and rehabilitate inner-city neighborhoods.

With his involvement with civil rights and with the MICCO, Fauntroy was making a great many political contacts. In 1967, he was appointed vice chairperson of the Washington, D.C., City Council by President Johnson, a position he held until 1969. At that time, all positions in the city were appointed rather than elected. In 1970, however, President Nixon signed into law the District of Columbia Delegate Act, providing the District of Columbia with an elective, nonvoting delegate to Congress. Fauntroy decided to run for the seat.

Although Fauntroy was challenged by two other Democratic opponents, he had strong support from Coretta Scott King, the widow of Martin Luther King, Jr., and from his political and religious contacts within the city. He easily won the primary and went on to defeat his Republican opponent. When Fauntroy was sworn into Congress on March 23, 1971, he was the first elected representative from Washington, D.C., since Reconstruction.

Although he had no vote in the House, Fauntroy could influence events; he could vote in committee and introduce legislation. He pushed for comprehensive legislation that would allow the District of Columbia to govern itself rather than rely on the federal government for leadership. He was a persuasive debater and, in December 1973, the District of Columbia Self-Government and Government Reorganization Act was made law. This gave the city limited self-rule and provided for an elected mayor and city council.

During his tenure in the House, Fauntroy chaired the District of Columbia committee's Subcommittee on Fiscal Affairs and Health. He also served on the Committee on Banking, Finance and Urban Affairs, and was chair of its Subcommittee on International Development Institutions and Finance. His agenda included helping the inner cities, minorities, and the poor. Although he had been successful in obtaining limited self-rule for Washington, D.C., he also felt that it was not enough and unsuccessfully pushed for statehood for the district, something that would give it full representation in Congress.

During the 97th Congress, from 1981 to 1983, Fauntroy was elected chair of the Congressional Black Caucus. With the other members of the caucus, he worked to combat drugs in the nation and protested the United States' investments in South Africa.

In 1990, Fauntroy stepped down from office to run for mayor of Washington, D.C., feeling he could more directly address the problems of his city in this position. He was defeated, but returned in good spirits to his ministry at the New Bethel Baptist Church. He also started Walter E. Fauntroy and Associates, a consulting firm that provides lobbying services. Kept busy with both his ministry and consulting service, Fauntroy told the *Washington Post* that "The chances are very slim that I would run for local office in the District" (Mabunda and Phelps 79).

Sources

Clay, William L. *Just Permanent Interests: Black Americans in Congress, 1870–1991*. New York: Amistad Press, 1992.

Estell, Kenneth. *African America: Celebrating 400 Years of Achievement*. Detroit, MI: Visible Ink Press, 1994.

"Former Black Members of Congress." *Congressional Times Journal*. <http://www.usbol.com/ctjournal/FrBlkCongMemList.html>. Accessed: 2/27/98.

Mabunda, L. Mpho, and Shirelle Phelps, eds. *Contemporary Black Biography: Profiles from the International Black Community*, Vol. 11. Detroit, MI: Gale Research, 1996.

Crystal Dreda Bird Fauset

Born: June 27, 1893, in Princess Anne, Maryland

Status: Died March 27, 1965, in Philadelphia, Pennsylvania

Education: Graduate, 1914, Boston Normal School, Boston, Massachusetts; B.S., 1931, Teachers College, Columbia University, New York, New York

Position: Teacher, 1914–1917; secretary for younger Negro girls, National Board, Young Women's Christian Association (YWCA), New York, New York, 1918–c. 1926; member, American Friends Service Committee (AFSC), 1927–c. 1931; social worker and administrator of Negro Affairs, YWCA, New York and Philadelphia, 1931–1933; founder and executive secretary, Institute of Race Relations, Swarthmore College, Philadelphia, Pennsylvania, 1933–1935; director, Negro Women's Activities, Democratic National Committee, 1936; assistant personnel director, Philadelphia Office, Works Progress Administration (WPA), 1936–1938; representative from the 18th District, Pennsylvania House of Representatives, 1938–1939; assistant state director, Education and Recreational Programs, WPA, Philadelphia, Pennsylvania, 1939–1941; appointed special consultant to the director, Office of Civilian Defense, Washington, D.C., 1941–1944; advisor on Negro affairs, Republican National Committee, 1944; co-organizer, United Nations Council of Philadelphia, 1945–1950; appointed to the board of directors, Small Business Opportunities Corporation, Philadelphia, Pennsylvania, 1963

Awards: Twice awarded the Meritorious Service Medal of the Commonwealth of Pennsylvania; named honorary member, Lincoln Dames

Early Years

Crystal Dreda Bird Fauset was the youngest of the nine children of Benjamin O. Bird and Portia E. Lovett Bird. She was born on June 27, 1893, in Princess Anne, Maryland, where her father was the principal of Princess Anne Academy for black students. Her father died when Fauset was barely four years old, and her mother, who had assumed Benjamin Bird's position as principal of the academy upon his death, passed away in 1900.

With her parents gone, Fauset was sent to live with her mother's sister, Lucy Groves, in Boston, Massachusetts, where she graduated from public school. Although Boston was very different from her home in Maryland, she did well in school. Upon graduation, she entered Boston Normal School, following in her parents' footsteps by becoming a teacher. In addition to her interest in teaching, Fauset was a talented singer and pianist and continued this interest all her life, often lecturing upon "Music in the Life of America" to many schools and groups (Smith 334).

Higher Education

Although Fauset graduated from Boston Normal School in 1914, it would be nearly 15 years before she would continue her own formal education. In 1914, a degree from a normal school was considered suitable for a woman, and it was the rare woman who even considered continuing her education—or who could gain admittance into a graduate school. However, by the late 1920s, higher education for women was becoming more accepted and Fauset returned to school while also working, receiving a bachelor's degree from Columbia University's Teacher's College in 1931.

Career Highlights

Upon her graduation from Boston Normal School, Fauset taught for three years in the public schools. By the end of 1917, however, the nation had entered the First World War, creating many employment opportunities for women. In 1918, Fauset left her teaching job to assume the position of secretary for younger Negro girls with the National Board of the Young Women's Christian Association (YWCA) in New York City. Her job studying racial relations involved a great deal of travel throughout the United States and even in Cuba. She found, according to an interview given later in 1938 to the *Philadelphia Record*, that the problems she saw "cannot be segregated—wherever I went, they appeared as inter-racial problems" (Smith 34).

An accomplished speaker with a dynamic personality, Fauset was asked to join the American Friends Service Committee in 1927 to promote and educate people about its programs within the African American community. She also returned to school at Columbia University and, in June of 1931, married Arthur Huff Fauset, who was the principal of Philadelphia's Singerley School. Unfortunately, the marriage was of short duration; Arthur Fauset filed for divorce in 1944 after several years' separation.

Fauset was becoming recognized as a spokeswoman for African Americans and, in 1933, founded Swarthmore College's Institute of Race Relations, serving as its executive secretary until 1935. Through her work with the Institute, she became convinced of the necessity of political involvement to initiate change. The Great Depression was ravaging America, particularly the black community, and Fauset became increasingly convinced that only political action would promote economic change. In 1936, as a result of her increasing interest in politics, Fauset accepted a position with the Works Progress Administration in the Philadelphia office and also served as the director of Negro women's activities of the Democratic National Committee. As the *Philadelphia Tribune* reported in 1938, "Her first real adventure into politics began when she became a member of the administrative staff of the W.P.A. in 1936" (Smith 34).

Her position with the Works Progress Administration in Philadelphia brought her into contact with the political community and, in 1938, Philadelphia Democrats asked if she would run for a seat in the Pennsylvania House of Representatives from Philadelphia's 18th District. With her election in November of 1938, Fauset became the first black woman in America to be elected to a state legislature. As the *Chicago Defender* wrote of her in April of 1939,

> Power surrounds the woman. It dwells within her, emanates from her, and yet, is very subtly hidden. Anyone who comes

> near Mrs. Fauset feels her greatness—in the sweep of her very alert glance, in the charm of her ready smile, in the warm sincerity of her hand clasp, and in her voice—like crisp staccato music. (Smith 34)

In November of 1939, although she had served less than a year, Fauset stepped down from her legislative seat to assume the position of assistant state director of the education and recreation programs with the WPA. By working with the WPA, she felt she would be able to reach more people in promoting equality and understanding between the races.

Fauset's many eloquent speeches and her involvement in politics had brought her national attention and, in 1941, soon after the United States entered World War II, President Franklin Delano Roosevelt called upon her to act as a special consultant to the director of the Office of Civilian Defense in Washington, D.C. Again traveling and speaking, as she had in many of her past jobs, Fauset also became a consultant on race relations to Roosevelt as part of his Black Cabinet, as well as a close friend of Eleanor Roosevelt and a consultant to Mayor Fiorello LaGuardia of New York.

Increasingly, however, Fauset was becoming disillusioned with the Democratic Party. She heartily opposed the poor treatment of black soldiers and the formation of segregated units during the war, but found the Democratic leadership turning a deaf ear to her protests. Her disappointment reached a peak in 1944. An October 22, 1944, article in *Time Magazine*, "The Old Magic," reported,

> Mrs. Crystal Bird Fauset, one-time friend of Eleanor Roosevelt, one-time member of the Pennsylvania Legislature (its first and only Negro woman) quit the Democratic National Committee's offices in Manhattan's Biltmore Hotel, walked up two blocks to Madison Avenue to join the G.O.P. at the Roosevelt Hotel. Said she: "Bob Hannigan [the Democratic National Committee leader] is a dictator—a man who is not willing to deal democratically with Negroes." ("The Old Magic")

Fauset quickly became as hardworking for the Republicans as she had been for the Democrats, supporting the Republican presidential candidate, Thomas E. Dewey, and becoming an advisor on Negro affairs to the Republican National Committee.

With the end of World War II, Fauset helped organize the United Nations Council of Philadelphia, and attended the founding conference of the United Nations in San Francisco in 1950 as an officer of the Philadelphia Council. In 1963, ever on the lookout for ways to economically benefit both black and white communities, she accepted the appointment by Mayor James Tate of Philadelphia to the board of directors of Philadelphia's Small Business Opportunities Corporation.

Crystal Fauset never really retired. Until her death from a heart attack on March 27, 1965, she continued to work to improve economic conditions and racial understanding by heading various committees and even, in 1957, unsuccessfully seeking an appointment as part of the U.S. delegation to mark Ghana's independence.

Sources

Hine, Darlene Clark, ed. *Black Women in America: An Historical Encyclopedia*, Vol. I, A–L. Brooklyn, NY: Carlson Publishing Co., 1993.

"The Old Magic." *Time Magazine*, 2 October 1944. *Time Almanac*, Reference Edition.

Ploski, Harry A., and James Williams, eds. *The Negro Almanac: A Reference Work on the African American*. Detroit, MI: Gale Research, 1989.

Smith, Jessie Carney, ed. *Notable Black American Women*. Detroit, MI: Gale Research, 1992.

Floyd H. Flake

Reproduced from AP/Wide World Photos

Born: January 30, 1945, in Los Angeles, California

Status: Pastor, Allen AME Church, Jamaica, New York

Education: B.A., 1957, Wilberforce University, Wilberforce, Ohio; graduate, Payne Theological Seminary; graduate studies, Northwestern University School of Business, Evanston, Illinois; graduate studies, doctor of ministry program, United Theological Seminary, Dayton, Ohio

Position: Pastor, African Methodist Episcopal Church, Jamaica, New York, 1976– ; U.S. representative from the Sixth Congressional District of New York, 1986–1997

Early Years

Floyd H. Flake was born in Los Angeles, California, on January 30, 1945. Soon after his birth, his family moved to Texas, where he grew up and attended the Houston public schools.

Higher Education

After graduation from high school in 1953, Flake attended Wilberforce University in Ohio, graduating in 1957. Flake wanted to enter the ministry, and after graduation from Wilberforce, he enrolled in the Payne Theological Seminary. Later, he was to do graduate studies in business administration at Northwestern University in Evanston, Illinois, and, during the late 1980s and early 1990s, he was enrolled in the doctor of ministry program at the United Theological Seminary in Dayton, Ohio. During this time, also, Flake married M. Elaine McCollins of Memphis, Tennessee; they later had four children: Aliya, Nailah, Rasheed, and Hasan.

Career Highlights

In 1976, Flake assumed the ministry of the African Methodist Episcopal (AME) Church in Jamaica, New York. When he first took over this ministry, the church had a congregation of 1,400 and a budget of $250,000. During the next 20 years, because of his active leadership, Flake's congregation grew to 6,452 members with a church budget of $22 million (*Congressional Black Caucus*).

Flake's involvement in politics came about indirectly from his involvement in the community as a pastor. The AME Church became the force behind a number of significant revitalization projects in the community. It built a 300-unit senior citizen complex, a Christian school, and a center to provide health care, Head Start programs, and other services to the community. Flake also provided the impetus to build 61 homes for low- and moderate-income families, and established a home care agency to help the elderly and disabled. All this meant that Flake had to become knowledgeable in cutting through the bureaucratic red tape surrounding construction and other issues concerning starting things on a community level. He also became well known within his district as a caring minister who got things done.

In the middle 1980s, the incumbent representative to the House, Joseph Addabbo, died while in office, and a special election was held to fill his seat for the remainder of his term. At the urging of his parishioners, Flake ran in the special election, but lost to Alton Waldon. In the next regular primary for Congress, Flake again ran. This time, he had even more support and easily defeated Waldon, then went on to win the regular election. Flake was sworn in in January, 1986, and assigned to the Banking, Finance and Urban Affairs Committee; the Small Business Committee; and the Select Committee on Hunger. As **William Lacy Clay, Sr.**, said, Flake's election "reflected a broad-based community effort to bring new, progressive leadership to the political front" (372).

Just as he had promoted housing in Jamaica, New York, Flake became active in Congress in promoting a national housing program and in improving education. In 1990, Flake introduced the **[George Thomas] Mickey Leland** Peace Dividend Housing Act to provide safe, decent, affordable housing. In addition, several of his proposals were included in the Housing Programs Reauthorization Act of 1991. He also became a leader in the war on drugs, having seen the negative impact drugs had had in both his own community and throughout the nation.

In the 1990s, Flake became chairman of several committees, and introduced, among other resolutions, House Resolution 1061, the Fair Employment Reinstatement Act, and House Resolution 1062, the Home Ownership Plan Encouragement Act. Reflecting his concern about the treatment of peoples worldwide, in 1991 he also introduced House Resolution 1328, which would authorize supplemental appropriations for Liberia.

Since his election in 1986, Flake has faced no serious challenger for his seat in Congress and, in 1997, was reelected by a huge majority to Congress. In this most recent race, Flake received 102,799 votes to his Republican challenger's 18,348 votes. In 1997, however, Flake announced his retirement from public office, resigning from Congress on November 15, 1997. Since then, he has assumed the full-time position of pastor at the Allen AME Church in Jamaica, New York.

Sources

Clay, William L. *Just Permanent Interests: Black Americans in Congress, 1870–1991*. New York: Amistad Press, 1992.

Congressional Black Caucus '93–'94 Guide. <http://www.sas.upenn.edu/African_Studies/Govern_Political/CBC_Guide.html>. Accessed: 3/5/98.

Gary A. Franks

Reproduced from AP/Wide World Photos, by Bob Child

Born: February 9, 1953, in Waterbury, Connecticut

Status: Business consultant

Education: B.A., 1975, Yale University, New Haven, Connecticut

Position: Executive in industrial and labor relations, Fairfield County, Connecticut, 1970s;

president, GAF Realty, Waterbury, Connecticut, 1980s; alderman, Waterbury, Connecticut, 1985–1990; vice chairman, zoning board, Waterbury, Connecticut, 1980s; U.S. representative from the Fifth Congressional District of Connecticut, 1990–1997; business consultant, 1997– ; candidate, U.S. Senate, 1998

Early Years

Gary Franks was born in Waterbury, Connecticut, on February 9, 1953. Franks's father was a worker in the brass mills of Waterbury with only a sixth-grade education, but he was determined that his six children would have the education he lacked. Franks attended Sacred Heart High School in Waterbury and was an honor student. He was also popular with his fellow students, being elected president of his senior class and named an all-state basketball player.

Higher Education

After graduation from high school, Franks entered Yale University in New Haven, Connecticut. As he had in high school, he played on Yale's basketball team and was twice chosen as captain by his teammates. In 1975, Franks graduated with honors from Yale.

Career Highlights

During the late 1970s, Franks worked as an industrial and labor relations executive for a number of companies, including Continental Can, Chesebrough Ponds, and Cadbury Schweppes. In the mid-1980s, however, with the real estate market booming in Connecticut, he left this field to establish his own real estate firm, GAF Realty, in his hometown of Waterbury, Connecticut.

Shortly after establishing his real estate firm, Franks entered local politics. He successfully ran for the position of alderman on the Waterbury Board of Aldermen and, during the next several years, became vice chair of the zoning board and a member of the Environmental Control Commission. In 1986, Franks entered the race for the office of state comptroller, running as a Republican. Although he lost this election to a Democrat, he led the field of Republicans. In 1987, he unsuccessfully ran for the chairmanship of the Connecticut State Republican Party, but again was defeated, finishing third in a field of nine candidates. Despite his losses, however, Franks was learning the ins and outs of politics and making contacts that would prove useful in the future.

In 1989, Franks announced that he would run for a seat in the House of Representatives from the Fifth Congressional District of Connecticut, challenging Democrat Toby Moffitt who had spent eight years in the House, from 1974 to 1982, before making an unsuccessful bid for the U.S. Senate. In an interview with *The New York Times*, Franks said, "My message will be different than what many people have heard from a black congressman" (Bigelow 83). Franks was a black candidate in a district that encompassed the wealthy, predominantly white towns in Fairfield County as well as blue-collar Waterbury, and he was also a Republican. As he said during campaigning, the people he met assumed he was a liberal Democrat. He would say, "'Wait, I'm a Republican!' [and] They'd turn around and say, 'Oh, in that case, we'll give you some thought'" (Bigelow 83–84).

The race was heated. Moffitt and his supporters attacked Franks for his weak stance on the Civil Rights Act of 1990 and his adherence to the traditional conservative positions of the Republican Party. Franks condemned the financial policies of the liberal Democrats, including Moffitt, saying, "The key to the American way is making people self-sufficient. The worst myth out there is that you can do this through policies that tax and spend, tax and spend, tax and spend" (Bigelow 83). Franks also attacked Moffitt as a carpetbagger. Moffitt had changed his residence from Branford, in the Third Congressional District, to Newtown, Connecticut. Franks charged that Moffitt did so only to run for Congress.

The national committees of both the Republican and Democratic Parties targeted the race for the Fifth District, considering it an important one. This meant that both Moffitt and Franks received the maximum amount of money permitted for their campaigns, as well as support from various national figures. Both Barbara Bush and William Bennett, the so-called "Drug Czar" of the Bush administration, came to Connecticut to speak on Franks's behalf, with positive results. When the votes were counted, Franks had won, becoming the first black Republican to be elected as a voting member of the House since 1935, and the highest ranking black Republican official in the United States.

In January of 1990, Franks was sworn in. From the start, he encountered criticism and opposition from many of the other African American members of Congress because of his conservative positions. As the *Associated Press* reported in 1998, Franks's "six years in Congress were stormy, marked by staff turnover, personal financial problems and highly publicized sparring with other members of the Congressional Black Caucus" (Robinson). Franks supported welfare reform, proposing the Parental Responsibility Act, a welfare reform initiative. It required states to enforce existing laws mandating the identification of the fathers of children of single mothers on welfare or else risk losing a portion of welfare monies provided by the federal government. He also introduced the Urban Entrepreneurial Opportunities Act, encouraging companies to invest in the rebuilding of urban areas by aiding urban entrepreneurs.

Franks was reelected in 1994 after an easy race. In 1996, however, he encountered defeat. Perhaps he had become too complacent, calculating that, having won twice before, he did not have to devote much time to a reelection campaign. He ignored interview requests and even failed to appear at some scheduled campaign events. Whatever the reason, Franks was out of office, and his Democratic opponent, Jim Maloney, was in.

After leaving the House in 1997, Franks again did some business consulting. Then, in 1998, he formally declared his intention to challenge incumbent Christopher Dodd for his seat in the United States Senate, saying, "He has been in Washington too long and he has lost . . . touch with the everyday problems and struggles of our hard working men and women right in this state" ("Franks Formally Runs . . ."). Christopher Dodd, who was first elected in 1974, received the news with equanimity.

Franks faced an uphill battle. Dodd had a campaign war chest of more than $2 million, four times what Franks raised. Dodd also has a reputation as an effective lawmaker and is the son of the late Senator Thomas Dodd, a revered figure in Connecticut and one of the prosecutors at the Nuremberg trials against the Nazis. However, as the Associated Press reported, "Franks had even changed his look, shaving his mustache. And he's stressing his working-class roots . . . and experience as a diaper-changing father of three" (Robinson). In addition, as Dick Foley, a former Connecticut Republican Party chairman, commented, "He's a determined fellow" (Robinson). Despite his tenacity, Franks was defeated by Dodd in the fall of 1998.

Sources

Bigelow, Barbara Carlisle, ed. *Contemporary Black Biography: Profiles from the International Black Community*, Vol. 2. Detroit, MI: Gale Research, 1992.

Clay, William L. *Just Permanent Interests: Black Americans in Congress, 1870–1991*. New York: Amistad Press, 1992.

Congressional Black Caucus '93–'94 Guide. <http://www.sas.upenn.edu/African_Studies/Govern_Political/CBC_Guide.html>. Accessed: 3/10/98.

Estell, Kenneth. *African America: Celebrating 400 Years of Achievement*. Detroit, MI: Visible Ink Press, 1994.

"Franks Formally Runs for Dodd's Senate Seat." Channel 8 News Online. *WTNH-TV News*. 1998. <http://www.wtnh.com/news/012098b.html>. Accessed: 3/3/98.

"National Elections '98." *The Washington Post*, 4 November 1998. <http://elections 98.washingtonpost.com/wp-srv/results98/national>. Assessed: 11/19/98.

Robinson, Melissa B. "Former Representative Running for Senate." *Nando.net.* Associated Press, 1998. <http://www.nando.net/newsroom/ntn/politics/012098/politics2_29787_noframes.html>. Accessed: 4/9/98.

G

Kenneth Allen Gibson

Reproduced from AP/Wide World Photos

Born: May 15, 1932, in Enterprise, Alabama

Status: President, Gibson Associates, Newark, New Jersey

Education: B.S., 1962, Newark College of Engineering, Newark, New Jersey

Position: Sixty-fifth Engineering Battalion, U.S. Army, 1956–1958; manual laborer, 1958–1960; engineer, Newark Housing Authority, Newark, New Jersey, 1960–1966; chief structural engineer, City of Newark, New Jersey, 1966–1970; mayor, Newark, New Jersey, 1970–1986; delegate, Democratic National Midterm Conference, 1974, 1978; president, U.S. Conference of Mayors, 1976–1977; president, Gibson Associates, Newark, New Jersey, 1987–

Early Years

Kenneth Allen Gibson was born on May 15, 1932, in Enterprise, Alabama, the eldest of the two sons of Willie and Daisy Gibson. Willie Gibson worked as a butcher, and Daisy was a seamstress. Although the Depression had hit the South hard, the Gibsons were industrious and they hoped to save enough to buy their own home.

An event occurred, however, when Gibson was five years old that took a serious bite out of the Gibsons' savings. Gibson was playing with a balloon that had a cardboard whistle attached and accidentally swallowed the whistle. It became lodged in his right bronchial tube and local doctors were unable to remove it. Finally, withdrawing most of their savings from the bank, Kenneth's father, Willie, took him by train to a hospital in Newark, New Jersey, where doctors were finally able to remove the whistle by a suction process. A local resident later related to Daisy Gibson, "You know, that's two times Ken Gibson has put Enterprise on the map. His election [as mayor of Newark, New Jersey] and the time he swallowed a whistle!" (Haskins 134–35).

When Gibson was seven years old, it looked as if the Gibsons would finally have enough money to build a house. But in Enterprise, it was not considered proper for a black man to own his own home while some white people could not. When Willie Gibson's boss heard about his ambitions, he cut his salary to $10 a week. Faced with this opposition to their dreams, the Gibsons decided to move north, planning to save more money and return later to finish their house.

In the fall of 1940, when Gibson was eight, Willie Gibson went north to look for work. He finally found a job at Swift and Company meatpackers in Kearny, New Jersey, close to Newark, and rented a one-room apartment for the family. They moved to Newark, and Daisy also found a job. According to Gibson,

> We never had too much money but we always had enough to eat. My father had two main principles. One, always take care of your family and, two, that he was the boss of the house. He was the authority figure, but we were buddies, too, and we played games together. I've seen father figures who were aloof, but he's been very close to us. I can't remember him hitting us. (Haskins 136)

Kenneth was a quiet, studious boy, but he wasn't one to back down from a challenge. He watched over his younger brother, Harold, and faced the bullies on the streets of Newark who tried to take the boys' lunch money. Both Gibson and his brother attended the Newark public schools, and when Gibson was 12 years old, he decided he wanted to be an engineer when he grew up.

Higher Education

Gibson attended Newark's Central High School and did well academically. He also played the saxophone in the school band. By the time he graduated, he had been accepted at the Massachusetts Institute of Technology, Stevens Institute, and the Newark College of Engineering (NCE). Gibson chose to go to the latter as the family had little money to spare for college, and he could live at home if he went to college in Newark.

Gibson also decided to get married when he graduated from high school, and the added financial burden forced him to drop out of NCE after only two months. For the next several years, he worked in a factory, playing the saxophone on weekends, and taking evening classes at NCE. In 1956, however, his studies were again interrupted when he was drafted into the army; he served two years with the 65th Engineer Battalion in Hawaii. During this time, his first wife and he divorced, their two young daughters becoming solely his responsibility.

When Gibson was discharged in 1958, he returned to Newark again to work on his engineering degree. He soon remarried. His second wife, Muriel, had a daughter by a former marriage, so Gibson was going to school, working, and trying to support a family of five at this time. At last, in 1962, he graduated with a bachelor's degree with honors in engineering, 12 years after finishing high school.

Career Highlights

Gibson had been working for the New Jersey Highway Department as an engineer, but when he received his degree, he obtained a job with the Newark Housing Authority. As an administrator with the housing authority, Gibson learned a great deal about the workings of the Newark city government, and observed firsthand the deterioration of the city's buildings. Newark was a city in trouble in the 1960s. Although its financial industry was strong, whites were fleeing for the suburbs. It had the highest crime rate of cities greater than 250,000. It had the greatest percentage of substandard housing, the second highest birth rate, infant-mortality rate, and population density in the nation for a city its size. In 1962, Hugh Addonizio, a former state legislator, had been elected mayor of the city, pledging to solve its problems, but he did little during his term.

In 1966, six weeks before the mayoral election, Gibson decided that he would run for mayor. He had no money, was virtually unknown, and had only his close friends to act as his staff. He decided, however, "that the best way to influence public policy is to be in a position to direct it" (Haskins 144).

Gibson faced opposition from six other candidates in the general primary, including incumbent mayor Hugh Addonizio. Although Gibson did not win, his position in the final tally was surprising even to him. He came in third, with 16,200, or 20 percent, of the votes. In a runoff election, Addonizio defeated runner-up Carlin to win reelection as mayor. The election, however, demonstrated to Gibson that there was support for his candidacy and that he would have a good chance of winning in 1970 if he worked hard.

During the next four years, Newark seemed to deteriorate even further. In 1967, riots tore the city apart. The riots benefited Gibson indirectly as they caused Addonizio's popularity to drop, and they showed black community leaders that there was a need for a strong black political organization.

Addonizio's popularity plummeted even further in 1969. In December of that year, Gibson, who was working as the city's chief structural engineer, reported the corruption he had observed at city hall to the state prosecutor in a letter. Gibson's letter, with supporting evidence, led to the indictment of the mayor and nine other city officials on 66 counts of extortion and income tax evasion. The trial date was set for June, 1970, when the election campaign for mayor would be in full swing.

In 1970, Gibson again declared himself a candidate for the office of mayor. This time, he had more support and money, and the incumbent, Addonizio, was facing serious charges in court. Although Addonizio had previously assumed a liberal position on racial matters, when faced with a black opponent he shifted his campaign track, attacking Gibson and his followers and trying to frighten white constituents. One of Gibson's black supporters was LeRoi Jones, a writer of plays, essays, and poems that emphasized black pride and solidarity and were often militant and anti-white in tone. Addonizio used Jones's writings as an example of the radical militancy whites would face should Gibson be elected. He called Gibson "part of a raw and violent conspiracy to turn this city over to LeRoi Jones and his extremist followers" (Haskins 152).

Gibson, however, continued to campaign quietly and steadily, calling Addonizio's charges inflammatory and "very dirty and low." Gibson had an impressive array of supporters, including Harry Belafonte, Stevie Wonder, **Julian Bond**, the Reverend Ralph Abernathy, **Richard Hatcher**, and **Carl Burton Stokes**, and although he expected a tight race, he was confident he would win. After all, the people of the city could not possibly want a corrupt mayor such as Addonizio for their leader.

On election day, June 16, 1970, Gibson's confidence paid off. He had received 95 percent of the black vote and almost 20 percent of the white vote, becoming the first black mayor of a major eastern city. In his victory speech, Gibson said,

> This is an important victory for the nation. This will be an administration of all the people—black, white, Puerto Rican, and all colors. We will work for everyone, and we will work on and on—right on, as we say! When Robert Treat founded the city of Newark over 300 years ago, I am sure he never and you never realized that someday Newark would have soul. (Haskins 153)

When Gibson took office, he thought he knew the problems he would face as mayor. But in going over the city's records, he saw that the situation was worse than he had expected. The Addonizio administration had overspent alarmingly, unbeknownst to the public. There was a $65 million dollar deficit in the city's budget. Just as he had worked to get his engineering degree, however, Gibson worked steadily and persistently to rehabilitate Newark.

Gibson's first effort was in the area of public health. In an attempt to reduce the alarming infant mortality rate in Newark, he instituted a comprehensive policy of testing and set up seven community health centers. He was highly criticized when he appointed John L. Redden, a white man, as chief of police. He had chosen Redden, however, because Redden had a reputation of incorruptibility, something Newark desperately needed. Gibson also improved the city's garbage pickup and street-sweeping services to improve the living conditions and appearance of the city.

Gibson had initially said that he would serve for one term, but as his first term of office neared its end, he found he had barely begun to tackle Newark's many problems. Therefore, in 1974, he ran for reelection and received 54 percent of the vote, defeating Anthony Imperiale, a state senator.

During his second term of office, Gibson, while continuing to promote health care, also focused on reducing Newark's high crime rate, which was first in the nation. By 1977, Newark was ranked as 23rd in the nation. In 1976, Gibson was elected as the first black president of the U.S. Conference of Mayors and, in that position, lobbied Washington on the plight of American cities, as well as frequently advising President Jimmy Carter. Elected mayor yet again, Gibson looked toward a higher position, and during the 1980s he made two unsuccessful attempts for election as governor of New Jersey.

Gibson's work as mayor was not without its detractors, but in the years he had been mayor, Newark had improved greatly. There were more jobs, tax cuts, and incentives for businesses to locate in the city. In 1982, his enemies got the upper hand for a time. Prosecutors charged him with creating a "no show" job, a token job, for a former city councilman, and Gibson was indicted. Despite the indictment, he won reelection during this time and, at the trial, the judge declared the prosecutor's case inadequate, saying, "It sounds to me that what I've heard in this case is that you [the prosecutor] started with a preconceived judgment and you are trying to weave everything into this" (Bigelow 98).

Although Gibson had improved conditions in Newark dramatically over the years, the city still had problems. Poverty plagued it and public education still needed further improvement. By 1986, Gibson had been in office 16 years, and many felt he had become entrenched in office. On May 13, 1986, the people of Newark turned against him; they did not reelect him.

Gibson felt his job as mayor was not finished; Newark was still not the city he had envisioned when taking office in 1970. But the voters had spoken. After his defeat, Gibson returned to the private sector and began Gibson Associates, a consulting firm that advises developers and investment bankers.

Sources

Bigelow, Barbara Carlisle, ed. *Contemporary Black Biography: Profiles from the International Black Community*, Vol. 6. Detroit, MI: Gale Research, 1994.

Haskins, James. *A Piece of the Power: Four Black Mayors*. New York: Dial, 1972.

Joint Center for Political Studies. *Profiles of Black Mayors in America*. Washington, DC/Chicago, IL: The Joint Center for Political Studies/Johnson Publishing, 1977.

Woodrow Wilson Goode

Reproduced from AP/Wide World Photos, by Scott Applewhite

Born: August 19, 1938, near Seaboard, North Carolina

Status: Deputy assistant secretary for regional and community services and representative, Region Three, Office of Intergovernmental and Interagency Affairs (OIIA), U.S. Department of Education; head, Goode Cause, Philadelphia, Pennsylvania; associate professor of political science and urban policy, Eastern College, St. Davids, Pennsylvania

Education: B.A., 1961, Morgan State University, Baltimore, Maryland; M.P.A., 1968, Wharton School, University of Pennsylvania, Philadelphia; recipient of 14 honorary degrees from various colleges and universities

Position: U.S. Army, 1962–1963; probation officer, supervisor in a building maintenance firm, and insurance claims adjuster, 1963–1966; executive director and president, Philadelphia Council for Community Advancement, Philadelphia, Pennsylvania, 1966–1978; head, Pennsylvania Public Utility Commission, 1978–1980; managing director, City of Philadelphia, 1980–1983; mayor, Philadelphia, Pennsylvania, 1984–1992; director, Regional Services Team, and representative, Region Two, Office of Intergovernmental and Interagency Affairs (OIIA), U.S. Department of Education, 1992–1997; deputy assistant secretary for regional and community services and representative, Region Three, OIIA, 1997– ; founder, head, Goode Cause, Inc.; associate professor of political science and urban policy, Eastern College, St. Davids, Pennsylvania

Early Years

Woodrow Wilson Goode was born on August 19, 1938, in a shack outside of Seaboard, North Carolina. His parents, who were sharecroppers, and their children lived in abject poverty until they moved to West Philadelphia, Pennsylvania, after World War II and found greater opportunities.

Goode grew up attending Philadelphia's public schools and was an honor student in high school. Although the family never had much, Goode said later that much of his strength and determination to succeed came from his early years and the poverty he had experienced.

Higher Education

After Goode graduated from high school, he attended Morgan State University, working to put himself through school. In 1961, he earned a bachelor's degree, becoming the first member of his family to graduate from college. After graduation, he entered the army, earning the rank of captain by the time he was discharged, and received a medal of commendation.

Goode was discharged from the army in 1963 and took a number of jobs in the following years. He also worked on his master's degree in public administration at the Wharton School of the University of Pennsylvania in Philadelphia; in 1968, he received an M.P.A.

Career Highlights

Goode first became involved in education and politics in 1967 in Philadelphia while working for the Philadelphia Council for Community Advancement, an organization established to assist nonprofit housing corporations. That year, he was a member of several advisory committees of the Philadelphia school district, and chairman of the teacher's selection and evaluation task force. In 1969, he was promoted to the position of executive director of the Philadelphia Council for Community Advancement and, in 1972, named "Outstanding Young Leader of the Year" by the Philadelphia Jaycees. Goode was rapidly becoming known in the city as someone who was committed to bettering its conditions.

In 1978, Goode was appointed head of the Pennsylvania Public Utility Commission by Pennsylvania governor Milton J. Shapp. In this position, Goode was in charge of regulating the state's utility rates. While serving in this position, Goode had to handle the delicate situation caused by an accident at the Three Mile Island nuclear plant in 1979. Not only did he have to ensure the public's safety and guard against a disruption in the state's power supply, but he had to handle all the adverse publicity generated by the accident. Goode proved himself more than able to handle pressure situations with intelligence and concern for the public.

In 1980, when Philadelphia mayor William J. Green was seeking a new managing director for the city, he turned to Goode, appointing him the first black city manager in Philadelphia's history. In this position, Goode had to oversee the day-to-day running of the city. Unlike previous managing directors, Goode worked directly with neighborhood leaders in trying to combat the city's problems. Because of this approach, he gradually became well known throughout the city and was looked upon favorably by most of its citizens.

In 1983, Goode decided to run for mayor of the city. In his campaign, he downplayed the race issue, trying to appeal to Philadelphia's white voters as well as its black voters. The *Wall Street Journal* called him "the ideal man to unite the city," and in the Democratic primary Goode garnered a substantial percentage of the white vote, as well as nearly 98 percent of the black vote (Bigelow 109). He then went on to win the general election, becoming the first African American mayor of Philadelphia.

The national economy was booming and, as mayor, Goode hoped to boost the economy of Philadelphia and to bring new business into the city. He devised a plan he called "Seizing Control of Our Destiny," involving the business leaders of the city, to lure new industry to Philadelphia. At the same time, Goode sought ways of reducing racial tensions in the city. He appointed a six-member cabinet to study the conditions of housing, unemployment, crime, and other factors that affected the African Americans of Philadelphia. Goode's programs seemed to confront all of the city's problems, and Philadelphia was filled with an optimism that it had not experienced in years. As G. Fred Dibona, Jr., an advisor of Goode, said to the *Wall Street Journal* soon after Goode took office, "Never before did a mayor come into office with more genuine support from all communities, from the business community, from the neighborhoods" (Bigelow 107). Everyone was behind him. Goode was even being considered for the position of vice president by presidential candidate Walter Mondale.

In 1985, however, things began to go sour for Goode. In May of that year, a black radical group, MOVE, took over a row house in West Philadelphia. Neighbors complained about their activities and the police moved in to evict them. When the police failed, Goode made the disastrous decision to drop a bomb on the roof of the house. "The resulting explosion and fire killed eleven people (including four children), destroyed 61 houses, and caused an estimated $8 million in damage" (Bigelow 109). The negative publicity extended beyond the city's limits to the national arena. Goode, initially denying responsibility, appointed a commission to investigate the bombing. Unfortunately, his own commission concluded that Goode himself had been "negligent, irresponsible and had 'abdicated his responsibilities as a leader'" (Bigelow 109).

In 1987, Goode was reelected, but only by a very narrow margin. The optimism that had carried him into office in 1983 was gone, and he had lost the trust of many in the city. He was in constant conflict with the city council, and critics charged him with being ineffectual as a leader. In addition, the national economy had experienced a drastic downturn with the stock market crash in October of 1987, and Philadelphia was among the many cities feeling the effect. Goode faced an increasing budget deficit and, with the city council opposed to many of his suggestions, was unable to raise revenue to cover the losses. The council voted against Goode's proposed tax increases and other methods of raising funds.

By 1990, Philadelphia's economy had spiraled out of control and was on the brink of bankruptcy. It was only narrowly able to avert this when the city obtained a $150 million loan from a group of banks and pension funds. The bailout, however, not only put the city deeper in debt, but also increased Goode's unpopularity. By the end of Goode's second term in office, even if he had not been prohibited from running for a third term by law, in all probability he would not have been able to gain reelection.

After leaving office, Goode thought of running for Congress, but his unpopularity remained with him, and he decided he had little chance of winning election. Instead, following the interest he had always had in improving education, he accepted the position of director of the Regional Services Team and acting secretary's representative for Region Two with the Office of Intergovernment and Interagency Affairs (OIIA) of the U.S. Department of Education. As representative of Region Two, Goode oversaw the department's interests in New York, New Jersey, Puerto Rico, and the Virgin Islands. In 1997, Goode was appointed deputy assistant secretary for regional and community services of OIIA and regional representative of Region Three, which includes Pennsylvania, Delaware, Maryland, the District of Columbia, Virginia, and West Virginia. At this writing, Goode continues in this position. In addition to his position with OIIA, Goode also founded and today oversees Goode Cause, Inc., of Philadelphia, an organization serving some 1,000 African American youths through a variety of sporting and mentoring programs. Goode also teaches political science and urban policy at Eastern College in St. Davids, Pennsylvania.

In many ways, the problems Goode faced as mayor of Philadelphia were not of his own making. He was an intelligent and compassionate mayor with a genuine feel for the people whom he governed. In an article in *Time Magazine*, Goode asserted that he was a victim of the times. As Dr. Sandra Featherman of Philadelphia's Temple University said, "I don't think he was a bad mayor; he tried hard to be a good mayor. But he was weak, not vindictive enough—and you have to be vindictive to manage something as complex as this city" (Bigelow 107).

Sources

Bigelow, Barbara Carlisle, ed. *Contemporary Black Biography: Profiles from the International Black Community*, Vol. 4. Detroit, MI: Gale Research, 1993.

Estell, Kenneth. *African America: Celebrating 400 Years of Achievement*. Detroit, MI: Visible Ink Press, 1994.

"Goode Named Deputy Assistant Secretary at Ed." *U.S. Department of Education*. 1997. <http://www.ed.gov/PressReleases/04-1997/goode.html>. Accessed: 3/13/98.

William Herbert Gray III

Reproduced from AP/Wide World Photos, by Denis Paquin

Born: August 20, 1941, in Baton Rouge, Louisiana

Status: President and chief executive officer, United Negro College Fund; pastor, Bright Hope Baptist Church, Philadelphia, Pennsylvania

Education: B.A., 1963, Franklin and Marshall College, Lancaster, Pennsylvania; M.Div., 1966, Drew Theological Seminary, Madison, New Jersey; M.A. in theology, 1970, Princeton University, Princeton, New Jersey; recipient of more than 50 honorary degrees from various colleges and universities

Position: Assistant pastor, senior pastor, Union Baptist Church, Montclair, New Jersey, 1964–1972; pastor, Bright Hope Baptist Church, Philadelphia, Pennsylvania, 1972– ; teacher of history and religion, St. Peter's College, Jersey City State College, Jersey City, New Jersey, Rutgers University, New Brunswick, New Jersey, and Montclair State College, Upper Montclair, New Jersey, 1960s–1970s; U.S. representative from the Second Congressional District of Pennsylvania, 1979–1991; president and CEO, United Negro College Fund, 1991– ; special advisor to President Bill Clinton on Haiti, 1994; awarded Medal of Honor by Haitian president Jean-Bertrand Aristide, 1995; awarded President's Award, National Conference of Black Mayors, 1997

Early Years

William Herbert Gray III was born on August 20, 1941, in Baton Rouge, Louisiana. Shortly after his birth, his family—which also included his father, William H. Gray, Jr.; mother, Hazel Yates Gray; and older sister, Marion—moved to St. Augustine, Florida. His father, who was an educator and a minister, had accepted the position of president of Florida Normal Industrial Institute (now Florida Memorial College); in 1944, he was named president of Florida A and M College in Tallahassee.

In 1949, William Gray, Jr., stepped down from the presidency of the college. When his father, Gray's grandfather, who had presided as pastor of the Bright Hope Baptist Church in Philadelphia, Pennsylvania, died, Gray's father moved the family to Philadelphia to step into the pastorship of the church. The family settled in North Philadelphia, where Gray grew up, attending the public schools of Philadelphia. In 1959, Gray graduated from Simon Gratz High School and entered Franklin and Marshall College in Lancaster, Pennsylvania.

Higher Education

Although Gray intended to follow in his father's and grandfather's footsteps and become a minister, while at Franklin and Marshall his political science professor, Sidney Wise, urged him to consider a career in politics. Wise even recommended him for a congressional internship with U.S. representative Robert Nix of Pennsylvania during Gray's senior year. Despite Wise's urging, however, Gray continued to pursue his interest in becoming a minister. In 1963, he graduated with a major in history from Franklin and Marshall. The following year, Gray became minister of Union Baptist Church in Montclair, New Jersey, a position he would hold until 1972.

However, Gray did not feel that he was finished studying. While carrying out his ministerial duties, he took graduate courses at the University of Pennsylvania and, in 1966, received a master of divinity from Drew Theological Seminary in Madison, New Jersey. He also studied at Temple University in 1966, and at Mansfield College at Oxford University in 1967. In 1970, Gray earned a second master's degree, this one in theology, from Princeton University in Princeton, New Jersey.

Career Highlights

In 1966, Gray was promoted from assistant pastor to senior pastor of the Union Baptist Church, with Martin Luther King, Jr., officiating at his installation ceremony. Gray was united with King not only through his religious vocation, but through his activism within the Montclair community. While he was minister at the Union Baptist Church, he founded a number of nonprofit organizations that built low- and moderate-income housing, and battled discrimination in the community. During this time, Gray was also teaching at a number of colleges and universities: St. Peter's College, Jersey City State College, Rutgers University, and Montclair State College.

In 1971, he married Andrea Dash; over the years the Grays would have three sons: William H. Gray IV, Justin, and Andrew.

In 1972, with the death of his father, Gray moved to Philadelphia and assumed the pastorship of the Bright Hope Baptist Church, which has a membership of more than 5,000. As he had in Montclair, Gray continued his activism, working against discrimination and establishing several nonprofit housing corporations. In 1976, he decided to enter the political arena, challenging the incumbent congressman, **Robert Nelson Cornelius Nix, Sr.**, for whom Gray had interned as a student. While Gray was becoming well known within the community, Nix still was able to defeat him in the primary. The race was close, however; Nix squeaked by with about 300 votes. With this kind of margin, Gray felt confident that he would be able to win the next contest, and in 1978 he did. That year, Gray defeated Nix in the primary, garnering 58 percent of the vote, and went on to defeat Republican Roland Atkins in the general election, becoming Pennsylvania's second black congressman.

Gray was sworn into the 96th Congress on January 3, 1979, and appointed to the Budget Committee, the Committee on the District of Columbia, and the Committee on Foreign Affairs. During the next 10 years, Gray found his work was cut out for him. Ronald Reagan assumed the presidency in 1981, and Gray, working with the other Democrats in the House, scrambled to save social programs Reagan was determined to cut under his theory of "Trickle Down" economics. Indeed, in 1981 and 1982, when he was vice chair of the Congressional Black Caucus, Gray joined with its members in creating proposals that expanded existing social programs in an attempt to help the nation's poor. In 1983, Gray sponsored a proposal to permit minority and female-owned businesses, as well as black colleges, a greater say in programs administered by the Agency for International Development. As a result, minorities and women received $300 million in AID contracts over the next three years (Ploski and Williams 391). In 1985, Gray was elected chairman of the Budget Committee and, in 1989, House Democratic whip—the number three position in the House of Representatives.

Besides championing the rights of the poor and of minorities, Gray also had a deep interest in Africa. Early in his career in the House, he authored the legislation creating the African Development Foundation to ensure direct American aid to African villages. He also authored the House versions of the Anti-Apartheid Acts of 1985 and 1986 that condemned apartheid in South Africa and limited American support to that country.

By 1991, Gray was one of the highest ranking African Americans to serve in the House. He had been reelected with little opposition during the previous 10 years, but, that year, Gray announced he was stepping down from office to accept the position of president and chief executive officer of the United Negro College Fund (UNCF). As he told the National Conference of Black Mayors in 1997, "There is nothing I'd rather be doing than helping young people attain their dreams of receiving a college education" ("Conference . . .").

After assuming the presidency of the UNCF on September 11, 1991, Gray set about strengthening the Fund. As the *Amsterdam News* reported in 1997, "Approximately one-third of the more than $1.2 billion raised in the College Fund's 53-year history has been collected during Gray's tenure" ("Conference . . ."). In addition to fund-raising, Gray cut costs and expanded the programs and services of the Fund. He moved the headquarters of the UNCF to Washington, D.C., and developed a new technology center that linked member colleges. Gray also established the Frederick D. Patterson Research Institute "to compile and analyze data on a host of issues affecting African American students from kindergarten though graduate school" ("United Negro . . ."). By 1997, the UNCF, now known as the College Fund/UNCF, was ranked as the number one nonprofit educational fund in America by *The Chronicle on Philanthropy*.

In 1994, at the request of President Bill Clinton, Gray accepted an appointment as a special advisor to the president of Haiti. In this position, he worked to restore democracy to

Haiti and, in 1995, was awarded the Medal of Honor by Haitian president Jean-Bertrand Aristide.

Gray continues today to minister to his parishioners of the Bright Hope Baptist Church and to oversee the College Fund, a task he feels is of vital importance. As he said in the *Washington Post*,

> If America is to prosper in the global marketplace and maintain our economic strength, we will have to rely on the skills and productivity of that 21st-century workforce. Thus we need to support the educational institutions that know how to take not just the best and brightest, but also the talented and intelligent, and give them the skills America will need. (Smith 284)

Sources

Clay, William L. *Just Permanent Interests: Black Americans in Congress, 1870–1991*. New York: Amistad Press, 1992.

"Conference of Black Mayors Honors Negro Fund President." *Amsterdam News*, 17 May 1997, 8.

"Former Black Members of Congress." *Congressional Times Journal*. <http://www.usbol.com/ctjournal/FrBlkCongMemList.html>. Accessed: 2/27/98.

Ploski, Harry A., and James Williams, eds. *The Negro Almanac: A Reference Work on the African American*. Detroit, MI: Gale Research, 1989.

Smith, Jessie Carney, ed. *Black Heroes of the 20th Century*. Detroit, MI: Gale Research, 1998.

"United Negro College Fund President to Speak at WSU." *Washington State University*. 11 September 1997. <http://www.wsu.edu/NIS/releases / mg111.htm>. Accessed: 5/12/98.

H

Grace Towns Hamilton

Reproduced from AP/Wide World Photos

Born: February 10, 1907, in Atlanta, Georgia

Status: Died July 17, 1992

Education: Graduate, 1923, Atlanta University High School, Atlanta, Georgia; B.A., 1927, Atlanta University, Atlanta, Georgia; M.A. in psychology, 1929, Ohio State University, Columbus, Ohio

Position: Secretary for Girls' Work, Young Women's Christian Association (YWCA), Columbus, Ohio, 1928–1929; teacher, Atlanta School of Social Work, Atlanta, Georgia, 1929; teacher, Clark College, Atlanta, Georgia, 1929; teacher, LeMoyne-Owen College, Memphis, Tennessee, 1930–1934; survey compiler, Works Progress Administration (WPA), Memphis, Tennessee, 1935–1936; hired to develop interracial programs on college campuses, Young Men's Christian Association (YMCA), Memphis, Tennessee, 1936–1941; appointed to the advisory board of trustees, Hughes Spaulding Hospital Authority, Atlanta, Georgia, 1944; executive director, Urban League, Atlanta, Georgia, 1943–1961; assistant director of Program Planning, Southern Regional Council, Atlanta, Georgia, 1954–1955; appointed to the Georgia Commission on the Status of Women, 1963; appointed by Lyndon B. Johnson to the Committee on Recreation and Natural Beauty, 1966; temporary director, Atlanta Youth Council, Atlanta, Georgia, 1966; owner, community relations firm, 1961–1967; legislator from the 31st District (Fulton County), Georgia State House of Representatives, 1965–1985

Awards and honors: Grace Towns Hamilton Lectureship established by Emory University, Atlanta, Georgia, 1989; Grace Towns Hamilton distinguished chair established by Emory University, Atlanta, Georgia, 1990

Early Years

Grace Towns Hamilton was born in Atlanta, Georgia, on February 10, 1907. She was the oldest of the four children of George A. Towns and Nellis McNair Towns. Her father was a professor at Atlanta University and made a comfortable living. He was vocal on the issues of equality and racial injustice, and Hamilton grew up in a household that supported education and activism. Hamilton's mother, although she considered her family her first job, was active in the community, supporting the Young Women's Christian Association (YWCA) and helping to found the "first organized child and service center in Atlanta" (Smith 445). In many ways, Hamilton led a life of privilege compared to most African Americans at the time. Her family was comfortably situated and removed by education—both her father and mother were highly educated—from the racial conflicts that were so prevalent. Hamilton attended the Atlanta University High School from 1919 to 1923.

Higher Education

When Hamilton graduated from high school, she enrolled at Atlanta University. As an undergraduate, she studied hard but was also active on and off campus. She belonged to the Atlanta Interracial Student Forum that worked to promote opportunities for dialog among students from different races in the Atlanta area. She also wrote for the student newspaper and was active, like her mother, in the YWCA.

When she graduated from Atlanta in 1927, she entered graduate school at Ohio State University in Columbus, Ohio. Working to support herself, she took a job as secretary of Girls' Work in the Negro branch of the Columbus YWCA. She graduated with a master's degree in psychology in 1929.

Career Highlights

After graduation, Hamilton returned home to Atlanta and began teaching at the Atlanta School of Social Work and then at Clark College. While teaching in Atlanta, she met and married Henry Cooke Hamilton. Soon after, Henry Hamilton was appointed dean and a professor of education at LeMoyne-Owen College in Memphis, Tennessee, and the couple moved to Memphis. Hamilton was also able to get a teaching position at LeMoyne and taught there for four years. In 1931, she gave birth to a daughter, Eleanor, the Hamiltons' only child.

Hamilton found that she did not enjoy teaching as much as she had hoped. She had been raised to voice her opinions and to work for racial equality. The Depression was at its height, and she decided to work with Roosevelt's Works Progress Administration in Memphis, conducting surveys of various workers. At the same time, she began to become involved politically in the Memphis area through her friendship with Charles Houston, chief counsel for the National Association for the Advancement of Colored People (NAACP). She also developed interracial programs on college campuses for the Young Men's Christian Association (YMCA) in Memphis from 1936 until 1941, when her husband Henry accepted a position with Morehouse College; the family then moved back to Atlanta.

In 1943, Hamilton found a job that utilized the skills she had developed working for the WPA and the YMCA: executive director of the Urban League in Atlanta. She oversaw surveys of the city's black community and reports based on those surveys, which influenced the city to increase funding to the black schools. For this work, Hamilton was named "Most Useful Citizen for 1945" by the Omega Psi Phi Fraternity.

At the same time Hamilton was promoting education, she was also working with the Urban League's Health Committee to improve housing and health facilities for blacks in the city. In 1944, the Urban League established a health center for blacks, and Hamilton was appointed to the advisory board of trustees of Hughes Spaulding Hospital, a teaching hospital for blacks. During the early 1950s, the Urban League also helped bring about the construction of public housing in the city.

Hamilton was becoming more and more well known throughout Atlanta. Although her position with the Urban League required that she not take a political stance, she was a familiar face to most local politicians. In 1954, she decided to take a leave of absence from the league to assume the assistant directorship of program planning for the Southern Regional Council, which was working to end discrimination; and she became actively involved with the NAACP and other political groups. As she became more politically involved, she held a number of appointed positions, such as on Georgia's Commission on the Status of Women and on the Georgia Committee on Children and Youth. In 1966, President Lyndon B. Johnson appointed her to the Committee on Recreation and Natural Beauty.

With all this political involvement, it was a logical next step for Hamilton to seek political office and, in 1965, she decided to run for a seat in the Georgia State Legislature. Redistricting in the state had created a new seat in Georgia's house of representatives, and when a special election was called to fill it in 1965, Hamilton ran. Voters knew her as someone who worked hard to promote equal housing, health, and job opportunities, and she won the election easily. With her election, Grace Towns Hamilton became the first black woman to be elected to the Georgia State Legislature.

Hamilton served in the legislature for nearly 20 years, always fighting for equality. In 1973, she was one of the architects of the new Atlanta city charter that provided for a greater voice for African Americans in the city. She championed fair housing and job opportunities, and set an example for other blacks to follow in civic involvement.

In 1984, however, she made a critical mistake. **Jesse Louis Jackson** had announced his candidacy for the presidency, a move that was heavily supported in Atlanta's black community. Hamilton, however, threw her support behind Walter Mondale, alienating her constituents. At the time, she was running for a 10th term in the legislature, and her support of Mondale became an issue in her campaign. Her opponent, Mabel Thomas, said that Hamilton had been in office too long and was "out of touch with her district" (Hine 521). The voters seemed to agree, and Thomas won both a primary and a runoff election.

Although she retired from the active political arena upon losing to Thomas, Hamilton actively supported many issues and candidates during her remaining years. In 1989, Emory University of Atlanta honored her years of community involvement by establishing the Grace Towns Hamilton lectureship, and, in 1990, the Grace Towns Hamilton distinguished chair.

On July 17, 1992, Grace Towns Hamilton, at age 85, died in Atlanta after a life of service to that city and to the state of Georgia. As **Julian Bond**, who would later serve as president of the NAACP, said of her,

> At a time when there was very little interracial cooperation and very little of any kind of discussion, she was a real pathfinder... She set a standard for civic involvement that was difficult for any of her peers to meet and will be difficult for any who come after her to meet. (Hine 520)

Sources

"Black Involvement in Politics: Grace Towns Hamilton." <http://www.lib.gsu.edu/spcoll/ggdp/hamilton.htm>. Accessed: 3/11/98.

Hine, Darlene Clark, ed. *Black Women in America: An Historical Encyclopedia*, Vol. I, A–L. Brooklyn, NY: Carlson Publishing Co., 1993.

Smith, Jessie Carney, ed. *Notable Black American Women*. Detroit, MI: Gale Research, 1992.

Jeremiah Haralson

Reproduced from the Collections of the Library of Congress

Born: April 1, 1846, near Columbus, Georgia

Status: Died c. 1916 in Colorado

Education: Self-educated

Position: State representative, Alabama State House of Representatives, c. 1869; state senator, Alabama State Senate, 1870–1874; U.S. representative from the First Congressional District of Alabama, 1875–1877; clerk, Federal Custom House, Baltimore, Maryland, c. 1877; clerk, Department of the Interior, c. 1878–1881; employee, Pension Bureau, Washington, D.C., 1882–1884; farmer, Louisiana, 1884–1904; pension agent, Arkansas, 1904

Early Years

Jeremiah Haralson was born the slave of planter John Haralson on April 1, 1846, on a plantation near Columbus, Georgia. Shortly after Jeremiah's birth, John Haralson moved his household to Alabama where Jeremiah remained a slave until the end of the Civil War in 1865. Haralson was intelligent and taught himself to read and write. He was called "a natural politician," and, upon being freed, almost immediately entered into politics. He was reported to have been an accomplished speaker and debater.

Career Highlights

Dark-skinned, unlike many African American politicians who were accepted into Congress at that time, "Haralson capitalized on the fact he was a 'pure-blooded' Negro" (Logan and Winston 286). In 1868, at the age of 22, he ran unsuccessfully for Congress. Although he was defeated, he actively participated in local and national election campaigns. Haralson ran as an independent for a seat in the Alabama State House of Representatives and was successful, serving for a brief time before running for the state senate. To discourage local white voters, he campaigned for the Democratic presidential candidate while secretly supporting the Republican candidate.

In 1870, Haralson was elected to the Alabama State Senate. During his four years in the senate, he alternately supported and opposed the candidacies of Ulysses Grant and Charles Sumner of Massachusetts for the presidency. A skillful speaker who had built a strong political base, he is said to have "emerged as perhaps the most feared Negro in the state legislature" (Logan and Winston 286).

In 1874, Haralson again decided to make a bid for Congress, running on a strong civil rights platform. The June 18, 1874, issue of the *Mobile Register* reported on one of his campaign appearances:

> Jere, black as the ace of spades and with the brogue of the cornfield, ascended the rostrum. A burly Negro, shrewd and fully aware of the strength of his people, insolent to his opponents and always advancing his line of battle while professing to desire nothing but the rights of his race, uncompromising, irritating and bold—Jere struck consternation to the scalawag soul. (Logan and Winston 286)

Haralson defeated liberal Republican Frederick G. Bromberg, but Bromberg challenged the election in the House, declaring that many of Haralson's votes were fraudulent and that his own supporters had been intimidated at the polls or prevented from voting entirely. In April of 1876, the House Committee on Elections ruled that, although some of Haralson's votes appeared invalid, he had still carried the election. The House confirmed the committee's decision and Haralson was sworn into the 44th Congress on March 4, 1875, and appointed to the Committee on Public Expenditures.

Representative Haralson was a very different person than State Senator Haralson. Gone was the oratory and lack of compromise. In the House, Haralson assumed a position of moderation and made no speeches. He favored amnesty for ex-Confederates and became a friend of Jefferson Davis, the former president of the Confederacy. In a letter, published January 29, 1876, in the *Mobile Register*, Haralson asked, "Is it not better for us in general, especially in the South, that there be good feeling between white and black?" (Logan and Winston 286). Although Haralson presented petitions from his constituents in Alabama on various issues and introduced several bills, his impact on Congress was minimal for one with such a strong personality.

In 1876, when Haralson returned to Alabama to run for reelection, he faced a district that had been redefined. It was now the only Alabama district with a black majority, and Haralson was challenged for the Republican nomination by **James Thomas Rapier**. Losing to Rapier, Haralson ran in the general election as an independent, but because of the split vote, both Rapier and Haralson lost to Democrat Charles M. Shelley. Although Haralson contested the vote in the House, it upheld Shelley's election; Haralson's congressional career was at an end.

Following his defeat, Haralson took a number of jobs, working for a time as a clerk at the Federal Custom House in Baltimore, Maryland; as a clerk in the Department of the Interior; and as an employee of the Pension Bureau in Washington, D.C. He tried for reelection in 1878, and again in 1884, but was unsuccessful.

After his defeat in 1884, Haralson moved to Louisiana and, for a time, became a farmer before moving to Arkansas where he worked as a pension agent. After 1904, Haralson essentially became a drifter, moving from Arkansas back to Alabama, and then on to Texas, Oklahoma, and, finally, Colorado. He reportedly mined coal in Colorado until 1916, when he was supposedly killed by wild animals.

Sources

Christopher, Maurine. *America's Black Congressmen.* New York: Thomas Y. Crowell, 1971.

Clay, William L. *Just Permanent Interests: Black Americans in Congress, 1870–1991.* New York: Amistad Press, 1992.

"Former Black Members of Congress." *Congressional Times Journal.* <http://www.usbol.com/ctjournal/FrBlkCongMemList.html>. Accessed: 4/28/98.

Logan, Rayford W., and Michael R. Winston, eds. *Dictionary of American Negro Biography.* New York: W.W. Norton and Co., 1982.

Patricia Roberts Harris

Copyright Washington Post, *reprinted by permission of D.C. Public Library, by Bob Grieser*

Born: May 31, 1924, in Mattoon, Illinois

Status: Died March 23, 1985, in Washington, D.C.; buried in Rock Creek Cemetery, Washington, D.C.

Education: B.A. summa cum laude, 1945, Howard University, Washington, D.C.; graduate studies, 1946–1949, University of Chicago, Chicago, Illinois; graduate studies, 1949, American University, Washington, D.C.; degree in law, 1960, George Washington University Law School, Washington, D.C.

Position: Assistant director, American Council of Human Rights, 1949–1953; executive director, Delta Sigma Theta, 1953–1959; member, research and appeals staff, U.S. Department of Justice, Washington, D.C., 1960–1961; lecturer, associate professor, professor, associate dean of students, Howard University Law School, Washington, D.C., 1961–1965, 1967–1969; U.S. ambassador to Luxembourg, 1965–1967; appointed dean, Howard University Law School, Washington, D.C., 1969; delegate to the 21st and 22nd General Assemblies of the United Nations, 1967–1969; law partner, Fried, Frank, Harris, Shriver, and Kampelman, Washington, D.C., 1970–1977; U.S. secretary of housing and urban development, 1977–1979; U.S. secretary of health, education and welfare, 1980; U.S. secretary of health and human services, 1980; ran for mayor of Washington, D.C., 1982; professor of law, George Washington University, Washington, D.C., 1983–1985

Awards and honors: Recipient of the Alumni Achievement Award, George Washington University, Washington, D.C., 1965; Distinguished Achievement Award, Howard University, Washington, D.C., 1966; Order of Oaken Crown, 1967

Early Years

Patricia Roberts Harris was born on May 31, 1924, in Mattoon, Illinois. Her father, who had been a waiter for the Central Illinois Railroad, abandoned her mother, Hildren Chiquita Roberts. Hildren was left alone to raise Harris and her brother, Malcolm Roberts. Harris once said, "We didn't have a lot of money [but] we believed in education and . . . in reading" (Smith 302).

Harris attended early public school in Mattoon, a predominately white town, learning the cruelty of racism. She attended high school in Chicago and, as an intelligent and hardworking student, received scholarship offers from five different colleges upon graduation.

Higher Education

Harris chose to accept the scholarship offered by Howard University in Washington, D.C. While an undergraduate, she became involved in battling racial discrimination, serving as vice chairperson of the student branch of the National Association for the Advancement of Colored People (NAACP) and joining in nonviolent protests of Washington restaurants that refused admittance to blacks. In 1945, she graduated summa cum laude from Howard and returned to Chicago to continue her studies on the graduate level at the University of Chicago.

While studying industrial relations at the University of Chicago, Harris also became active in the Young Women's Christian Association. In 1949, she returned to Washington, D.C., where she continued her studies at American University and worked as assistant director for the American Council of Human Rights.

In 1953, Harris accepted the position of executive director of Delta Sigma Theta, a national black sorority, and held the job until 1959. During this time she met and married William Beasley Harris, a Washington lawyer. He encouraged her to study law and, in 1957, she began classes at the George Washington University School of Law. The field of law seemed to suit Harris. She shone in her classes, was a member of the law review, and was elected to the national legal honor society, the Order of the Coif. Graduating first in her class in 1960, Harris accepted a job with the appeals and research staff of the criminal division of the Department of Justice. In 1961, she resigned to accept the position of dean of students at

Howard University and to teach part time in its law school.

Career Highlights

Civil rights, however, was becoming the important issue of the day, and Harris felt she should become involved. She had spoken on the topic numerous times, and was gratified when she received an appointment from President John F. Kennedy to cochair the National Women's Committee for Civil Rights, which coordinated the activities of nearly 100 women's civil rights groups in the United States. During the same time, Harris was given a full-time teaching position at Howard University at the rank of associate professor.

In 1965, Harris was appointed U.S. ambassador to Luxembourg by President Lyndon B. Johnson, making her the first black woman to be appointed to an ambassadorship. Taking a leave of absence from Howard, she served in this post until 1967. When she received the appointment, she was keenly aware of what was occurring and said, "I feel deeply proud and grateful the President chose me to knock down this barrier, but also a little sad about being the 'first Negro woman' because it implies we were not considered before" (Bigelow 100).

Upon her return from Luxembourg, Harris continued teaching at Howard with the rank of professor, and also served as a delegate to the 21st and 22nd General Assemblies of the United Nations. In 1969, she again had to face the recognition of "first Negro woman" when she was appointed the first black female dean of Howard University's Law School. Unfortunately, her tenure as dean was of short duration and was filled with upheaval. During the year she served, the school experienced a student uprising. Harris encountered conflicts with both faculty and administration and so, in 1970, she resigned to join a Washington law firm, Fried, Frank, Harris, Shriver, and Kampelman.

For seven years, Harris worked as a corporate lawyer, but also served on the boards of a number of associations and corporations. In 1977, she again became a "first" when President Jimmy Carter appointed her to the cabinet position of secretary of housing and urban development, making her the first black woman to be appointed to a cabinet position. During her confirmation hearing in the Senate, Harris confronted the charge that she was not in touch with those she might be serving, responding,

> You do not understand who I am . . . I am a black woman, the daughter of a Pullman car waiter. I am a black woman who even eight years ago could not buy a house in parts of the District of Columbia. I didn't start out as a member of a prestigious law firm, but as a woman who needed a scholarship to go to school. If you think I have forgotten that, you are wrong. (Smith 305)

In many ways, Harris felt, the federal government itself had contributed to the problems her agency had to face. She battled long and hard for funding for the various programs her department administered, and attacked discrimination in housing and employment. In her many speeches and presentations before various governmental groups, she expressed her concern for the plight of those discriminated against in American society. About minority unemployment, for example, she said, "I am concerned that an entire generation may grow up without the opportunity to hold a decent job. We cannot allow that to happen" (Smith 305). In 1980, Harris was appointed to head the Department of Health, Education, and Welfare (renamed Health and Human Services), where she continued her battle to help the American public.

In addition to promoting programs to help the disadvantaged, Harris also spoke up frequently for women's rights: "I want to hear the Speaker of the House addressed as Madam Speaker and I want to listen as she introduces Madam President to the Congress assembled for the State of the Union" (Smith 305). Thus it was no surprise to her acquaintances when, in 1982, two years after she had stepped down from her cabinet position with the defeat of Jimmy Carter, Harris decided to run for the office of mayor of Washington, D.C. Although she was a popular candidate, many, again, felt she was out of touch with lower income African Americans. She lost to incumbent mayor, **Marion S. Barry, Jr.**

After her defeat as mayor, Harris returned to teaching, this time at George Washington University. She held this position at the time of her death from cancer on March 23, 1985.

Sources

Bigelow, Barbara Carlisle, ed. *Contemporary Black Biography: Profiles from the International Black Community*, Vol. 2. Detroit, MI: Gale Research, 1992.

Estell, Kenneth. *African America: Celebrating 400 Years of Achievement.* Detroit, MI: Visible Ink Press, 1994.

New Grolier Multimedia Encyclopedia. Novato, CA: The Software Toolworks, Inc./Grolier, Inc., 1993.

Smith, Jessie Carney, ed. *Black Heroes of the 20th Century.* Detroit, MI: Visible Ink Press, 1998.

Alcee Lamar Hastings

Courtesy of the Office of Congressman Alcee Lamar Hastings

Born: September 5, 1936, in Altamonte Springs, Florida

Status: U.S. representative from the 23rd Congressional District of Florida

Education: B.A., 1958, Fisk University, Nashville, Tennessee; attended Howard University School of Law, Washington, D.C.; J.D., Florida A and M University, Tallahassee, Florida, 1963; admitted to the bar of Florida, 1963

Position: Attorney, 1963–1976; circuit judge, Florida, 1977–1979; U.S. district court judge, Southern District of Florida, 1979–1989; U.S. representative from the 23rd District of Florida, 1993–

Early Years

Alcee Lamar Hastings was born in Altamonte Springs, Florida, on September 5, 1936. As a teenager, he attended Crooms Academy in Florida.

Higher Education

He then attended Fisk University in Nashville, Tennessee, graduating in 1958. He studied law at Howard University Law School in Washington, D.C., and received his juris doctor degree from Florida A and M University in Tallahassee, Florida (*Congressional Black Caucus*).

Career Highlights

Hastings worked as an attorney for 17 years before exchanging his lawyer's suit for a judge's robe. In 1977, he became a circuit judge in Florida. Two years later, he was appointed U.S. district court judge of the Southern District of Florida by President Jimmy Carter, which made him Florida's first black federal judge.

In 1981, Hastings's career as a judge was threatened. That year, he tried a case involving two mobsters from Miami. After the trial, Hastings was indicted by a grand jury on the charge that he had accepted $150,000 in bribes for a reduction in the mobsters' sentences. Although Hastings was acquitted of these charges in 1983, a special investigating committee for the 11th U.S. Circuit Court of Appeals found that he had fabricated the evidence that had led to his acquittal, perjuring himself. Since Hastings was a federally appointed judge, the committee submitted their findings to Congress, recommending that Hastings be impeached (the only method to remove a federal judge, who is appointed for life).

As in a lower court, impeachment within Congress occurs in two stages. The House, like a grand jury, hears the case and decides whether to recommend impeachment; the Senate then tries the individual accused. In Hastings's case, the House voted 413 to 3 for impeachment on the charges of accepting bribes and perjury. After hearing the facts of the case, the Senate then voted 69 to 26 in favor of impeachment.

Hastings appealed the decision of the Senate and, on September 17, 1992, U.S. district judge Stanley Sporkin ruled that the trial was invalid. The Senate had chosen that the case be heard by a panel of 12 members, rather than the whole Senate. Sporkin ruled that the trial should have taken place before the entire Senate, as is generally required in an impeachment. The case then went to the United States Supreme Court for a final ruling.

Although Hastings was in the midst of defending himself, even after he was stripped of his judgeship in 1989, he continued to seek public office. In 1990, he ran for secretary of state of Florida, but was defeated. When the congressional district boundaries were redrawn as a result of the 1990 census, Hastings decided to run for Congress from the newly created 23rd District, which was made up of seven Florida counties, including the heavily populated Dade County. He ran for the nomination against Democrat Lois Frankel, a white state representative, calling her a wealthy outsider. Hastings relied on his record as a civil rights supporter as an attorney and judge, ignoring the fact that he had been impeached by the United States Senate. As the *Congressional Quarterly Weekly Report* said of him, "Where do you start in attempting to characterize Alcee Hastings? Without question he is charming, inspirational, brilliant, gutsy, and charismatic. He is also profane, audacious, proud, brazen, and pardon me for saying it, slick" (Phelps 84). Hastings was able to defeat Frankel, then go on to win election against his Republican opponent, Ed Fielding.

In January of 1993, when Hastings was just about to be sworn into office in the House of Representatives, the United States Supreme Court rendered its decision; Hastings was impeached. That same month, Hastings was sworn into the very body that had impeached him; a United States district court had ruled on January 4 that, despite his impeachment, Hastings was not barred from holding public office.

Hastings was assigned to the Merchant Marine and Fisheries Committee and the Foreign Affairs Committee. A liberal, he started to do what he had promised during his campaign: eliminate discrimination and work for increased jobs and better health care. During his first term, Hastings vocally supported the "César Chavez Workplace Fairness Act," which sought to prevent striking workers from being fired or replaced. He also worked to restore funds that had been cut from the Medicare program, and secured funds for road repairs and improvements for his district in Florida.

Alcee Hastings has been called "one of the more colorful and more interesting members" of Congress (*Congressional Times Journal*). Few would dispute this as he holds the unique position of serving in the body that once impeached him.

Despite his earlier problems, Hastings has had no trouble being reelected for office. As representative, he continues to follow his agenda against discrimination and violent crime, and for better health care.

Sources

"Biographical Sketch of Congressman Alcee L. Hastings." *U.S. House of Representatives.* <http://www.house.gov/alceehastings/bio.html>. Accessed: 3/6/98.

Congressional Black Caucus '93–'94 Guide. <http://www.sas.upenn.edu/African_Studies/Govern_Political/CBC_Guide.html>. Accessed: 3/10/98.

Phelps, Shirelle, ed. *Contemporary Black Biography: Profiles from the International Black Community*, Vol. 16. Detroit, MI: Gale Research, 1998.

Richard Gordon Hatcher

Reproduced from UPI/Corbis-Bettmann

Born: July 10, 1933, in Michigan City, Indiana

Status: Attorney, Gary, Indiana

Education: B.S., 1955, Indiana University; degree in criminal law, with honors, 1959, Valparaiso University, Valparaiso, Indiana

Position: Law clerk, East Chicago, Illinois, 1959; attorney, Michigan City, Indiana, 1961; deputy prosecuting attorney, Lake County Criminal Court, Indiana, 1961; staff member, juvenile court, Gary, Indiana, 1961; attorney, Gary, Indiana, 1961– ; member, city council, Gary, Indiana, 1963–1966; mayor, Gary, Indiana, 1967–c. 1975

Early Years

Richard Gordon Hatcher was born in Michigan City, Indiana, on July 10, 1933, the 12th of 13 children. The Depression had devastated the country economically and, soon after Hatcher was born, his father, Carlton Hatcher, lost his job. Carlton Hatcher was forced to move his family to "the Patch," a slum area of the city, and to earn a living by pushing a junk cart through the alleys, collecting paper, scraps of cloth, and bits of metal to sell. Despite their poverty, Hatcher's parents were proud and very religious. As Hatcher later said, "I have some rather strong feelings about the kind of strength and support that one draws from a belief in God, and that belief has always served me well" (Haskins 52).

When Hatcher was about three years old, an accident occurred. His parents had gone to church and he was playing a game with a friend in the street. The game consisted of one boy throwing a rock at another, trying to come as close as he could without hitting the other boy. But Hatcher was hit in his left eye; when his parents returned home, he was crying and in pain. They had no money for a doctor, but scraped together what they could to obtain the care he needed. After a year of seeing various specialists, Hatcher lost his eye.

The accident brought Hatcher and his father closer together; and their closeness was made even stronger when Hatcher's mother died in 1947 from cancer. His father was his mentor and guide through his youth, helping him understand the racism so prevalent in the city and country at the time. As Hatcher commented,

> If I were to try to look to the single person who provided me with the kind of continuous encouragement, support, and inspiration that is so essential to every young person, it would just have to be my father. (Haskins 54)

Hatcher attended public school in Michigan City, and hoped to continue his education and get a college degree. Although poor, his father encouraged him in this goal. When Hatcher graduated from Elson High School in 1951, however, he learned from his father that there was just no money for college.

That summer, Hatcher worked at Pullman Standard, where his father was also employed. He saved money for college. He also was able to get a small athletic scholarship for football at Indiana University, and two local churches took up collections for him. By the end of the summer, Hatcher had just enough money for his first year of college; the next three years were financed in much the same way.

Higher Education

Indiana University was a shock to Hatcher. He found that the black schools of Michigan City had left him unprepared academically for college, and he had to work twice as hard as other students to succeed. He also enrolled in math classes at a high school on campus so that he could catch up.

Hatcher had to face blatant discrimination on the campus. Most black students were excluded from campus activities, and were not permitted to eat in the campus restaurants; they could buy food to take out, but could not eat it there. Hatcher engaged in his first sit-in as a result of this policy. He and a group of other black students sat-in and picketed the most popular campus restaurant and succeeded in integrating it.

During Hatcher's senior year, it looked as if all he had worked for and tolerated would be lost. Toward the end of the first semester, a group of his friends found some firecrackers in his desk and set them off in the hallway of the dormitory. Although Hatcher had not been a part of the group, he refused to reveal their identities and was expelled. But he was determined to finish college and, after a summer and one semester of suspension, returned to finish his senior year, graduating in 1955.

Hatcher entered Valparaiso University Law School because he knew he could work at a nearby mental hospital while in graduate school to support himself. He did well in his studies and, in 1958, took his first step into politics, seeking the Democratic nomination for Michigan Township justice of the peace. There were 10 other candidates, but only he had any law background. He came in fourth, having learned a great deal about politics.

In 1959, Hatcher graduated from Valparaiso with honors in criminal law. While he studied for the bar exam, he worked in an East Chicago office as a clerk for lawyer Henry Walker.

Career Highlights

Once Hatcher had passed the bar exam, he set up his own practice in 1961 in Michigan City. Many of his clients were poor and unable to pay his fees, so he also accepted an appointment as part-time deputy prosecutor in the criminal court at the county seat. Because of a lack of money, he closed his law office after only a few months.

Hatcher was becoming more involved with the civil rights movement as a member of the NAACP. He acted as one of the NAACP's attorneys in an unsuccessful lawsuit against the Gary, Indiana, school system for failing to integrate its schools. He also marched in various protests, and joined in founding a group called Muigwithania, an organization with the goal of reforming politics in Gary.

By 1963, blacks comprised more than 55 percent of Gary's population of some 200,000. However, the city was run by a Democratic machine that was predominantly white. Graft was rampant, and organized crime was called "Gary's second largest industry" (Haskins 61). The midtown section of the city, where most of the blacks lived, was a horrible slum. Most of Gary's citizens felt reform was impossible.

Hatcher set up a law practice in the Gary office of Muigwithania member Jackie Shropshire and, in 1963, declared his intention to seek the nomination for councilman at large on the Gary City Council. He found that the local Democratic Committee would not support him. As he said,

> They were not especially anxious to welcome any new aspirants for office who had no past history of working with them. We had a number of wonderful volunteers—people who worked very hard. They didn't know all the political rules so they just worked with people and we won the election. (Haskins 62–63)

Hatcher ran as an independent Democrat and, although attacked as a "radical," managed to get 99 percent, a record number, of the black vote. Hatcher set another record when, within a year, he became the first freshman councilman to be elected president of the city council.

Although Hatcher was having an effect upon Gary from his position on the city council, he felt change was occurring too slowly. He decided to run for mayor; from that position, he would be able to institute needed changes more quickly. The Muigwithanians got to work on a campaign as soon as Hatcher announced his intentions and, in December of 1966, Hatcher received a big boost to his ambitions. He was one of eight city leaders from across the country to be invited to dine with Vice President Hubert Humphrey, and to discuss disenchantment of the poor and blacks with the Johnson administration. The dinner gave Hatcher much-needed publicity in Gary, demonstrating his leadership qualities.

Hatcher formally announced his candidacy for mayor on January 13, 1967. He would be confronting incumbent mayor Martin Katz, also a Democrat. Katz had the backing of the Democratic organization, while Hatcher had to raise his own funds. Previously, Katz had run a campaign sympathetic to the city's black population. Faced with a black candidate, however, he played upon the ignorance and fear of the white population of Gary, calling Hatcher a radical, an extremist, and an advocate of black power. Hatcher responded coolly to Katz's attacks, pointing out that he did not believe in separation but, rather, in the pooling of resources, whether they came from blacks or whites.

In the primary, Katz and a third candidate, Konrady, split the white vote, while Hatcher received 70 percent of the black vote. Although Hatcher had won the party's nomination, the local Democratic Party refused to support him, joining with his Republican opponents in attacking him.

Hatcher received support from the local black community and from many prominent national Democratic leaders. When Hatcher's campaign was nearly out of money—the local Democratic Party would not fund his campaign—he called upon national leaders for help. The National Democratic Club in Washington, D.C., held a fund-raiser for him, and various national leaders spoke on his behalf.

As the election neared, Hatcher learned of a scheme that, if successful, would prevent his winning. Election officials who opposed him had added 3,000 false names to the white voter rolls and removed 5,286 names from the black voter rolls. A Democratic committeewoman from the 12th precinct, Marian Tokarski, felt she could not keep silent about this, even though she did not support Hatcher. She went to Hatcher with her story, then to the FBI and the Justice Department.

When election day dawned, tensions were high in Gary. Blacks turned out in record numbers to vote. When the polls closed, Hatcher had beaten his Republican opponent by nearly 2,000 votes, becoming Gary's first black mayor.

Over the next four years, Hatcher labored tirelessly to rehabilitate Gary, building up its police force, organizing crime prevention units, luring business and federal money to the city, and improving inner-city housing areas. Grants were obtained to build the first new public housing in Gary since 1953 and three new parks, two of which were in the barren inner-city area. Although Hatcher faced opposition every step of the way, his improvements spoke for themselves and helped him gain reelection in 1971.

Hatcher faced death threats, disunion—one suburb threatened to secede from the city—name calling, and bald hatred during his time as mayor of Gary. This did not stop him, however; he kept his original goal of improving the city ever in mind. As he said early in his years as mayor, "What's important is whether our society can respond in a legitimate way to the black man in *any* position. What's on trial in Gary is the American system" (Haskins 87).

Sources

Haskins, James. *A Piece of the Power: Four Black Mayors*. New York: Dial, 1972.

Joint Center for Political Studies. *Profiles of Black Mayors in America*. Washington, DC/Chicago, IL: The Joint Center for Political Studies/Johnson Publishing, 1977.

Augustus Freeman Hawkins

Reproduced from AP/Wide World Photos

Born: August 31, 1907, in Shreveport, Louisiana

Status: Retired

Education: B.A. in economics, 1931, University of California at Los Angeles (UCLA); attended the University of Southern California's Institute of Government

Position: Real estate broker, 1930s; member, California State Assembly, 1934–1963; U.S. representative from the 29th Congressional District of California, 1963–1990

Early Years

Augustus Freeman Hawkins was born on August 31, 1907, in Shreveport, Louisiana, the youngest son of Nyanza and Hattie Freeman Hawkins, who had four other children. His father, a pharmacist, decided to move his business to Los Angeles when Hawkins was 10. Hawkins grew up in that city, clerking at his father's drugstore, working part-time as a postal clerk, and attending public high school. He did well in school and was able to enter the University of California at Los Angeles on a work scholarship.

Higher Education

Hawkins's work scholarship provided him with a job as a janitor at UCLA, cleaning the girls' gymnasium. Hawkins graduated in 1931 with a bachelor's degree in economics, hoping to continue studying in graduate school as a civil engineer. But by the time he graduated, the Depression had set in and money was scarce. His father's pharmacy was struggling, so Hawkins could not count on help from his father in funding his education. For a time, he tried his hand at various businesses while attending the University of Southern California's Institute of Government.

Career Highlights

With a partner, Hawkins started an automobile appliance store that quickly failed. He then went into the real estate business with his brother Edward and was more successful. As a businessman, Hawkins began to take a greater interest in both local and national politics. During Franklin Roosevelt's 1932 campaign for the presidency, Hawkins worked hard in his area to turn out the vote for the Democrats. The Republicans had had their shot at trying to end the Depression; only the Democrats seemed to offer new hope.

As he became more widely known, Hawkins began to think of running for office himself and, in 1934, ran for the California State Assembly from the 62nd District, challenging Frederick Roberts, a black Republican who had held the office for 16 years. Hawkins ran on a ticket of change. One of his promises was to lower the fares on the local streetcars but, after taking office, he found he could not deliver. This experience taught him, he later said, "never to be irresponsible with campaign promises" (Christopher 222).

Many felt that Hawkins's election was an accident—he was young and virtually unknown compared to Roberts—and that he would not last in office. But Hawkins was to retain his assembly seat for nearly 30 years, until he decided to run for Congress. During his time in the California assembly he labored hard on behalf of his constituents, working for slum clearance and low-cost housing, minimum wage for women, and workers' compensation for domestics, among other things. Hawkins was helped in his political endeavors by his wife, Pegga Adeline Smith, whom he had married in 1941. Until her death in 1966, Pegga Hawkins participated actively in organizing and promoting her husband's political career locally and nationally.

In 1962, Hawkins decided to run for a seat in Congress. His opponent charged that Hawkins was being pushed into Congress by the Democrats because they did not wish to see a black person in the speaker's seat in Sacramento, a position for which he would have qualified as a senior assemblyman. Hawkins refuted the charge, saying, "I ran for Congress because many of the issues with which I am deeply concerned, such as Medicare and low-cost housing, transcend to the national level. I felt that as a congressman I could do a more effective job than in the assembly" (Christopher 223).

When Hawkins took his congressional seat in 1963, the issues of civil rights and the Vietnam War were becoming the prime concerns of many in the country, and Hawkins actively tackled them. As one constituent said, "He won't be popping off like [**Adam Clayton**] **Powell** [**Jr.**], but you can bet your boots that Gus will deliver the goods" (Christopher 223). Quietly and forcefully, during his tenure in Washington, Hawkins confronted and fought for some of the most important legislation of the 1960s. He authored and successfully pushed for the Juvenile Justice and Delinquency Prevention Act, the Community Service Act, and the Civil Rights Act that called for black equality and established the Equal Employment Opportunity Commission.

Hawkins's district included Watts in Los Angeles, the site of one of the most violent riots of the 1960s. With uncanny foresight, Hawkins said after the Watts riots on May 12, 1967,

> Let us face head-on the fact that sporadic violence in our slum ghettos can be expected . . . for we are limited in providing solutions by the economic and ideological limits fixed by those jealous of giving up power or spending money on such intangibles as race relations, preventive programs and a better society . . . it is not that we lack the capacity to avoid a decade of disorders but the will—the will to redirect such institutions as our schools, to provide saturation programs to overcome long-existing deficiencies, and to admit the disadvantaged into the mainstreams of American society. Many public agencies don't even want the poor involved in community action for their own benefit out of insatiable fear the poor may gain power to change conditions, including perhaps some public officials. (Christopher 224)

Throughout the next two decades, Hawkins continued to push for social and economic reform, authoring the Fair Housing Act. He also was one of the leading critics of United States involvement in the Vietnam War and of some of the more horrific actions of the U.S. and South Vietnamese military in Vietnam. In July 1970, he and William R. Anderson, representative from Tennessee, protested the "savage mistreatment" of prisoners in the Con Son prison of South Vietnam, which they had discovered on a fact-finding trip to South Vietnam. Shortly after their disclosure of conditions there, the Con Son prison was closed.

During his tenure in the 99th Congress, Hawkins saw passage of an amendment he had written to the Higher Education Act giving more resources to minority colleges, and he saw the passage of his bill to continue the School Lunch and Nutrition Program. These two pieces of legislation are typical of those he supported throughout his congressional career. They were both aimed at closing the gap separating black from white, helping African Americans achieve a more equal status in the United States.

These legislative moves, however, were a mere drop in the bucket to Hawkins. Toward the end of his career of nearly 56 years in public office, Hawkins was still warning of the growing frustration and violence that plagued the United States:

> Congress seems to be bent on finding ways to crush dissent and social change which it has helped to encourage . . . Expedient appeals based on law and order and supported by strong police-state force may temporarily achieve civic quietness, but the problems which give rise to unrest and disorders will remain. People will not willingly accept unemployment, starvation, and exploitation. (Christopher 227)

In 1990, at the age of 83, Augustus Hawkins decided to retire, having served for over half a century. Although not the most public of figures in Congress, Augustus Hawkins had achieved respect for his understanding, intelligence, and perception.

Sources

Christopher, Maurine. *America's Black Congressmen.* New York: Thomas Y. Crowell, 1971.

Clay, William L. *Just Permanent Interests: Black Americans in Congress, 1870–1991.* New York: Amistad Press, 1992.

Charles Arthur Hayes

Born: February 17, 1918, in Cairo, Illinois

Status: Died April 8, 1997, in Hazel Crest, Illinois

Education: Graduate, 1935, Sumner High School, Cairo, Illinois

Position: Machine operator, Cairo, Illinois; president, Local 1424, United Brotherhood of Carpenters and Joiners of America, 1940–1942; member, grievance committee, United Packinghouse Workers of America (UPWA), 1943; field representative, UPWA, 1949; union official, District One, UPWA, 1954–1978; director of Region 12 and international vice president, United Food and Commercial Workers International Union, 1979–1983; U.S. representative from the First Congressional District of Illinois, 1983–1992

Early Years

Charles Arthur Hayes was born in Cairo, Illinois, on February 17, 1918. When he graduated from Cairo's Sumner High School in 1935, he was facing a bleak future. The Depression was at its height and, although he was intelligent, he had no money to continue his education. The job market at the time was nearly nonexistent.

Franklin Delano Roosevelt had been elected in 1932 by voters hoping that he would be able to pull the nation out of the economic doldrums that had prevailed since the stock market crash in 1929. By 1935, when Hayes graduated, the effects of Roosevelt's New Deal were just beginning to be felt, although millions were still unemployed. Hayes was among the lucky, acquiring a job as a machine operator in Cairo.

Career Highlights

During the prosperity of the 1920s, the influence of labor unions had weakened, undercut by a number of legislative acts from Congress. By 1935, unions had little influence. As Carman et al. point out in their *A History of the American People*, ". . . by 1930 all that remained of the American labor movement was a small group of craft-unions in the A.F. of L. and the Railroad Brotherhoods" (562). But the New Deal of Roosevelt sought to strengthen the power of the workers by encouraging them to unionize. The New Deal labor policy did this in a number of ways:

> It supported collective bargaining by giving both moral and legal aid to workers who wanted to unionize their industries . . . It provided relief for those who could not work [and] . . . Finally, the New Deal imposed and enforced certain minimum standards for workers who were employed. (Carman et al. 610)

For workers such as Hayes, the New Deal policies provided both good news and opportunity. Almost as soon as he began working, Hayes, with others, began to organize Local 1424 of the United Brotherhood of Carpenters and Joiners of America. Once organized, Hayes served as its president from 1940 until 1942.

Hayes had a real flair for union work; he was intelligent and got along well with people. In 1943, he was asked to become a member of the grievance committee of the United Packinghouse Workers of America (UPWA), a union with which he would work for the next 36 years. In 1949, he became a field representative for the UPWA and, from 1954 until 1968, served as its District One director. In 1968, the UPWA merged with the meat cutters' unions, and Hayes assumed the position of district director and international vice president.

In 1979, Hayes became the international vice president and director of Region 12 of the United Food and Commercial Workers International Union. Hayes would retain these positions until his retirement in 1983 to run for Congress.

Throughout many years with the unions, Hayes had worked consistently to better working conditions and to provide more opportunities for both minorities and women, fighting discrimination and segregation in hiring and promotions. He also attempted to bring as many minorities as he could into positions of leadership in the unions. With this kind of record, it was a natural progression, then, for him to enter the political arena.

In April of 1983, Harold Washington stepped down from his congressional seat representing the First District of Illinois, South Central Chicago, to assume the position of mayor of Chicago. Local political leaders scouted for candidates to fill Washington's vacant seat; among the candidates nominated was labor leader Charles Arthur Hayes.

The battle for the nomination was intense. There was a field of 14 candidates from which to choose, some much more well-known than Hayes. Among them was Al Raby, who had been a civil rights leader and had aided Washington in his run for mayor. Another, Lu Palmer, was a community activist and was well known among constituents because he was a local radio host. Despite this formidable opposition, Hayes prevailed after Washington announced he would support Hayes. Hayes was able to sweep the primary with 45 percent of the votes and take the vacant seat in an August election.

On September 12, 1983, Charles Hayes was sworn into the 98th Congress. He was appointed to the Committee on Education and Labor, the Small Business Committee, and, later, the Post Office and Civil Service Committee.

In Congress, as he had done for nearly 50 years, Hayes championed labor and education. He introduced a number of pieces of legislation to encourage young people not to drop out of school, and to provide them with job training and support services. As chairman of the Subcommittee on Postal Personnel and Modernization, he oversaw the improvement of both working conditions and services in the post office. He consistently opposed apartheid in South Africa and, in 1984, joined a demonstration outside South Africa's embassy in Washington to protest its dehumanizing policy of segregation.

Although Hayes successfully ran for reelection a number of times, in 1992, he was finally defeated when opposed by Bobby L. Rush, who was a member of Chicago's city council at the time. After his retirement from Congress, Hayes returned to Hazel Crest, Illinois, where, five years later on April 8, 1997, he died of complications from lung cancer at the South Suburban Hospital. During his lifetime, Charles Arthur Hayes built a solid reputation in Congress and in the workplace through his support of unions and the working people of America.

Sources

Carman, Harry J., Harold C. Syrett, and Bernard W. Wishy. *A History of the American People, Volume II—Since 1865*, 3rd ed. New York: Alfred A. Knopf, 1952.

Clay, William L. *Just Permanent Interests: Black Americans in Congress, 1870–1991*. New York: Amistad Press, 1992.

"Former Black Members of Congress." *Congressional Times Journal*. <http://www.usbol.com/ctjournal/FrBlkCongMemList.html>. Accessed: 2/18/98.

J

Jesse Louis Jackson

Reproduced from AP/Wide World Photos

Born: October 8, 1941, in Greenville, South Carolina

Status: President, National Rainbow Coalition, Inc.

Education: Attended University of Illinois, Chicago, Illinois, 1959–1960; B.A., 1964, North Carolina A and T College, Greensboro, North Carolina; attended Chicago Theological Seminary, Chicago, Illinois, 1964–1966; ordained a minister in the Baptist church, 1968; recipient of numerous honorary degrees from various colleges and universities

Position: Field representative, Council on Racial Equality (CORE), 1964; Chicago coordinator, Operation Breadbasket, 1966–1967; national director, Operation Breadbasket, 1967–1971; founder and executive director, Operation PUSH, 1971–1986; founder, PUSH-Excel and PUSH for Economic Justice, 1971; founder, national president, National Rainbow Coalition, Inc., 1986– ; statehood senator, Washington, D.C., 1991–1997; host, "Voices of America" with Jesse Jackson, 1989– ; special envoy for the promotion of democracy in Africa, 1998

Early Years

When Jesse Jackson's mother, Helen Burns, discovered she was pregnant, she shocked her Greenville, South Carolina, neighborhood by declaring that she would bear the child out of wedlock. Earlier, she had caught the eye of her next-door neighbor, Noah Robinson, and the two had fallen in love. There was one insurmountable obstacle to their marriage, however; Noah was already married, with a wife and three children. Burns's son, Jesse Burns, born on October 8, 1941, would not find out who his father was until he was nine or 10 years old. He would have to endure the taunts of other children who teased that he was "a nobody" without a father. In many ways, this made Jesse determined that someday, somehow, he would be somebody.

When Jesse was two years old, Helen Burns married Charles Jackson, who gave Jesse his name. Charles tried hard to make Jackson feel he belonged. "I never told him I was not his father," he said, "because I didn't want him to grow up thinking he was different" (Haskins 12). But Jackson knew.

As a boy, Jackson attended the segregated schools of Greenville, walking five miles to the black elementary school, even though there was a white school within two blocks of his home. With his family, he also attended the Longbranch Baptist Church each Sunday for services. When Jackson was nine years old, he gave his first public speech at a Christmas pageant at church. The congregation was so impressed by his devoutness and his speaking ability that they sent him to a national Sunday school convention in Charlotte, North Carolina, to represent the church. As he grew up, Jackson became a familiar figure in the Longbranch church, presenting an oral report once each month before the congregation. Even at an early age, Jackson had accepted and made his faith an important part of his everyday life.

Jackson and his young friends frequently encountered the discrimination that was rampant at that time in the South. He and his friends would try to rationalize the separation between blacks and whites:

> We would say we didn't want to eat because we weren't hungry, or we didn't want to drink water because we weren't thirsty, or we didn't want to go to the movie theater because we didn't want to see the picture. Actually we were lying because we were afraid. (Haskins 15)

Jackson was popular with other young people his age and, in the ninth grade, was elected president of the honor society and president of his class. Throughout his years at the all-black Sterling High School in Greenville, he continued to pursue the class offices. One of his high school teachers, Mrs. Norris, recalled that "Whatever office was available, Jesse would be there signing his name" (Haskins 20). And he usually won. He was also a good athlete, playing football, basketball, and baseball in high school. He dreamed of being a professional football player. But that dream came crashing down at the end of his senior year in high school. One of Jackson's chief competitors was a boy named Dickie Dietz, the top quarterback at the all-white Greenville High School across town from Sterling High. In 1959, after graduating, both boys were approached by a scout for the New York Giants. Jackson discovered that while he was offered $6,000 a year to play for the Giants, Dietz had been offered $95,000 a year. Jackson knew that Dietz wasn't a better player than he, but Dietz was white. Jackson refused the offer and decided to continue his education, accepting an athletic scholarship at the University of Illinois.

Higher Education

Jackson attended the University of Illinois from 1959 to 1960, but could not achieve his goal of being a quarterback on the college football team. He was told there were no black quarterbacks, and there would be no black quarterbacks. Black players were expected to be halfbacks or ends.

Jackson also disliked the tacit segregation on the campus. As he said, "We [the black students] were reduced to a subculture at Illinois ... The annual interfraternity dance was the social event of the fall, but the three black fraternities weren't invited" (Haskins 27). Then in February, 1960, Jackson's attention was riveted on an event occurring in Greensboro, North Carolina. Four college students from North Carolina Agricultural and Technical College in Greensboro were staging a sit-in at a local Woolworth's, attempting to desegregate the lunch counter. The event made national news and electrified Jackson. These students were instituting meaningful change and he wanted to be part of the movement. At the end of his freshman year, Jackson transferred to North Carolina A and T College.

The sit-in had been organized by the Congress of Racial Equality (CORE). When Jackson arrived at A and T, he immediately joined the group. He was soon in a leadership position, organizing marches and protests almost daily. He did not neglect his studies or his school; in fact, he was an honors student and became president of the student body.

In June of 1963, Jackson was arrested for the first time, on the charge of inciting a riot in downtown Greensboro. His girlfriend and wife-to-be, Jacqueline Davis, stood by him during this time. Jackson had met Jacqueline Davis through the civil rights movement. She was a freshman from Virginia, and the first time they spoke, Jackson told her, "Hey, baby, I'm going to marry you!" Later, the two were married in a quiet ceremony at Jackson's parents' home in Greenville.

Jackson continued working in the civil rights movement. His senior year, 1964, he was elected president of the newly formed North Carolina Intercollegiate Council on Human Rights, and became a field representative for CORE. His responsibilities included attending a number of workshops led by Dr. Martin Luther King, Jr., and his staff. In King, Jackson saw ideals that incorporated all he believed in: fighting for justice and ministering to his faith.

After graduation, Jackson and his family, which now included daughter Santita, moved north to Chicago, where Jackson enrolled at the Chicago Theological Seminary. At the seminary, Jackson seemed to be involved in everything. He joined the basketball, baseball, and football teams; studied hard; and joined King's Southern Christian Leadership Conference (SCLC).

When Martin Luther King, Jr., announced that he intended to stage a protest march in Selma, Alabama, and called for supporters from all over the United States, Jackson dashed through the halls of the seminary recruiting students to participate in the protest. They piled into a number of cars and drove through the night to reach Selma in time for the march.

The following day, the nation watched the protest on television and was horrified to see the marchers savaged by Alabama State Troopers and white crowds. But the march got the notice of President Lyndon B. Johnson, who called upon Congress to pass a voting rights law.

During the march, Jackson came to the attention of Dr. King and his supporters from the Southern Christian Leadership Conference and, at first, he irritated them. Jackson was everywhere, barging in wherever King was. The SCLC leaders were especially taken aback when, during a number of speeches held on the steps of Brown Chapel in Selma, Jackson also stood up and spoke. But they decided to keep an eye on him; his rhetoric had moved the crowds and he seemed to be a young man who was going places.

During 1966, the SCLC decided to extend its economic program, Operation Breadbasket, northward. In January of that year, Martin Luther King, Jr., flew to Chicago for a rally to promote the program and, as usual, Jackson was in the forefront, organizing. He gathered local ministers, urging their support, and marched through white neighborhoods. Jackson became so caught up in the civil rights activities in Chicago that he dropped out of the Chicago Theological Seminary; later, in June of 1968, he was ordained in the Baptist church, and in 1969 the seminary granted him an honorary degree. But in 1966 Jackson's formal schooling ended, and he began the crusade for equality that would consume his life.

Career Highlights

In the years following the SCLC march in Chicago, Jackson worked steadily to promote the SCLC's Operation Breadbasket, serving as its coordinator in Chicago for a year. In addition, early in 1968, Jackson, as well as other leaders of the SCLC, began to plan a Poor People's Campaign that would include a march on Washington, D.C., to call attention to the thousands of poor and jobless in the country. The march was successful beyond their hopes. King moved all with his rhetoric, stirring them with his memorable "I Have a Dream" speech. Those attending built a tent city, Resurrection City, next to the Lincoln Memorial and named Jackson its city manager. But King had to leave the march to go to Memphis, Tennessee, where sanitation workers were staging a strike; his followers, including Jackson, accompanied him.

On April 4, 1968, the day after giving a stirring speech at the Mason Temple in Memphis, King, along with his followers, was preparing to leave the Lorraine Motel, where the group was staying, to go to dinner. As King stepped out on the balcony of the motel, a shot rang out and he crumpled. Below, Jackson stood stunned. As Ralph Abernathy, King's closest aide, ran to King's side, crying, "Oh, my God, Martin's been shot," everyone came running. Hosea Williams, another staff member, recalled, "Jesse crawled up the staircase sometime after the photographers arrived . . . I can't remember him crying. He just stood there. Then I think he ran to the phone to call Coretta [Dr. King's wife]" (Haskins 55).

What ensued over the next several days infuriated and embittered SCLC members. Suddenly Jesse Jackson was on all the television news shows claiming he was the last man to speak to Dr. King. The story escalated to Jackson, rather than Abernathy, cradling the dying Dr. King in his arms. The leadership of the SCLC was enraged, particularly when, in 1969, *Playboy* stated, "Jesse Jackson [is the] fiery heir apparent to Martin Luther King . . . He was talking to King on the porch of the Lorraine Motel in Memphis when the fatal shot was fired and cradled the dying man in his arms" (Haskins 55). Jackson, whether they wished it or not, was fast becoming the successor to Martin Luther King in the public's eye.

Jackson was now the national director of Operation Breadbasket, but had lost much of the support of the SCLC. In 1971, matters came to a head. That year, Jackson staged a Black Expo in Chicago to aid black business owners. There were rumors of Jackson refusing to share the proceeds from this with the SCLC, and Ralph Abernathy, the new head of the SCLC, went to Chicago to investigate. Although Abernathy found the charges were unfounded, he felt Jackson was a wild card who needed to be controlled. Abernathy imposed a 60-day suspension from the SCLC on Jackson and ordered him to move to Atlanta, Georgia, where the SCLC could watch him.

Faced with these disciplinary measures, Jackson broke with the SCLC and started his own organization, Operation PUSH (People United to Save Humanity). It would be, according to Jackson, "a rainbow coalition of blacks and whites gathered together to push for a greater share of economic and political power for all poor people in America in the spirit of Dr. Martin Luther King, Jr." (Haskins 58). Operation PUSH continued the same agenda in Chicago that Operation Breadbasket had begun. Jackson also promoted improved education through PUSH-Excel that worked to keep inner-city young people in school and to provide jobs for them.

After PUSH was organized in 1971, Jackson decided to enter the political arena to try to bring about change. That year, he mounted a campaign against Mayor Richard J. Daley, forming a third party, the Bread 'n Butter Party. But Jackson was up against stiff opposition on two fronts. He lacked solid backing in the black community because he had alienated many of the local black leaders by announcing his candidacy without consulting them. Jackson also faced the formidable Democratic "machine" of Daley, and Daley won easily by a wide margin. Having had a taste of politics, however, Jackson made the decision to try harder in the future.

During the 1970s, Jackson continued to promote PUSH in Chicago, despite the fact that it had encountered a number of problems; paramount among them was the fact that the government, suspecting misappropriation of funds, was investigating its financial records. But nothing came of the investigation. Jackson continued with his work and began earning an international reputation.

In 1979, he traveled to South Africa to speak against the apartheid there, and to the Middle East to push for peace negotiations between the PLO and Israel. Although he was tolerated in South Africa, Jackson met outright hostility in Israel. Many felt he was endorsing the terrorist tactics of the PLO when he met with Yasir Arafat, the leader of the PLO.

By 1983, Jackson felt he was ready to move on to national politics. On November 3, 1983, he announced his intention to run for president at a rally held in Washington, D.C., at the Washington Convention Center, saying,

> . . . let the word go forth from this occasion that this candidacy is not for blacks only . . . I would like to use this candidacy to help build a new rainbow coalition of the rejected that will include whites, blacks, Hispanics, Indians, and Native Americans, Asians, women, young people, poor people, old people, gay people, laborers, small farmers, small business-persons, peace activists and environmentalists . . . Together the old minorities constitute a new majority. (Haskins 80)

With that, Jackson's Rainbow Coalition was born, with Jackson as its first (and only) candidate.

Jackson's campaign was given a boost when, in 1984, he flew to Syria and successfully negotiated the release of Lt. Robert O. Goodman, an American pilot who had been shot down and taken hostage. Jackson was praised by Ronald Reagan for his efforts and gained a great deal of credibility as a candidate.

Eight days before the New Hampshire primary, however, Jackson made a fatal mistake. In February, 1984, Milton Coleman, a black reporter for the *Washington Post,* reported that Jackson had made a negative comment about Jewish people, denigrating both them and New York City. Although he publicly apologized, the damage was done—his campaign was tarnished. In the New Hampshire primary, Jackson finished fourth with only 5 percent of the vote. The charge of anti-Semitism would haunt Jackson throughout his campaign. Despite this, by the time the Democratic National Convention was held, Jackson had won 384 delegates, a respectable showing.

By 1988, when Jackson again ran for the presidency, he had learned a few things. He had moved his home from Chicago to Washington, D.C., and was making contacts. His National Rainbow Coalition had more money and was better organized. By the end of the various primaries, Jackson had won a number of them, including an unexpected victory in the state of Michigan. Although his chances for a nomination for president at the National Democratic Convention were poor, Jackson was hoping to be asked to fill the vice presidential spot on Michael Dukakis's ticket. Dukakis then angered Jackson by announcing, before he had notified Jackson, that he had chosen Texas senator Lloyd Bentsen. After an apology and discussion, Dukakis agreed to have Jackson introduce him at the convention; in return, Jackson would campaign on Dukakis's behalf.

Although Jackson chose not to run again for the presidency in 1992 or 1996, he continues to be an active and vocal presence in politics. In 1991, he ran and was elected "statehood senator" for the District of Columbia, a position established by the city to promote the statehood of Washington, D.C., in Congress. In February, 1998, Jackson returned to Africa as the president's and secretary of state's special envoy for the promotion of democracy in Africa. During this trip, Jackson visited Kenya, the Democratic Republic of the Congo, and Liberia.

In his various speeches, Jackson urges his supporters to tell themselves, "I am somebody!" Throughout his life, Jackson has believed that he is somebody. As the next presidential campaign approaches, it is quite likely Jackson will again set out to make that "somebody" president of the United States; in April of 1998, Jackson was busy testing the waters in Ohio for a third presidential bid.

Sources

Haskins, James. *I Am Somebody!: A Biography of Jesse Jackson*. Hillside, NJ: Enslow Publishers, 1992.

LaBlanc, Michael L., ed. *Contemporary Black Biography: Profiles from the International Black Community*, Vol. 1. Detroit, MI: Gale Research, 1992.

"Special Envoy Jesse Jackson Travels Again to Africa." *Africa News Online*. Washington, DC: U.S. Department of State, 1998. <http://www.africanews.org/usafrica/stories/19980206_feat3.html>. Accessed: 5/4/98.

Maynard Holbrook Jackson, Jr.

Reproduced from UPI/Corbis-Bettmann

Born: March 23, 1938, in Dallas, Texas

Status: Founding chairman, Atlanta Economic Development Corporation; chairman, Atlanta Urban Residential Finance Authority

Education: B.A. in history and political science, 1956, Morehouse College, Atlanta, Georgia; LL.B. cum laude, 1964, North Carolina Central University School of Law, Durham; admitted to the bar of Georgia, 1965

Position: Claims examiner, Ohio State Bureau of Unemployment Compensation, Cleveland, Ohio, 1957–1958; salesman, associate district sales manager, P. F. Collier, Inc., Boston, Massachusetts, Cleveland, Ohio, and Buffalo, New York, offices, 1958–1961; general attorney, National Labor Relations Board, Atlanta, Georgia, 1964–1967; managing attorney and director of community relations, Emory Community Legal Service Center, Atlanta, Georgia, 1968–1969; vice mayor, Atlanta, Georgia, 1970–1974; senior partner, Jackson, Patterson and Parks, Atlanta, Georgia, 1970–1973; mayor, Atlanta, Georgia, 1973–1981, 1989–1997; Atlanta-based law partner, Chapman and Cutler, Chicago, Illinois, 1980s; founding chairman, Atlanta Economic Development Corporation; chairman, Atlanta Urban Residential Finance Authority

Early Years

Maynard Holbrook Jackson, Jr., was born in Dallas, Texas, on March 23, 1938. His father, Maynard Jackson, Sr., was a Baptist minister, and his mother, Irene Dobbs Jackson, a teacher. Both of Jackson's parents were educated and involved in their communities; his father was the first black candidate to run for a position on a board of education in Texas. Later, his mother would become chair of the foreign language department at North Carolina Central University in Durham, North Carolina.

Jackson began school in Texas and, when he was seven, the family moved to Atlanta, Georgia, where his father became the minister at the Friendship Baptist Church. Jackson continued in the Atlanta schools, excelling in his studies. After he had finished his sophomore year in high school in 1952, Jackson was accepted at Atlanta's Morehouse College as a Ford Foundation early admissions scholar.

Higher Education

Although Jackson was only 14 years old when he entered college, he did well, majoring in history and political science. During his undergraduate years, he lived at home and, for a time, considered following in his father's footsteps by becoming a minister, but college changed his mind. Jackson graduated from college at the age of 18 when most young people are graduating from high school.

When he graduated, he accepted a job as a claims examiner with the Ohio State Bureau of Unemployment Compensation in Cleveland, where he worked for a year. In 1958, he became an encyclopedia salesman with P.F. Collier, Inc., rising to the district sales manager position and working for a time in the Boston, Massachusetts, and Buffalo, New York, offices of the company. But being a salesman or even a manager held no challenge for Jackson and, in 1961, he decided to return to school, enrolling in North Carolina Central University's school of law. Again, Jackson shone academically, graduating cum laude in 1964.

Career Highlights

When Jackson graduated, he returned to Atlanta, Georgia, where he accepted a position as a general attorney with the National Labor Relations Board. In 1968, he joined the Emory Neighborhood Law Office as managing attorney and director of community relations, providing legal assistance to those who normally would have been unable to afford it. That same year, Jackson decided to enter the political arena and ran in the Democratic primary for a seat in the United States Senate. As an unknown, Jackson had little chance of winning, particularly since he was running against Herman Talmadge who was known as the "number-one power in Georgia" (Bigelow 114). Few were surprised by his loss to Talmadge, but Jackson had carried the city of Atlanta and had gained support from the poor and from organized labor. Jackson felt that, perhaps, the time had at last come for a black politician to be elected in Georgia.

In 1969, Jackson entered the race for vice mayor of Atlanta against Milton Farris, a white businessman with a long record of service on Atlanta's board of aldermen. Again, many predicted Jackson had no chance, but, this time, he was able to gain the support of Atlanta's black community as well as one-third of the white vote, defeating Farris. Jackson was sworn in as Atlanta's first black vice mayor on January 5, 1970.

During his term of office as vice mayor, Jackson spent much of his time mobilizing support for a run for mayor in 1973. He also cofounded the law firm of Jackson, Patterson and Parks, the first black law firm in Georgia's history (Bigelow 114). In March of 1973, Jackson announced that he would enter the race for mayor. He faced two other candidates: the incumbent mayor, Sam Massell, and Leroy Johnson, a black state senator. Even during the primary, however, the race narrowed to one between Massell and Jackson. Massell, who was white, played on the racial fears of the white citizens of Atlanta, charging that if Jackson were elected he would institute preferential hiring of blacks for city jobs. Massell's campaign, however, did not work; he received only 19.8 percent of the vote to Jackson's 46.6 percent and, in a runoff, Jackson received an even higher 59.2 percent of the total vote. Jackson had garnered 95 percent of the black vote and 24 percent of the white (Joint Center 59).

Over the next four years, Jackson would change the face of Atlanta. He replaced the board of aldermen with a biracial city council and divided the city into 24 planning districts that held public meetings. The people of Atlanta felt they finally had representation in their government that truly reflected the city's makeup.

Jackson, of course, faced opposition from many different quarters. When construction of a new airport was proposed, many in the white community criticized his attempts to involve minority businesses in its construction. In 1974, Jackson tried to fire John Inman, the chief of police, because he felt Inman discriminated against blacks. Although he was able to get Inman demoted, Jackson was not able to be rid of him entirely. Jackson was also criticized for his appointment of A. Reginald Eaves as public safety commissioner; critics charged that Eaves packed the police department with blacks and used his influence inappropriately. Again, Jackson was able to weather the criticism, pointing to the decreased crime rate under his administration.

With the changes Jackson had brought to Atlanta, he was able to win easily a second term in office in 1977. But his second term was clouded by the killings that were going on in the city. In 1981, a serial killer was discovered on the loose, and citizens were alarmed. Jackson and the Atlanta police called in the FBI and, at last, Wayne B. Williams was captured and convicted of the crimes.

During Jackson's second term in office, the city council changed the Atlanta city charter so that mayors were permitted only two consecutive terms in office. In 1982, former congressman and UN representative **Andrew Jackson Young, Jr.**, was elected to office. For the next seven years, Jackson devoted himself to the practice of law, working in the Atlanta office of the Chicago firm of Chapman and Cutler.

In 1989, Jackson decided to run again for mayor. His decision was welcomed by many. During his earlier administration, he had brought the city together and had lured business and industry to the area. After the stock market crash of 1987, people felt Atlanta needed someone like Jackson to help the city recover from the recession. Jackson easily won, but as he said in an interview in the *Christian Science Monitor* after he was sworn into office, "It's tougher this time around. There are fewer state and federal dollars and . . .issues on my plate that weren't even mentioned in the 1981 budget" (Joint Center 115). Atlanta faced increasing crime, drugs, and the spread of AIDS.

Not one to shy from issues, Jackson again tackled the problems of the city, working to build housing for the poor and to bring money back into the city. In 1994, the city sponsored the Super Bowl and, in 1996, the Summer Olympic Games. When Jackson was first elected to office in 1973, he told *The New York Times*, "We have risen from the ashes of a bitter campaign to build a better life for all Atlantans" (Joint Center 114). During the 1990s, Jackson brought Atlanta back from the ashes of a recession and worked to build a better life for his constituents.

Sources

Bigelow, Barbara Carlisle, ed. *Contemporary Black Biography: Profiles from the International Black Community*, Vol. 2. Detroit, MI: Gale Research, 1992.

Estell, Kenneth. *African America: Celebrating 400 Years of Achievement*. Detroit, MI: Visible Ink Press, 1994.

Joint Center for Political Studies. *Profiles of Black Mayors in America*. Washington, DC/ Chicago, IL: The Joint Center for Political Studies/Johnson Publishing Co., 1977.

William Jennings Jefferson

Born: March 14, 1947, in Lake Providence, Louisiana

Status: U.S. representative from the Second Congressional District of Louisiana

Education: Graduate, 1969, Southern University, Baton Rouge, Louisiana; law degree, 1972, Harvard University Law School, Cambridge, Massachusetts

Position: Clerk for U.S. District Judge Alvin B. Rubin, 1972–1973; legislative assistant to U.S. Senator J. Bennett Johnson of Louisiana, 1973–1975; attorney, founding partner,

Jefferson, Bryan and Gray, New Orleans, Louisiana, 1976–1981; state senator, Louisiana State Senate, 1979–1991; U.S. representative from the Second Congressional District of Louisiana, 1991–

Awards and honors: A.P. Tureaud Community Legal Services Award; twice named "Legislator of the Year" by the Alliance for Good Government

Early Years

William Jennings Jefferson was born on March 14, 1947, in Lake Providence, Louisiana.

Higher Education

After graduating from high school in 1965, Jefferson attended Southern University in Baton Rouge, then went on to Harvard University's law school, graduating in 1972.

Career Highlights

In 1991, after being elected as the first black congressman from Louisiana since 1874, William J. Jefferson said, "I've always wanted to be in the arena where the decisions are being made" (McCoy 25). In many ways, Jefferson's early years were spent in preparation for assuming a seat in the House, his first jobs training him in the ways of politics.

Immediately after law school, Jefferson accepted a position clerking for U.S. District Judge Alvin B. Rubin. In 1973, he applied for a position as a legislative assistant to U.S. Senator J. Bennett Johnson of Louisiana. Under Johnson, Jefferson learned the ins and outs of political life and made some valuable contacts in both the state and national governments.

In 1976, Jefferson returned to Louisiana and, with two fellow attorneys, founded the practice of Jefferson, Bryan and Gray in New Orleans. While with the firm, Jefferson specialized in litigation, municipal law, public finance, and corporations. In addition to his private cases, he received the A.P. Tureaud Community Legal Services Award for legal services he provided to the community (*Congressional Black Caucus*).

In 1979, Jefferson ran for and won a seat in the Louisiana State Senate, an office he would hold until he ran for Congress in 1991. In the state senate, Jefferson served on the State Bond Commission and the Senate Finance Committee, and was later named chairman of the Senate and Governmental Affairs Committee. During his time there, he was twice named "Legislator of the Year" by the Alliance for Good Government.

In 1990, Congresswoman Lindy Boggs announced her retirement from the House. With her seat from the Second Congressional District available, Jefferson threw his hat into the ring along with 11 other candidates. During the primary and ensuing run-off election, the race narrowed to a contest between Jefferson and Marc Morial. Although Jefferson's strong state legislative record spoke for him, Morial was a tough opponent. He was the son of former New Orleans mayor Dutch Morial. However, when the time came to choose, most voters came down on the side of Jefferson. As the New Orleans *Weekly Gambit* said in its recommendation of him,

> The run-off election for Lindy Boggs' Second Congressional District seat offers a choice between a bright young attorney and an experienced legislative leader. The young attorney, Marc Morial, is politically astute beyond his years. The legislative leader, Senator William Jefferson, has a strong record of accomplishments . . . It's a tough decision, but we recommend State Senator William Jefferson. . . . (Clay 377)

In 1991, Jefferson was sworn in as the first black congressman from Louisiana since 1874. Because of New Orleans's ties to the fishing industry, he was assigned to the Merchant Marine and Fisheries Committee, as well as the

Public Works Committee, the Education and Labor Committee, and the House/Senate Conference Committee. At last, Jefferson was truly in an arena where decisions were being made.

During his first term in Congress, Jefferson was chosen by his fellow freshman Democrats as their whip, and was also elected secretary of the Congressional Black Caucus. While interested in human rights, Jefferson also was concerned with any legislation affecting his city of New Orleans. As he said in 1991, "My goals are tied closely to the needs of the city" (McCoy 25).

Jefferson easily won reelection in 1992 to the 103rd Congress, and was assigned a position on the powerful Committee on Ways and Means, and to the Committee on the District of Columbia. In the 104th Congress, he was assigned to the House Oversight Committee, the National Security Committee, and the Joint Printing Committee.

Jefferson is a knowledgeable and conscientious legislator and sees no difficulties ahead in future races for Congress. Although he spends much of his time in Washington, D.C., he and his wife, Andrea, live part of the year in New Orleans; most of his five children have graduated from college.

Sources

Clay, William L. *Just Permanent Interests: Black Americans in Congress, 1870–1991*. New York: Amistad Press, 1992.

Congressional Black Caucus '93–'94 Guide. <http://www.sas.upenn.edu/African_Studies/Govern_Political/CBC_Guide.html>. Accessed: 3/5/98.

"Jefferson, William J." *Encarta Online*. Microsoft Corp., 1998. <http://encarta.msn.com/index/concise/0vol49/0B0B7000.asp>. Accessed: 4/21/98.

McCoy, Frank. "Freshman on the Hill." *Black Enterprise*, April 1991, 25.

Eddie Bernice Johnson

Courtesy of the Office of Congresswoman Eddie Bernice Johnson

Born: December 3, 1935, in Waco, Texas

Status: U.S. representative from the 30th Congressional District of Texas

Education: Nursing diploma, 1955, St. Mary's College, Notre Dame University, South Bend, Indiana; B.S. in nursing, 1967, Texas Christian University, Fort Worth, Texas; M.P.A., 1976, Southern Methodist University, Dallas, Texas; recipient of five honorary degrees from various colleges and universities

Position: Psychiatric nurse, Dallas Veterans Administration Hospital, Dallas, Texas, 1956–1972; state representative, Texas State Legislature, 1972–1977; regional director, Department of Health, Education and Welfare, 1977–1979; founder Eddie Bernice Johnson and Associates, Inc., Dallas, Texas, 1981– ; assistant to the president, Sammons Enterprises, Dallas, Texas, 1981–1986; state senator, Texas State Senate, 1986–1992; U.S. representative from the 30th Congressional District of Texas, 1993–

Awards and honors: Juanita Craft Award in Politics, NAACP, 1989; Scholar Award, United Negro College Fund, Dallas chapter,

1992; Family Advocacy Award, The Family Place, Dallas, Texas, 1992

Early Years

The Dallas Morning News once described Eddie Bernice Johnson as "tough, shrewd and unswervingly devoted to her principles" ("Biography ..."). What they failed to mention was that Johnson is also a caring legislator, and that care has permeated all she has accomplished throughout her life.

Eddie Bernice Johnson was born in Waco, Texas, on December 3, 1935. Growing up in the South, Johnson was keenly aware of the inequities surrounding her during the 1930s and 1940s. She dreamed of doing something in the field of medicine but, at that time, no college in Texas accepted black students.

Higher Education

When Johnson graduated from high school, she enrolled in St. Mary's College at Notre Dame University in South Bend, Indiana, and studied nursing. In 1955, she received a diploma in nursing; it would be nearly 12 years before she would continue her higher education. By the time she returned to school, Texas colleges and universities had opened their doors to black students. In 1967, she received a bachelor of science degree in nursing from Texas Christian University and, in 1976, a master's in public administration from Southern Methodist University in Dallas, Texas.

Career Highlights

When Johnson received her degree in nursing from Notre Dame, she returned to Texas and found a job as a psychiatric nurse at the Dallas Veterans Administration Hospital in Dallas. During that time, she rose to the position of chief psychiatric nurse and worked as a registered nurse at St. Paul Hospital in Dallas; she was also vice president of the Visiting Nurse Association of Dallas. Her vocation would lead her in later years to take a keen interest in health care issues on both the state and national levels.

In 1972, Johnson decided to enter politics and ran for the Texas legislature. She was not the favored candidate, but she won a landslide victory and became the first black woman elected to public office from Dallas since 1935. This was only the beginning of a long line of "firsts" that she would achieve during her career in public office. In her second term as state representative, she became the first woman in the history of Texas to chair a major House committee, the Labor Committee.

In 1977, Johnson stepped down from her seat in the Texas legislature to accept the appointment by President Jimmy Carter of regional director for the Department of Health, Education and Welfare. When Ronald Reagan became president, Johnson resigned her position and went into business for herself. She founded Eddie Bernice Johnson and Associates in 1981, a business consulting firm. The firm was a success and continues to be to the present day.

In 1986, Johnson returned to politics, running for the Texas State Senate. Again, her victory marked a number of "firsts": she became the first woman and the first African American representing the Dallas area to be elected to the Texas senate since Reconstruction.

Johnson was to remain in the Texas senate for six years. During that time, she pursued the issues that had always been of concern to her: health care, community services, education, and women's and minority issues. But it was difficult, as she said in an interview in the *Chicago Tribune*, "When you see who's in the important huddles, who's making the important decisions, it's men" (Mabunda 143). Johnson was a black woman in a white, male political world, and fighting for what she felt was important was an uphill battle. Despite this, however, Johnson was able to sponsor several significant bills. One bill established goals for the government of Texas to work with "socially disadvantaged" businesses. Johnson was also able to push through legislation aimed at creating fair housing in the state.

In 1992, Johnson's decision to run for Congress was not received without criticism. She had served on the state committee overseeing the redistricting of the state in conformance with the 1990 census. One new district, the 30th, was made up of 50 percent African Americans and 17 percent Hispanics. When Johnson announced that she would seek a seat representing this district, she was accused of having engineered the redistricting to assure herself a seat in Congress. The *Texas Monthly* named her one of the state's 10 worst lawmakers. In response, Johnson told *The Dallas Morning News*, "I wanted a district that any black could win in. It's clear that my opponent uses that as a major issue against me, but just as much as it is a major issue against me, it is also a major issue for me because these people are so pleased to be enfranchised" (Mabunda 144). Despite the outcry, Johnson received an overwhelming vote of confidence from the people of the 30th District, and she defeated her opponent with 74 percent of the vote in the general election. With her election, Johnson became the first black woman from Dallas in the Texas house delegation and the first black woman from Texas to serve in the house since **Barbara Charline Jordan** had been elected in the 1970s.

When Johnson was sworn into Congress, she pursued the same areas of interest she had while serving on the state level: improved health care and equal opportunities for all. In 1993, she again was the subject of criticism when Congress was considering the North American Free Trade Agreement (NAFTA). She was accused of having traded her vote in return for the promise that two aircraft would be built by companies in her district. Johnson, however, countered by explaining that she was for NAFTA because it would create all kinds of jobs within her district, not because the government had promised her anything.

During her time in Congress, Johnson has served as the Congressional Black Caucus whip, as well as its second vice chair. She has also served as the Democratic deputy whip in the House and is the highest ranking Texan on the House Committee on Transportation and Infrastructure. In 1998, she was elected to her fifth term in office, and to this day continues to work toward her goals with care.

Sources

"Biography of Congresswoman Eddie Bernice Johnson." *U.S. House of Representatives*. <http://www.house.gov/ebjohnson/bio.htm>. Accessed: 3/6/98.

Mabunda, L. Mpho, ed. *Contemporary Black Biography: Profiles from the International Black Community*, Vol. 8. Detroit, MI: Gale Research, 1995.

"National Elections '98." *The Washington Post*, 4 November 1998. <http://elections98.washingtonpost.com/wp-srv/results98/national/>.

Barbara Charline Jordan

Reproduced from AP/Wide World Photos, by Rusty Kennedy

Born: February 21, 1936, in Houston, Texas

Status: Died January 17, 1996; buried in Texas State Cemetery, Austin, Texas

Education: B.A. magna cum laude, 1956, Texas Southern University, Houston; LL.B., 1959, Boston University School of Law, Boston, Massachusetts; admitted to the bars of Massachusetts and Texas, 1959; recipient of 25 honorary degrees from various colleges and universities

Position: Attorney, Houston, Texas, 1960–1964; administrative assistant to Judge Bill Elliot, County Judge of Harris County, Texas, 1964–1965; state senator, Texas State Senate, 1966–1972; U.S. representative from the 18th Congressional District of Texas, 1973–1979; professor, Lyndon B. Johnson School of Public Affairs, University of Texas, Austin, Texas, 1979–1995; special counsel for ethics, appointed by Texas governor Ann Richards, 1991; chairwoman, U.S. Commission on Immigration Reform, 1994

Awards and honors: Spingarn Medal, NAACP, 1992; Presidential Medal of Freedom, 1994

Early Years

Barbara Charline Jordan was born on February 21, 1936, in Houston, Texas, the youngest daughter of Benjamin and Arlyne Jordan. Benjamin Jordan was a Baptist minister; thus, the church would play an important role in Jordan's life.

Growing up in segregated Houston, Jordan attended all-black schools, graduating from the Phillis Wheatley High School in 1952. While in high school, Jordan was popular with the other students, but by her senior year she outshone many of them, liking the fact that she was different. As she later said, "I always liked to have some award of something . . . I decided that I was not going to be like the rest, [but] my point of reference was other black people. It seemed an impossibility to make any transition to that larger world out there" (Jordan and Hearon 61, 64).

Higher Education

After high school, Jordan enrolled at Texas Southern University, an all-black school. In many ways, the university seemed a continuation of Phillis Wheatley High School. Many of her friends were also enrolled at the school, and she joined Delta Sigma Theta sorority and the debate team. Her debate team became the first from a black university to compete in the annual debate tournament held at Baylor University, following the 1954 United States Supreme Court decision in the case of *Brown v. The Board of Education*, Topeka, Kansas. During that tournament, Jordan won first place in junior oratory.

The Supreme Court decision of 1954 prompted Jordan to think about her own future. She decided that she wanted to go to law school and applied to Boston University. Her father encouraged her in her ambitions, only saying, "This is more money than I have ever spent on anything or anyone. But if you want to go, we'll manage. But if I pay for you to go up there, there won't be any money for you to come home for Thanksgiving, Christmas, Easter. Once you get there, you're there" (Jordan and Hearon 83). Jordan decided this was something she had to do and traveled to Massachusetts to study law, despite the separation from her family.

Law school and Boston University were a cultural shock to Jordan. As she said,

> I realized, starkly, that the best training available in an all-black, instant university was not equal. Separate was not equal, no matter what face you put on it . . . I really can't describe what that did to my insides and to my head. I said I'm being educated, finally. I'm doing sixteen years of remedial work in thinking. (Jordan and Hearon 73)

At Boston University, for the first time, Jordan had to work hard to keep up with her classes and make up for things she had missed earlier in her education. She also faced discrimination not as a black but as a woman studying a profession that was dominated by men at that time. It frustrated her that she was not called on often in class; the "ladies" were often overlooked. But she delighted in the fact that she was finally learning, thinking, being challenged. In 1959, after three years of hard work, Jordan completed law school, graduating as one of only two women in her class; that same year, she was admitted to both the Massachusetts and Texas bars.

Career Highlights

When Jordan returned to Houston, she found it difficult to get started in the practice of law. She had little money and taught part time at Tuskegee to earn more. Then she and two friends opened a law office. With the civil rights issues becoming more critical—many of Jordan's early cases dealt with these—she began to get more and more involved in politics. During John F. Kennedy's campaign for the presidency, Jordan worked on voter registration and turnout and eventually became speaker of the Harris County Democratic Party.

Change, however, was slow in Texas, especially in terms of equal rights. In 1962, Jordan decided that the only way to institute change was to be where changes could be made: in public office. Borrowing the $500 filing fee from a friend, Jordan entered the race for a seat in the Texas State Legislature.

The race was a hard and discouraging one. One man, a professor from Rice University, visited Jordan's campaign headquarters and told her, "You know it's going to be hard for you to win a seat in the Texas Legislature. You've got too much going against you: You're black, you're a woman, and you're large. People don't really like that image." Jordan replied, "Well, I can't do anything about the first two elements" (Jordan and Hearon 116). She felt, however, once people got to know her, they would look beyond these superficialities. She set out to acquaint the voters with who she was, speaking at every opportunity. Despite her efforts, however, she lost this election and lost again in 1964.

During 1964 and 1965, Jordan worked as an administrative assistant for Judge Bill Elliott of Harris County, as well as project coordinator for a nonprofit group set up to help the unemployed. In 1966, she again made a run for office and, this time, her hard work paid off.

The campaign for office was a contentious one. Her main contender, Charles Whitfield, introduced the element of race into the election when he posted flyers that said, "So this race points up the question, Shall we have a seat for a member of the NEGRO race or shall we consider other factors such as qualifications and experience in order to give Harris county its most effective voice in the 11th District?" (Jordan and Hearon 133). In many ways, this gave Jordan ammunition to wage an effective campaign and to win by a margin of two to one, upon which she became the first black woman in the Texas legislature and the first black person to serve since 1883.

Jordan was determined to do well in the legislature and studied the laws and the procedures of the House, just as she had studied twice as hard as anyone while in law school. Her work paid off for her. As an article in *Ebony* pointed out, "She not only dazzled [the legislature] with her intellectual brilliance but also with her knowledge of their kind of rough-and-tumble politics. . . . She never permitted the men of the 'club' to feel uncomfortable around her" (Smith 386). Jordan learned her lessons well, becoming an extremely effective legislator. During her time in the Texas senate, Jordan sponsored much of Texas's environmental legislation and worked for equality. In 1972, she was named president pro tempore and Governor for a Day. During her day as governor, Jordan proclaimed September, 1972, Sickle Cell Disease Control Month in Texas.

That same year, Jordan decided to run for Congress in Texas's newly created 18th Congressional District. In the race, she faced Republican Paul Merritt. Running on her state senatorial record, Jordan had no difficulty defeating him. When she took her seat in 1973, she became the first black Texan to sit in the

House of Representatives. She was appointed to the Judiciary Committee, the Government Operations Committee, and the Steering and Policy Committee.

Just as she had when entering the Texas senate, Jordan studied for her new position, attending an orientation conference for freshmen representatives held at the John F. Kennedy Institute of Politics. Almost immediately, Jordan had to draw upon all her knowledge and experience because of the breaking Watergate scandal. As a member of the House Judiciary Committee, she was called upon to examine Gerald Ford who had been chosen to replace Spiro Agnew as Richard Nixon's vice president. She had a great many questions about his civil rights record and, at the final vote, joined with seven other committee members in voting against him.

In 1974, Jordan was a member of the the Judiciary Committee as it undertook one of the most difficult tasks ever to face it: whether to proceed with impeachment proceedings against Richard Nixon. In a public speech on television, Jordan asked,

> Has the President committed offenses and planned and directed and acquiesced in a course of conduct which the Constitution will not tolerate? That is the question. We know that. We know the question. We should now forthwith proceed to answer the question. It is reason and not passion which must guide our deliberations, guide our debate, and guide our decisions. (Jordan and Hearon 191–92)

Jordan did not like the idea of impeachment, but she felt it was a necessary constitutional safeguard and appropriate in this instance. As she said, "I didn't like the idea of working to impeach a President. I didn't like doing that; I wished that it had not been necessary to do that . . . When the roll was called . . . I could barely get my 'yes' out" (Jordan and Hearon 200). Before actual impeachment hearings could begin, however, Nixon resigned as president, and Gerald Ford assumed the office.

The drama of Watergate had brought Jordan national attention, support, and approval. In the coming years, she would have no difficulty seeking reelection or being heard on issues within the House. In 1975, Jordan sponsored legislation that extended the Voting Rights Act of 1965 to include Hispanics and other minorities. She was able to obtain passage of the Consumer Goods Pricing Act of 1975, as well as a bill repealing anti-trust exemptions that artificially hiked consumer prices on certain goods. In 1976, she delivered the keynote address to the Democratic National Convention, becoming the first black person and the first woman to do so.

In December of 1977, Jordan announced that she would be retiring from Congress at the end of her term. She had received an invitation to speak at Harvard University, which started her thinking about herself and her own life. "I believed that in order to free myself to move fully in a new direction, I would of necessity have to leave elected politics and pursue the platform wherever I could find it" (Jordan and Hearon 250). Jordan felt she could do more in the private sector. Jordan may also have been influenced by her health, which was not good; later, in 1988, she would be diagnosed with multiple sclerosis.

After leaving office, Jordan accepted the position of professor at the Lyndon B. Johnson School of Public Affairs at the University of Texas in Austin. She also continued to contribute politically when needed. In 1991, Texas governor Ann Richards appointed her special counsel for ethics and, in 1994, Jordan served as chairwoman on the U.S. Commission on Immigration Reform. Because of her work on this commission, she was awarded the Presidential Medal of Freedom by President Clinton in 1995.

During the last years of her life, Jordan fought a losing battle with leukemia and, on January 17, 1996, died from pneumonia that was complicated by her disease. After her death she was remembered and continues to be remembered for her many talents and accomplishments. As a young girl, Jordan recalled, "I felt at that time . . . I was saying, 'I'm not going to be like the rest'" (Jordan and Hearon 1), and she certainly was not "like the rest."

Sources

"Barbara Jordan." Legislative Biographies. <http://www.glue.umd.edu/~cliswp/Politicians/Leg/Bios/legbioj.htm>. Accessed: 2/27/98.

Estell, Kenneth. *African America: Celebrating 400 Years of Achievement*. Detroit, MI: Visible Ink Press, 1994.

"Former Black Members of Congress." *Congressional Times Journal*. <http://www.usbol.com/ctjournal/FrBlkCongMemList.html>. Accessed: 2/25/98.

Jordan, Barbara, and Shelby Hearon. *Barbara Jordan: A Self-Portrait*. Garden City, NY: Doubleday and Co., 1979.

"A Short Biography: From the Good Hope Memorial Service." *Armadillo*, 22 January 1996. <http://www.rice.edu/armadillo/Texas/Jordan/goodhopebio.html>. Accessed: 3/31/98.

Smith, Jessie Carney, ed. *Black Heroes of the 20th Century*. Detroit, MI: Visible Ink Press, 1998.

K

Sharon Pratt Dixon Kelly

Copyright Washington Post, *reprinted by permission of D.C. Public Library*

Born: January 30, 1944, in Washington, D.C.

Status: Author

Education: B.A., 1965, Howard University, Washington, D.C.; J.D., 1968, Howard University, Washington, D.C.

Position: House counsel, Joint Center for Political Studies, Washington, D.C., 1970–1971; attorney, Pratt and Queen, Washington, D.C., 1971–1976; professor, Antioch School of Law, 1972–1976; associate general counsel, Potomac Electric Power Co. (PEPCO), Washington, D.C., 1976–1979; director of consumer affairs, PEPCO, 1979–1983; vice president, PEPCO, 1983–1986; national treasurer, Democratic National Committee, 1985–1989; vice president of public policy, PEPCO, 1986–1990; mayor, Washington, D.C., 1991–1995; fellow, Institute of Politics, Kennedy School, Harvard University, Cambridge, Massachusetts, 1995; author, 1995–

Early Years

Sharon Pratt Dixon Kelly was born Sharon Pratt on January 30, 1944, in Washington, D.C. When she was four years old, her mother, Mildred Pratt, died. Her father, Carlisle Pratt, took Kelly and her older sister Benaree to live with his mother and sister. Carlisle Pratt was a former superior court judge in Washington and his own career as an attorney proved to be an inspiration to Kelly who, even as a child, knew she wished to follow in his footsteps. When she was still in elementary school, he gave her a copy of Black's *Law Dictionary* as a birthday present.

Pratt grew up attending the segregated schools of Washington, D.C., and graduated from Roosevelt High School.

Higher Education

Pratt graduated with a bachelor's degree from Howard University in 1965 and continued in the university's law school. While attending law school, she met and married Drew Arrington Dixon; the couple would have two children, Aimee Arrington Dixon, born in 1968, and Drew Arrington Dixon, born in 1970 (Dixon and Kelly would later divorce in 1982). In 1968, Kelly graduated from Howard Law School, having achieved her lifelong ambition to become a lawyer like her father.

Career Highlights

From 1970 to 1971, Kelly worked as house counsel for the Joint Center for Political Studies in Washington, D.C., then, in 1971, she established a private law practice, Pratt and Queen. During the time she practiced privately as an attorney, Kelly also taught at Antioch School of Law. In 1976, she left both positions to join the Potomac Electric Power Company (PEPCO) in Washington, D.C., as associate general counsel. Over the next 14 years, Kelly would rise in the echelons of PEPCO, becoming director of consumer affairs in 1979, vice president in 1983, and vice president of public policy in 1986, initiating programs to assist low-income and senior citizens.

Kelly also was becoming more involved in politics. In 1985, she made history when she became the first woman to serve as national treasurer of the Democratic National Committee, a post she held until 1989. She had previously served as a Democratic national committeewoman in 1971 and as general counsel to the committee from 1976 to 1977. In addition, she was cochair of the Rules Committee, and a member of the Ad Hoc Credentials Committee and of the Judicial Council at the Democratic National Convention of 1980.

During this time, **Marion S. Barry, Jr.**, was mayor of Washington, D.C., but his administration increasingly was coming under fire. Because of this, Kelly (then Sharon Pratt Dixon) decided to enter the race for mayor. As the *Washington Post* reported, "Dixon [Kelly], who was the first candidate to announce for mayor, showed extra-ordinary courage from the outset. She was willing to go up against an incumbent who had a political machine and would be a formidable fund-raiser" (LaBlanc 58). Barry was accused of putting his friends and relatives on the city's payrolls and of other misuses of his office. In January of 1990, however, Barry's administration crumbled when he was caught by the FBI using cocaine in a sting operation. In November, 1990, Barry was convicted and sentenced to six months in prison, a $5,000 fine, and one year of probation—which effectively removed him from the mayoral race.

With Barry out of the picture the field was wide open, and a number of candidates joined Kelly in the race. She was running from the position of an outsider, someone who was not a professional politician. *Time* noted that, of the candidates running, Kelly "was the only candidate who created a perception that she was different and that the other candidates were part of the problem and she was the one to solve it" (LaBlanc 59). She was photographed with a shovel, saying, "I'll clean house with a shovel, not a broom" (Hine 676). During her campaign, she promised to cut 2,000 mid-level managers and $130 million from Washington's budget. Although she was virtually unknown, Kelly managed to pick up the endorsement of the *Washington Post*, and in both the primary and general elections walked away with the votes, establishing two records. She became the first woman to be elected mayor of Washington, D.C., and the first native-born Washingtonian to be elected as mayor.

When Kelly assumed the office of mayor, she expected problems, but she was optimistic. Her life was changing; not only was she assuming the office of mayor of one of the most important cities in the United States but, in 1991, she married New York City businessman James Kelly III. From the beginning, however, her administration met with trouble. The city government was still loyal to Marion Barry and resistant to the changes Kelly wished to make. In 1991, too, riots struck the city in the Mount Pleasant area, intensifying the pressure on her. During her second year of office, Barry's supporters attempted to recall her from office. This caused Kelly to back away from the tough reforms she had proposed when entering office and to mistrust advice given to her by members of the city government.

Kelly turned her attention to Congress, attacking the federal government for creating the city's financial plight and championing statehood for the district. In return, the federal government accused Kelly of withholding information about the city's finances and of providing erroneous information. The city's deficit, meanwhile, was ballooning, and city services were declining. Although Kelly obtained money from Congress for the city government, it was merely a drop in the bucket.

In the meantime, Marion Barry, having served his sentence on drug possession, had run for and won a seat on Washington's city council. In 1994, when Kelly came up for reelection, both city council member John Ray and Marion Barry challenged her. With the city government in disarray, Barry was easily able to defeat her in the Democratic primary, winning 47 percent of the vote. Kelly stepped down from office in 1995.

After serving as mayor of Washington, Kelly all but retired from public office. She worked on a book, *Spirit for a New America*, which covered the changing political and moral climate of America. In an interview with *Ebony* magazine in 1996, Kelly stated that while she is still "supportive of the [Democratic] party . . . traditional kinds of politics is certainly not attractive to me. . . We are ready to enter a new millennium. We can't be trapped by the same old way of thinking . . . [but] I don't have a desire to go back to what I was doing" (Townsel et al.).

Sources

Estell, Kenneth. *African America: Celebrating 400 Years of Achievement*. Detroit, MI: Gale Research, 1994.

Hine, Darlene Clark, ed. *Black Women in America: An Historical Encyclopedia*, Vol. I, A–L. Brooklyn, NY: Carlson Publishing Co., 1993.

LaBlanc, Michael L., ed. *Contemporary Black Biography: Profiles from the International Black Community*, Vol. 1. Detroit, MI: Gale Research, 1992.

"Sharon Pratt Kelly." *Washington City Paper*. Washington Free Weekly, Inc. 1996. <http://www.washingtoncitypaper.com/lips/bios/kellybio.html>. Accessed: 3/13/98.

Townsel, Lisa Jones, Kevin Chappel, and Muriel L. Whetstone. "Sharon Pratt Kelly: Teaching and Writing a Book." *Ebony*, May 1996, 92.

L

John Mercer Langston

Reproduced from Oberlin College Archives, Oberlin, Ohio

Born: December 14, 1829, in Louisa County, Virginia

Status: Died November 15, 1897, in Washington, D.C.; buried at Woodlawn Cemetery, Washington, D.C.

Education: B.A., 1849 Oberlin College, Oberlin, Ohio; advanced studies in theology and oratory, Oberlin College, Oberlin, Ohio, 1849–1852; read law with Judge Philemon Bliss, Elyria, Ohio; admitted to the Ohio bar in September, 1854

Position: Elected clerk of Brownhelm Township, Lorain County, Ohio, 1855; appointed inspector general, Freedmen's Bureau, 1868; founded the law department, Howard University, Washington, D.C., 1868; dean, law department, Howard University, 1869–1875; vice president, Howard University, 1874; acting president, Howard University, 1875; member, District of Columbia Board of Health, 1871–c. 1876; U.S. minister to Haiti, 1877; U.S. chargé d'affaires to Santo Domingo, 1883–1885; president, Virginia Normal and Collegiate Institute (now Virginia State University), Petersburg, Virginia, 1885–1887; U.S. representative from Virginia, 1890–1891

Early Years

John Mercer Langston was born in Louisa County, Virginia, on December 14, 1829. His father, Ralph Quarles, was a white plantation owner, and his mother, Lucy Langston, was a freed woman of mixed black and Native American heritage. John was their fourth child and at age five, following the death of both his parents in 1834, he was sent with his older brothers to live in Ohio, in accordance with his father's will. In the north, his father had felt, the children would have greater educational opportunities than in Virginia.

While his brothers lived in foster homes, John was taken in by William Gooch, one of the executors of his father's estate who lived in Chillicothe, Ohio. After several years, Gooch decided to move his family west to Missouri, but John's brothers did not want John taken to a slave state. So John lived with another white family in Dayton, Ohio, and later attended a private school in Cincinnati.

Higher Education

Oberlin College, founded in 1833 in Oberlin, Ohio, was one of the first institutions of higher learning to open its doors to black students. Following in the footsteps of his older brother, Charles, Langston entered Oberlin in 1845, receiving a bachelor's degree in 1849 with the intention of entering law school. While waiting for responses to his applications to two law schools, Langston continued to take courses at Oberlin in theology and oratory; but both law schools denied him admission because of his race.

At that time, a degree from a law school was not the only road to law practice. A student could read law for a number of years with an established lawyer and, after passing an examination, be admitted to the bar of the state in which he wished to practice. Since he could not gain admission to a school of law, Langston chose this route, reading law with Judge Philemon Bliss of Elyria, Ohio. On September 13, 1854, having successfully passed his examination, he was admitted to the Ohio bar.

Career Highlights

The fall of 1854 was a momentous one for John Mercer Langston. After setting up his law practice in Brownhelm, Ohio, in September he bought a farm and, on October 25, married his college sweetheart, Caroline Wall. A captivating host, Langston quickly made his home a gathering place for those interested in local or national politics, and in abolition. Langston joined the Liberty Party, an abolitionist group, and was elected on their ticket as township clerk of Brownhelm. Many believe Langston was the first African American to be elected to office by a mixed black and white constituency.

In 1856, Langston and his family, which now included a son, Arthur Dessalines Langston, moved to Oberlin where, as in Brownhelm, he became active in local politics. In 1857, Langston was elected to the city council of Oberlin and, in 1860, to the Oberlin Board of Education. During this time, two more sons and a daughter—Ralph, Frank, and Nettie—were born to the Langstons.

A staunch abolitionist, Langston wished to contribute when the Civil War began, but he also had to think of his wife and children. According to historian Maurine Christopher, Langston hired a substitute to fight in his place in the war, as was a common practice at that time (141). Like so many other black leaders of the day, Langston did help recruit black men for the Union and, in 1864, was elected head of the National Rights League, a group advocating equal rights and black suffrage. So eloquent an orator was he that he was frequently asked to speak on issues concerning emancipation and was consulted by Presidents Abraham Lincoln and Andrew Johnson.

In 1867, Langston was offered the position of inspector general of the Freedmen's Bureau, which had been formed immediately after the war to organize schools and provide aid to the formerly enslaved African Americans. The following year, 1868, Langston founded the law department at Howard University in Washington, D.C., serving as its dean from 1868 to 1875. Because much of his work had shifted to the nation's capital, he moved his wife and children to Washington in 1871.

Langston was no longer a small-town lawyer, but an influential force in national politics and a respected scholar. In 1874, he was named vice president of Howard University, and the following year he became acting president. He resigned all his positions at Howard in 1875, however, when, against his protests, the board of trustees elected a white man as president of the university over Langston and other black candidates. Langston felt that a university for black students should be led by a black president.

During his time at Howard, Langston had kept his hand in politics, supporting Republican Rutherford B. Hayes during his campaign for president. When Hayes's campaign was successful, Langston was rewarded with an appointment as minister to Haiti in 1877 and as the United States chargé d'affaires to Santo Domingo, Dominican Republic, from 1883 to 1885.

With the election in 1884 of Democrat Grover Cleveland, Langston lost his diplomatic appointment and tendered his resignation as of January 31, 1885, although he remained at his post until July 1 of that year until a successor could replace him. On his return to the United States, Langston accepted the position of president of Virginia Normal and Collegiate Institute (now Virginia State University) in Petersburg, Virginia. Langston had at long last returned to the state in which he had been born.

Langston's tenure at Virginia Normal was not an easy one. Although he was a consummate diplomat, even Langston had difficulty balancing and mediating between the demands of the all-white state board of education and the black board of visitors, the advisory body to the institute. Fed up with the conflicts between the two, and by faculty politics, Langston resigned in 1887.

Soon after he left Virginia Normal, Langston, a Republican, was approached by a group of local political independents and asked to run for the House of Representatives from Virginia's Fourth Congressional District. Langston accepted, and his candidacy met with vitriolic opposition from his former party. Local Republicans even persuaded the great Frederick Douglass to write a letter of opposition to Langston's candidacy. Both black and white voters met with countless delays and harassment at the polls on election day, so when Langston's opponent, Democrat Edward Venable, was declared the winner, Langston challenged the election results.

Many elections across the country were being challenged at the time, which is the reason Congress took so long to consider Langston's suit. But the delay allowed him to rally his support, especially in Washington, and on September 23, 1890, Congress at last voted 151 to 1 to set aside Venable's election and to seat Langston in his stead. The Democrats of the House had been incensed by the challenge and refused to vote, then boycotted Langston's swearing-in ceremony. Because the challenge had taken so long, Langston had only a few days to get a feel for his new position; Congress recessed its first session on October 1, 1890, and most members returned to their districts to launch reelection campaigns.

When the second session of the 51st Congress convened in January of 1891, Langston attended as a lame duck; he had been unsuccessful in his second campaign, losing to James Epes, a Democrat. Although Langston suspected that this election had also been tainted, power had shifted to the Democrats and he felt a challenge would fail.

During the remainder of his term, Langston served on the Committee on Education. As a member of that committee, he unsuccessfully pushed for the establishment of a national industrial university for African Americans. He also spoke out in support of the enforcement of the 15th Amendment, passed in 1870, giving black citizens the vote. Since its passage, numerous states had enacted poll taxes, literacy requirements, and other "Jim Crow" laws that prevented black suffrage. Langston also attempted to nominate several black candidates to the United States Naval Academy, but the secretary of the navy at that time, Benjamin Tracy, refused to act on his recommendations.

When Langston's term ended on March 3, 1891, he all but retired from the political arena. Although he was a delegate to both the Virginia and the national Republican conventions, when asked to run again in the Fourth District, he declined, feeling that a black candidate no longer had any chance of winning. Not until nearly 100 years later, in the 1970s, did a black candidate, **Lawrence Douglas Wilder**, succeed in Virginia politics.

Langston divided his time during his retirement years between Petersburg, Virginia, and Washington, D.C., where he had built a house near Howard University. He kept in touch with his political friends, but spent much of his time writing. A collection of his speeches, *Freedom and Citizenship*, was published in 1883, and his autobiography, *From the Virginia Plantation to the National Capitol*, in 1894. On November 15, 1897, one month short of the age of 68, Langston passed away at his home in Washington, D.C., and was buried in Washington's Woodlawn Cemetery. Despite the opposition he faced in life, John Mercer Langston was remembered and honored by many after his death. The town of Langston, Oklahoma, home of Langston University, was named for him, and his boyhood home in Dayton, Ohio, was designated a national historic landmark on May 15, 1975. His great-nephew, the esteemed poet Langston Hughes, carried his name.

Sources

Christopher, Maurine. *America's Black Congressmen*. New York: Thomas Y. Crowell, 1971.

"Former Black Members of Congress." *Congressional Times Journal*. <http://www.usbol.com/ctjournal/FrBlkCongMemList.html>. Accessed: 1/21/98.

"John Mercer Langston (1829–1897)." *Oberlin College Archives*. <http://www.oberlin.edu/~EOG/OYTT-images/JMLangston.html>. Accessed: 1/21/98.

Kestenbaum, Lawrence. *Political Graveyard: A Database of Historic Cemeteries*, rev. 1/13/98. <http://www.potifos.com/tpg.html>. Accessed: 1/17/98.

Neyer, Constance. "Black Governors Buried in History." *Hartford Courant*, 1 February 1998, A1, A12.

Ploski, Harry A., and James Williams, eds. *The Negro Almanac: A Reference Work on the African American*. Detroit, MI: Gale Research, 1989.

Smith, Jessie Carney, ed. *Black Firsts: 2,000 Years of Extraordinary Achievement*. Detroit, MI: Visible Ink Press, 1994.

Smythe, Mabel M., ed. *The Black American Reference Book*. Englewood Cliffs, NJ: Prentice-Hall, Inc., 1976.

William Alexander Leidesdorff

Reproduced from the San Francisco History Center, San Francisco Public Library

Born: 1810 in Concordia, St. Croix, Danish West Indies (now the United States Virgin Islands)

Status: Died May 18, 1848, in San Francisco, California

Education: Unknown

Position: Appointed U.S. vice consul to Mexico, 1845; built and operated first hotel in San Francisco (then Yerba Buena), California, 1846; organized first horse race in San Francisco, and operated first steamboat, the *Sitka*, to sail San Francisco Bay, 1847; cattle and horse rancher, Mexico, 1844–1848; importer-exporter, San Francisco, California, 1846–1848; chairman, San Francisco Board of Education, San Francisco, California, 1848

Early Years

Little is known of the childhood and youth of William Alexander Leidesdorff, who was born in 1810 of a Danish father and an African mother, Anna Marie Sparks. His father, who was a wealthy plantation owner on the island of St. Croix in the Danish West Indies (now the United States Virgin Islands), evidently provided Leidesdorff with a good education. As an adult, he was fluent in a number of languages and had a shrewd eye for business.

Before setting out on his own, however, Leidesdorff worked for his father, sailing ships laden with cotton to various ports in the United States. In 1841, a failed love affair motivated Leidesdorff to leave St. Croix and his father's business and sail to California to seek his fortune like so many others at that time.

Career Highlights

California had been colonized by Spain and by 1800 was one of the tattered remnants of Spain's once-great empire in the New World. In 1821, Mexico won its independence from Spain and later acquired California. By 1841, when William Leidesdorff arrived in California on his ship, the *Julia Ann*, California was a mélange of Mexicans, Spaniards, and settlers from the United States, or Californios, as the Mexicans called them.

Yerba Buena (or San Francisco as it was renamed in 1847 after being seized by the United States in 1846) had been established by the Spanish in 1776 as a settlement of trading posts near the Mission of San Francisco de Asis. Its great bay was a natural harbor for ships. Leidesdorff saw its advantages and set up a trade route with Hawaii and other ports of call.

Ever on the lookout for ways to make money, Leidesdorff became a Mexican citizen in 1844 to obtain extensive land holdings. He acquired 35,000 acres of land from the Mexican government and established a ranch, Rio Del Rancho Americana, where he raised horses and cattle. In 1845, despite his Mexican citizenship, Leidesdorff was named United States vice consul to Mexico by Colonel Thomas David Larkin, the U.S. consul to Mexico. His appointment made Leidesdorff the first black diplomat in the history of the United States.

In 1846, Leidesdorff built the first hotel in Yerba Buena, on two 300-foot lots at the corner of Clay and Kearney Streets that he had purchased upon his arrival in California. That same year, he also built an import-export warehouse at the foot of California Street. Dealing in the tallow and hides from his own ranch and those of others, Leidesdorff was creating his own small empire.

The following year, 1847, Leidesdorff built a house on Montgomery Street. Seeing the advantages of the new steam-powered ships, that same year he also bought the 37-foot-long steamship *Sitka*, the first steamship ever to sail the waters of San Francisco Bay. For this, Leidesdorff was heralded as the "Robert Fulton of the West."

San Francisco had been claimed for the United States by John C. Fremont in 1846 during the Mexican War. The settlers welcomed the U.S. soldiers, wining and dining and entertaining them. William Leidesdorff was among those who welcomed the occupation by the soldiers. Not only did he do his share of entertaining, arranging a formal ball at his home for the U.S. leaders, he also organized a horse race in 1847, which is believed to have been the first horse race in San Francisco.

All was going very well indeed for Leidesdorff. Like so many who had gone west to seek their fortunes, he was busy gathering his wealth. He was also helping to build the small town that was fast becoming a booming metropolis as gold had just been discovered not far from Leidesdorff's own ranch. There was even talk of California becoming a state. A man of influence, in April of 1848, Leidesdorff was named chairman of the city's board of education, which opened California's first public school.

Then tragedy struck. The city was hit by a typhus epidemic and, on May 18, 1848, William Leidesdorff was numbered among its victims. When he died, his estate was deeply in debt because of the speculation in which he had been engaged. His legacy was not one of debts, however; gold was later discovered on his ranch.

William Leidesdorff was esteemed by his fellow San Franciscans even after his death. In 1856, a street was named for him that, appropriately, runs through San Francisco's financial district.

Sources

Haskins, James. *African American Entrepreneurs*. New York: John Wiley and Sons, 1998.

Smith, Jessie Carney, ed. *Black Firsts: 2,000 Years of Extraordinary Achievement*. Detroit, MI: Visible Ink Press, 1994.

George Thomas "Mickey" Leland

Reproduced from UPI/Corbis-Bettmann

Born: November 27, 1944, in Lubbock, Texas

Status: Died August 7, 1989, near Gambela, Ethiopia

Education: B.S. in pharmacy, 1970, Texas Southern University, Houston, Texas

Position: Instructor of clinical pharmacy, Texas Southern University, Houston, Texas, 1970–1972; state representative, Texas State Legislature, 1973–1978; U.S. representative from the 18th Congressional District of Texas, 1979–1989

Early Years

George Thomas "Mickey" Leland was born in Lubbock, Texas, on November 27, 1944, but grew up and attended school in Houston.

Higher Education

In 1966, Leland entered Texas Southern University in Houston, majoring in pharmacy. During his college years, he became active in the civil rights movement, which, in turn, generated his interest in politics. Like so many others at that time, Leland felt that if permanent changes were to occur, African Americans needed to have a strong voice in both local and national government decision making.

Career Highlights

After graduating from Texas Southern University, Leland taught clinical pharmacy at the university for two years, then, in 1972, entered his first political race for state representative. Although he was virtually unknown, Leland's sincerity and strong beliefs in civil rights won him the office and, in 1973, he was sworn into the Texas State Legislature where he would serve until 1978.

During his time in the Texas house, Leland worked to expand civil rights. He also became involved in national politics as a member of the Democratic National Committee, and he was a delegate to the Texas Constitutional Convention in 1974. In 1977, **Barbara Charline Jordan**, who was then congresswoman from the 18th Congressional District of Texas, announced that she would not be seeking reelection. This came as a surprise to many, but gave Leland the opportunity to seek national office.

In a race replete with candidates, Leland headed the pack, winning the Democratic primary in 1978; and, in the fall of that year, he carried the general election. When he assumed his seat in Congress, he was assigned to the Interstate and Foreign Commerce (later, Energy and Commerce) Committee, and the Post Office and Civil Service Committee. During his time in office, Leland would also serve on the Committee on the District of Columbia, become chair of the Subcommittee on Postal Operations and Services, and chair the Congressional Black Caucus during the 96th Congress. In 1984, he established the Select Committee on World Hunger, serving as its chair.

Leland was concerned about the disenfranchised and poor around the world. During the 1980s, he sponsored the Homeless Person's Survival Act. Although it did not pass the House, a number of its provisions were incorporated into the Stewart B. McKinney Homeless Assistance Act that was passed. He also fought against apartheid in South Africa, urging stronger sanctions against that country, and was deeply concerned about the various tribal wars that disrupted the continent of Africa. As chairman of the Select Committee on World Hunger, he made frequent trips to Africa, visiting areas that were in dire need of help from America.

On August 7, 1989, Leland was on such a trip, intent upon visiting a camp of starving refugees. That day, the plane that carried him as well as his congressional staff members, State Department officials, and his Ethiopian escorts, crashed in a mountainous region near Gambela, Ethiopia, killing all on board. The loss of Leland, with his interest in alleviating hunger around the globe, was a loss for the world.

Sources

Clay, William L. *Just Permanent Interests: Black Americans in Congress, 1870–1991*. New York, NY: Amistad Press, 1992.

Estell, Kenneth. *African America: Celebrating 400 Years of Achievement*. Detroit, MI: Visible Ink Press, 1994.

"Former Black Members of Congress." *Congressional Times Journal*. <http://www.usbol.com/ctjournal/FrBlkCongMemList.html>. Accessed: 2/27/98.

"George Thomas (Mickey) Leland." *U.S. House of Representatives*. <http://www.house.gov/leland.htm>. Accessed: 5/21/98.

John Lewis

Courtesy of the Office of Congressman John Lewis

Born: February 21, 1940, in Troy, Alabama

Status: U.S. representative from the Fifth Congressional District of Georgia

Education: B.S., 1961, American Baptist Theological Seminary, Nashville, Tennessee; B.A. in religion and philosophy, 1967, Fisk University, Nashville, Tennessee; recipient of numerous honorary degrees from various colleges and universities

Position: Chairman, Student Nonviolent Coordinating Committee (SNCC), 1963–1966; associate director, Field Foundation, mid-1960s; project director, Southern Regional Council, 1970s; director, Voter Education Project, 1970s; director, ACTION, 1977–1980; community affairs director, National Consumer Co-op Bank, Atlanta, Georgia, 1980s; councilman, Atlanta City Council, Atlanta, Georgia, 1981–1986; U.S. representative from the Fifth Congressional District of Georgia, 1987– ; recipient of the Martin Luther King, Jr., Non-Violent Peace Prize

Early Years

John Lewis was born the son of sharecroppers on February 21, 1940, just outside Troy, Alabama. Growing up poor and black in rural Alabama during the 1940s taught Lewis hard lessons on inequality and segregation. He attended the segregated public schools in Pike County, Alabama, and, after graduating from high school, entered the American Baptist Theological Seminary in Nashville, Tennessee.

Higher Education

Lewis intended to study for the ministry but, early in the 1960s, became involved in the civil rights movement that was just beginning in the South. After graduation in 1961, Lewis volunteered to participate in the Freedom Rides, challenging interstate bus terminals across the South. It would be six years before he would finish his education; he would graduate with a bachelor's degree in religion and philosophy from Fisk University in Nashville, Tennessee, in 1967.

Career Highlights

In 1961, it was dangerous to be in the civil rights movement in the South, and Lewis was in for his share of violence. During his time as a Freedom Rider, he suffered numerous beatings at the hands of angry mobs. By 1963, he had been named one of the "Big Six" leaders of the civil rights movement, despite his youth. When the Student Nonviolent Coordinating Committee was organized by Lewis and others at a meeting held at Shaw University in Greensboro, North Carolina, he was elected chairman, a position he would hold until 1966.

Lewis was one of the planners and a keynote speaker of the 1963 March on Washington. During the following year, Lewis worked throughout the South, organizing protests, voter registration drives, and community action programs. Along with Hosea Williams, a fellow activist, he led the march across the Edmund Pettus bridge in Selma, Alabama, on "Bloody Sunday," March 7, 1965. Alabama state troopers descended upon the marchers, attacking and beating them, horrifying a nation that was watching the events unfold on television. This march and the march between Selma and Montgomery, Alabama, eventually led to Congress's enactment of the Voting Rights Act of 1965.

Although Lewis left SNCC in 1966, he continued to work within the civil rights movement as associate director of the Field Foundation and by working on voter registration drives for the Southern Regional Council. This latter work led to his appointment as director of the Voter Education Project (VEP). During his time with VEP, the organization was able to add nearly 4 million voters to the rolls throughout the nation (*Congressional Black Caucus*).

Lewis's efforts brought him to the attention of President Jimmy Carter, who offered him an appointment as director of ACTION, a federal volunteer agency. In this position, Lewis directed nearly 250,000 volunteers throughout the country. In 1980, he left ACTION to become community affairs director of the National Consumer Co-op Bank of Atlanta, Georgia.

With his shift to the National Consumer Co-op Bank, he left activism behind and began looking at the political arena. In 1981, he was elected to the Atlanta City Council. During his tenure on the city council, Lewis strongly advocated for ethics in government and for neighborhood preservation ("Biography . . .").

In 1986, Lewis gave up his seat on the city council to run for Congress from Georgia's Fifth Congressional District, which is made up of the entire city of Atlanta, as well as parts of Fulton, DeKalb, and Clayton Counties. With his background of civil rights activism and service, Lewis had little trouble being elected and took his seat in Congress in January of 1987. Since that time, Lewis has been reelected with little opposition and, at the time of this writing, continues to represent his Georgia constituency in the House.

Lewis has been called "one of the most courageous persons the Civil Rights Movement has ever produced," and during his time in public office continued to pursue the same sorts of goals he had worked for during the 1960s and 1970s ("Biography . . ."). In Congress, Lewis initially served on the Public Works Committee and on the Interior and Insular Affairs Committee; more recently, he was named to the powerful House Ways and Means Committee and the Democratic Steering Committee; and he has served as chief deputy Democratic whip. Lewis continues to push for those things he feels are important: the protection of human rights, the securing of personal dignity, and the building of what he calls "The Beloved Community."

Sources

"Biography of Congressman John Lewis." *U.S. House of Representatives*. <http://www.house.gov/johnlewis/bio.html>. Accessed: 3/6/98.

Clay, William L. *Just Permanent Interests: Black Americans in Congress, 1870–1991*. New York: Amistad Press, 1992.

Congressional Black Caucus '93–'94 Guide. <http://www.sas.upenn.edu/African_Studies/Govern_Political/CBC_Guide.html>. Accessed: 3/5/98.

Estell, Kenneth. *African America: Celebrating 400 Years of Achievement*. Detroit, MI: Visible Ink Press, 1994.

Jefferson Franklin Long

Reproduced from the Collections of the Library of Congress

Born: March 3, 1836, near Knoxville, Georgia

Status: Died February 4, 1901, in Macon, Georgia; buried at Lynwood Cemetery, Macon, Georgia

Education: Self-educated

Position: Owner, tailor, J.F. Long and Son, Macon, Georgia, c. 1865–1901; chairman, Georgia Republican State Convention, 1869; U.S. representative from Georgia, 1871

Early Years

Jefferson Franklin Long was born a slave on March 3, 1836, near Knoxville, Georgia, to a black mother and a white father. Little is known of his early years. At some point, Long learned to read, write, and calculate; in all probability, he was self-educated. Schooling was forbidden to slaves and, even after the Civil War, was not freely available to blacks in the South. By 1865, the end of the Civil War, Long owned a tailoring business in Macon, Georgia.

Career Highlights

Under the plan for the Reconstruction of the South, passed by Congress in 1867, the South was divided into five military districts. Each state was to hold a constitutional convention under military supervision, elect new officials, and draw up a new state constitution. And when the new state government had ratified the 14th Amendment, its representatives could be admitted to Congress at congressional discretion. The military occupation of the South allowed an opportunity for black leaders to seek political office and promote equal rights. Jefferson Long, who was a well-liked businessman in Macon, Georgia, was one such leader.

His business prospering, Long sought to enter the political arena in Georgia. By 1867, he had become active in the Republican Party, encouraging the registration of black voters and working to advance the goals of the Georgia Educational Association, which, like the Freedmen's Bureau, worked to establish schools and to aid newly freed black citizens. He also worked to improve the working conditions of the newly freed slaves who were laborers or tenant farmers. Rising rapidly in the state Republican ranks, Long held a position on its central committee and chaired its 1869 convention in Macon. That same year, Long was nominated to represent the Fourth Congressional District of Georgia.

Georgia's attempts at readmission to the Union had not been without violence and strife. The United States Congress had denied the state's readmission in 1868 after a group of white conservatives had forcibly expelled 28 black members from Georgia's legislature and declared that those who had one-eighth or more Negro blood were not eligible for public office. In 1869, Congress voted to restore the black legislative members to their seats in Georgia's state house. Once the black members of Georgia's legislature had reclaimed their seats, they re-petitioned Congress for Georgia's admission. Among those nominated for Congress by the legislature was Jefferson Long, who campaigned to fill a seat for the third (and last) session of the 41st Congress.

Long's campaign, like those of most black candidates in Georgia at the time, was met with threats and violence. He persevered, however, telling one crowd in Macon on election eve, "If you will stand by me, we will take the polls tomorrow and we will hold them" (Christopher 27). Although many African Americans who attempted to vote the next day were attacked by angry mobs of whites, Long prevailed, winning the election by 900 votes. He became the second black man to be seated in Congress (after **Joseph Hayne Rainey** in 1870) on January 16, 1871.

Although his tenure in Congress would last only until March of that year, Long did as much as he could to further the cause of equality. Frederick Douglass had described Long in the *New National Era* of Washington, D.C., as being of "light brown complexion with manly, independent carriage . . . [giving] the impression of a man activated by a high sense of duty and of the position he occupies" (Christopher 28). And although he was a junior member of Congress and had served less than a month in that body, on February 1, 1871, Long rose to address Congress, becoming the first black representative to speak from the floor of the House.

A bill was before the House that would, if passed, ease the restoration of the political rights of former confederates. Long opposed this bill strongly, arguing that, if passed, it would only exacerbate the violence by whites toward blacks in the South. He spoke movingly of the terror and mayhem that had already been inflicted upon black citizens in Georgia by the Ku Klux Klan and other white secret societies, and of how, because of the influence of these terrorists, there was no justice to be had: "When we take the men who commit these outrages before judges and juries we find that they are in the hands of the very Ku Klux themselves, who protect them" (Christopher 28). Unfortunately, despite Long's passionate oratory, the bill was passed a few days later and became law, although it went unsigned by President Ulysses S. Grant.

Long's term of office expired on March 3, 1871, and he returned to Georgia. He had no hope of winning reelection, however. The conservative forces were regaining power within the state and, by 1872, had full control of Georgia's government. Blacks who attempted to vote were dissuaded by intimidation and violence. An African American who considered running for public office was guaranteed a death sentence.

Although Long's brief career in public office had come to an end, he continued his political activities for several more years. He urged blacks to vote for independent Democrats, arguing that the conservative Republicans in power were intent upon denying equality to blacks. Seeing his efforts fail, however, and witnessing the withdrawal of federal troops from the state in 1877—opening the door even wider to white abuse and domination—Long retired from the political arena disheartened and disillusioned.

Jefferson Franklin Long spent his remaining years working at his tailoring business, J.F. Long and Son, in Macon, Georgia, where, on February 4, 1901, he quietly died at his home.

Sources

Christopher, Maurine. *America's Black Congressmen*. New York: Thomas Y. Crowell, 1971.

"Former Black Members of Congress." *Congressional Times Journal*. <http://www.usbol.com/ctjournal/FrBlkCongMemList.html>. Accessed: 3/12/98.

Kestenbaum, Lawrence. *Political Graveyard: A Database of Historical Cemeteries*, rev. 1/13/98. <http://www.potifos.com/tpg.html>. Accessed: 1/17/98.

John Roy Lynch

Reproduced from the Collections of the Library of Congress

Born: September 10, 1847, in Vidalia, Louisiana

Status: Died November 2, 1939, in Chicago, Illinois; buried in Arlington National Cemetery, Arlington, Virginia

Education: Read law; admitted to the Mississippi bar, 1896; admitted to the Washington, D.C., bar, 1897; admitted to the Illinois bar, 1911

Position: Photographer's assistant, Natchez, Mississippi, 1867–c. 1869; appointed justice of the peace, Natchez, Mississippi, 1869; representative, Mississippi State Legislature, 1870–1872; speaker of the house, Mississippi State Legislature, 1872–1873; U.S. representative from the Sixth Congressional District of Mississippi, 1873–1877, 1882–1883; temporary chair, Republican National Convention, 1884; appointed auditor of the treasury for the Navy Department, 1889–1893; lawyer, Washington, D.C., 1898–1899; major and pay-master of volunteers during the Spanish-American War, 1899–1911; lawyer, Chicago, Illinois, 1911–c. 1939

Early Years

John Roy Lynch was born into slavery on September 10, 1847, on Tacony plantation near Vidalia, Louisiana, the son of a slave woman, Catherine, and a white planter named Patrick Lynch. Although his father had left instructions in his will that Catherine and her children were to be freed upon his death, his wishes were not honored. Instead, Catherine and all her children were sold to Alfred Davis and moved to Natchez, Mississippi.

Sometime during his early years, while still a slave, Lynch learned to read and write. In 1863, when federal troops captured Natchez, where he lived during the Civil War, Lynch took advantage of his new-found freedom to seek further schooling. He attended night school in Natchez and, during the day, worked as a photographer. Always ambitious, he soon had his own profitable studio and enough money to invest in real estate. By 1867, when he actively entered the political arena, Lynch was a prosperous man.

Higher Education

It was only later, from 1893 to 1896, after Lynch's political opportunities had dried up with the reestablishment of white rule in Mississippi, that Lynch was able to extend his education. During those years, he read law and, in 1896, was admitted to the Mississippi bar. Later, he also would qualify for the bar in Washington, D.C., and, in 1911, be admitted to the Illinois bar.

Career Highlights

John Lynch was one of the youngest members of the Natchez, Mississippi, Republican Club when the Civil War ended in 1865. Despite his age of 18, he still threw himself wholeheartedly into Republican activities, seizing the new opportunities afforded by the war for black participation in government. In 1868, he was elected by the club to present its views to Governor Adelbert Ames on the new Mississippi state constitution and the proposed list of those who would hold office. Lynch was astounded in going over the list to find his name on it for the position of justice of the peace. Despite the risk of alienating some of his fellow Republicans in Natchez who felt he had talked Ames into nominating him, Lynch accepted the position and was sworn in in April of 1869.

Shortly after accepting this position, Lynch, along with his political rival, H.P. Jacobs, was nominated for the Mississippi house of representatives. Both were elected in November of 1869, and Lynch resigned his position as justice of the peace in December to take his seat in the legislature early in 1870.

Although only 22 years old when he took his seat, Lynch was not reticent about voicing his opinions. During his years in the legislature, he worked to establish a public school system and aided in the reconstruction of the state government and in the reform of the state penal system. In 1872, despite stiff opposition, he was elected speaker of the Mississippi house.

During the fall of 1872, Lynch decided to try for higher office, running successfully for a seat in Congress from the Sixth Congressional District of Mississippi against Democrat Hiram Cassidy. When he left for Washington, the *Jackson Clarion* praised him, reporting on the testimonial given by his fellow state legislators:

> His bearing in office had been so proper and his rulings in such marked contrast to the partisan conduct of the ignoble whites of his party who have aspired to be the leaders of the blacks that the conservatives cheerfully joined in the testimonial. (Christopher 58)

John Roy Lynch was only 25 years old when he took his seat in the 43rd Congress in 1873. He was appointed to the Committee on Mines and Mining and the Committee on Expenditures in the Interior Department. During his term of office, however, his main interest was the passage of what would become the Civil Rights Act of 1875. Like other black congressmen and senators, Lynch sought in his speeches to quell the fears of the white members of Congress who felt that the bill might lead to a mixing of the races. Should the bill be passed, Lynch said,

> those who fear this will find that there is no more social equality than before . . . that the whites and blacks do not intermarry any more than they did before the passage of this bill. In short, they will find that there is nothing in the bill but the recognition by law of equal rights of citizens before the law. (Clay 34)

Unfortunately, although the bill was passed, it was later nullified by the Supreme Court.

When Lynch returned to Mississippi in 1875, he found that, as in other southern states, the Democrats were slowly regaining control politically through intimidation and harassment. In his reelection campaign, Lynch was able to retain his seat in Congress, but only by a narrow margin as black voters stayed away from the polls out of fear.

During his second term of office, in the 44th Congress, Lynch worked against a bill calling for separate schools for blacks and whites. In addition, while he defended the Republican administration of Governor Ames of Mississippi, he unsuccessfully called upon Congress to do something about the rising tide of violence by Democrats in southern elections.

By 1876, when Lynch ran for a third term in Congress, these same southern Democrats were able to exert enough control to defeat him. Lynch lost his seat to James R. Chalmers, a former Confederate general. When Lynch contested the election, the House refused to hear his case.

In 1880, however, when Lynch again challenged Chalmers and contested the outcome, the House did vote to hear him and ruled in Lynch's favor. Lynch was seated in the 47th Congress on April 29, 1882. During the short time he had left in office—since his appeal had taken so long—Lynch supported legislation that would benefit his state. He voted for a bill to pay war reparation fees to the Protestant Orphan Asylum in Natchez for damage caused by federal troops, and he voted to divide Mississippi into two federal judicial districts.

Lynch tried for reelection in 1882 and again in 1884 and 1886, but southern Democrats had firmly regained control in Mississippi. There no longer were open opportunities for blacks in either state or federal politics. Returning to Washington, from 1889 to 1893 Lynch held the post of auditor of the treasury for the Navy Department.

In 1893, Lynch began reading for the bar and was admitted to the Mississippi bar in 1896. Seeing little opportunity for a black lawyer in the state, however, he moved back to Washington, D.C., and, after passing its bar in 1897, opened a law firm there in 1898. The following year, though, he left his firm when offered a position by President William McKinley. Lynch was appointed a major in the army and paymaster of volunteers during the Spanish-American War and served as paymaster and captain in the regular army after the war. In 1911, he resigned from the army at the rank of major and moved to Chicago to practice law once again.

During his later years, in addition to speaking, Lynch chronicled his own life and challenged historian James Ford Rhodes's views on black history. Lynch's *The Fact of Reconstruction*, which presented Lynch's views on the era, was published in 1913. *Some Historical Errors of James Ford Rhodes* appeared in 1922; his autobiography, *Reminiscences of an Active Life* was published posthumously.

On November 2, 1939, John Roy Lynch died at the age of 92. His life had been a full one. Until **A. Michael "Mike" Espy** was elected to Congress in 1986, John Roy Lynch was the only black congressman from the state of Mississippi. By dint of hard work, Lynch had risen from slavery to hold one of the highest offices in the United States. As *The New York Times* said in its obituary of him, Lynch was "one of the most fluent and forceful speakers in the politics of the 1870s and 80s" (Clay 35). Because of his distinguished career in the army, Lynch was buried at Arlington Cemetery in Washington, D.C.

Sources

Christopher, Maurine. *America's Black Congressmen.* New York: Thomas Y. Crowell, 1971.

Clay, William L. *Just Permanent Interests: Black Americans in Congress, 1870–1991.* New York: Amistad Press, 1992.

"Former Black Members of Congress." *Congressional Times Journal.* <http://www.usbol.com/ctjournal/FrBlkCongMemList.html>. Accessed: 2/13/98.

M

Thurgood Marshall

From the Collection of The Supreme Court Historical Society, by Joseph D. Lavenburg

Born: July 2, 1908, in Baltimore, Maryland

Status: Died January 24, 1993; buried at Arlington National Cemetery, Arlington, Virginia

Education: Graduate cum laude, 1930, Lincoln University, Oxford, Pennsylvania; LL.B. magna cum laude, 1933, Howard University Law School, Washington, D.C.; recipient of numerous honorary degrees from various colleges and universities

Position: Attorney, Baltimore, Maryland, 1933–1936; attorney, National Association for the Advancement of Colored People (NAACP), Baltimore branch, Baltimore, Maryland, 1934–1936; special counsel, NAACP, New York, New York, 1936–1940; chief, legal staff, NAACP, 1940–1961; circuit judge, U.S. Court of Appeals for the Second Circuit, 1961–1965; U.S. solicitor general, 1965–1967; justice, United States Supreme Court, 1967–1991

Awards and honors: Spingarn Medal, NAACP, 1946

Early Years

Thurgood Marshall was born Thoroughgood Marshall in Baltimore, Maryland, on July 2, 1908. He was named after his paternal grandfather who had fought for the Union during the Civil War. His parents, William Canfield Marshall and Norma Williams Marshall, were economically comfortable. His father worked as a waiter on the Baltimore and Ohio Railroad, and Marshall's mother taught school in Baltimore. Shortly after Marshall was born, the family moved to Harlem in New York City, where Marshall spent his first five years. In 1913, William Marshall left the railroad and got a job as a steward in the restaurant of the Gibson Island Club, an all-white country club in Baltimore, so the family returned to Maryland.

After the family's move back to Baltimore, Marshall, who had been very shy, changed. As his Aunt Denmedia recalled, "One day . . . he stopped crying and became a pretty tough guy. Now, I don't know what caused the change. Maybe the boys slapped his head" (Haskins 8). The neighborhood in which the Marshalls lived was respectable, but, as Marshall later said, "behind us there were back alleys where the roughnecks and the tough kids hung out" (Haskins 9).

As soon as they were old enough, both Marshall and his older brother, Aubrey, got part-time jobs. Marshall first ran errands for the neighbors, then shined shoes. By the time he was an adolescent, he was working as a delivery boy for a hatmaker. It was while working at this job that Marshall had his first serious encounter with racism. He was carrying a stack of hatboxes, piled so high he could not see over them. He was waiting for the trolley, and when it arrived, he started to step up into it when suddenly his arm was grabbed and he heard a man say, "Nigger, don't you never push in front of no white lady again." Dropping the boxes, Marshall whirled around and punched the small white man who had grabbed his arm; soon the two were fighting. A policeman, who happened to know Marshall, arrived to break up the fight and was willing to listen to Marshall's side of the story. Not knowing who to believe, the policeman arrested them both. Marshall, however, was rescued by his employer, Mr. Schoen, who paid his fine and assured him he still had a job.

Both Marshall and his brother attended Douglass High School in Baltimore, an all-black school. Marshall did well in school, getting good grades without much effort, and in the summers worked on the New York-to-Washington run of the Baltimore and Ohio Railroad. Upon graduation, Marshall followed Aubrey to Lincoln University, an all-black university near the small town of Oxford, Pennsylvania.

Higher Education

Marshall entered the same class as the noted poet Langston Hughes, who had also come to Lincoln, and who became a good friend. Marshall had loved high school, and he found college even more exhilarating. He wasted no time making friends and enjoyed going to parties, playing cards, and going to Philadelphia to restaurants and clubs. Marshall and a number of other students also devoted a great deal of energy to making life difficult for the school administration, organizing strikes against the school, especially over the food and rules. The students felt this was the only way they could get the attention of the uninterested, all-white faculty.

During this time, Marshall fell in love with Vivien Burey, a student at the University of Pennsylvania he had met while on one of his frequent jaunts to Philadelphia. Despite the qualms of both Marshall's and Vivien's parents, the two managed to convince them that it would be better for them to get married and, in June, just after Marshall finished his junior year, they were married. Vivien, whom everyone called Buster, dropped out of school and got a job as a secretary in Oxford, where the couple had rented a small apartment.

Marshall had intended to become a dentist and had majored in predentistry at Lincoln, but in his senior year he realized he wanted to become a lawyer. In 1930, Marshall graduated cum laude and began to search for a law school. To afford law school, the Marshalls had to move in with his parents in Baltimore. Marshall would have preferred to attend the nearby University of Maryland, but the university did not accept black students at that time, so he applied to and was accepted at the closest one, Howard University Law School in Washington, D.C.

Marshall started law school just as the Great Depression was being felt throughout the country. In many ways, he and his wife were fortunate. She had been able to find a job as a secretary in Baltimore, and the couple had moved out of his parents' home into a small apartment on Druid Hill Avenue in the city. Marshall commuted to Washington to school, and sold insurance after his classes each day. Despite the grueling schedule, Marshall loved law school and, in 1933, first in his class, he graduated magna cum laude with his degree in law.

Career Highlights

After passing the Maryland bar exam, Marshall joined a small law firm in Baltimore, but he soon became bored with divorce work, property claims, and the other minor cases the firm handled. What he really wanted to do, as he said years later, was "straighten out all this business about civil rights" (Haskins 41). Civil rights cases, however, were difficult to prosecute at that time, and most people had no money. His interest in civil rights led him to join a number of civic organizations, including the Baltimore branch of the National Association for the Advancement of Colored People (NAACP).

In 1934, Marshall at last got a chance to work on the sort of case he liked. That year, a former professor, Charles Hamilton Houston, who was chief counsel for the NAACP, asked him to help with a civil rights case. Houston had Marshall named the NAACP's legal counsel in Baltimore. The case involved a young man, Donald Murray, who wanted to attend the University of Maryland's Law School. He had applied to the school and been rejected because of his color. At that time, the state provided scholarships to out-of-state universities for black students who wished to attend law school. But the $200 was not enough for Murray to attend an out-of-state college, and he wanted to seek a court order to force the University of Maryland's board of regents to admit him. Although the court order was granted and Murray was preparing to enter school, the university was appealing the court order. Marshall and Houston presented the NAACP's arguments on Murray's behalf before the Maryland Court of Appeals in late 1935 and, in January of 1936, the court ruled that, as a public agency, the university had to admit Murray; Marshall had won. However, the decision applied to one school in one state, and both Marshall and Houston wanted to see the decision repeated throughout the country, so the two searched for other cases similar to Murray's.

The Murray case had taken a great deal of Marshall's time, leaving him few moments for his private law practice. In 1936, he confided to Houston that he wanted to concentrate on the civil rights cases, if he could earn a living that way. So Houston invited Marshall to join him at the New York offices of the NAACP as his assistant for $150 a month, a modest sum even in those days. It was not enough for Marshall to afford to move his wife to New York, so again he commuted, this time between New York and Baltimore.

The next several years were spent tracking down civil rights cases and doggedly following them through the courts. Then, in 1940, Charles Hamilton Houston announced his retirement from the NAACP, and Marshall was named his replacement as chief counsel of the NAACP in New York. The modest raise of $200 a year was just enough to enable him to have Buster moved to New York, and the couple rented an apartment in Harlem.

Over the next 15 years, Marshall traveled throughout the country. His work, in many ways, was a preparation for the greatest case of his life. In 1949, the Reverend Oliver Brown, a schoolteacher and minister in Topeka, Kansas, attempted to enroll his daughter in the Sumner Elementary School, an all-white school. When her enrollment was denied, Brown called upon the NAACP for help in combating the ruling. What Marshall had to prove was that segregation was harmful and unlawful, which would essentially overturn the case of *Plessy v. Ferguson* that had earlier established the concept of "separate but equal" facilities for blacks and whites. Marshall rallied experts in all fields to aid in the case, and after gradually working its way through the court system, *Brown v. Board of Education, Topeka, Kansas,* arrived before the United States Supreme Court. After arguments were heard from both sides, and months of deliberations had passed, on May 17, 1954, the Court handed down its decision on the case. The justices had voted 9 to 0 in favor of desegregation, a decision that would have a major impact on the country for years to come.

While 1954 was a year of professional triumph for Marshall, in other ways it was a terrible year. During that year, Marshall found out that his wife had cancer. All through the fall and winter of 1954, Marshall took charge of her care and barely left her side. When she died in February, 1955, he said, "I thought the end of the world had come. I had no thoughts on remarriage" (Haskins 99). After his wife's death, Marshall threw himself into his work, burying his grief in endless days of traveling, giving speeches, and attacking segregation on every legal front he could find. He eventually found a sympathetic shoulder in Cecilie "Cissy" Suyat, a Hawaiian woman who had come to work at the NAACP in 1948. The couple was married in 1956 and later had two children: Thurgood, Jr., and John.

The publicity of his cases had brought Marshall national prominence and, in 1961, President John Kennedy offered him an appointment as circuit judge in the U.S. Court of Appeals for the Second Circuit. Although there were many objections to Marshall's appointment, he was confirmed by the Senate. During his time as circuit judge, Marshall made 112 decisions, none of which were overturned by the Supreme Court.

In 1965, Lyndon B. Johnson asked Marshall to accept the appointment of solicitor general of the United States. The solicitor general, among other things, decides which cases will be heard by the Supreme Court. Marshall accepted, knowing that in this position he could continue the fight for civil rights. Again, there were objections, but Marshall was sworn in on August 24, 1965. At the swearing-in ceremony, Johnson said, "Thurgood Marshall symbolizes what is best about our American society: the belief that human rights must be satisfied through the orderly process of law" (Haskins 125). At that time, there was a great deal of speculation that Johnson was grooming Marshall for a seat on the Supreme Court. And, in fact, in 1967, Johnson nominated Marshall for a position on the Court.

Although Marshall's appointment was again criticized, and many in Congress tried to block it, he was confirmed. When Marshall was sworn in as the first black member of the highest court in the land, President Johnson said that his appointment "was the right thing to do, the right time to do it, the right man and the right place" (Smith 487).

Marshall remained on the Supreme Court bench for the next 24 years. He became the voice of liberals in the Court, and the voice for civil rights. He also became known for his biting sarcasm. In 1981, during an argument on the death penalty, Justice Rehnquist commented that the inmate's repeated appeals had cost the state a great deal of money. Turning to him, Marshall dryly said, "it would have been cheaper to shoot him right after he was arrested, wouldn't it?" ("Thurgood Marshall." This Person in Black History.).

In 1991, at the age of 82, Marshall announced his retirement from the Court. He said, "I am old. I'm getting old and coming apart" ("Thurgood Marshall." Voice of America.). Two years later, on January 24, 1993, Marshall died at the age of 84. Earlier, when asked how he wished to be remembered, he replied that he wanted people to say of him, "he did what he could with what he had" ("Thurgood Marshall." Voice of America.). Looking back on Marshall's life, one can say he did much more than just "what he could."

Sources

Estell, Kenneth. *African America: Celebrating 400 Years of Achievement*. Detroit, MI: Visible Ink, 1994.

Haskins, James. *Thurgood Marshall: A Life for Justice*. New York: Henry Holt and Co., 1992.

"Marshall, Thurgood." *Biography Online Database*. <http://www.biography.com/find/bioengine/cgi?cmd+1&rec+7132>. Accessed: 4/11/98.

"Marshall, Thurgood." *Encyclopedia Britannica*. <http://blackhistory.eb.com/micro/378/26.html>. Accessed: 3/18/98.

Smith, Jessie Carney, ed. *Black Heroes of the 20th Century*. Detroit, MI: Visible Ink Press, 1998.

"Thurgood Marshall." <http://tqd.advanced.org/3337/tmarsh.html>. Accessed: 4/23/98.

"Thurgood Marshall, Supreme Court Justice." <http://provost.ucsd.edu/marshall/advising/acad4.htm>. Accessed: 3/18/98.

"Thurgood Marshall." This Person in Black History. <http://www.ai.mit.edu/~isbell/HFh/black/e...nd_people/html/001.thurgood_marsall.html>. Accessed: 4/23/98.

"Thurgood Marshall." Voice of America. <http://www.kaiwan.com/~mcivr/thurgood.html>. Accessed: 4/23/98.

Donald F. McHenry

Born: 1936, in St. Louis, Missouri

Status: University research professor of diplomacy and international affairs, Georgetown University, Washington, D.C.; president, IRC Group, Washington, D.C.

Education: B.A., 1957, Illinois State University, Normal, Illinois; M.S., 1959, Southern Illinois University, Carbondale, Illinois; postgraduate studies, Georgetown University, Washington, D.C.

Position: Teacher, professor at various universities, 1960–1963; employee dealing in U.S. foreign policy, Department of State, 1963–1973; guest scholar, Brookings Institute, Washington, D.C., 1971–1972; international affairs fellow, Council on Foreign Relations, New York, New York, 1971–1972; project director, Humanitarian Policy Studies, Carnegie Endowment for International Peace, Washington, D.C., 1973–1976; member, President Jimmy Carter's transition team, 1976; U.S. deputy representative to the United Nations Security Council, 1977–1979; U.S. permanent representative to the United Nations, 1979–1981; university research professor of diplomacy and international affairs, Georgetown University, Washington, D.C., 1982– ; president, IRC Group, Washington, D.C., c. 1982–

Early Years

Donald F. McHenry was born in 1936 in St. Louis, Missouri, but grew up in East St. Louis, Illinois.

Higher Education

In 1957, he received a bachelor's degree from Illinois State University in Normal, Illinois, and two years later was awarded a master's degree from Southern Illinois University in Carbondale, Illinois. Later, he did postgraduate work at Georgetown University in Washington, D.C.

Career Highlights

After graduating from and teaching at Southern Illinois University in Illinois and teaching at Howard and American Universities in Washington, D.C., in 1963 McHenry joined the United States Department of State, where he held a variety of positions related to U.S. foreign policy. Midway through his career with the State Department, he was awarded the department's Superior Honor Award for his outstanding work.

In 1971, McHenry took a leave of absence from the State Department. He became a guest scholar at the Brookings Institute, a think tank in Washington, D.C., and also served as international affairs fellow on the Council on Foreign Relations in New York City. In 1973, McHenry was offered the position of project director in Humanitarian Policy Studies at the Carnegie Endowment for International Peace in Washington. He resigned from the Department of State to accept this position.

McHenry was becoming well known in scholarly and diplomatic circles and, in 1976, Jimmy Carter asked him to be a member of his transition team as he moved into the office of president. McHenry accepted, again working with the State Department during the transition. With the transition complete, Carter then appointed McHenry deputy representative for the United States at the United Nations Security Council.

McHenry's background in foreign service and international law served him well in the United Nations and, in 1979, he was appointed U.S. permanent representative to the United Nations, a post he held until January 20, 1981, when President Ronald Reagan took office. Since that time, McHenry has taught on the university level and has served as a member of the board of governors of the United Nations Association of the United States of America. Presently, he is university research professor of diplomacy and international affairs at Georgetown University, Washington, D.C., as well as president of the IRC Group, an international consulting firm. He is the author of *Micronesia: Trust Betrayed.*

Sources

"Donald F. McHenry." *United Nations Association of the United States of America.* 1997. <http://www.unausa.org/about_UNAUSA/mchenry.htm>. Accessed: 3/18/98.

"Donald McHenry." Background Information. *Columbia University.* <http://www.cc.columbia.edu/cu/secretary/trustees/bio/McHenry.html>. Accessed: 5/4/98.

Cynthia Ann McKinney

Reproduced from AP/Wide World Photos, by Doug Mills

Born: March 17, 1955, in Atlanta, Georgia

Status: U.S. representative from the Fourth Congressional District of Georgia

Education: B.A., 1978, University of Southern California, Los Angeles; doctoral candidate in international relations, The Fletcher School of Law and Diplomacy, Tufts University, Medford, Massachusetts, 1998

Position: Diplomatic fellow, Spelman College, Atlanta, Georgia, 1984; teacher of political science, Clark Atlanta University, Atlanta, Georgia, and Agnes Scott College, Decatur, Georgia, 1985–c. 1987; state representative, Georgia State Legislature, 1988–1992; board member, HIV Health Services Planning Council of Metro Atlanta, 1991–1992; U.S. representative from the Fourth Congressional District of Georgia, 1993–

Early Years

Cynthia Ann McKinney was born in Atlanta, Georgia, on March 17, 1955. Her father, Billy McKinney, was a veteran Georgia state representative, and her mother, Leola McKinney, was a nurse at Grady Hospital in Atlanta. McKinney grew up surrounded by politics because of her father's position.

Higher Education

McKinney attended Atlanta's public schools and, upon graduating, entered the University of Southern California in Los Angeles, earning a bachelor's degree in 1978.

Career Highlights

In 1984, McKinney accepted a position at Spelman College in Atlanta as a diplomatic fellow. She also taught political science at Clark Atlanta University. Later, moving to DeKalb County, she taught at Agnes Scott College. Just as she had when she was younger, McKinney took an interest in local politics and in helping with campaigns. In 1987, she decided to run for a seat in the Georgia house of representatives.

During her four years in the Georgia legislature, McKinney earned a reputation for working on civil rights issues and pushing for increased opportunities for both minorities and women. She fought for a fair reapportionment of Georgia districts and gained national attention in the process. In addition to her legislative work, McKinney also was a member of the board of the HIV Health Services Planning Council of Metro Atlanta.

In 1992, McKinney declared her intention to run for a seat in the House from the 11th Congressional District of Georgia, a predominantly black district. Although the race was a tough one, McKinney had years of experience in the state legislature plus political savvy she had gained from her father, and she won in a landslide victory.

In 1993, McKinney was sworn into the House of Representatives, becoming Georgia's first African American congresswoman. She was assigned to the House Committee on Banking and Financial Services and the International Relations Committee. From the start, she took a leading role. In 1993, she was elected whip for Region Eight by the Democratic Caucus, she was the first freshman representative to head the Women's Caucus Task Force on Children, Youth and Families; and she took an active role in the Congressional Black Caucus.

During McKinney's first term in Congress, the district lines in Georgia and many other states were redrawn as a result of decisions by the United States Supreme Court challenging the constitutionality of the Voting Rights Act. When McKinney returned to Georgia to run for re-election, she was running in the newly created Fourth Congressional District. This district is one of Georgia's largest, encompassing 22 counties, and includes much of Georgia's rural heartland, as well as a number of metropolitan areas, excluding Atlanta. Whereas the 11th District had been predominantly black, the new district held a majority of white voters. Many predicted that McKinney could not win from such a district, but she proved them wrong. As *The New York Times* reported, "The assumption was that, come Election Day, whites would be chosen to replace the redistricted Representatives . . . but all were reelected" (Ayres). In her second year in Congress, McKinney was appointed to the prestigious National Security Committee, as well as the International Relations Committee. On the floor of the House, she sponsored the Arms Transfers Code of Conduct forbidding the sale of arms to dictatorships, which finally passed in 1997.

Over the years, McKinney's influence has grown in the House. In 1998, because of her continuing interest in Africa, President Clinton invited her to serve on the official American delegation sent to the inauguration of Liberian President Charles Taylor. McKinney has been described as intelligent, charismatic, and effective as a member of the House. She also has no hesitation about speaking out when she feels it is appropriate. In May, 1998, McKinney made national news when she and her guests received "disparate treatment" at a White House event.

McKinney was attending a reception held by President Clinton for Prime Minister Romano Prodi of Italy. She was escorting a Pakistani man and his daughter to the reception. According to *The New York Times*, "Ms. McKinney said security guards and Secret Service agents failed to recognize or acknowledge that she was a member of Congress, just as they had at a White House event in 1996" (Alvarez). In a letter to Clinton, McKinney wrote, "I am absolutely sick and tired of having to have my appearance at the White House validated by white people" (Alvarez). Members of the White House staff apologized to McKinney for the rudeness.

In 1998, McKinney again faced a race for reelection. She was challenged by Republican Sunny Warren, a personnel management specialist who is black. Yet McKinney's effectiveness as a legislator, her articulateness, and her knowledge of the issues served her well; she retained her seat in the House.

Sources

"About Congresswoman Cynthia McKinney." *U.S. House of Representatives*. <http://www.house.gov/mckinney>. Accessed: 3/13/98.

Alvarez, Lizette. "House Member Describes Snub at White House." *The New York Times on the Web*. <http://archives.nytimes.com/archives/>. 9 May 1998.

Ayres, B. Drummond, Jr. "Political Briefing; 3 Rare Battles Loom in the South." *The New York Times on the Web*. <http://archives.nytimes.com/archives/>. 17 April 1998.

Congressional Black Caucus '93–'94 Guide. <http://www.sas.upenn.edu/African_Studies/Govern_Political/CBC_Guide.html>. Accessed: 3/10/98.

"National Elections '98." *The Washington Post*, 4 November 1998. <http://elections98.washingtonpost.com/wp-srv/results98/national/>. Accessed: 11/19/98.

"Women We've Helped to Elect: Congresswoman Cynthia A. McKinney." *Emily's List*. 1997. <http://www.emilyslist.org/about/players/play_mckinney.htm>. Accessed: 3/6/98.

Carrie Pittman Meek

Courtesy of the Office of Congresswoman Carrie Pittman Meek

Born: April 29, 1926, in Tallahassee, Florida

Status: U.S. representative from the 17th Congressional District of Florida

Education: B.S. in biology and physical education, 1946, Florida A and M University, Tallahassee, Florida; M.S. in public health and physical education, 1948, University of Michigan, Ann Arbor, Michigan; graduate studies at Florida Atlantic University, Boca Raton, Florida; recipient of five honorary degrees

Position: Teacher, Bethune-Cookman College, Daytona Beach, Florida, 1949–1958; teacher and coach, Florida A and M University, Tallahassee, Florida, 1958–1961; professor, Miami-Dade Community College, Miami, Florida, 1961–1968; associate dean for community services and assistant to the president, Miami-Dade Community College, Miami, Florida, 1968–1979; special assistant to the vice president, Miami-Dade Community College, Miami, Florida, 1982; state representative, Florida State Legislature, 1979–1982; senator, Florida State Senate, 1982–1993; U.S. representative from the 17th Congressional District of Florida, 1993–

Awards and honors: Eminent scholar's chair named in her honor, Florida A and M University; recipient of the LeRoy Collins Lifetime Achievement Award; recipient of United Way's Public Policy Leadership Award

Early Years

Carrie Pittman Meek was born one of 12 children on April 29, 1926, in Tallahassee, Florida. Her mother, Carrie Pittman, was a domestic and also took in laundry, and her father, William Pittman, was a sharecropper. The family lived at near-poverty level, but as Meek was later to say, "We were poor, but we didn't know it" (Bigelow 193).

Growing up in racially segregated Florida in the 1920s and 1930s taught Meek a great deal. She said, "I have experienced extreme, rigid and very painful segregation and racism from childhood" (Bigelow 192). But she didn't see herself as a victim; she dreamed of being an important person when she grew up. Carrie

Pittman, her mother, "inspired us to really want to go to school. She used to tell me stories [about] how she came up, and how hard it was, but how much we could do" (Bigelow 193).

Meek attended the racially segregated public school in Tallahassee. While in high school, she competed and did well in athletics, a pursuit she would follow in college and further.

Higher Education

When Meek graduated from high school, she continued her education at Florida A and M University, which, at that time, was an all-black school. While following her love of athletics and lettering in track and field, she majored in biology and physical education with the aim of becoming a teacher, "because that was about the only thing open to [black women] in those days" (Bigelow 193). When she graduated in 1946, no college in Florida accepted blacks for graduate studies, so she traveled north to the University of Michigan in Ann Arbor, where she earned a master's degree in physical education and public health in 1948. Later, while teaching and working, she would continue her education, taking graduate classes at Florida Atlantic University in Boca Raton, Florida.

Career Highlights

Upon graduation from the University of Michigan, Meek returned home to teach. She found a job at **Mary McLeod Bethune**'s Bethune-Cookman College in Daytona Beach, Florida. Bethune inspired Meek in many ways, showing her that women did not have to take a second place in life. As Meek later said, ". . . Bethune. . . was a very regal woman. Mrs. Bethune was the first feminist I had a chance to know, only we didn't call it that back then. She brought Madame Nehru and Eleanor Roosevelt . . . to campus to speak to us and that made a big impression on me" (Bigelow 193).

Meek was also inspired by a man named Virgil Hawkins. He was trying to break the color barrier at the University of Florida at the time. Meek and others joined with him to protest racism.

After teaching and coaching basketball at Bethune-Cookman, Meek moved on to a job at her alma mater, Florida A and M University, where she taught biology and physical education for three years, from 1958 to 1961. In 1961, she accepted a teaching position at Miami-Dade Community College in Miami, Florida. Meek enjoyed teaching: "What means most to me," she said, "is to see some of the students I taught, who everyone else had destined to failure, come back as a whopping success" (Bigelow 193).

At the same time that she was teaching, Meek was also trying to be a good single parent to her three children: Lucia, Sheila, and Kendrick. She had been through two divorces and, at times, struggled: "Just sometimes a tire blowing out or the car not starting one day can be a disaster when you don't have anyone" (Bigelow 193–94).

Meek, however, was finding success at Miami-Dade College. After teaching there a number of years while also developing its athletic program, Meek was named associate dean for Community Services and assistant to the president of the college. With greater contact with the community outside the college, and her involvement with Miami's Model City program in the 1960s, Meek began to think about assuming a greater role in politics. She said, "Now I know where [community empowerment] is at. It's in Tallahassee, it's in Washington, and it's with the local and municipal governments. Only government can bring equity to blacks" (Bigelow 194). Government was the agency that had the money and power, and Meeks realized that if she truly wished to effect change she would have to become a part of it.

In 1979, Dade County State Representative Gwen Cherry was killed in a car accident. Meek decided that it was time for her to enter the political arena. Despite the fact that many discouraged her from running for the position, telling her she had no chance of winning, Meek defeated a field of 12 opponents in a special election. The following year, in the regular election, she was elected to a full term. In 1982, Meek successfully ran for the state senate.

As a state senator, Meek fought for the things in which she believed. During her final term in the state senate, she served as the chairperson of the educational subcommittee of the Appropriations Committee. In that position, she was in control of Florida's nearly $10 billion education budget and was able to push for the educational programs she felt were needed by the state. She also fought for affordable housing and help for minority-run businesses. Meek keenly remembered her own upbringing, hoping to make things better for those who came after her.

After more than a dozen years in the state government, Meek decided to run for Congress. She had become known far beyond her own district and stood a good chance of winning the seat. Running in the 17th Congressional District, which was predominantly Democratic and black, Meek faced two other candidates, both black men; but her work on the state level spoke for her, and she was able to sweep the primary by 83 percent of the vote and go on to win in the general election.

Meek was sworn in to the House of Representatives on January 5, 1993. She was assigned to the Committee on Appropriations and, although a freshman representative, immediately made her opinions known on the issues of education, social services, and affordable housing. One of her first pieces of legislation was a bill to provide retirement security for such domestic workers as gardeners, nannies, and cleaning personnel. This was passed by Congress and signed into law by President Clinton. When Hurricane Andrew struck her home state of Florida, devastating sections of it, Meek was one of those in the forefront fighting to provide federal assistance.

Meek continues to hold her seat in Congress and fight for equality for men and women, black and white. Her service to the public has been honored many times, most recently by Florida's business and community leaders when they awarded her the LeRoy Collins Lifetime Achievement Award "... for her lifelong commitment to improving the quality of life for Florida's citizens and its future generations" ("Representative Carrie Meek: Biography").

Sources

Bigelow, Barbara Carlisle, ed. *Contemporary Black Biography: Profiles from the International Black Community*, Vol. 6. Detroit, MI: Gale Research, 1994.

Congressional Black Caucus '93–'94 Guide. <http://www.sas.upenn.edu/African_Studies/Govern_Political/CBC_Guide.html>. Accessed: 3/10/98.

"Representative Carrie Meek: Biography." *U.S. House of Representatives*. <http://www.house.gov/meek/bio.html>. Accessed: 3/6/98.

Ralph Harold Metcalfe

Reproduced from the Collections of the Library of Congress

Born: May 29, 1910, in Atlanta, Georgia

Status: Died October 10, 1978, in Chicago, Illinois; buried in Holy Sepulchre Cemetery, Worth, Illinois

Education: Ph.B., 1936, Marquette University, Milwaukee, Wisconsin; M.A. in physical education, 1939, University of Southern California, Los Angeles, California

Position: Awarded silver medal in track, 1932 Olympics; awarded a gold and a silver medal in track, 1936 Olympics; track coach and teacher of political science, Xavier University, New Orleans, Louisiana, 1936–1942; first lieutenant, U.S. Army Transportation Corps, 1942–1945; director, civil rights department, Chicago Commission on Human Relations, 1945–1949; commissioner, Illinois State Athletic Commission, 1949–1952; elected Third Ward committeeman, 1952; elected to the Chicago City Council, Chicago, Illinois, 1955; U.S. representative from the First Congressional District of Illinois, 1971–1978

Early Years

Ralph Harold Metcalfe was born in Atlanta, Georgia, on May 29, 1910. When he was still a young child, his family moved to Chicago, Illinois, where Metcalfe attended public school. While in high school, he became interested in running and joined the track team, a decision that would eventually establish a place for him in the history of sports.

Higher Education

After graduating from high school, Metcalfe attended Marquette University in Milwaukee, Wisconsin. During his college years, he pursued his interest in track. In 1932, he competed in the Olympics, receiving a silver medal in track. While training for the 1932 Olympics, he broke three world records: the 100-meter, 200-meter, and 220-yard records; and while training for the 1936 Olympics, he was nicknamed the "world's fastest human." In 1936, he and gold medalist Jesse Owens became the first African Americans to win gold medals in the Olympics.

After graduating from Marquette University in 1936, Metcalfe continued his education at the University of Southern California, graduating in 1939 with a master's degree in physical education.

Career Highlights

Metcalfe taught political science and coached the track team for six years at Xavier University in New Orleans. With the entrance of the United States into World War II, however, he resigned his teaching position and joined the army. For three years, from 1942 until 1945, he fought with the Army Transportation Corps as a first lieutenant.

When Metcalfe was discharged from the army, he returned to his hometown of Chicago. He was hired as the director of the civil rights department of the Chicago Commission on Human Relations and worked to improve racial relations in the city. In 1949, he was appointed commissioner of the Illinois State Athletic Commission, a post he held until 1952.

Metcalfe was becoming more and more involved in Chicago politics and, as part of the Democratic "machine" in Chicago, he could count on support for his political efforts. In 1952, he was elected Third Ward committeeman and, in 1955, was elected to the Chicago City Council. During his term on the city council, Metcalfe was elected president pro tempore of the council and chaired the council's housing committee, fighting for housing programs for lower income residents. For nearly 20 years, during the height of the civil rights movement, Metcalfe was a strong voice for equality on the Chicago City Council.

In 1970, longtime congressman **William Levi Dawson** announced that he would be stepping down from his seat in Congress. Such was Dawson's power with the Chicago "machine" that he could name his successor with the confidence that that person would be elected. Dawson named Ralph Metcalfe, who easily won the election in the all-black First District in November of 1970, a few days before Dawson's death.

When Metcalfe was sworn into Congress on January 3, 1971, he was appointed to the Committee on Merchant Marine and Fisheries and to the Interstate and Foreign Commerce Committee. That same year, Metcalfe became one of the founding members of the Congressional Black Caucus, a group formed to promote minority rights in Congress and in national legislation. As Representative **William Lacy Clay, Sr.**, writes of the caucus, "The thirteen black members of Congress were uniquely situated and sharply primed to lead an all-out assault on the institution of racism" (122).

With his background in housing matters, Metcalfe worked in Congress to promote federal housing programs and to eliminate "redlining," the practice of denying loans and insurance to low-income neighborhoods. He also attempted to improve the safety of low-income housing projects and to help minority-owned businesses. Unlike William Dawson, who had toed the line for Chicago's political machine while in Congress, Metcalfe did not, and frequently spoke out for African American equality.

In 1972, Metcalfe went head to head with Chicago's machine over police brutality. Charging that the police had unfairly brutalized minority citizens, he conducted a public forum in Chicago to allow people to testify to their experiences. His final break with the machine came, however, when he refused to support Mayor Richard J. Daley in his run for mayor in 1975. Daley, to get even, supported a Democratic challenger, Erwin A. France, against Metcalfe in his 1976 reelection primary; but Metcalfe had the support of black neighborhoods and won the election. In 1978, Metcalfe ran unopposed for the Democratic nomination, but died on October 10, 1978, a month before the actual election. Because of his defiance of the Chicago political machine and his willingness to challenge both it and the racial inequality in the city, Metcalfe stands as a symbol of independence for African Americans in Chicago.

Sources

Clay, William L. *Just Permanent Interests: Black Americans in Congress, 1870–1991*. New York: Amistad Press, 1992.

"Former Black Members of Congress." *Congressional Times Journal*. <http://www.usbol.com/ctjournal/FrBlkCongMemList.html>. Accessed: 2/18/98.

Kestenbaum, Lawrence. *Political Graveyard: A Database of Historical Cemeteries*, rev. 1/13/98. <http:www.potifos.com/tpg.html>. Accessed: 1/17/98.

Kweisi Mfume

Courtesy of the NAACP Archives

Born: October 24, 1948, near Baltimore, Maryland

Status: President and chief executive officer, National Association for the Advancement of Colored People (NAACP)

Education: Graduate, 1974, Community College of Baltimore, Baltimore, Maryland; B.S. magna cum laude, 1976, Morgan State University, Baltimore, Maryland; M.A., 1984, Johns Hopkins University, Baltimore, Maryland

Position: Assistant professor, Morgan State University, Baltimore, Maryland; radio host,

"Black Reflections"; disc jockey, then program director, WEAA-FM radio, Baltimore, Maryland; councilman, Baltimore City Council, Baltimore, Maryland, 1979–1986; U.S. representative from the Seventh Congressional District of Maryland, 1987–1996; president and CEO, NAACP, 1996–

Early Years

Frizzell Gray, who would later change his name to Kweisi Mfume, was born in Turners Station, Maryland, on October 24, 1948. Turners Station was a tiny town about 10 miles south of Baltimore. The Gray family consisted of Mfume; his three sisters; his mother, Mary Elizabeth William Gray; and his stepfather, Clifton Gray. They lived in Turners Station until 1960 when Mfume's mother separated from his stepfather; she then moved the children to Baltimore.

Life in Baltimore was hard for the Grays. They were always short of money; Mfume sold newspapers to try to help out. They were often aided by a friend of the family, Rufus Tate. Then, in 1964, when Mfume was 16, Mary Gray was diagnosed with fatal cancer. The night she died, Tate visited the house to offer his condolences and to reveal to Mfume that he was his biological father. Stunned by the two events, Mfume didn't know which way to turn. The family was broken up; his sisters went to live with his grandmother, and Mfume was sent to live with his two uncles. Mfume had to support himself, as well as go to school, and he tried to help with the costs of his sisters. More and more, he began to hang out on the streets of Baltimore, dropping out of high school and joining a gang.

On the streets, Mfume started running numbers; it earned him a great deal more money than a legitimate job. He was picked up by the police several times and seemed to be headed for a life of crime. Then, while hanging out on the street, he met Congressman **Parren James Mitchell**, who chastised him and told him to stop being part of the problem and to start becoming part of the solution. In addition to this event during his life on the streets, he claims to have seen his mother's face before him. These events prompted him to change his life (Smith 473).

Higher Education

Mfume earned a graduate equivalence diploma (GED), then entered the Community College of Baltimore. He also began working as a disc jockey in a local radio station. At the same time, he became involved in local politics, campaigning for various candidates and discussing local issues on his radio show, "Black Reflections." He also decided to change his name to better reflect his African heritage, choosing Kweisi Mfume, which means "conquering son of kings."

After receiving an associate's degree from the Community College of Baltimore in 1974, Mfume entered Morgan State University. As a student, he lobbied with the student government to begin a university radio station, WEAA-FM, which provided Mfume with another opportunity to express himself. Mfume graduated magna cum laude in 1976 and was offered a position at Morgan State teaching political science and communications and serving as program director of the radio station. As he had earlier, Mfume used the radio to discuss local issues. A caller suggested that, since he seemed to have little faith in Baltimore's city council, he should run for a council seat. Mfume took the suggestion seriously and, in 1978, ran from the Fourth District of Baltimore. Despite the fact that his campaigning had almost no funding, his door-to-door campaigning impressed people, and he was able to narrowly defeat his opponent.

During the next seven years, Mfume served on the Baltimore City Council and, at the same time, attended school, earning a master's degree in liberal arts from Johns Hopkins University in 1984.

Career Highlights

Mfume's "street smarts" were put to good use as a councilman; he knew the city and its problems intimately and became known as someone who fought for his constituents. During his time in office, Mfume introduced legislation requiring the city to divest itself of investments in apartheid South Africa, as well as legislation aiding minority businesses. Then, when Parren Mitchell left his seat in Congress, Mfume entered the race in the Seventh Congressional District.

Mfume faced a crowded field. His opponents pointed out Mfume's past on the streets, his police record, and the fact that he had fathered five sons out of wedlock; but Mfume, in turn, reminded voters that he had turned his life around and that he had a solid legislative record. The advantage of his background was that he knew the problems indigenous to urban areas firsthand and was, as **William Lacy Clay, Sr.**, pointed out in 1992, "an articulate, forthright advocate for the needs of people" (380). Despite the opposition, Mfume was able to pull ahead easily in the polls and win the election.

Mfume assumed his seat in Congress in January, 1987, and was elected deputy whip of the freshman Democrats in the House. During his first month in Congress, he was elected treasurer of the Congressional Black Caucus and, by 1993, would ascend to chairman of the caucus.

Mfume was assigned to a number of committees. Through his committee work and on the floor of the House over the years, Mfume set out to help minority businesses and strengthen civil rights in general. He cosponsored the Americans with Disabilities Act. He sponsored the minority contracting and employment amendments to the Financial Institutions Reform and Recovery Act and was the author of the Minority Business Development Act. He also coauthored the Civil Rights Act of 1991 to include Americans employed in other countries. During his tenure in Congress, he had no fear about challenging other members of Congress and Presidents Reagan, Bush, and Clinton.

With his strong record in Congress, Mfume had little trouble being reelected time and again. He was known in Congress as a vocal, articulate supporter of civil rights, although he would like to have seen more and swifter changes. As he said in an interview in *U.S. News and World Report* in 1996, "It's difficult to bring about the kind of change I want as an individual member of Congress" (Smith 474). So when Mfume was elected to the position of president and chief operating officer of the National Association for the Advancement of Colored People (NAACP) in December of 1995, he resigned his seat in Congress to accept the NAACP's offer. He assumed that position on February 15, 1996.

When Mfume took over the leadership of the NAACP, it was facing a large deficit and declining membership. During his first year, through cutbacks and assiduous fund-raising and membership drives, Mfume was able to erase the debt and increase membership. Since that time, he has expanded the scope of the NAACP's mission to include everyday urban problems, and has reached out to other organizations, creating networks of support. In 1996, the same year he assumed the leadership of the NAACP, he also published his autobiography, written with Ron Stodghill II, *No Free Ride: From the Mean Streets to the Mainstream*, a book that serves as an inspiration for the downtrodden.

Sources

Clay, William L. *Just Permanent Interests: Black Americans in Congress, 1870–1991*. New York: Amistad Press, 1992.

Congressional Black Caucus '93–'94 Guide. <http://www.sas.upenn.edu/African_Studies/Govern_Political/CBC_Guide.html>. Accessed: 3/10/98.

"Kweisi Mfume." *Congressional Times Journal*. <http://www.usbol.com/ctjournal/Bios/kmfume.html>. Accessed: 2/27/98.

"Kweisi Mfume, President and CEO of the NAACP." *NAACP Online*. <http://www.naacp.org/president/kbio.html>. Accessed: 5/12/98.

Mfume, Kweisi, and Ron Stodghill II. *No Free Ride: From the Mean Streets to the Mainstream*. New York: Ballantine, 1996.

"Representative Kweisi Mfume." *Project Vote Smart*. 1995–1998. <http://www.vote-smart.org/congress/104/md/md-rs-a/md-07-ab.html>. Accessed: 5/21/98.

Smith, Jessie Carney, ed. *Black Heroes of the 20th Century*. Detroit, MI: Visible Ink Press, 1998.

Arthur Wergs Mitchell

Reproduced from the Collections of the Library of Congress

Born: December 22, 1883, near Lafayette, Alabama

Status: Died May 9, 1968, in Petersburg, Virginia

Education: Attended Tuskegee Institute, Tuskegee, Alabama; attended Columbia University Law School, New York, New York; admitted to the Washington, D.C., bar, 1927

Position: President, Armstrong Agricultural School, West Butler, Alabama, early 1900s; lawyer, Washington, D.C., 1927–1928; lawyer and real estate investor, Chicago, Illinois, 1928–1942; U.S. representative from the First Congressional District of Illinois, 1935–1943; farmer, Petersburg, Virginia, 1943–1968

Early Years

Arthur Wergs Mitchell was born on December 22, 1883, on a small farm just outside the little town of Lafayette, Alabama. Life was hard for young Mitchell; he was up each day early to do chores and then attend the small schoolhouse for black children where he learned to read and write. He knew he did not want to be a farmer and that education was the best way to accomplish his goals.

Higher Education

In 1897, when he was 14 years old, Mitchell walked and hitchhiked to Booker T. Washington's Tuskegee Institute in Tuskegee, Alabama. He worked as he had at home on the institute's farms and got a job as an office boy for Booker T. Washington to afford his education.

After studying at Tuskegee, Mitchell taught at a number of schools for African Americans and, for a time, served as president of Armstrong Agriculture School in West Butler, Alabama, where he followed the precepts of his mentor, Booker T. Washington. After working a few years, he decided to return to school to study law.

After studying briefly at Columbia University's law school in New York, Mitchell passed the examination for the bar in Washington, D.C., and set up his own law practice in that city. At the same time, Mitchell began to explore politics, working with the Republicans in Washington, who, in 1928, sent him to Chicago to campaign for the presidential bid of Herbert Hoover. Mitchell liked the people and politics of Chicago and decided to relocate there with his wife, Annie.

Career Highlights

Once in Chicago, practicing law and dabbling in real estate, Mitchell saw that the real power in the city lay with the Democrats. The effects of the Great Depression were beginning to be felt across the nation, and many people believed that the Republicans were not doing much to help. Mitchell felt that the remedies being offered by the Democrats, even in the early days of Roosevelt's New Deal, were better than those suggested by the Republicans, so he switched his political allegiance. Mitchell sought the Democratic nomination for U.S. representative from Illinois' First Congressional District, but lost the nomination to Harry Baker, a white man who was an old party favorite. Before the election could be held, however, Baker died and Mitchell was named the Democratic candidate to run against **Oscar Stanton De Priest**, the Republican incumbent.

De Priest had been elected from the mostly Republican First District and had held his congressional seat for a number of years. However, following the Republicans of the House, De Priest voted against various New Deal proposals that would have helped his constituents, thereby disappointing them. Thus, in November of 1934, Arthur Mitchell was easily able to unseat De Priest and win election to the 74th Congress. With his victory over De Priest, Mitchell became the first black Democrat to be elected to Congress.

Although many African Americans in Chicago who had supported Mitchell hoped that he would provide a much-needed voice for them in Congress, he pointed out that nearly 20,000 whites had also voted for him and that he planned to represent his entire district. Mitchell owed his political fortune to the Chicago political "machine," which dictated that he take a conservative track. However, although Mitchell was conservative, he did consider the interests of his black constituents. Less than a month after taking his congressional seat, on January 3, 1935, he introduced an anti-lynching bill to the House. There were a number of such bills before the House that were stronger than Mitchell's proposal, particularly one that was already supported by the NAACP, but his proposal reassured his constituents.

In 1937, an event occurred that was to affect Arthur Mitchell strongly and place his name in history books. While traveling to Hot Springs, Arkansas, from Chicago in April of that year on the Chicago, Rock Island, and Pacific Railroad, Mitchell was forced by a conductor to move from his first-class Pullman compartment to a "Jim Crow" car when the train crossed into Arkansas. According to the suit that Mitchell filed later against the railroad, the conductor called him "vile names too opprobrious and profane, vulgar and filthy to be spread upon the record . . ." (Christopher 181). Mitchell was forced to continue his journey in an old and dirty railroad car reserved for blacks.

Mitchell complained to the Interstate Commerce Commission and sued the Illinois Central and Rock Island Railroads in the Cook County, Illinois, court for $50,000, maintaining that since trains cross state lines, they should not have to abide by the Arkansas law that required "separate but equal" cars for black and white passengers. His case was dismissed by the Illinois federal courts and the Interstate Commerce Commission, so Mitchell appealed to the United States Supreme Court. In *Mitchell v. United States et al.*, the Supreme Court ruled in April, 1941, that black passengers had the right to the same accommodations and treatment accorded white passengers. Mitchell's case was yet another small step toward the equality for which African Americans had been fighting in America, although it would be years before segregation on interstate transportation would be prohibited altogether. As Mitchell said, "It's a step in the destruction of Mr. Jim Crow himself" (Christopher 182).

Mitchell's pursuit of this case and the publicity it received, as well as his increasing support of bills calling for black equality, alienated him from the conservative Chicago Democratic machine. In 1942, when it was time to consider running for reelection, he lost the party's endorsement and faced a primary contest against a conservative candidate from the Democratic Party in Chicago.

Mitchell's wife, Annie, was ill, and Mitchell could see no future in politics in Chicago. Rather than running again for office, he decided to retire to a home that he had built in Virginia. As he said in his farewell speech to Congress, "I go . . . to dedicate anew my life and every bit of energy I possess to working out better understanding between the two races in the South . . ." (Christopher 183).

After his retirement from Congress, Mitchell spent much of his time farming his land in Virginia, lecturing, and traveling about the South in support of such groups as the Southern Regional Council. His wife died soon after their move to Virginia and, in 1947, Mitchell married Clara Smith, a teacher. He continued working to promote a better understanding between the races and, by the time of his death on May 9, 1968, in Petersburg, Virginia, had lived long enough to see the positive results of his work and the work of others manifested in the civil rights movement of the 1950s and 1960s.

Sources

"Black Game." *Time Magazine*, 17 August 1936. *Time Almanac*, Reference Edition. Fort Lauderdale, Fl: Compact Publishing, 1994.

Christopher, Maurine. *America's Black Congressmen*. New York: Thomas Y. Crowell, 1971.

Clay, William L. *Just Permanent Interests: Black Americans in Congress, 1870–1991*. New York: Amistad Press, 1992.

"Former Black Members of Congress." *Congressional Times Journal*. <http://www.usbol.com/ctjournal/FrBlkCongMemList.html>. Accessed: 2/13/98.

Review of *The New Deal's Black Congressman: A Life of Arthur Wergs Mitchell*, by Dennis S. Nordin. <http://www.system.missouri.edu/upress/spring1997/nordin.htm>. Accessed: 2/13/98.

Charles Lewis Mitchell

Born: November 10, 1829, in Hartford, Connecticut

Status: Died April 13, 1912, in Boston, Massachusetts; buried in Dover, Massachusetts

Education: Self-educated

Position: Typesetter, Hartford, Connecticut; printer, *The Liberator*, Boston, Massachusetts, 1853–1863; private, sergeant in the Union army, 1863–1865; representative, Massachusetts General Court, 1866–1867; inspector of customs in Boston, 1869–1877; clerk, customhouse of Boston, 1871–1909

Early Years

Charles Lewis Mitchell was born on November 10, 1829, in Hartford, Connecticut. His family was free and, like so many black persons of the time, keenly aware of the value of education. Mitchell was taught to read and write at an early age, and this ability helped him gain a job as a typesetter at a press in Hartford.

Career Highlights

Seeking greater opportunity, Mitchell moved to Boston, Massachusetts, in 1853 and obtained a job as a printer on William Lloyd Garrison's abolitionist newspaper, *The Liberator*. Mitchell worked for Garrison for 10 years, actively supporting the abolitionist cause both in his work on *The Liberator* and in his own personal actions.

When the Civil War began in 1861, there was little Mitchell could do; at that time, black recruits were not being accepted. In 1863, however, when black regiments were finally being formed, Mitchell, then 33, enlisted as a private in the 55th Massachusetts Infantry. He was transferred from the 55th and stationed at Morris Head, South Carolina, and by 1864 had been promoted to the rank of sergeant overseeing his regiment's printing. Later that year, he was transferred back to the 55th Infantry with which he actively entered battle. On November 30, 1864, he was injured, losing his right foot during a battle at Honey Hill, South Carolina. He spent the remainder of the war in various hospitals and received a disability discharge on October 20, 1865. He was granted a disability pension of nearly $30 a month for the rest of his life.

Returning to Boston, Mitchell saw an opportunity to promote the equality for which he had fought so ardently in the war. He had, according to a contemporary account, the "Stateliest step of the soldier," and had garnered the respect of various Republicans in the city. In November, 1866, after running for the state legislature with little opposition, Mitchell was elected to a one-year term in the Massachusetts General Court (the lower house of the legislature). When he took his seat, he became the first black state representative in the United States.

Mitchell was sworn in with Edward G. Walker, another African American who had won election. The two men kept up a friendly argument for years over who was actually the first black man to serve in a state legislature, although most accounts accord that honor to Mitchell. While Mitchell's term of office lasted only a year, he and Walker spoke often in the legislature on the need for equality between the races.

When his term expired, Mitchell kept his hand in local politics and was rewarded in April, 1869, with an appointment as an inspector of customs in Boston. In 1871, he was promoted to the position of clerk in the customhouse of Boston, a job he would hold until his retirement in 1899 at the age of 70.

To the end of his life, Mitchell held the respect of many. In 1879, he had the honor of being one of the pallbearers at William Lloyd Garrison's funeral. During the Spanish-American War (1898), Mitchell recruited black men to form Company L to fight in the war.

After his retirement, Mitchell led a quiet life with his wife, Nellis Brown Mitchell, at their home in Boston; they had no children. It was there, on April 13, 1912, that Charles Mitchell died of apoplexy.

Sources

Christopher, Maurine. *America's Black Congressmen.* New York: Thomas Y. Crowell, 1971.

Kestenbaum, Lawrence. *Political Graveyard: A Database of Historical Cemeteries*, rev. Jan. 13, 1998. <http://www.potifos.com/tpg.html>. Accessed: 1/17/98.

Logan, Rayford W., and Michael R. Winston, eds. *Dictionary of American Negro Biography*. New York: W.W. Norton and Co., 1982.

Ploski, Harry A., and James Williams, eds. *The Negro Almanac: A Reference Work on the African American*. Detroit, MI: Gale Research, 1989.

Parren James Mitchell

Reproduced from the Collections of the Library of Congress

Born: April 29, 1922, in Baltimore, Maryland

Status: Retired

Education: Graduate, 1940, Douglass High School, Baltimore, Maryland; B.A., 1950, Morgan State College, Baltimore, Maryland; M.A., 1952, University of Maryland, Baltimore

Position: Commissioned officer, 92nd Infantry, U.S. Army, 1942–1946; instructor of sociology, Morgan State College, Baltimore, Maryland, 1953–1954; supervisor of probation, Supreme Bench of Baltimore City, Baltimore, Maryland, 1954–1957; executive secretary, Maryland Human Relations Commissions, 1963–1965; director, Baltimore Community Action Agency, Baltimore, Maryland, 1965–1968; professor of sociology and assistant director, Urban Affairs Institute, Morgan State University, Baltimore, Maryland, 1968– ; president, Baltimore Neighborhoods, Inc., 1969; U.S. representative from the Seventh Congressional District of Maryland, 1971–1987; chairman, Minority Business Enterprise Legal Defense and Education Fund, Washington, D.C., 1980s–1990s

Early Years

Parren James Mitchell was born in Baltimore, Maryland, on April 29, 1922. At that time, Baltimore had a large African American community and schools were segregated. Mitchell, a quiet, studious young man, did well in school and, in 1940, graduated from Douglass High School with plans to attend college. However, World War II intervened and Mitchell was drafted. In the army, Mitchell's intelligence again shone, and he was commissioned an officer and company commander with the 92nd Infantry Division.

Higher Education

When Mitchell was discharged in 1946, he continued his education as he had planned. Enrolling in Morgan State College, in Baltimore, he received his bachelor's degree in 1950. He then enrolled at the University of Maryland, receiving a master's degree in 1952, and decided to teach on the college level where he felt he could positively influence young people.

Career Highlights

Parren Mitchell began teaching at his alma mater, Morgan State College, in 1953 and, in 1954, accepted a job as supervisor of probation for the Supreme Bench of Baltimore City, a position he would hold until 1957. With civil rights becoming an important issue in the late 1950s, Mitchell wanted to contribute more directly, and in 1963 he accepted the position of executive secretary of the Maryland Human Relations Commission. One of the functions of this commission was to oversee the implementation of Maryland's public accommodations law. In 1965, he became director of Baltimore's Community Action Agency, which oversaw the city's anti-poverty program. In 1968, he returned to his teaching at Morgan State College, where he was named professor of sociology and assistant director of the college's Urban Affairs Institute.

The same year that Mitchell returned to teaching, he also began actively to enter politics. Although he had many political connections because of the positions he had held, he had never run for office; but in 1968, he challenged Congressman Samuel N. Friedel in a Democratic primary for Friedel's seat from the Seventh District of Maryland. The Seventh District had a large Jewish population, and Friedel had represented them for nearly 20 years. With the backing of the Jewish population, Friedel easily defeated Mitchell in the primary and went on to win reelection to Congress.

Having swum in political waters, Mitchell was not about to give up so easily. He continued his teaching and community work in the city. In 1969, he was named president of Baltimore Neighborhoods, Inc., and the following year decided to challenge Friedel again.

The campaign of 1970 was far different from that of 1968. Although Friedel was Jewish, running in a heavily Jewish district, Mitchell was not his only challenger. Friedel was also challenged from within the Jewish community by a Democrat, Carl Friedler. Friedel and Friedler waged a no-holds-barred campaign that virtually ignored Mitchell. When the votes were tallied, however, their battle had caused a split in the votes and the election of Mitchell by the tiniest of margins. In the general election, Mitchell fared better, beating his Republican opponent, Peter Parker, by nearly 20,000 votes. When Parren Mitchell was sworn into Congress on January 3, 1971, he became the first black congressman from the state of Maryland.

Mitchell was named to the Budget and Banking and Urban Affairs Committees and, later, to the Committee on Small Business. Eventually, in 1981, he would become chairman of this latter committee. As he had in Baltimore, and would throughout his career in Congress, Mitchell worked to support legislation that would help minorities and young people. He supported the creation of additional summer jobs for young people, strongly backed the Small Business Administration, and opposed establishing a sub-minimum wage for people 18 and younger.

The year that Mitchell took his seat in Congress, 12 other African Americans had been elected to the House. With this many seats, they felt they had a chance to influence legislation if they were organized. As a result of this thinking, the Congressional Black Caucus came into being, with Mitchell as one of its founding members. The caucus hoped at that time to force President Richard Nixon into better enforcement of civil rights legislation, and over the years the caucus has tackled a variety of issues that have affected minorities throughout the United States.

It was also during his time as congressman that Mitchell had an unexpected influence on a young man who would later sit in his seat in the House. While in Baltimore, Mitchell encountered a black youth lounging on a street corner. After a conversation with him, Mitchell told the young man to "stop being part of the problem and to start becoming part of the solution" (Smith 473). The young man was **Kweisi Mfume**. Taking Mitchell's words to heart, he did indeed change his life and even forged a successful career in politics.

In 1972, when Mitchell faced his first run for reelection in the House, the campaign was vastly different than those he had waged in 1968 and 1970. During the two years Mitchell had been in office, Maryland had redrawn its district boundaries, as is required every 10 years according to census results. The Seventh Congressional District now held a majority of black voters, and Mitchell had no difficulty being reelected, nor would he encounter any serious challenges for the next 14 years. In 1986, when he announced he would retire from office, Mitchell did so voluntarily, not because there was any threat from a contender for his seat in the House. Kweisi Mfume, the young man Mitchell had inspired, then ran successfully for Mitchell's vacant seat.

After Mitchell stepped down from office in 1987, at the age of 65, he turned his attention to supporting community and business causes in Maryland. He was also named chairman of the Minority Business Enterprise Legal Defense and Education Fund, based in Washington, D.C. In March of 1996, Mitchell suffered a severe heart attack. Since that time, he has retired from many of his activities, although he still supports a variety of causes.

Sources

Clay, William L. *Just Permanent Interests: Black Americans in Congress, 1870–1991*. New York: Amistad Press, 1992.

"Former Black Members of Congress." Parren James Mitchell." *Congressional Times Journal*. <http://www.usbol.com/ctjournal/FrBlkCongMemList.html>. Accessed: 2/21/98.

"Mitchell Suffers Stroke." *Congressional Times Journal*, rev. 8 March 1996. <http://www.usbol.com/ctjournal/Mitchellstroke.html>. Accessed: 4/14/98.

Smith, Jessie Carney, ed. *Black Heroes of the 20th Century*. Detroit, MI: Visible Ink Press, 1998.

Carol Moseley-Braun

Courtesy of the Office of Senator Carol Moseley-Braun

Born: August 16, 1947, in Chicago, Illinois

Status: Education advisor, U.S. Department of Education

Education: B.A., 1967, University of Illinois, Chicago, Illinois; J.D., 1972, University of Chicago law school, Chicago, Illinois

Position: Legal intern, associate attorney, Chicago, Illinois, c. 1970–1973; assistant U.S. attorney, Chicago, Illinois, 1974–1977; state representative, Illinois State Legislature, 1978–1988; radio talk show host, WXOL, Chicago, Illinois, 1980s; recorder of deeds, Chicago, Illinois, 1988–1992; U.S. senator from Illinois, 1993–1998; advisor, U.S. Department of Education, 1999–

Awards and honors: Best Legislator Award, 1980, 1982, Independent Voters of Illinois

Early Years

Carol Moseley-Braun was born on August 16, 1947, in Chicago, Illinois. Her father, Joseph Moseley, was a policeman, and her mother, Edna A. Davie Moseley, was a medical technician. With two incomes, the Moseley family was economically comfortable, but emotionally, the family was in turmoil. Joseph Moseley frequently took out the stresses of his job on the family, beating his wife and children. When Moseley-Braun was 16, her mother divorced her father. Joseph moved to California, and Edna took the children and moved in with her mother. While the family had emotional security from within, they faced economic hardship and violence from without, living for two years in a poverty-ridden, crime-filled black neighborhood in Chicago known as the "Bucket of Blood" (Smith 482).

Even after moving from this neighborhood, Moseley-Braun felt its effects. She said later in the *Washington Post*, "When you get a chance to see people who are really trapped and don't have options and you've got all these blessings, you've got to be a pretty ungrateful person not to want to do something" (Smith 482).

Higher Education

After graduating from high school, Moseley-Braun went on to the University of Illinois at Chicago, graduating in 1967. She then entered the University of Chicago School of Law and clerked as a legal intern to earn money for school. In 1972, she graduated with a degree in law, and the following year married Michael Braun, a white law student whom she had met at the law school.

Career Highlights

After graduating, Moseley-Braun worked as an associate attorney for a year. Then, in 1974, she entered public life, working as an assistant U.S. attorney for the northern district of Illinois. This position taught her a great deal about how government functions, and in 1977 she decided to run for public office. She won a seat in the Illinois legislature from the 25th District of Illinois, the Hyde Park area of Chicago.

During her 10-year tenure in the state legislature, Moseley-Braun proved to be an effective and vocal legislator. She quickly became known as an ardent supporter of civil rights and education legislation. She also supported efforts to ban government investments in South Africa. In 1980 and 1982, she was awarded the Best Legislator Award by the Independent Voters of Illinois, and in 1983 **Harold Washington**, Chicago's mayor, designated her his floor leader in the House. In 1986, Moseley-Braun made a bid for the lieutenant governorship of Illinois but, according to the *Washington Post*, was blocked from the position by Harold Washington.

After a year of confronting a number of upheavals in her personal life—her mother became ill, her brother died from drug and alcohol abuse, and she and her husband divorced—Moseley-Braun successfully ran for recorder of deeds/registrar of titles for Cook County, becoming the first black woman elected to an executive position in the county. During her time in this position, she effectively reorganized and increased the efficiency of the office, which managed a budget of $8 million.

In 1991, however, an event occurred that changed the course of Moseley-Braun's career. That year, Illinois state senator Alan J. Dixon cast one of the deciding votes to confirm **Clarence Thomas**, who had been accused of sexual harassment by attorney Anita Hill, as associate justice of the United States Supreme Court. As the *Congressional Quarterly Weekly Report* noted, "The vote enraged liberal activists, including feminists who urged Moseley-Braun—considered a rising star in Democratic circles—to risk the contest" (Benenson 740).

Dixon was entrenched in the Senate, not having lost an election in 42 years. He was challenged in the primary by both Moseley-Braun and Al Hofeld, a wealthy Chicago lawyer. Many felt that Moseley-Braun, whose campaign was woefully underfinanced, had little chance against either Dixon or Hofeld. Dixon had his years of experience and the backing of the Democratic machine in Illinois; Hofeld had money. Dixon spent much of his campaign countering claims by Hofeld that Dixon was a part of a Congress "corrupted by business special interests" (Benenson 740). Hofeld spent more than $4 million in commercials attacking Dixon. Dixon, in turn,

> spent more than $1 million, [and] mostly responded in kind with a barrage of ads aimed at tarnishing the little-known Hofeld. Dixon cast Hofeld as a rich dilettante trying to buy a Senate seat . . . But even as Dixon cast doubt on his upstart challenger, he diminished the "hail fellow" image that had been the basis of his popularity. (Benenson 740)

Moseley-Braun, meanwhile, running an underfinanced campaign—she spent less than $500,000—went directly to the voters for support. Reminding black voters of her years in the legislature, during which she had supported human rights, she also appealed to women, condemning Dixon's support of Clarence Thomas. In the final week of the primary campaign, a televised debate between Dixon, Hofeld, and Moseley-Braun clinched the victory for her. While Dixon and Hofeld vituperously attacked one another, Moseley-Braun focused on the issues, coming across as knowledgeable and confident. In the election, Moseley-Braun won 47 percent of the vote in Cook County and finished strongly in other areas, defeating both Dixon and Hofeld. In the general election, Moseley-Braun faced Republican Rich Williamson, also an attorney, and easily won, becoming the first black woman to be elected to the United States Senate.

Moseley-Braun's first term in the Senate was not without criticism. Called a "symbolic senator," her campaign was investigated for keeping poor records on donations. She was also harshly condemned by fellow Democrats when she visited Nigeria's military leader, General Sani Abacha, who had been accused of human rights violations. In Chicago, her popularity fell with constituents when she endorsed legislation to try teens as adults, and when she supported Richard M. Daley over two black contenders for the office of mayor of Chicago.

She achieved national attention, however, with her vehement opposition to Senator Jesse Helms of North Carolina when he proposed to renew the patent on the United Daughters of the Confederacy flag insignia. Speaking with deep emotion, Moseley-Braun condemned the proposal, saying, "This vote is about race . . . and the single most painful episode in American history . . .[The Confederate flag] has no place in our modern time . . . no place in this body . . . no place in our society" (Smith 486).

Moseley-Braun faced a tough campaign for reelection, and was defeated in the fall of 1998. Yet even her detractors admit that she had some victories during her term in the Senate. Moseley-Braun made history when she took her seat and, as she said, showed "the way for our entire country to the future" (Smith 482). After her defeat, she was appointed an advisor to the U.S. Department of Education on a part-time basis by U.S. secretary of education Richard W. Riley.

Sources

Benenson, Bob. "Incumbent Tremors in Illinois." *Congressional Quarterly Weekly Report*, 21 March 1992, 739–44.

Estell, Kenneth. *African America: Celebrating 400 Years of Achievement*. Detroit, MI: Visible Ink Press, 1994.

"Former Sen. Carol Moseley-Braun to Become Education Advisor." *AP News Service*, 1999. <http://abcnews.go.com/wire/US/AP19990106_174.html>. Accessed: 1/8/99.

"National Elections '98." *The Washington Post*, 4 November 1998. <http://elections98.washingtonpost.com/wp.siv/results98/national/>. Accessed: 11/19/98.

Smith, Jessie Carney, ed. *Black Heroes of the 20th Century*. Detroit, MI: Visible Ink Press, 1998.

Constance Baker Motley

Reproduced from UPI/Corbis-Bettmann

Born: September 14, 1921, in New Haven, Connecticut

Status: Senior U.S. district judge, Southern District of New York

Education: Graduate, with honors, New Haven High School, 1939; attended Fisk University, Nashville, Tennessee, 1941–1942; B.A. in economics, 1943, New York University, New York, New York; LL.B., 1946, Columbia Law School, Columbia University, New York, New York; recipient of more than 20 honorary degrees from various colleges and universities

Position: Employed by the National Youth Administration, 1930s; law clerk for Thurgood Marshall, chief counsel of the Legal Defense and Education Fund, National Association for the Advancement of Colored People (NAACP), 1946–1950; associate counsel, NAACP Legal Defense and Education Fund, 1950–1964; senator, New York State Senate, 1964–1965; president, Borough of Manhattan, New York, New York, 1965–1969; appointed judge of the U.S.

District Court for the Southern District of New York by President Lyndon B. Johnson, 1966; chief judge, U.S. District Court for the Southern District of New York, 1982–1990; senior judge, U.S. District Court for the Southern District of New York, 1990–

Early Years

Constance Baker Motley was born in New Haven, Connecticut, on September 14, 1921. Her parents, Willoughby Alva Baker and Rachel Huggins Baker, were born and raised on the Caribbean island of Nevis and immigrated to the United States before Motley was born. Willoughby Baker worked as a chef in one of the fraternities at Yale University in New Haven. Although the black community in New Haven was small at the time of Motley's birth, she grew up with a strong sense of her heritage. The minister in the Episcopal church her family attended gave history lessons in Sunday school.

Motley went to the public schools in New Haven, entering New Haven High School at the age of 15. Several incidents during these years shaped Motley's views on civil rights. On one occasion, Motley and a group of young black people went to Bridgeport, Connecticut, for a picnic and roller skating. But they were refused admittance to the roller-skating rink because of their color. Another time, she and some friends went to Milford, Connecticut, to swim and were denied admittance to the public beach because of their race. These incidents led Motley not only to believe firmly in racial equality, but also to involve herself in civil rights at an early age. While still in high school, Motley became president of the New Haven Youth Council and secretary of the New Haven Adult Community Council, both formed to promote racial equality.

Higher Education

After graduation from high school, Motley worked for the National Youth Administration (NYA), one of Franklin Roosevelt's New Deal programs. The NYA was organized to help young men and women who had left school, furnishing part-time clerical work in academic offices and granting funds to help them continue their education. Motley had sought the job because, with the Depression at its height and her father unable to help, it looked as if it would be impossible for her to continue her education. As Motley said in her "Some Recollections of My Career," her parents "thought I should be a hairdresser. I even thought I should be an interior decorator when I was in the eighth grade" (Smith 779).

After working for more than a year with the NYA, however, Clarence Blakeslee, a successful contractor whom she had met in the course of her work, was so impressed by her intelligence and skills that he offered to fund her education. In February of 1941, Motley entered Fisk University and attended for a year before transferring to New York University, where she studied economics and graduated with a bachelor's degree in 1943. She immediately entered law school, receiving her degree in law in 1946. That same year, she married Joel Wilson Motley, who was an insurance broker. On May 13, 1952, they would have a son, Joel, who would follow in his mother's footsteps by studying law at Harvard University Law School.

Career Highlights

During her final year in law school, Motley searched for a job, but the racial inequities she had encountered as a girl were still a barrier. As she recounts,

> My first job interview was an accurate sign of the times . . . When I appeared for my interview, a balding middle-aged white male appeared at a door leading to the reception room where I was standing. The receptionist had not even asked me to have a seat. Even after the door to the reception room quickly closed, she still did not invite me to sit down. She knew as well as I that the interview was over. (Hine 823)

Experiences such as this only strengthened Motley's determination to work for civil rights, and she did find a job that suited her perfectly.

Motley had heard of an opening for a law clerk with the National Association for the Advancement of Colored People (NAACP). When she went for an interview, she met **Thurgood Marshall**, for whom she would be working. At the time, Marshall was chief counsel for the NAACP's Legal Defense and Education Fund. During their interview and after, Marshall encouraged Motley to pursue her dreams, telling her stories of other successful black women. She later recounted that "Over the years, he told me about every successful African-American woman he encountered" (Hine 823).

Motley's work involved a great deal of research, and Marshall urged her to take the New York bar exam so that she could use the New York City Bar Association library; she easily passed the examination. Her work also involved a great deal of travel, particularly after she was promoted to associate counsel for the Legal Defense and Education Fund in 1950. "During the course of my work with the NAACP . . . I traveled around the country trying school and other kinds of desegregation cases. One of the early cases in which I appeared as a trial lawyer was a case in Mississippi [*Bates v. Batte*], involving the equalization of black teachers' salaries . . ." (Smith 780). Motley was at the center of things during one of the most significant periods for civil rights in the history of the United States. In 1954, she would help write the briefs filed for the landmark case of *Brown v. Board of Education of Topeka, Kansas*, in which the Supreme Court declared school segregation and the "separate but equal" statutes regarding education unconstitutional. As Motley later wrote, "The *Brown* decision was the catalyst which changed our society from a closed society to an open society and created the momentum for other minority groups to establish public interest law firms to secure their rights" (Smith 780).

Motley's involvement in civil rights cases only increased during the turbulent 1960s. She personally argued cases against the Universities of Mississippi, Georgia, and Alabama, and Clemson College in South Carolina. Because of her legal skills in such landmark civil rights cases, Motley was becoming a well-known figure. In 1964, she was asked to run for the New York State Senate to fill the unexpired term of state senator James Watson. With her election in February of that year, she made history, becoming the first black woman to be elected to a senate seat in New York State.

While in the New York State Senate, Motley continued her push for civil rights, arguing for equality in employment, housing, and education. In February of the following year, however, she was elected to the position of Manhattan Borough president in a special election and stepped down from the senate to take that position. Although black men had been elected to this position, Motley was the first woman to hold the office of borough president.

Because of the public nature of the cases Motley had tried over the years, in 1966, then-attorney general Ramsey Clark suggested to President Lyndon Johnson that Motley be nominated to fill a vacancy on the Federal Court of Appeals for the Second Circuit. However, "the opposition to my appointment," Motley later wrote, "was so great, apparently because I was a woman, that Johnson had to withdraw my name" (Hine 824). Johnson then nominated Motley as a U.S. district judge to the United States District Court for the Southern District of New York. Although this, too, met with opposition on the federal level, Motley did receive the votes necessary from the Senate and was sworn in in August of 1966, becoming the first African American woman to be appointed to a federal judgeship. As always, Motley was forced to battle against sexism:

> When I was introduced as a new judge at a Second Circuit Judicial Conference, the master of ceremonies said, "And now

> I want to introduce Connie Motley who is doing such a good job on the District Court." In contrast, everyone else was introduced with a full-blown curriculum vitae. (Hine 824)

In 1982, Motley was appointed chief judge of the Southern District of New York and, in 1990, became senior U.S. district judge of that district, one of the largest in the nation, where she continues to serve.

Over the years, Motley has received recognition and honors from many quarters. She has received more than 20 honorary degrees from various colleges and universities. In 1965, she received the Elizabeth Blackwell Award from Hobart and William Smith College. Her alma mater, Columbia Law School, presented her with its Medal for Excellence in 1987, and the New York State Bar Association awarded her its Gold Medal Award in 1988. Most recently, in 1995, she was the recipient of the New York Women's Bar Association's 12th Florence E. Allen Award.

In both her speeches and her writings, Motley continues the struggle for equality, urging young African Americans to become involved, particularly in law. As she said in 1992,

> Lawyers are natural leaders and activists in the black community. More and more blacks will become involved in policy-making agencies, in government, in politics, in business and diplomacy—in areas where blacks have not been before and where decisions and changes are going to be made. (Smith 781)

Sources

Hine, Darlene Clark, ed. *Black Women in America: An Historical Encyclopedia*, Vol. II, M–Z. Brooklyn, NY: Carlson Publishing Co., 1993.

"Law Alumna Motley Given Allen Award." *Columbia University Record*, 9 June 1995. <http://www.columbia.edu/cu/record/record2031.22html>. Accessed: 3/11/98.

Smith, Jessie Carney, ed. *Notable Black American Women*, Vol. 1. Detroit, MI: Gale Research, 1992.

N

Robert Nelson Cornelius Nix, Sr.

Reproduced from AP/Wide World Photos

Born: August 9, 1905, in Orangeburg, South Carolina

Status: Died June 22, 1987, in Philadelphia, Pennsylvania

Education: Graduate, Townsend Harris High School, New York, New York; graduate, 1921, Lincoln University, Chester County, Pennsylvania; law degree, 1924, University of Pennsylvania Law School, Philadelphia

Position: Lawyer, Nix and Nix, Philadelphia, Pennsylvania, 1925–c. 1958; elected committeeman of the 44th Ward, Philadelphia, Pennsylvania, 1932; special deputy attorney general, Pennsylvania Department of Revenue, and special assistant deputy attorney general, Commonwealth of Pennsylvania, 1934–1938; U.S. representative from the Second Congressional District of Pennsylvania, 1958–1979; committeeman of the 32nd Ward, Philadelphia, Pennsylvania, 1979–1987

Early Years

Robert Nelson Cornelius Nix was born in Orangeburg, South Carolina, on August 9, 1905. His father, Nelson Nix, had been a slave who, upon gaining his freedom, had devoted himself to education; he earned a doctorate in mathematics and eventually became the dean of faculty at South Carolina State College in Orangeburg.

Feeling that his son would not receive an adequate education in Orangeburg, Nelson Nix and his wife Sylvia decided to send him to New York City for most of his education. In the early 1900s, schools in the South were segregated and the quality of education in the black schools was often poor. So Robert Nix traveled north and lived with relatives in New York, where he attended Townsend Harris High School.

Higher Education

Upon graduation from Townsend Harris High School, Nix entered Lincoln University in Chester County, Pennsylvania. As an undergraduate, he was an outstanding student and captain of the football team. Nix graduated from Lincoln in 1921 and entered the University of Pennsylvania Law School, graduating in 1924 and establishing a law practice in Philadelphia the following year.

Career Highlights

Almost from the start of his professional career, Nix involved himself in politics. In 1932, he was elected committeeman from the 44th Ward of Philadelphia and, from 1934 until 1938, served as a special deputy attorney general in the Department of Revenue of the Commonwealth of Pennsylvania, then as a special assistant deputy attorney general.

Earlier, he had married Ethel Lanier and they had had one son, Robert Nix, Jr., who would join his father in the law firm and, in January of 1968, receive an appointment to a judgeship in Philadelphia. Professionally, Nix was occupied with the business of his law firm, which was doing well, and with his duties as committeeman. Then in 1958, he was approached by the white-run Philadelphia Democratic political machine to run for office in a predominantly black congressional district in Philadelphia. The previous holder of that office, Representative Earl Chudoff, had decided to step down to accept a position as judge in Philadelphia. During the fall of 1957, a special election was held to fill the remainder of Chudoff's term in Congress, and Nix was able to defeat Republican Cecil Moore, taking his seat in the 86th Congress on May 20, 1958.

When Nix entered Congress, there were only three other black representatives: **William Levi Dawson** of Illinois; **Adam Clayton Powell, Jr.,** of New York; and **Charles Coles Diggs, Jr.,** of Michigan. In some ways, Nix was a disappointment to the others. Civil rights issues were becoming crucial in the eyes of these black legislators, but Nix did not share their need to promote a "national black agenda" (Clay 90). Nix himself stated that he was a "congressman first, a Democrat second, and a black third" (Clay 90). Although consistently reelected to his seat during the next 20 years, Nix continually had to confront charges that his interests lay only with the white political machine of Philadelphia, as well as charges of absenteeism. Yet he was a strong supporter of the 1964 Civil Rights Bill allowing equal access to public accommodations and supporting school desegregation. Similarly, a year earlier, when black activists were organizing the March on Washington, Nix spoke in support of the march, quelling other legislators' fears that it would result in riots and bloodshed, and asking Congress to

> examine your attitudes toward the August 28 march in terms of the total cause of which that event is only a symbol. I urge you to take into consideration the fact that all man's civil and personal rights are of paramount importance at present; that they are not . . . subject to being rationed at the will of some so-called master group. I ask you to accept the inevitable; not because it is inevitable . . .but because it is right and no other course will protect the Negro or the Nation's future. (Christopher 217)

During his time in office, Nix served on the Veterans Affairs Committee, Foreign Affairs Committee, and the Committee on Merchant Marine and Fisheries. In 1977, he was elected chairman of the Committee on the Post Office and Civil Service, becoming the third African American to chair a standing committee of the House of Representatives.

Nix's election to the chair of the Post Office and Civil Service Committee was not without strong opposition. A number of younger, white members of the committee contended that, at 68, he was too old for the position and unfit for it because of his "record of inactivity" (Clay 91). However, the Congressional Black Caucus, a group formed earlier by black congressional members, came to Nix's defense and succeeded in having him elected to the position. Unfortunately, they came to believe that their support had been somewhat misplaced. As former representative **William Lacy Clay, Jr.,** wrote, "I never dreamed . . . that he would totally abdicate his authority and surrender the power vested in a chairman . . . His election as chairman accrued no particular benefits to those of us struggling to increase the power of blacks in the House" (Clay 91). Nix's term as chairman was characterized by neglect, Clay asserted; Nix did not exert himself to wield the authority he had been given and, in the eyes of the Black Caucus, allowed himself to be manipulated both by the white members of the committee and by President Carter, who was calling for changes in the Civil Service laws that would effectively reduce job security. Since many African Americans held Civil Service positions, opposing Carter's plans was of key importance to the Black Caucus.

During his time in office, although he alienated many fellow black members of Congress, Nix did accomplish a number of things. In 1967, he came to the defense of Adam Clayton Powell, Jr., when Congress voted to deny Powell his seat. In 1975, he led an investigation on the misuse of funds by defense contractors, and he later introduced an amendment requiring the Defense Department to submit to Congress information on the names and fees paid to agents negotiating arms sales for American arms manufacturers.

In 1976, Nix had been challenged in his run for reelection by Democrat **William H. Gray III** of Philadelphia and had barely survived a primary, winning reelection against his Republican opponent. But Gray was young and bright, and as an ordained minister, he presented an example of the kind of moral leadership for which people were searching. In 1978, when Nix again came up for reelection, despite the fact that he was the senior black congressman in the United States, he could not rally the support he needed to seize the nomination from Gray for election to an 11th term. Finishing his term in March of 1979, Nix returned to his law firm and to local politics. He was elected committeeman of the 32nd Ward in Philadelphia, a post he retained until his death on June 22, 1987.

Although Nix often infuriated the more radical black members of Congress with his conservative stances and frequent inattention to his duties, his more than 20 years in Congress allowed him to serve often as the voice of moderation, placating white members of Congress, especially during the turbulent years of the civil rights marches and protests. As he himself urged in one speech, "Let us exercise the dignity, the statesmanship, the rationality of a great race of people . . ." (Christopher 220).

Sources

Christopher, Maurine. *America's Black Congressmen.* New York: Thomas Y. Crowell, 1971.

Clay, William L. *Just Permanent Interests: Black Americans in Congress, 1870–1991.* New York: Amistad Press, 1992.

"Former Black Members of Congress." *Congressional Times Journal.* <http://www.usbol.com/ctjournal/FrBlkCongMemList.html>. Accessed: 2/18/98.

Eleanor Holmes Norton

Courtesy of the Office of Congresswoman Eleanor Holmes Norton

Born: June 13, 1937, in Washington, D.C.

Status: Congressional representative for the District of Columbia

Education: B.A., 1960, Antioch College, Yellow Springs, Ohio; M.A. in American studies, 1963, Yale University, New Haven, Connecticut; J.D., 1965, Yale University, New Haven, Connecticut; recipient of more than 60 honorary degrees from various colleges and universities

Position: Lawyer, assistant director, American Civil Liberties Union, New York, New York, 1965–1970; head, New York City Commission on Human Rights, New York, New York, 1970–1977; chairperson, Equal Employment Opportunity Commission, 1977–1981; senior fellow, Urban Institute, Washington, D.C.; professor of law, Georgetown University, Washington, D.C., 1982–; congressional representative for the District of Columbia, 1991–

Early Years

Eleanor Holmes Norton was born on June 13, 1937, in Washington, D.C. Growing up in the nation's capital and going to its segregated schools gave Norton a keen sense of the injustice of segregation and discrimination.

Higher Education

After finishing high school, Norton entered Antioch College in Ohio, graduating in 1960. She then entered Yale University where she worked simultaneously on a master's degree in American studies and a degree in law. It was during this time that she joined the Student Nonviolent Coordinating Committee (SNCC) and, like so many other African Americans at that time, worked for desegregation and equality in the civil rights movement. She participated in the Mississippi Freedom Democratic Party and, in 1963, was a member of the national staff of the March on Washington.

That same year, 1963, Norton completed her master's degree at Yale and, in 1965, received her degree in law. Since her graduation, Yale Graduate School has awarded her the Yale Wilbur Cross Medal as an Outstanding Alumnus, and Yale Law School has awarded her its Citation of Merit in recognition for the work she has done since leaving school.

Career Highlights

In 1965, Norton accepted a position with the American Civil Liberties Union (ACLU) in New York City. Some of the cases that she handled during her years with the ACLU caused controversy, particularly among her African American friends, because she was a staunch defender of the Constitution. In 1968, as a lawyer for the ACLU, she was called upon to represent former Alabama governor George Wallace, who was known for his racial bias. Wallace had been denied permission to hold a political rally at Shea Stadium in New York City and had called upon the ACLU to defend him. After her successful defense of Wallace, Holmes was named assistant director of the ACLU of New York City.

In 1970, Holmes left the ACLU to accept the position of head of New York City's Commission on Human Rights. She was appointed by Mayor John V. Lindsay and received national attention in the position. In 1977, President Jimmy Carter offered her the appointment of chairperson of the U.S. Equal Employment Opportunity Commission (EEOC), a post she held until 1981 when President Ronald Reagan took office. During this time, the *Ladies Home Journal* named her one of the 100 most important women in America, and *Washington Magazine* listed her as one of the most powerful women in Washington (*Congressional Black Caucus*).

When Norton took over the EEOC, it was a morass of mismanagement. Within two years, however, she had untangled the bureaucratic red tape and transformed it into an efficient and productive agency, increasing its productivity by 65 percent (Hine 886).

After leaving office when Carter stepped down from the presidency, Norton first worked as a senior fellow at the Urban Institute then, in 1982, accepted the position of professor of law at Georgetown University in Washington, D.C. In 1990, she decided to seek elective office, running for congressional representative from the District of Columbia. As delegate from Washington, D.C., Norton was denied a vote in the House even though she could vote in committee, a situation she set out to change. In 1993, she initiated a debate in the House on the issue of statehood for the District that emphasized the lack of democratic participation that Washington, D.C., has in the national government. As a result of this and other discussions, Norton won the right to vote on the House floor in the Committee of the Whole for the first time in the history of the District of Columbia ("Congresswoman Eleanor Holmes Norton"). In 1995, however, when the majority of power shifted to the Republicans, the vote was reversed, "an injustice she strives to reverse for her constituents who are the only Americans to pay federal taxes without full representation . . ." ("Congresswoman Eleanor Holmes Norton"). During her first term in office, Norton also was able to increase the amount of federal funds to the District of Columbia. In addition, she threw her support behind passage of the Civil Rights Act of 1991, and expanded police protection in Washington.

In 1992, Norton successfully ran for reelection under the slogan "Full Rights to Match Our Full Responsibilities." During the 103rd Congress, Norton was elected chair of the Post Office and Civil Service Subcommittee and chair of the District of Columbia Subcommittee on Judiciary and Education, becoming the first second-term member of Congress to chair two subcommittees. She also became the first delegate from the District of Columbia to serve on a joint committee of Congress.

Now in her fifth term in Congress, Norton continues to fight for full representation for the District of Columbia. In addition to serving on the boards of a number of corporations and nonprofit foundations, Norton also continues to teach at Georgetown University. She is married to Edward Norton and has two children, Katherine and John.

Sources

Congressional Black Caucus '93–'94 Guide. <http://www.sas.upenn.edu/African_Studies/Govern_Political/CBC_Guide.html>. Accessed: 3/10/98.

"Congresswoman Eleanor Holmes Norton." *U.S. House of Representatives*. <http://www.house.gov/norton/bio.htm>. Accessed: 3/11/98.

"Eleanor Holmes Norton." *Georgetown Law School*, rev. 8 August 1997. <http://www.law.georgetown.edu/faculty/vitas/norton.html>. Accessed: 5/7/98.

Estell, Kenneth. *African America: Celebrating 400 Years of Achievement*. Detroit, MI: Visible Ink Press, 1994.

Hine, Darlene Clark, ed. *Black Women in America: An Historical Encyclopedia*, Vol. I, A–L. Brooklyn, NY: Carlson Publishing Co., 1993.

O

James Edward O'Hara

Courtesy of Regenstein Library, University of Chicago

Born: February 26, 1844, in New York, New York

Status: Died September 15, 1905, in New Bern, North Carolina; buried at Greenwood Cemetery, New Bern, North Carolina

Education: Attended law classes, Howard University, Washington, D.C., 1860s; admitted to the bar of North Carolina, 1873

Position: Schoolteacher, c. 1860; delegate and embossing clerk, North Carolina constitutional convention, 1868; representative, North Carolina State Legislature, 1868–1869; lawyer, Enfield, North Carolina, 1973–c. 1882; elected chairman, Halifax Board of Commissioners, 1973; U.S. representative from the Second Congressional District of North Carolina, 1883–1887; lawyer, New Bern, North Carolina, 1888–1905

Early Years

James Edward O'Hara was born in New York, New York, on February 26, 1844. According to various sources, his father was an Irish seaman, and his mother a black woman from the West Indies. Little is known of his youth; the family moved to the West Indies in 1850, and O'Hara presumably grew up and obtained some schooling there. He could read and write and had enough learning so that sometime before the Civil War ended, when he came to the United States and settled in North Carolina, he became a schoolteacher and began reading law.

After the end of the Civil War, O'Hara became involved in North Carolina politics. In 1868, he was employed by the North Carolina State Constitutional Convention as an embossing clerk. That same year, O'Hara was elected to the North Carolina legislature as a representative, serving until 1869. He then traveled to Washington, D.C., to study law at Howard University's Department of Law. He took a number of classes at Howard but did not graduate, returning instead to North Carolina where he finished reading for the bar. He was admitted to the bar of North Carolina in 1873. He then settled in Enfield, North Carolina, and established a practice of law, at the same time serving as chairman of the Halifax County Board of Commissioners.

Career Highlights

O'Hara, however, had higher aspirations. He entered the race for a seat in Congress in 1874, but lost the district nomination to Republican John A. Hyman. In 1878, O'Hara tried again, but a challenge from fellow Republican James H. Harris split the vote, giving the election to Democrat William H. Kitchin. That year, O'Hara challenged the election's results in the House. Unfortunately, while he was waiting to be heard by Congress, a fire destroyed his home and all the evidence he had collected to support his challenge. Having no evidence to present, O'Hara tried to unseat Kitchin through the courts, but the courts rejected his challenge, as had Congress.

In 1880, O'Hara again tried for Congress, but lost the nomination to Orlando Hubbs. In 1882, O'Hara was at last successful. Running unopposed for the Republican nomination, he was able to defeat his Democratic opponent by a wide margin and, on March 4, 1883, O'Hara was sworn into the 48th Congress as the only African American member of Congress for that year; **Robert Smalls** would join him a year later in March of 1884. O'Hara was assigned to the Committee on Expenditures on Public Buildings.

Vocal in his opinions and energetic in pushing for what he felt was needed, O'Hara introduced legislation into his very first session of Congress. He unsuccessfully sponsored a bill that would reimburse the depositors in the Freedmen's Savings Bank and Trust Company for their losses due to the bank's failure 10 years earlier. He proposed a civil rights constitutional amendment, but the House failed to even consider it. He also tried to add an amendment to the proposed Interstate Commerce Act before Congress that would have banned segregation on trains and provided for equal accommodations, regardless of color, in passenger cars.

In the election of 1885, O'Hara again won election, but when he returned to Congress for the 49th session, he had no luck getting legislation passed. During this session, he proposed that the monies paid to Robert Smalls and his crew for the capture of the Confederate ship *Planter* be increased. In 1887, he inserted a proviso into a District of Columbia appropriations bill to assure that no discrimination in salary be made between male and female teachers of similar abilities.

The winter, 1887, session was to be O'Hara's last in Congress. In the election in 1886, dissension among the black Republicans of the Second Congressional District of North Carolina had produced a challenger to O'Hara, Republican Israel B. Abbott. The Democrat in the race, Furnifold McLendel Simmons, was able to benefit from this split, winning the congressional seat with 45 percent of the vote.

O'Hara returned to New Bern, North Carolina, where he resumed the practice of law, eventually forming a partnership with his son, Raphael. Although he remained active in local Republican politics, he did not run for office again.

Sources

Christopher, Maurine. *America's Black Congressmen*. New York: Thomas Y. Crowell, 1971.

Clay, William L. *Just Permanent Interests: Black Americans in Congress, 1870–1991*. New York: Amistad Press, 1992.

"Former Black Members of Congress." *Congressional Times Journal*. <http://www.usbol.com/ctjournal/FrBlkCongMemList.html>. Accessed: 4/28/98.

Logan, Rayford W., and Michael R. Winston, eds. *Dictionary of American Negro Biography*. New York: W.W. Norton and Co., 1982.

Major Robert Odell Owens

Born: June 28, 1936, in Memphis, Tennessee

Status: U.S. representative from the 11th Congressional District of New York

Education: B.A. in mathematics, 1956, Morehouse College, Atlanta, Georgia; M.S. in library science, 1957, Atlanta University, Atlanta, Georgia; recipient of honorary doctorates from Atlanta University, 1988, and Audrey Cohen College of Human Services, 1990

Position: Community coordinator, Brooklyn Public Library, Brooklyn, New York; chair, Brooklyn Congress of Racial Equality; vice president, Metropolitan Council on Housing, Brooklyn, New York; adjunct professor, Columbia University, New York, New York; commissioner, New York City Community Development Agency, New York, New York; state senator, New York State Senate, 1974–1982; U.S. representative from the 11th Congressional District of New York, 1983–

Early Years

Major Robert Odell Owens was born in Memphis, Tennessee, on June 28, 1936.

Higher Education

After graduating from high school, Owens attended Morehouse College in Atlanta, Georgia, where he majored in mathematics. The following year, he received a master's degree in library science from Atlanta University.

Career Highlights

After completing his graduate studies, Owens moved to Brooklyn, New York, and began work for the Brooklyn Public Library. Over the years, he held a number of positions with the library, eventually becoming a noted scholar and expert on library education and information development. One position in particular that guided him to politics was his role as community coordinator for the library. This brought him into contact with many different people and groups in Brooklyn.

Owens's entry into public service, however, really began during the civil rights movement of the 1960s. During this time, in addition to working on the campaigns of a variety of Democratic candidates, he held the position of chairman of the Brooklyn Congress of Racial Equality (CORE). He also began to become involved in the problems of the city in which he lived, serving as vice president of the Metropolitan Council on Housing, a tenants' rights group, and eventually as commissioner of New York City's Community Development Agency.

In 1973, Owens declared his intention of running for the New York State Senate in the newly created 17th Senatorial District. Owens was by this time well known to the people of this district and won easily. During his eight years in the state senate, Owens continued to work for civil rights, governmental reform, and improvement of his district.

In 1982, **Shirley Anita St. Hill Chisholm** announced her retirement from the House of Representatives. Owens declared that he would run for her seat, but unlike his campaigns for the New York senate, he met serious opposition. Owens had spent a great deal of time denouncing the party regulars; it seemed they decided who would run and who would not. He also was not popular with either the career politicians or their supporters because of his efforts to institute reforms in government. In his race for the House, he did not have the support of Shirley Chisholm or Brooklyn borough president Howard Golden. As a result, many thought his was a losing race.

Owens was running against State Senator Vander Beatty, who had the money, power, and support to finance a tough campaign. However, during the campaign, it was revealed that Beatty had ties to some "unsavory political characters, including some who had been convicted of felonies" (Clay 265). That information, along with the endorsements of the *Amsterdam News* and the *Village Voice*, was enough to defeat Beatty. In the election, Owens garnered 54 percent of the vote.

Once in Congress in 1983, Owens was appointed to the Education and Labor Committee and the Government Operations Committee. Owens had long had an interest in improving education, and he set to work to further that goal, which earned him the title of the "Education Congressman" by those in his district. In addition to pushing for better schools and teachers, Owens also championed child abuse prevention and worked on gun control, sponsoring legislation that would require a seven-day waiting period for handgun purchases. He also was one of the sponsors of the Americans with Disabilities Act (ADA), which prohibits discrimination in employment and other areas against those who are disabled.

Since his election in 1982, Owens has faced no serious challenge to his reelection. In addition to his other assignments, he has served as a senior member of the House Education and Labor Committee and chair of the Sub-Committee on Select Education and Civil Rights.

Sources

Clay, William L. *Just Permanent Interests: Black Americans in Congress, 1870–1991*. New York: Amistad Press, 1992.

Congressional Black Caucus: '93–'94 Guide. <http://www.sas.upenn.edu/African_Studies/Govern_Political/CBC_Guide.html>. Accessed: 3/10/98.

P

Carrie Saxon Perry

Born: August 10, 1931, in Hartford, Connecticut

Status: Resident of Hartford, Connecticut

Education: B.S., 1953, Howard University, Washington, D.C.; studied at Howard School of Law, Washington, D.C., 1953–1955

Position: Social worker, Hartford, Connecticut, 1950s; administrator, Community Renewal Team of Greater Hartford, Hartford, Connecticut, 1960s; executive director, Amistad House, Hartford, Connecticut, 1970s; state representative, Connecticut State Legislature, 1980–1987; mayor, Hartford, Connecticut, 1987–1991

Early Years

Carrie Saxon Perry was born on August 10, 1931, in Hartford, Connecticut, the only child of Mabel Lee Saxon. Despite the fact that Saxon and her mother lived in poverty, her mother and grandmother encouraged her to follow her dreams. Saxon attended public school in Hartford, graduating from high school in 1949 and enrolling at Howard University in Washington, D.C.

Higher Education

Saxon studied political science at Howard University, then studied for two years at Howard's School of Law before returning to Hartford, Connecticut, where she obtained a job as a social worker. Soon after her return to Hartford, Perry met and married James Perry, Sr., whom she later divorced. The couple had one son, James Perry, Jr.

Career Highlights

In addition to raising her son, Perry was busy building her career. She was appointed administrator for the Community Renewal Team of Greater Hartford and, soon after, became executive director of Amistad House. Her jobs, which concerned helping the poor, increasingly involved contacts with various politicians and political groups in Hartford. She saw that she would have to become directly involved in politics herself to help those in need, and in 1976 she made a bid for a seat in the Connecticut State Legislature.

The race was a tough one, and Perry had virtually no support. Her opponent pounded at her lack of experience, a charge Perry answered by saying,

> I have a right to go up there and make a fool of myself. I'll never know until I get up there. If you're going to always judge people—women, blacks, Indians, whatever—against a white person who has had more advantages, more opportunities, and a quicker starting time, then we should never participate in anything. (Smith 838)

The race was a tight one. As the returns came in election night, it looked as if Perry had been able to pull off a victory:

> I was not endorsed by a single soul. I won on the machine. We were partying, just dancing and everything, and then they came in with the absentee ballots and said, "You Lost." It was kind of crushing. (Smith 838)

Although she had lost, the race proved to her that her constituents in Hartford were looking for a new voice and, in 1980, she ran again. Once again, Perry had no support from any group or politician, and as before her opponent charged her with a lack of experience. This time, however, she was victorious by a narrow margin and would run successfully three more times.

Although Perry was a freshman legislator in 1980, she was appointed assistant majority leader of the House. Perry made human rights her prime agenda. She had grown up in the inner city and knew firsthand what poverty was like. As chair of the House Subcommittee on Bonding, she was able to push through the funding for a project called Riverfront Recapture, which was aimed at rehabilitating the riverfront area in Hartford. She also persuaded the legislature to rid itself of investments in South Africa and pushed for better education and housing for Hartford's citizens.

Perry was also building a political base. Representing the Democratic Party of Connecticut, she attended both the 1984 and 1988 National Democratic Conventions. She was becoming better known both in Hartford and throughout the state, always recognizable wearing a stylish hat.

In 1987, Perry decided to run for mayor of Hartford, feeling she could contribute more directly to the city, which was in deep financial and social trouble. As she later said, "I thought about it. And the fact that Mount Everest is there, why not climb it? It was a challenge, an opportunity" (Smith 838).

Again, the race was a tough one, but now she had political experience and support. She was able to defeat her opponent, a white male Republican, by nearly 3,000 votes. On November 3, 1987, Perry was sworn in as the 60th mayor of Hartford and the first black female mayor of both Hartford and New England.

The Hartford that Perry faced had many problems, problems with which Perry was all too familiar from growing up in the city. Touted as the insurance capital of the world in a state that had the highest per capita income in the United States, Hartford did not share in that bounty. Twenty-two percent of its residents fell below the poverty line, and the city had the fourth highest crime rate in the country (Smith 838). Although nearly half of its population was made up of minorities, few of those in power came from minority groups. The city needed change; as Perry said,

> I believe that you have to force change. It doesn't always have to be by violence. You rebel, you organize, you force issues, you threaten the status quo, you show numbers, you promise upheaval: there are numbers of things you have to do. You have to be committed to long distance and accept the fact that it doesn't happen overnight, and that you're doing it probably for another generation. (Smith 839)

Perry set to work creating after-school and day care programs, improving housing, and trying to pull new business into the city. She created Operation Break, a job training program aimed at those living in public housing. In addition to job training, the program also offered drug rehabilitation, remedial education, and English as a second language. She also attempted to resuscitate Hartford's failing school system (a task that has yet to be accomplished; in 1997, it became the first school system in the country to be taken over by a state legislature in an attempt to force improvement).

Although active and dynamic, Perry was facing something even she could not fix: a state- and nationwide recession. The stock market had crashed in 1987, just as she was taking office, and Connecticut was among one of the hardest hit states. Job layoffs were in the thousands, and companies were fleeing the state despite tax breaks offered by the legislature. When Perry faced reelection, her opponent took advantage of the fact that the economy was declining under her leadership. As a result, she lost the election.

Although still active in the Democratic Party, Perry has returned to the private sector, at least for now. But she presented and continues to present an example for women and for black women, in particular, to emulate. As she said in a speech in 1990,

> It is very lonely being a woman in politics. We have to become much more comfortable with these positions. Women, African-American women in particular, have to consider public office as a position that is most honorable. (Smith 839)

Sources

Hine, Darlene Clark, ed. *Black Women in America: An Historical Encyclopedia*, Vol. II, M–Z. Brooklyn, NY: Carlson Publishing Co., 1993.

Smith, Jessie Carney, ed. *Notable Black American Women*, Vol. 1. Detroit, MI: Gale Research, 1992.

Pinckney Benton Stewart Pinchback

Born: May 10, 1837, in Macon, Georgia

Status: Died December 21, 1921, in Washington, D.C.; buried at Metairie Ridge Cemetery, New Orleans, Louisiana

Education: Attended Gilmore High School, Cincinnati, Ohio, 1846–1848; attended Straight University, New Orleans, Louisiana, 1885–1886; admitted to the bar of Louisiana, 1886

Position: Cabin boy, then steward on various riverboats, 1849–1862; member, First Louisiana Volunteer Infantry, 1862–1863; organized the First Cavalry, Corps D'Afrique (also known as the Louisiana Native Guards), 1863; organized the Fourth Ward Republican Club, New Orleans, Louisiana, 1867; member, Louisiana delegation, Republican National Convention, Chicago, Illinois, 1868; senator, Louisiana State Senate, 1868–1871; partner, Pinchback and Antoine, New Orleans, Louisiana, 1869–1871; publisher, *Louisianian*, 1869–1881; lieutenant governor of Louisiana, 1871; elected congressman at large for Louisiana, 1872 (denied seat); governor of Louisiana, December 9, 1872–January 13, 1873; elected to the United States Senate, January 14, 1873 (denied seat); appointed surveyor of customs, New Orleans, Louisiana, 1882; helped organize the American Citizens' Equal Rights Association, 1890; delegate, Republican National Convention, 1892; U.S. marshall, New York, New York, c. 1893

Early Years

Pinckney Benton Stewart Pinchback was born on May 10, 1837, in Macon, Georgia, the son of a freed black woman, Eliza Stewart, and a white plantation owner, Major William Pinchback. Pinchback, the eighth child of the couple, had arrived earlier than expected. Eliza Stewart and Major Pinchback were en route from Virginia to a new home in Holmes County, Mississippi, where Major Pinchback had purchased a large plantation.

Pinchback's early years reflected a life of rare privilege for a young black child at that time, but he was aware of the disparity of treatment between whites and blacks and of the inequality that existed outside his father's plantation. He came to know well the running of the plantation and the cycles of planting and harvesting, as evidenced by references to them in his many speeches later in life.

Although Pinchback probably had been taught to read and write by his father, until the age of nine he had had no formal education. The opportunity for education was denied a black child in Mississippi, or even a quadroon, one-fourth black, as Pinchback was. Because of this, in 1846, when Pinchback's brother Napoleon was 16 and he himself was nine, both were sent north to Cincinnati, Ohio, where they attended Gilmore High School. Pinchback's schooling ended abruptly, however, in 1848, when he and Napoleon were called home because his father was mortally ill. Shortly after their arrival, Major Pinchback died, leaving his family nearly destitute.

Higher Education

Pinchback was 48 years old before he would be able to return to his education—after he had achieved the most notable accomplishments of his life. In 1885, he decided that he wanted to become a lawyer, although from his various experiences, he probably knew more about Louisiana and United States law than did many with formal degrees. In 1880, he had helped establish the law department of Straight University in New Orleans, a "university for the education of persons of color," and served on its board of trustees (Haskins 251). It was natural for him, therefore, to choose this university for his own education, and in 1885 he entered its law department, graduating only a year later, in 1886, in its first graduating class. That same year, Pinchback was admitted to the Louisiana bar. Much had happened, however, between the time Pinchback had halted his early education upon the death of his father and this culminating degree in law.

Career Highlights

Major William Pinchback was not formally married to Eliza Stewart. Such a marriage would have renounced the mores of the day. Nevertheless, the major considered himself a family man and cared deeply for Eliza and their children. It was a shock then when, upon his death, his white heirs descended upon his plantation and confiscated his wealth and lands, leaving nothing to Eliza and her children but the very real possibility of being sold into slavery. With the help of one of the administrators of Major Pinchback's estate, Eliza and the children fled to Cincinnati, Ohio, out of reach of the major's heirs, but penniless.

Napoleon, the eldest of the children, would have been expected to provide for the family but, possibly because of the sudden changes in the family's circumstances and the prospect of such a burden descending upon him, he became mentally unstable (Haskins 10). This left Pinchback, the only other male in the family, to provide for them. He was 12 years old at the time and was forced to grow up quickly.

Pinchback, being very light-skinned, could have passed for white and taken advantage of opportunities and jobs available to whites that were denied to blacks. He chose to recognize his African heritage, however. This meant that the jobs open to him because of his age and color were menial, degrading, and low-paying.

For more than 10 years, Pinchback worked on the river, first as a cabin boy on the Ohio River, then as a steward on the big riverboats plying the Missouri and Mississippi Rivers. During this time, he learned the trade of gambling from George Devol and three compatriots of Devol, all of whom worked the riverboats scamming "suckers" out of their money. According to various accounts, Devol and his henchmen, along with "Pinch," as Devol called him, were forced to jump ship at Yazoo City, Mississippi, to escape the rage of those they had bilked. This willingness to take risks—along with the ego that accompanies risk-taking—was typical of Pinchback.

When Pinchback had made his way from Yazoo City to New Orleans, he encountered the brother of a woman he had supposedly married (he had had the marriage annulled and subsequently married Nina Emily Hawthorne in 1860). But the brother was angry at how Pinchback had treated his sister, and a fight ensued. Having been captured by Union forces, New Orleans was under the control of federal military authorities, who arrested Pinchback. He was tried for assault and attempted murder and sentenced to two years in the workhouse.

Pinchback was able to obtain his release for the sum of $500 in July, 1862, and decided to enlist in the Union army, joining the First Louisiana Volunteer Infantry, a white regiment. He was then authorized by his commanding officer, General Benjamin F. Butler, to form a new company and recruit black soldiers for it. The "Corps D'Afrique," also called the Louisiana Native Guards, was an elite company of men. But Pinchback had been denied promotion because of his color, so he resigned on September 10, 1863. He then applied to Major General N.P. Banks, commander of New Orleans, for permission to form a black cavalry company. He was verbally appointed captain and formed the First Cavalry Regiment Corps D'Afrique. Again he was denied a promotion in rank, so Pinchback left the Corps and returned to Cincinnati where his family still lived.

The end of the Civil War spelled opportunity to Pinchback. After traveling with his wife through Alabama, encouraging the newly freed blacks to vote and participate in the new government that was being formed, he returned to New Orleans. Pinchback settled, started a cotton brokerage firm with C.C. Antoine, and jumped enthusiastically into politics, organizing the Fourth Ward Republican Club. In 1868, he served as a delegate to both the Louisiana constitutional convention and the Republican National Convention, which was held in Chicago, Illinois. That same year, Pinchback was elected to the Louisiana State Senate, serving as its president pro tempore and, upon the death of Lieutenant Governor Oscar J. Dunn in November, 1871, was promoted by the senate in 1872 to fill that position. In 1872, Pinchback also decided to run for congressman at large on the Republican slate and won the election. His opponent, however, contested the election results.

In 1872, Governor Henry C. Warmoth was asked to step down from office to await impeachment proceedings. This meant that Pinchback, as lieutenant governor, would assume the position of acting governor. With this move, Pinchback became the first black governor in the United States, a feat not emulated until the 1989 election of Virginia governor **Lawrence Douglas Wilder,** who was the first black governor elected to office. Although Pinchback's term as governor was brief—from December 9, 1872, to January 13, 1873—it assured him a place in history and also caused problems for him later.

The day after Pinchback stepped down as governor, the Louisiana legislature elected him to the United States Senate. He was bound for Washington as both a representative and a senator for Louisiana, but Pinchback's right to either office was being strenuously challenged. Many were outraged at his dual claims to office and were crying favoritism because he was black. James Beck of Kentucky said, "I know that many rights are accorded to men because of race, color or previous condition, but I never knew that even a Negro could be both a representative in Congress and a senator at the same time" (Christopher 110).

Pinchback's opponents for both seats charged election irregularities, but Pinchback also fell prey to a sort of catch-22. His credentials for the House had to be signed by the governor of Louisiana to be accepted. But Pinchback himself had been governor and his own signature was on the election certificate. This, the House felt, was unacceptable. Pinchback argued eloquently on his own behalf, pointing out that the House had accepted his signature as valid on the credentials of the other representatives from Louisiana, so why not on his? His challenger for the seat, George Sheridan, had had his credentials signed by ex-Governor Warmoth before the votes for the Senate seat had been tallied.

Despite Pinchback's arguments, on March 3, 1875, the House voted 121 to 29 to uphold Sheridan's claim over his. On March 8, 1876, the Senate voted 32 to 29 against seating him, although it did award him payment for the time he had been in Washington and for travel expenses, nearly $17,000.

When Pinchback returned to New Orleans, Radical Reconstruction was rapidly winding down and whites were regaining control of southern government. Rutherford B. Hayes had swept into office on the promise of the removal of federal troops from the South; in effect, handing control of the state governments over to the conservative Democrats. This slammed the door on the participation of blacks in politics. Embittered by his rejection by both the House and Senate, and seeing most of his political opportunities quickly drying up, Pinchback turned to other interests. In 1877, Pinchback joined the Democratic Party and was appointed the surveyor of customs for New Orleans in 1882. He participated as much as he could in the local political arena, and for a brief period of time he and his family lived in New York City where he held the position of U.S. marshall. They then moved to Washington, D.C., where Pinchback died on December 21, 1921, at the age of 84.

Sources

Christopher, Maurine. *America's Black Congressmen*. New York: Thomas Y. Crowell, 1971.

Estell, Kenneth. *African America: Celebrating 400 Years of Achievement*. Detroit, MI: Visible Ink Press, 1994.

Haskins, James. *The First Black Governor: Pinckney Benton Stewart Pinchback*. Trenton, NJ: African World Press, 1973.

New Grolier Multimedia Encyclopedia. Novato, CA: The Software Toolworks, Inc./Grolier, Inc., 1993.

Adam Clayton Powell, Jr.

Reproduced from AP/Wide World Photos

Born: November 29, 1908, in New Haven, Connecticut

Status: Died April 4, 1972, in Miami, Florida

Education: Graduate, 1924, Townsend Harries Preparatory School of the College of the City of New York; attended City College of New York, New York; B.S., 1930, Colgate University, Hamilton, New York; attended Union Theological Seminary, 1930; M.A. in religious education, 1931, Teachers College, Columbia University, New York, New York; ordained as a minister, 1930

Position: Assistant minister and business manager, Abyssinian Baptist Church, New York, New York, 1930–1935; pastor, Abyssinian Baptist Church, 1936–1971; elected to the New York City Council, 1941; publisher and editor, *The People's Voice*, 1941–1945; member, New York State Office of Price Administration, 1942–1944; member, Manhattan Civilian Defense, 1942–1945; U.S. representative from the 22nd (later, the 18th) Congressional District of New York, 1945–1967, 1969–1970

Awards and honors: state office building and avenue in Harlem, New York, named for him

Early Years

Adam Clayton Powell, Jr., was one of the most flamboyant and outspoken congressmen in the history of the House of Representatives. He didn't conform to the stereotype of most black politicians, and didn't want to. He proclaimed, "I'm the first bad Negro they've had in Congress," and made enemies left and right. But Powell would also become one of the strongest defenders of civil rights and would fight long and hard for racial equality during his time in office.

Powell was the grandson of a former slave named Sally, who was part black and part Cherokee Indian, and a white slave owner whose last name was Powell. His father, who missed being born into slavery by one month, was light-skinned like Powell and was high-spirited as a youth. As Powell said of him, "He was, according to his own account, a bum, a drunkard, a gambler, a juvenile delinquent, and possibly more" (Haskins 10). But Adam Clayton Powell, Sr., saw the light one morning after a particularly raucous night and turned to the church. Powell's father returned to school, graduating from Howard University Law School. He then entered Wayland Seminary and College in Washington, D.C., and was ordained as a minister in the Baptist church.

Adam Powell, Sr., married Mattie Schaefer in 1890, and together they moved to New Haven, Connecticut, where he was offered the ministry of the Immanuel Baptist Church. His salary was good and his family comfortable. In 1898, the couple had a daughter, Blanche, and 10 years later, on November 29, 1908, a son, Adam Clayton Powell, Jr.

Soon after Powell was born, his father accepted a ministry in New York at the Abyssinian Baptist Church on West 40th Street in New York City. At the time, the Abyssinian Baptist Church had the largest black congregation in the world.

The Powells at first lived on West 134th Street in Harlem. Harlem was then an almost totally white community filled with Irish, Italian, and Jewish families. While Powell's mother and father busied themselves with church activities, he was often cared for by their black housekeeper, Josephine. It was she who taught him to write the alphabet. Powell was often ill as a child with severe respiratory ailments—a weakness that would haunt him all his life—so, although a mischievous boy, he was unable to play as roughly as other boys his age. Powell's father often took him fishing, an activity Powell would love all his life. In essence, he was an only child as his sister married when he was six years old.

From the time he learned to read, Powell was an avid reader. He was a bright child, and after he entered school he was frequently moved ahead; Powell graduated from high school when he was 16.

By this time the Powells had moved to a house on West 136th Street in Harlem. But Harlem was changing; it was no longer dominated by whites, and racial tensions were felt in the area. Because of his light skin, Powell felt pressure from both sides. Later in life, he related a tale of how, when he was a boy, his father sent him on an errand, and he ran into a group of black youths who asked him if he was white or black. Never having really thought about it and seeing how light his skin was in comparison to theirs, he answered, "White!" whereupon they beat him up. The next night, on another errand, he was stopped by a group of white boys and, remembering his lesson from the night before when asked the same question, he answered, "Colored!" and he again was beaten (Haskins 15–16).

During the 1920s, Powell's father persuaded his congregation to move the Abyssinian Baptist Church to Harlem. Powell was 15 years old when the new church was dedicated in 1923, and he fell in love with the new buildings, which he had helped build. He later said,

"This was my church. It was my eternal mother" (Haskins 17).

Higher Education

After graduating from high school, Powell began college at the City College of New York at his father's insistence; but Powell discovered girls and was caught up in the wildness of the Roaring 20s. His brother-in-law, C.D. King, spoke of that time: ". . .he didn't do so well. Going to parties, smoking, drinking, chasing and being chased by girls, and generally having a good time caused Adam to flunk three subjects his first term" (Haskins 18). Powell's father pulled some strings to keep him in school another semester, but during that time his sister Blanche, whom Powell adored, died of a ruptured appendix, and he threw in the towel. The following summer, Powell worked as a kitchen helper but spent all his money on gambling, women, and liquor.

In the fall, his father forced him to go to Colgate University in Hamilton, New York. Away from all the temptations of the city, Powell settled down a bit and graduated with a bachelor of science degree in 1930. He had planned on becoming a surgeon, but increasingly he was drawn to the church and finally decided to follow his father into the ministry.

One weekend during his time at Colgate, Powell drove to New York to a party and met a young actress and dancer named Isabel Washington. She was separated from her husband and had a young child, but Powell fell in love with her, much to his father's dismay. When Powell graduated from Colgate, his father gave him a trip to Europe as a graduation present, hoping that Powell would forget Isabel during his trip. Powell, however, after graduating from the Teachers College of Columbia University in 1931, married Isabel.

Career Highlights

When Powell graduated from Colgate, he had been ordained in the church and made assistant minister and business manager of his father's Abyssinian Baptist Church. He soon rose to the position of minister and began making a name for himself. In addition to his post-graduate studies, Powell tackled the misery and need created by the Depression. He set up a free food pantry, a job referral service, and literacy classes at the church.

As he worked, Powell could see that racism caused as many problems as the Depression, and he began speaking out against it. He created a "Don't Buy Where You Can't Work" campaign in the city, calling for boycotts of businesses that would not hire black employees. He also held rent strikes and organized mass meetings, where his charismatic personality and eloquence convinced people that institutional racism had to be abolished. With the influence he was building, it was natural for him to turn to politics to try to institute change.

In 1941, Powell became New York's first black city councilman. During that time, he was also the publisher and editor of *The People's Voice*, a weekly newspaper that he used as a forum for his views. In 1942, he was appointed a member of the New York State Office of Price Administration, a post he held until 1944, and of Manhattan's Civilian Defense. In 1945, disillusioned with the life of a politician's wife and with Powell's womanizing, his wife Isabel divorced him. That same year, Powell married Hazel Scott, a nightclub pianist.

In 1944, Powell won a seat in Congress from the 22nd District of New York (later, the 18th), and became one of two African Americans in the House of Representatives. The other, **William Levi Dawson**, a representative from Chicago, was a quiet man who walked the party line laid down by the "machine" in Chicago. He promoted moderation; Powell was exactly the opposite.

From the moment Powell took his seat in Congress on January 3, 1945, he let everyone know that he was there to institute change. In 1945, Washington, D.C., was a segregated city and Congress was a segregated body. Although Dawson had abided by the segregation laws, not using the congressional dining room, gymnasium, or barbershop, or inviting black journalists to sit in the congressional gallery, Powell had no intention of following in his footsteps. He insisted on taking black friends and associates to lunch in the congressional dining room and ordered his black staff members to eat there, as was his privilege as a congressman. He similarly challenged the congressional barbershop and gymnasium and exposed racial slurs in Congress. One southern congressman had consistently used the word "nigger" in his speeches, and the House stenographer had discreetly changed it to "Negro" in the *Congressional Record*. Powell insisted that the congressman's exact words be recorded, causing quite a stir and no small embarrassment for the southern congressman.

During his first term of office, Powell served on the Indian Affairs, Invalid Pension, and Labor Committees. In 1947, he was appointed to the Education and Labor Committee and, from 1955 until 1961, the Committee on Interior and Insular Affairs. But Powell's real battles occurred on the floor of the House where he fought for civil rights and black equality. He introduced legislation banning lynching and the poll tax, as well as discrimination in the armed forces, housing, employment, and transportation. He habitually attached an anti-discrimination amendment to most legislation; so frequently, in fact, that it came to be called the "Powell Amendment."

In 1956, although a staunch Democrat, Powell supported Eisenhower, a Republican, in his run for presidential reelection against Adlai Stevenson. This provided an important boost for Eisenhower among black voters. "The Negro Vote," a *Time Magazine* article, published October 22, 1956, reports Powell's decision and notes his influence:

> Lightly as Negro intellectuals may regard Powell, he is a politician of indisputable influence. He has served six consecutive House terms, is pastor of one of Harlem's biggest churches . . . and, above all, has a demonstrated talent for bypassing the intellectuals and communicating directly with the Negro man-in-the-street. ("The Negro Vote")

Powell felt that the Democrats' platform on civil rights was too weak, and that Eisenhower's push for desegregation was stronger.

In 1958, some of the problems that would plague Powell's later years began to surface. That year, he was tried for income tax evasion, but faced a hung jury and was released. Four years earlier, Powell's second marriage had fallen apart; Hazel had moved to Paris and divorced Powell in 1956. In 1960, Powell married Yvett Marjorie Flores Diago, a young Puerto Rican divorcee who worked on his staff in Washington.

In 1961, Powell assumed the chairmanship of the Committee on Education and Labor, a position that allowed him to effect legislation on civil rights. The legislation that came from the committee formed the basis of the social policies of both Kennedy's "New Frontier" and Johnson's "Great Society." The bills Powell managed to push through were sweeping in their effects upon society, changing the minimum wage, establishing anti-poverty legislation, and providing for a National Defense Education Act that benefited generations of students.

However, Powell also had problems in the committee; charges were made that he was misusing his authority, and he was criticized for taking trips abroad at the public's expense and for refusing to return to his district where a judgment against him for slander would have forced him to make payment or face arrest. He was often absent from Congress, and there were rumors of kickbacks from former employees and, again, income tax evasion. In January of 1967, Powell was stripped of his chairmanship by the House Democratic Caucus and censured by the full House, which refused to seat him until an investigation was made by the Judiciary Committee.

Although the committee recommended Powell be censured, fined, and deprived of his seniority, the House ignored these recommendations and voted to exclude him altogether from Congress. Powell, however, quickly won back his seat in a special election held on April 11, 1967, to fill the vacancy left by his exclusion.

Powell was again reelected in the regular election held in November of 1967, but when he appeared in Congress the House refused to reinstate his seniority. In protest, Powell refused to take his seat when the 91st Congress convened in 1969 and appealed their decision to the Supreme Court.

In June of that year, the Supreme Court ruled that the House had acted unconstitutionally when it deprived Powell of his seat, and also noted that it could not deprive him of his 22 years' seniority. Powell resumed his seat in Congress, but, as writer Tony Chapelle points out, "Even then, he was docked $25,000 to repay the illegal kickback [monies he had taken]."

By 1970, Powell's luck had run out. His constituents were tired of his excesses and of listening to the charges against him. As Chapelle notes, "He had no permanent friends, only permanent interests. At some points, he aligned with traditional civil rights groups, then when it suited his purposes he'd accuse them of being made up of Uncle Toms not worthy of African Americans' support . . . Ultimately, Powell used up his political currency" (Chapelle). Powell lost the June, 1970, primary when he ran for reelection, and then failed to get on the ballot as an Independent. The following year, in 1971, he resigned from his ministry at the Abyssinian Baptist Church.

After his loss, Powell retired to Bimini but died in Miami on April 4, 1972; his ashes were scattered in Bimini. Although his excesses had brought him down, he was still mourned by millions who remembered that, during the middle of the century, his was almost the only voice for black Americans. To them, he had been, as the *New York Amsterdam News* said, "Harlem's Black Knight in shining armor" (Haskins 142).

Sources

Chapelle, Tony. "Adam Clayton Powell, Jr.: Black Power between Heaven and Hell." *The Black Collegian Online*. The Black Collegian Services, Inc., 1997. <http://www.black-collegian.com/adam.html>. Accessed: 3/31/98.

Christopher, Maurine. *America's Black Congressmen*. New York: Thomas Y. Crowell, 1971.

Clay, William L. *Just Permanent Interests: Black Americans in Congress, 1870–1991*. New York: Amistad Press, 1992.

"Former Black Members of Congress." *Congressional Times Journal*. <http://www.usbol.com/ctjournal/FrBlkCongMemList.html>. Accessed: 2/18/98.

Haskins, James. *Adam Clayton Powell: A Portrait of a Marching Black*. Trenton, NJ: African World Press, 1993.

"The Negro Vote." *Time Magazine*, 22 October 1956.

Time Almanac, Reference Edition. Fort Lauderdale, FL: Compact Publishing, 1994.

New Grolier Multimedia Encyclopedia. Novato, CA: The Software Toolworks, Inc./Grolier, Inc., 1993.

Smith, Jessie Carney, ed. *Black Heroes of the 20th Century*. Detroit, MI: Visible Ink Press, 1998.

Georgia Montgomery Davis Powers

Born: October 19, 1923, in Springfield, Kentucky

Status: Retired

Education: Graduate, 1940, Central High School, Louisville, Kentucky: attended Louisville Municipal College, Louisville, Kentucky, 1940–1942; attended Central High School's night school in business, Louisville, Kentucky; awarded honorary doctor of law degree May 7, 1989, University of Kentucky, Lexington; awarded honorary doctor of humane letters May 21, 1989, University of Louisville, Louisville, Kentucky

Position: Chairperson of a number of election campaigns, 1962–1967; elected to the Jefferson County Democratic Executive Committee, 1964; co-organizer, Allied Organizations for Civil Rights, 1964; co-organizer, Kentucky

Christian Leadership Conference, 1965; supervisor, U.S. Census Bureau, Louisville, Kentucky, c. 1966–1967; restaurant and dry cleaning business owner, 1969–1974; state senator from the 33rd District, Kentucky State Legislature, 1968–1988

Early Years

Georgia Davis Powers was born Georgia Montgomery on October 19, 1923, in Springfield, Kentucky, the second of nine children and the only daughter of Ben Montgomery and Frances Walker Montgomery. Both of Powers's parents could read and write, and they valued education. Her father had a third-grade education and her mother had finished the eighth grade. As Powers wrote in her autobiography, *I Shared the Dream*, "The eighth grade was about as far as a Black child could go in Washington County [Kentucky] . . . My parents were determined that their children would go to school . . ." (17).

While Ben Montgomery worked as a farm laborer, Powers's mother stayed home and raised the children. Ben was very light-skinned with blond hair, and most people thought he was white, which caused problems when he took his wife and children, who were darker, out in public. To protect his children from the abuse they met on those occasions, he resisted going out much socially.

On March 18, 1925, when Georgia Powers was 17 months old, a tornado hit Jimtown, a rural part of Springfield where the family was living. Powers and her brother Jay were napping in a bedroom, and "Suddenly, a whirling funnel of wind whipped through our house, flipping the bed upside down and blowing my mother and father outside. . . we were directly in the path of the storm" (Powers 14). Their house was destroyed and the family moved to Louisville near Powers's Aunt Mary, who found them a small house to rent in the Limerick area of the city. Four years later, in May, 1929, the Montgomerys bought a house on Grand Avenue in a racially mixed neighborhood.

With their parents to push them, the Montgomery children did well in the public schools in Louisville. Powers attended Louisville's Central High School. When she was 15 years old, a 25-year-old neighbor lured her to his home and raped her. Shaken and frightened, Powers did not tell anyone of the incident. At that time, there were no rape counselors to help girls like Powers, and rape was thought to be the victim's fault.

When she graduated from Central High School in 1940, she knew her parents did not have the money for college tuition. With the help of teachers, however, Powers was able to qualify for a two-year scholarship from Alpha Kappa Sorority to Louisville Municipal College.

Higher Education

Powers did well at Louisville Municipal College, but when her scholarship ran out after two years, she did not know how she would continue her education. She was determined not to wind up in the traditional kinds of jobs allotted to black women: cleaning houses or waiting on people. She had been dating a young man, Robert Jones, who was pressuring her to marry him. She had turned him down a number of times, because she also did not wish to follow the traditional path of stay-at-home housewife and mother. But as the fall semester of her junior year neared, Powers saw no alternative way to get the money for school, so she agreed to marry Jones if he would pay her tuition for college. Powers subsequently thought better of the idea, but her father insisted that since she had given her word, she had to go through with the marriage. Powers and Robert Jones were married in August, 1942.

When it came time for him to provide the money for Powers's tuition, Jones reneged on his promise, saying that, as a woman, Powers had no need for an education. America had entered World War II and Jones was in the Army Signal Corps. As soon as he left for an assignment in New Jersey, Powers filed for divorce. Soon after, Powers and Norman "Nicky" Davis met at a U.S.O. dance in Louisville, and after corresponding for a number of months (during which time Powers moved to Buffalo, New York, to work with a friend, Esther Jones, whom she had met in Louisville) they were married in Texas—where Davis was stationed at the time.

While Nicky was in the army, fighting abroad, Powers remained in Buffalo, working first as a riveter then as an expediter at Curtiss-Wright. When Davis returned from the war, Powers persuaded him to move back to Louisville so she could be close to her family. There, she took courses in business at Central High School's night school, and she and Davis adopted a son, Billy.

Career Highlights

During the next 10 years, Powers held a number of jobs. For a time, she and Davis lived in California and Powers trained to operate IBM data processing machines while her husband worked for the California Gas Company. With the illness and death of Powers's brother, Carl, however, the family once again returned to Louisville, Kentucky.

During the 1960s, the issue of civil rights was on everyone's mind, and Georgia Powers was no exception. Through her church in Louisville, she met a number of people involved in the budding civil rights movement, and in 1962 she was asked to help with the campaign of Wilson Wyatt, who was running for the Senate. Powers proved so adept at campaigning that she was soon organizing volunteers to work for a number of other candidates. In 1964, she was elected to the Jefferson County Democratic Executive Committee, but she resigned in 1966 because she felt the committee was unresponsive to the kinds of issues that it needed to confront.

In 1964, Powers was one of the organizers of the Allied Organizations for Civil Rights in Louisville. While organizing a march, she met Dr. Martin Luther King, Jr., who was to become a significant factor in her life. In her autobiography, *I Shared the Dream*, she recounts how she had an affair with King that lasted until his death in 1968. In fact, she had a room at the Lorraine Motel in Memphis, Tennessee, where he was killed, and heard the shots that killed him and saw his slain body.

Powers worked tirelessly for black civil rights. She marched in the Selma-to-Montgomery, Alabama, march in 1965. She campaigned for open housing in Kentucky in 1967 and the next year ran for the Kentucky State Senate. During her campaign, she was unable to get endorsement from the local Democratic Party, although she was running as a Democrat. She was able to obtain endorsements from various unions and professional associations, however, strengthening her position. Winning by nearly 4,000 votes, Powers became the first black person and the first woman to be elected to the Kentucky State Senate. Powers's victory was not without controversy. The Republican mayor of Louisville charged voter fraud, but few listened to him.

During her 20-year tenure in office, Powers focused on civil rights issues. The first bill she introduced as a freshman senator was indicative of those to follow; it was a bill calling for fair housing in the state. Other bills she sponsored over the years battled against racial, sexual, and age discrimination in hiring and called for improved education, low-cost housing, and an increased minimum wage.

In 1969, Powers bought a restaurant and a dry cleaning business, but sold them in 1974 because she did not have the time to devote to them. In 1984 and 1988, she served as the Kentucky chairperson for Jesse Jackson's campaign for the presidency and, for 20 years, was the secretary of the Democratic Caucus.

In 1988, at the age of 65, Powers decided it was time to step down. As she said, "It was time for someone else to run, a younger person with fresh ideas, and I need more free time" (Smith 868). After divorcing Norman Davis in 1968, she had married James F. Powers in 1973, and she wished to devote more time to her marriage and her other social interests. Her resignation from the Kentucky State Senate did not mean total retirement for her. In addition to involving herself in the campaigns of various politicians, in 1994 she was one of the organizers of QUEST (Quality Education for All Students), a group organized to fight for improved education. As she wrote in her autobiography, "I am greatly concerned about public education. Changes are needed, but those changes must be made within the framework of integrated systems" (321). At this writing, she still lives in Louisville, Kentucky, with her husband and continues fighting for this and other causes that concern the nation.

Sources

"Civil Rights March in Frankfort, 1964." Kentucky Department of Public Information Collection, rev. 2/17/98. <http://www.kdla.state.ky.us/arch/king.htm>. Accessed: 4/14/98.

Hine, Darlene Clark, ed. *Black Women in America: An Historical Encyclopedia*, Vol. II, M–Z. Brooklyn, NY: Carlson Publishing Co., 1993.

Ploski, Harry W., and James Williams, eds. *The Negro Almanac: A Reference Work on the African American*. Detroit, MI: Gales Research, 1989.

Powers, Georgia Davis. *I Shared the Dream: The Pride, Passion and Politics of the First Black Woman Senator from Kentucky*. Far Hill, NJ: New Horizona Press, 1995.

Smith, Jessie Carney, ed. *Notable Black American Women*, Vol. 1. Detroit, MI: Gale Research, 1992.

R

Joseph Hayne Rainey

Reproduced from the Collections of the Library of Congress

Born: June 21, 1832, in Georgetown, South Carolina

Status: Died August 2, 1887, in Georgetown, South Carolina; buried in the Baptist Cemetery, Georgetown, South Carolina

Education: Self-educated

Position: Barber, 1840s; conscripted steward on a Confederate blockade-runner, 1861–1862; barber, St. Georges, Bermuda, 1862–1866; representative for Georgetown, South Carolina, constitutional convention, 1868; state senator, South Carolina State Senate, 1870; U.S. representative from the First Congressional District of South Carolina, 1870–1879; first black representative to preside over a session of the House of Representatives, May, 1874; agent of internal revenue, South Carolina, 1879–1881; broker, banker, Washington, D.C., 1882–1886

Early Years

Joseph Hayne Rainey was born on June 21, 1832, in Georgetown, South Carolina, of parents who were of mixed heritage. His father, Edward Rainey, a successful barber, had been able to purchase his family's freedom before Rainey's birth. By the time Rainey was 14 years old, he had joined his father in his profession of barber. That same year, 1846, the family moved to Charleston, South Carolina, where father and son continued to work as barbers. Rainey also was able to obtain some education.

With the start of the Civil War, Rainey was conscripted as a steward on a Confederate blockade runner. A year earlier, in Philadelphia, he had married a woman named Susan. In 1862, he seized the opportunity to escape the Confederacy, together with Susan, aboard a ship to Bermuda, where slavery had been abolished in 1834.

Rainey and his wife settled in St. Georges, Bermuda, to await the outcome of the Civil War in the United States. He once again took up his trade as a barber and, as he had done in Charleston, spent time educating himself. He stayed abreast of news concerning the war, which ended in 1865, through sailors on the ships that frequently docked at the island.

Career Highlights

Following the war, Rainey and his family felt it was safe to return to South Carolina and chose to settle in Georgetown, his birthplace. There, Rainey quickly became involved in postwar politics. Like the majority of southern African Americans at the time, he joined the Republican Party (the southern Democratic Party, at the time, was known as the "party of rebellion" and was composed primarily of conservative, white ex-Confederates). Rainey, although self-educated, was intelligent with a quiet dignity. A natural leader, he gained the recognition of other Republicans and, soon after joining the party, became a member of its executive committee. In 1868, he attended the South Carolina constitutional convention, representing Georgetown.

Under the Radical or congressional Reconstruction begun in 1867, the Confederate states were mandated to allow blacks to vote, as well as to campaign for and, if elected, serve in public office. At this time, former Confederates were not permitted to vote or serve in office. In much of the South, Radical Reconstruction was overseen by federal troops. Given the political climate of the time, in 1870 Rainey campaigned for a seat in the South Carolina State Senate. Victorious, he assumed his seat that same year and was appointed chairman of the Finance Committee.

In February, 1870, Congressman Benjamin F. Whittemore resigned his seat in the House of Representatives amid charges of corruption. The South Carolina legislature called for a special election to fill this vacancy, and Joseph Rainey was nominated as the Republican candidate. The election, although heated, ended with Rainey defeating his Democratic opponent, C.W. Dudley, by nearly 9,000 votes. Rainey resigned from the state senate and headed for Washington, D.C., representing South Carolina's First Congressional District.

When Joseph H. Rainey was sworn into the 41st Congress on December 12, 1870, he became the first black man to be elected to and seated in the House of Representatives. Earlier, in 1868, John Willis Menard had been the first black man to be elected to Congress, but the House voted against seating him. Rainey, however, was admitted and was appointed to the Committee on Freedmen's Affairs.

Like his counterpart in the Senate, **Hiram Rhodes Revels**, Rainey spoke eloquently in favor of civil rights and against the charges of "black rule," attempting to allay the fears of both the white congressmen and the white South Carolinians who felt, because of the past, that blacks now in power might take revenge by legislating reverse discrimination. On March 5, 1872, Rainey spoke before the House on this issue:

> [The South Carolina] constitution towers up in its majesty with provisions for the equal protection of all classes of citizens. Notwithstanding our majority there, we have never attempted to deprive any man in that state of the rights and immunities to which he is entitled under the Constitution of the Government. You cannot point to me a single act passed by our Legislature, at any time, which had a tendency to reflect upon or oppress any white citizen of South Carolina. (Meltzer 113)

In 1872, Rainey was reelected to his seat in Congress, running unopposed. Again, civil rights was the issue of main concern to him. He was pressed by others in Congress to support an amnesty for former Confederates, but he strenuously declined unless civil rights measures promoting racial equality were also passed.

As a member of the Committee on Indian Affairs, Rainey was chosen to replace House Speaker James G. Blaine during a debate on appropriations to aid Indians. Rainey thus became the first African American to preside over a House session in May, 1874.

Rainey was to be elected to the House twice more, serving three full terms in office. In the 1876 election, however, Rainey's Democratic opponent, John S. Richardson, charged that Rainey had obtained his seat fraudulently. He claimed that the presence of federal troops in South Carolina and the existence of black political clubs in the state intimidated voters. Richardson presented a certificate of election to Congress demanding that he be seated in Rainey's stead. Richardson's certificate of election had been signed by the governor of South Carolina. Rainey pointed out to the House Committee on Election that his own certificate of election had been signed by the South Carolina secretary of state, the only official authorized to sign such a certificate.

While awaiting the decision of the Committee on Election, Rainey was permitted to take his seat in the House. However, in May, 1878, the committee ruled that many irregularities had taken place during the election and that the seat was to remain vacant. Rainey would have to run again to regain his seat.

By 1878, however, South Carolina was a very different place than it had been in 1870 when Rainey first was elected to Congress. In 1876, conservative elements had taken control of the state government and federal intervention by the military was weakening. Like so many other southern states in which whites were regaining control, South Carolina was busily instituting "Black Codes," laws restricting the freedom and rights of black citizens. In effect, these codes made African Americans slaves in all but name. White supremacy had also been given a boost by the Supreme Court in its decision in *United States v. Reese* (1876), which struck down the provisions in the federal law that guaranteed voting rights. Rainey returned to this atmosphere in 1878 to run again for his seat in the House, and Richardson soundly defeated him.

When Rainey left the House on March 3, 1879, he had been promised the position of clerk of the House of Representatives by his fellow Republicans. But when the next session of Congress convened, the Democrats had seized control of the House and the appointment went to a Democrat. While still seeking to obtain the promised appointment, Rainey worked for two years as an agent for internal revenue in South Carolina, and he traveled often to Washington. He also attempted to start a brokerage and banking firm in Washington during this time, which was unsuccessful. In 1886, financially depleted and in frail health, Rainey returned to Georgetown, where his wife opened a hat business to support the family. The following year, on August 2, 1887, at the age of 55, Joseph Hayne Rainey died. *The Charleston News and Courier* wrote in its obituary of him that, besides Robert Brown Elliott, Rainey was the most intelligent of South Carolina's black Reconstruction politicians (Christopher 37).

Sources

Christopher, Maurine. *America's Black Congressmen*. New York: Thomas Y. Crowell, 1971.

"Former Black Members of Congress." *Congressional Times Journal*. <http://www.usbol.com/ctjournal/FrBlkCongMemList.html>. Accessed: 2/21/98.

Kestenbaum, Lawrence. *Political Graveyard: A Database of Historical Cemeteries*, rev. 1/13/98. <http:www.potifos.com/tpg.html>. Accessed: 1/17/98.

Meltzer, Milton. *The Black Americans: A History in Their Own Words, 1619–1987*. New York: Thomas Y. Crowell, 1984.

Charles Bernard Rangel

Reproduced from AP/Wide World Photos, by David Pickoff

Born: June 11, 1930, in New York, New York

Status: U.S. representative from the 15th Congressional District of New York

Education: B.S., 1957, New York University, New York, New York; J.D., 1960, St. John's University School of Law, Jamaica, New York; admitted to the bar of New York, 1960

Position: U.S. Army, 1948–1952; lawyer, private practice, New York, New York, 1960–1961; assistant U.S. attorney, Southern District of New York, 1961–1962; legal counsel to a number of organizations, 1963–1966; state representative, New York assembly, 1966–1970; U.S. representative from the 16th (later, 15th) District of New York, 1970–

Early Years

Charles Bernard Rangel was born on June 11, 1930, in the Harlem section of New York City. At that time, drugs and crime were growing social concerns in Harlem, and Rangel became aware of the tremendous negative impact of drugs on people and society. His early experience led to the anti-drug position that he would take in his political career.

Rangel attended public schools near his home in Harlem and later attended DeWitt High School in the Bronx section of New York City. He dropped out of high school in his junior year and, after working in a number of boring, low-paying jobs, joined the army in 1948. The Korean War was taking place at the time, and Rangel was sent to Korea.

While stationed in Korea, Rangel earned both a Purple Heart and a Bronze Star when he rescued more than 40 soldiers trapped behind enemy lines. Although Rangel saw opportunities in the army, he had no desire to make it a career. Pervasive discrimination against blacks was evident, and he realized that his advancement would be limited as few African Americans gained promotion. In addition, leaving the army would give him the opportunity to attend college through the G.I. Bill.

Higher Education

When Rangel was discharged from the army in 1952, he returned to New York, where he completed high school quickly and obtained his diploma. In 1954, he entered New York University's School of Commerce. Rangel did well at NYU and graduated in 1957. He received a scholarship to attend graduate school at St. John's University in Jamaica, New York, where he studied law. Rangel graduated from St. John's University in 1960 and was admitted to the bar that same year.

Career Highlights

In 1960, Rangel began practicing law in his old neighborhood in Harlem. He also joined the Carver Club, the Harlem political machine that supported the election of minority candidates. Many of the cases Rangel handled that year involved civil rights issues, and he gained recognition for his work in this area. In 1961, Attorney General Robert F. Kennedy offered him the position of assistant U.S. attorney for the Southern District of New York. Recognizing the opportunity to increase his political visibility as well as his income, Rangel accepted the offer—and served in this position until 1962.

After stepping down as U.S. attorney, Rangel acted as counsel for a number of groups, such as New York City's Housing and Redevelopment Board and the National Advisory Commission on Selective Service. He also continued his work with the Carver Club, devoting long hours supporting the election of minority candidates. In 1965, Rangel decided that he would run for office and entered the race for state representative of central Harlem's 72nd District. Rangel's popularity in the district and his extensive involvement with the Carver Club assured his victory in the election.

When Rangel took his seat in the New York assembly in 1966, he brought with him his life experiences from the streets of Harlem. He took strong stances on issues that affected his constituents regarding social programs and job opportunities. He also continued to build his political base, becoming friendly with Nelson Rockefeller, who was then governor of New York State.

After four years in the assembly, Rangel decided the time was right to aim for Congress. Adam Clayton Powell, Jr., who represented the 16th Congressional District of New York (Rangel's assembly district in Harlem), was under increasing fire from his constituents and from Congress. During the late 1960s, Powell had been censured and fined by Congress for various ethical improprieties, and then frequently became absent from House sessions. Rangel knew he had a tough fight ahead of him, though, because Powell was an extremely charismatic figure who remained popular despite the charges against him.

Rangel ran a hard race. His record in the New York assembly spoke for him, and he was able to draw upon the strong political base he had built over the years; but he was running against a man who, in many ways, had become an icon of success for Harlem. The results of the primary election indicate how tight the race was; Rangel defeated Powell by a mere 150 votes. In the general election, however, Rangel went on to easy victory, garnering 80 percent of the vote (Bigelow 203).

When Rangel took his seat in Congress in 1970, he was assigned to the Select Committee on Crime. Drugs were becoming an issue of growing concern to the people and the government of the United States, and Rangel quickly became one of the most vocal opponents of drug trafficking. In 1971, he was one of the leaders who fought for passage of an amendment giving the president authority to cut military and financial aid to countries that did not cooperate with the United States in attempting to reduce the drug trade. Throughout his career in Congress, drug abuse and drug trafficking remained prime concerns for Rangel. Later, he chaired the Congressional Drug Abuse and Control Caucus. As he once commented, "Not one ounce of opium or coca, which are used to make heroin and cocaine and crack, is grown here on U.S. soil. Ending foreign supplies must become as important to the administration as stopping communism. It's not communists killing our kids; it's drugs" (Bigelow 205).

During his first term in office, the boundaries of the 16th District that Rangel represented were redrawn; it became the 15th District and included a portion of New York City's predominantly white West Side in addition to central Harlem. When Rangel's first term neared an end, he faced not only a changed district, but a strong challenger in Livingston Wingate, who had directed an anti-poverty organization in Harlem and was well known and liked in the area. Despite the fact that many former supporters of Adam Clayton Powell, Jr., threw themselves behind Wingate, Rangel was victorious in both the primary and the general election.

When Rangel returned to the House, he continued his battle against drugs and worked for equality, championing various social programs. He was a founding member of the Congressional Black Caucus during his first term of office and, in 1974, was elected its chairman.

He also was appointed a member of the House Judiciary Committee, which was a position that brought him to national attention during the time that the committee was holding impeachment hearings against President Richard Nixon.

Over the years, Rangel has made his mark in Congress and in the country. In addition to his war on drugs, he was the principal author of the Federal Empowerment Zone project to revitalize urban neighborhoods, and he authored the Low Income Housing tax credit, which made financing available for affordable housing. Rangel has sponsored legislation making thousands of jobs available to underprivileged young people and veterans, and in 1998 he fought for the revitalization of America's public schools.

Rangel has not faced a serious challenge to his seat in Congress, and he has established a record of sound leadership. During the 1980s, he authored the Rangel Amendment, which utilized the United States tax code to penalize American companies operating in apartheid South Africa. The amendment resulted in many American companies and organizations ridding themselves of stocks and other economic investments in South African companies. As senior member of the Trade Subcommittee of the Committee on Ways and Means, as well as a member of its Human Resources Subcommittee, Rangel was named a member of President Clinton's Export Council, which is working toward the inclusion of developing countries in Africa and the Caribbean in the global trade market. He has served as deputy Democratic whip, as well.

Charles Rangel is nearing the 30-year mark in his tenure in Congress and has yet to slacken his efforts on behalf of minorities and the underprivileged in this country and around the world.

Sources

Bigelow, Barbara Carlisle, ed. *Contemporary Black Biography: Profiles from the International Black Community*, Vol 3. Detroit, MI: Gale Research, 1993.

Clay, William L. *Just Permanent Interests: Black Americans in Congress, 1870–1991*. New York: Amistad Press, 1992.

"Congressman Charles B. Rangel." *New York State Democratic Committee Home Page*. <http://www.nydems.org/elected/rangel.html>.

Estell, Kenneth. *African America: Celebrating 400 years of Achievement*. Detroit, MI: Visible Ink Press, 1994.

"Rangel Is Longtime Advocate of U.S.-Africa Trade." *Africa News Online*, 2 December 1997. <http://www.africanews.org/usaf/stories/19971202_feat4.html>. Accessed: 4/2/98.

James Thomas Rapier

Born: November 13, 1837, in Florence, Alabama

Status: Died May 31, 1883, in Montgomery, Alabama; buried in Calvary Cemetery, St. Louis, Missouri

Education: Attended a school for black children in Nashville, Tennessee, for six years, c. 1847–c. 1853; attended school in Buxton, Ontario, Canada, c. 1855; attended a normal institute in Toronto, Ontario, Canada, c. 1856; received teaching certificate, 1863

Position: Teacher, Buxton, Ontario, Canada, 1863; reporter, Nashville, Tennessee, 1864; delegate, Tennessee constitutional convention, 1865; cotton farmer, Alabama, 1865–1883; publisher and editor, *Montgomery Sentinel*, Montgomery, Alabama, 1866–c. 1871; platform committee chairman, Alabama Republican State Convention, 1866; delegate, Alabama constitutional convention, 1867; U.S. commissioner for Alabama, International Exposition, Paris, France, 1867; Republican candidate for Alabama secretary of state, 1870; tax assessor, State of Alabama, 1871; U.S. representative from the Second Congressional District of Alabama, 1873–1875; U. S. commissioner for Alabama, Fifth International Exposition, Vienna, Austria, 1873; collector of internal revenue for the Second District of Alabama, 1878–1883

Early Years

James Thomas Rapier was born on November 13, 1837, in Florence, Alabama. His mother, Susan, was a free black woman, and his father, John H. Rapier, was a former slave and a man of modest circumstances who worked as a barber. James was the youngest of the four sons born to John and Susan Rapier.

John Rapier hoped to improve his sons' lives, and knowing that improvement lay in education, he sent James and one of his brothers to a Negro school in Nashville, Tennessee, for six years. After James finished at the school, he worked on boats plying the Mississippi for two years, but he wanted to do more. Knowing that educational opportunities were limited for African Americans in the United Sates, James went to Canada where he attended a school in an experimental black community in Buxton, Ontario.

Higher Education

There is some dispute regarding Rapier's higher education. Historian Maurine Christopher writes that Rapier was sent "to Montreal College in Canada, the University of Glasgow in Scotland, and Franklin College in Nashville, Tennessee" (Christopher 126). However, there was no Montreal College in Montreal at the time (the University of Montreal was not founded until 1878), and there was and is no Franklin College in Nashville. Far more likely, as other sources assert, is the idea that Rapier attended a teacher-training institute in Toronto, Ontario, Canada, and that that was the extent of his education. Regardless of where he studied, however, as he entered his professional life, James T. Rapier was an educated, insightful man with a dedication to helping others.

Career Highlights

After obtaining his teaching certificate, James Rapier taught for a brief time in the community that had earlier helped him with his own education, Buxton, in Ontario, Canada. But Canada was not involved in the strife that plagued the United States, and Rapier wished to do more to help further equality for blacks in the United States. In 1864, Rapier left his position in Canada, traveled to Tennessee, and settled in Nashville, a town familiar to him from his early schooling. He found a job as a reporter for a northern newspaper and took his first steps into the world of politics.

On April 9, 1865, Lee surrendered the Confederacy to Grant at Appomattox Courthouse in Virginia. Suddenly, new opportunities were available to those who previously had been enslaved. Like so many other black leaders of the day, Rapier worked for black enfranchisement. He was the keynote speaker at the Tennessee Negro Suffrage Convention in Nashville in 1865 and, later that year, was a delegate to the Tennessee constitutional convention.

Home for Rapier, however, was Alabama. Disheartened by Tennessee's failure to grant the vote to blacks, Rapier returned to Alabama and to his family. He leased 550 acres of land and planted cotton on it, a successful venture that funded his other interests. Because of his education, prosperity, and past political experience, Rapier became involved in politics again and spoke out for equality. In 1866, he became the publisher and editor of the *Montgomery Sentinel*, the voice of Republicanism for that area.

Rapier worked diligently for black enfranchisement, serving as the platform committee chairman for the 1866 Alabama Republican State Convention. While promoting the vote for blacks, he wisely opposed the move to disenfranchise whites who had aided the Confederacy, recognizing that such a move would alienate most whites against equality.

Because of his sound leadership, in October, 1867, Rapier was elected a delegate to Alabama's constitutional convention. The following year, however, his political career came to an abrupt halt. Embittered by his continuing success and mounting influence, in September, 1868, his political enemies accused Rapier of conspiring to burn down the

Tuscumbia Female Academy near his family home in Florence, Alabama. Rapier fled for his life to Montgomery where he all but disappeared until the accusation was proven false.

Finally free of the charges against him, Rapier again entered politics, working for black rights. In 1870, he was nominated as the Republican candidate for secretary of state, the first African American to run for a state office in Alabama. Although defeated, in 1871 Rapier was offered a federal appointment as a tax assessor, which he accepted.

In August of 1872, Rapier was nominated as the Republican candidate for the Second Congressional District of Alabama. After a bitter and sometimes violent campaign, he was declared the victor and, on December 1, 1873, was sworn into the House of Representatives as Alabama's second black representative (the first was **Benjamin Sterling Turner** from the First Congressional District of Alabama, who served from 1871 to 1873). Upon being seated, Rapier was assigned to the Committee on Education and Labor.

During his term in Congress, Rapier took an active role in the battle for black equality, condemning the past and present treatment of African Americans and discrimination in Washington, D.C. In one eloquent speech before the House, he said,

> I am subjected to far more outrages and indignities in coming to and going from the Capitol in discharge of my public duties than any criminal in the country providing he be white. Instead of my position shielding me from insult, it too often invites it. (Christopher 129)

Unlike other black representatives in the House who found all their goals thwarted, Rapier was able to accomplish several of his. On June 20, 1874, President Ulysses S. Grant signed into effect Rapier's Montgomery Port Bill, which made Montgomery a federal port of delivery, thereby aiding the faltering Alabama economy. Rapier also worked to obtain educational funding for Alabama and strenuously pushed for passage of a new Civil Rights Act.

By the summer of 1874, when Rapier returned to Alabama to campaign for reelection, violence against blacks was mounting, and there were, as in other states, a growing number of white secret societies intent on stopping African Americans from voting or running for office. The election of 1874 was rampant with violence, bribery, and fraud, and when the smoke cleared, Rapier had been defeated by Jeremiah Williams, an ex-Confederate army major. Rapier returned to the lame-duck session of Congress and was able to witness the passage of the Civil Rights Act for which he had worked so hard, although it had been modified.

In 1876, Rapier moved to Lowndes County, Alabama, the Fourth District, to run again for Congress. Lowndes County was the only district that had retained a black majority of voters after the state had been redistricted by a Democratic state legislature. Because of a split vote, however, the election went to the Democratic candidate, and Rapier all but retired from politics.

In 1878, Rapier was appointed collector of internal revenue for the Second District of Alabama and spent most of his remaining years in this position, in addition to campaigning on behalf of Republican candidates. In 1883, he was forced by ill health to resign from his position as collector, and he died of tuberculosis on May 31, at the age of 46. James T. Rapier never married; he devoted his life to furthering the cause of racial equality and to alleviating the plight of southern blacks.

Sources

Christopher, Maurine. *America's Black Congressmen*. New York: Thomas Y. Crowell, 1971.

Clay, William L. *Just Permanent Interests: Black Americans in Congress, 1870–1991*. New York: Amistad Press, 1992.

"Former Black Members of Congress." *Congressional Times Journal*. <http://www.usbol.com/ctjournal/FrBlkCongMemList.html>. Accessed: 2/13/98.

Smith, Jessie Carney, ed. *Black Firsts: 2,000 Years of Extraordinary Achievement*. Detroit, MI: Visible Ink Press, 1994.

Hiram Rhodes Revels

Reproduced from the Library of Congress, courtesy of the U.S. Senate Historical Office

Born: September 1 or September 27, 1822 or 1827, in Fayetteville, North Carolina

Status: Died January 16, 1901, in Aberdeen, Mississippi; buried in Holly Springs, Mississippi

Education: Educated at a seminary in Indiana; attended Knox College, Galesburg, Illinois, 1856–1857; ordained as a minister in the African Methodist Episcopal Church, Baltimore, Maryland, 1845

Position: First black member of the United States Senate, 1870–1871; first president, Alcorn Agricultural and Mechanical College, Lorman, Mississippi, 1871–1874 and 1876–1882; Mississippi secretary of state ad interim, 1873

Early Years

Few accurate official records were kept on the births and deaths of free blacks during the early nineteenth century. Depending upon the sources consulted, which are equally divided, Hiram Rhodes (Rhoades) Revels was born on September 1 or September 27 in either 1822 or 1827. What is known is that he was born of free parents in Fayetteville, North Carolina. His parents were of mixed African, Indian (Croatan), and Scottish heritage. His father was a Baptist minister.

Educational opportunities were limited for African Americans, and Revels, like other black boys at that time, was expected to learn a trade. A series of repressive laws in the southern states against free blacks limited not only their freedom of movement but also the educational opportunities available to them.

In the 1820s Nat Turner, a Virginia slave, came to believe that he was divinely ordained to lead his fellow slaves out of bondage. In 1831, after a solar eclipse that he construed as a "sign," he and seven other slaves murdered Turner's master, Joseph Travis, and Travis's entire faimly. Gathering more slaves from surrounding plantations, the group then went on a two-day rampage, killing 55 white persons. Although Turner and 16 companions were later captured and hanged, the rebellion stunned the South. In panic, almost every southern state quickly enacted harsher slave codes restricting the movements of blacks and forbidding their education.

On March 8, 1838, therefore, Revels entered into an apprenticeship to work in the barbershop of his brother, Elias B. Revels. Revels knew that education was the road to betterment, however. When his brother died unexpectedly in 1841, ending his apprenticeship, Revels traveled north to seek his education. He settled at last at a Quaker school in Liberty, Indiana, in 1844.

The Quakers, also known as the Society of Friends, had long protested slavery. One of their missions was to establish schools that were open to all people. Many prominent black leaders of that time received their early education in Quaker schools.

Higher Education

Having completed his education at the Quaker school, Revels moved to Baltimore, Maryland, where he was ordained a minister in the African Methodist Episcopal (AME) Church. However, he wanted "something more than a mere business education" (noted in an autobiographical sketch he dictated to his eldest daughter before his death) so he entered the Union County Quaker Seminary in Indiana, where he was the only black student.

For the next 15 years, Revels carried his ministry to black congregations throughout the Midwest, traveling to Ohio, Indiana, Illinois, Tennessee, Kentucky, Missouri, and Kansas. During this time, he married Phoeba Bass of Zanesville, Ohio. He also sought opportunities to further his education and attended Knox College in Galesburg, Illinois, on a scholarship.

His ministry in the Midwest was not without hazards. Revels wrote, "At times, I met with a great deal of opposition. I was imprisoned in Missouri in 1854 for preaching the gospel to Negroes, though I was never subjected to violence" (Christopher 2). After the years of danger, he and his family finally settled in Baltimore, Maryland, where he assumed the pastorship of a local church and became the principal of a school for black young people in 1860.

Career Highlights

The outbreak of the Civil War in 1861 energized Revels. Although Maryland was a border state with divided loyalties, Revels eagerly set to work for the Union cause, helping to organize and enlist men for the two Maryland regiments of black troops. Revels was sent by the AME Church to Missouri to organize a school for African Americans in St. Louis. He continued his recruitment efforts and organized black volunteers into a regiment from Missouri in 1863. But merely recruiting men to fight was not enough for Revels. Giving up his civilian ministry, Revels applied and was accepted for active duty as a chaplain for a Mississippi regiment of free blacks fighting for the Union. He was respected by his superior officers for his calm demeanor and governing ability and, as a result, was appointed provost marshall of Vicksburg, Mississippi, for a short time.

At the conclusion of the Civil War, Revels returned to his ministry and was assigned briefly to churches in Leavenworth, Kansas, and New Orleans, Louisiana. In 1866, he was given a permanent pastorship in Natchez, Mississippi, where he settled with his wife and five daughters, continued his ministerial work, and founded schools for black children.

The end of the Civil War ushered in the Reconstruction period, when the hegemony of upper-class whites in the South was interrupted, and groups that in the past had little or no voice in the management of their state's government suddenly were empowered. Under Reconstruction, southern states were ordered to form new governments, write new constitutions, elect new officials, and register black men to vote. Often, as in Mississippi, this reorganization was overseen by military troops sent by the federal government. While many white "carpetbaggers" from the North and "scalawags" from the South managed to acquire power in the new governments, Reconstruction also provided an opportunity for black men of education and influence to try to help shape the new South.

In 1868, Hiram Revels was elected to the position of alderman in Natchez, and in 1869 he was elected to represent his area, Adams County, in the Mississippi State Senate. One of the most pressing issues before the newly formed senate was the election of replacement representatives to the United States Congress and Senate, as those who had held office before the Civil War were now barred from reclaiming their seats. On January 20, 1870, after a heated debate, Revels was elected by a vote of 81 to 15 to fill the unexpired senatorial term of Jefferson Davis, the former president of the Confederacy.

Revels's election did not go unchallenged on the federal level. In fact, it met with considerable opposition from within the Senate. Opponents to Revels's election first challenged his credentials. They also argued that, according to the Supreme Court decision in the case of Dred Scott, Revels, a black man, could not be counted as a citizen before the passage of the 14th Amendment in 1866 and its ratification in 1868. Since election to the Senate required that the person elected have nine years' prior citizenship, they argued, Revels could not be seated, having been a citizen by law for only two to four years.

Supporters of Revels countered this argument by stating that the Dred Scott decision applied only to those blacks who were of pure African blood. Revels was a mulatto, as evidenced by his light skin, so he was exempt, they said, and had been a citizen all his life. This argument prevailed, and on February 25, 1870, Revels, by a vote of 48 to 8, became the first black man ever to be seated in the United States Senate.

Always the voice of compromise and moderation, although a staunch advocate of equality among blacks and whites, Revels tried to reassure the members of the Senate who still might have held doubts about his or any black person's participation in the government. In his first speech to the Senate on March 16, 1870, in a plea to reinstate the black legislators of the Georgia general assembly who had been illegally ousted by white representatives, he said, "I maintain that the past record of my race is a true index of the feelings which today animate them. They aim not to elevate themselves by sacrificing one single interest of their white fellow citizens" (Ploski 18).

This plea for reason was to characterize Revels's career in the Senate. Although he served on both the Committee on Education and Labor and the Committee on the District of Columbia, the general business of the Senate at that time frequently focused on the ongoing Reconstruction. While others called for punishment or monetary fines against ex-Confederates, for example, Revels argued for amnesty for them and a restoration of full citizenship, provided they swore an oath of loyalty to the United States.

Revels's term lasted only a little over a year, until March 3, 1871, but during that time he quietly, persistently—although for the most part unsuccessfully—worked for equality. He spoke against an amendment proposed by Senator Allen G. Thurman to keep the schools of Washington, D.C., segregated. He nominated a young black man, Michael Howard, to the United States Military Academy, although Howard was subsequently denied admission. Revels was successful, however, in championing the cause of black workers who had been barred by their color from working at the Washington Navy Yard.

Revels was praised in the newspapers for his oratorical abilities. His conduct in the Senate, along with that of the other African Americans who had been seated in the House of Representatives, also prompted a white contemporary, James G. Blaine, to say, "The colored men who took their seats in both Senate and House were as a rule studious, earnest, ambitious men, whose public conduct would be honorable to any race" (Smythe 38).

When Revels's term in the Senate ended, he went home to Mississippi and accepted an appointment as the first president of Alcorn Agricultural and Mechanical College (now Alcorn State University) in Lorman, Mississippi, where he also taught philosophy. Alcorn, which was founded in 1871, was the first land-grant college for black students in the United States. During 1873, Revels took a leave of absence from Alcorn to serve as Mississippi's secretary of state ad interim, resigning as president of Alcorn in 1874 because of political pressure. Republican governor Adelbert Ames, a political foe of Revels, had been plotting to remove

Revels from the presidency. To forestall this move, Revels resigned, although both faculty and students protested his resignation. With the election in 1876 of a Democratic governor, John M. Stone, who was more favorably disposed toward him, Revels was reappointed to the position of president of Alcorn, where he remained until his retirement in 1882.

In addition to his involvement in state politics and his position at Alcorn, Revels remained active in his ministry. For a time, he served as editor of the *Southwestern Christian Advocate* and taught theology at Shaw College (now Rust College), founded in 1866 in Holly Springs, Mississippi, where Revels and his family made their home. Hiram Revels died on January 16, 1901, while attending a church conference in Aberdeen, Mississippi. At his funeral in Holly Springs, Revels was honored as a minister, a scholar, and the first black man to sit in the United States Senate.

Sources

Christopher, Maurine. *America's Black Congressmen*. New York: Thomas Y. Crowell, 1971.

Family Encyclopedia of American History. Pleasantville, NY: The Reader's Digest Assoc., 1975.

"Former Black Members of Congress." *Congressional Times Journal*. <http://www.usbol.com/ctjournal/FrBlkCongMemList.html>. Accessed: 1/21/98.

"Hiram Rhoades Revels." <http://www.ils.unc.edu/nc/HiramRevels.html>. Accessed 1/21/98.

"Hiram Rhodes Revels." *North Carolina Encyclopedia*. State Library of North Carolina. <http://www.cler.state.nc.us/nc/bio/afro/revels.html>. Accessed: 1/21/98.

Kestenbaum, Lawrence. *Political Graveyard: A Database of Historic Cemeteries*, rev. 1/13/98. <http://www.potifos.com/tpg.html>. Accessed: 1/17/98.

Lamson, Peggy. *The Glorious Failure: Black Congressman Robert Brown Elliott and the Reconstruction of South Carolina*. New York: W.W. Norton and Co., 1973.

New Grolier Multimedia Encyclopedia. Novata, CA: The Software Toolworks, Inc./Grolier, Inc., 1993.

Ploski, Harry A., and James Williams, eds. *The Negro Almanac: A Reference Work on the African American*. Detroit, MI: Gale Research, 1989.

Smythe, Mabel M., ed. *The Black American Reference Book*. Englewood Cliffs, NJ: Prentice-Hall, Inc., 1976.

Carl Thomas Rowan

Copyright Washington Post, *reprinted by permission of D.C. Public Library, by Bernie Burton*

Born: August 11, 1925, in Ravenscroft, Tennessee

Status: Journalist, commentator

Education: Graduate, valedictorian, 1942, Bernard High School, McMinnville, Tennessee; attended Tennessee State University, Nashville, Tennessee, 1942–1943; attended Washburn University, Topeka, Kansas, 1943–1944; B.A. in mathematics, 1947, Oberlin College, Oberlin, Ohio; M.A. in journalism, 1948, University of Minnesota

Position: Commissioned officer, U.S. Navy, 1943–1946; freelance writer, correspondent, *Baltimore Afro-American*, *Minneapolis Spokesman*, *St. Paul Recorder*, 1947–1948; copy editor, *Minneapolis Tribune*, Minneapolis, Minnesota, 1948–1950; staff reporter, *Minneapolis Tribune*, Minneapolis, Minnesota, 1950–1961; deputy assistant secretary for public affairs, U.S. Department of State, Washington, D.C., 1961–1963; U.S. ambassador to Finland, 1963–1964; director, United States Information Agency, 1964–1965; syndicated columnist, *Chicago Daily News*, 1965–1978, *Chicago Sun Times*, 1978– ; radio commentator, "The Rowan Report," Westinghouse Broadcasting Co.; radio and television commentator, Post-Newsweek Broadcasting Co.; panelist, "Agronsky and Co." and "Inside Washington" television shows; frequent panelist on "Meet the Press"

Awards and honors: Sidney Hillman Award, 1952; named one of "America's Ten Outstanding Young Men" by the U.S. Chamber of Commerce, 1954; Anti-Defamation League of B'nai B'rith communications award, 1964; "Washington Journalist of the Year," Capital Press Club, 1978; American Black Achievement Award, *Ebony*, 1978; George Foster Peabody Award, 1978; Alfred I. Dupont-Columbia University Silver Baton, 1987; Spingarn Medal, NAACP, 1997

Early Years

Soon after Carl Thomas Rowan was born on August 11, 1925, his family moved from Ravenscroft, Tennessee, to McMinnville, Tennessee, where he grew up. Rowan's early years were filled with poverty and want. The family lived in a house with no electricity, as Rowan mentions in his autobiography, *Breaking Barriers*. His father, Thomas David Rowan, worked as an unskilled laborer stacking lumber, and his mother, Johnnie B. Rowan, took in laundry. Rowan and the other children of the family worked in menial jobs around town to try to supplement what their parents earned.

Times were hard, but Rowan escaped through books and education. When he was in high school, one teacher in particular, "Miss Bessie," helped him pursue his love of learning. In those days, not only were the schools segregated, but blacks usually were not permitted in libraries. This was true in McMinnville, but Miss Bessie would smuggle books out of the library for Rowan to read, encouraging him in his dreams. As Rowan says in *Breaking Barriers*, Miss Bessie taught him that, "If you don't read, you can't write, and if you can't write, you can stop dreaming" (LaBlanc 208).

Higher Education

Rowan excelled in school and graduated in 1942 from Bernard High School in McMinnville as valedictorian of his class. Hoping to continue his education, Rowan went to Nashville, where his grandparents lived, to attend college. He found a job as a hospital attendant and enrolled in Tennessee State University, which at the time was an all-black college. In 1943, a professor at the university recommended that he take the examination to be admitted into the officer-training program for the U.S. Navy. Joining the navy would enable Rowan to obtain the education he wanted.

Rowan took and passed the examination and joined the navy in 1943. He was assigned to the officer-training program at Washburn University in Topeka, Kansas, where he was one of the first 15 African Americans to be admitted to the V-12 officer training program. As a continuation of the program, Rowan attended Oberlin College in Oberlin, Ohio, and later the Naval Reserve Midshipmen School in Fort Schuyler, Bronx, New York. After he completed the training and received his commission, Rowan was assigned to sea duty, working as deputy commander of the communications division.

The navy taught him a great deal. As he later wrote, "When you are plucked out of a totally Jim Crow environment at age seventeen and thrown into a totally white environment where more is at stake than your personal life, you mature rapidly" (LaBlanc 209). Rowan had seen much of the country and the world during his three years in the navy. He had liked his officer-training stint at Oberlin College, and at the end of World War II, when he was discharged from the navy in 1946, he decided to continue his education there. Oberlin was one of the first colleges to accept black students.

Rowan majored in mathematics and graduated in 1947.

After finding a job as a freelance writer for the Negro newspaper chain, the *Baltimore Afro-American*, Rowan continued his education at the University of Minnesota, where he majored in journalism. In addition to writing for the *Afro-American*, he also wrote for two other black newspapers, the *Minneapolis Spokesman* and the *St. Paul Recorder.*

Career Highlights

Rowan graduated in 1948 with a master's degree in journalism and was hired by the *Minneapolis Tribune* as a copy editor. In 1950, he was promoted to the rank of reporter, becoming the paper's first black reporter.

Following his promotion, Rowan came to national attention for a series of articles he wrote about discrimination in the South. A friend in the navy, also a writer, advised him to "tell all the little things it means to be a Negro in the South, or anyplace where being a Negro makes a difference" (LaBlanc 209). During the next several months, Rowan traveled more than 6,000 miles as he wrote the series, which was published in 1951 and entitled "How Far from Slavery." The series earned him the Sidney Hillman Award in 1952 for the best newspaper reporting and later was published in book form under the title *South of Freedom* (1952).

In the wake of the United States Supreme Court's historic decision in *Brown v. Board of Education* of Topeka, Kansas, which abolished "separate but equal" education, Rowan commenced a second series of articles entitled "Jim Crow's Last Stand." In these articles, he discussed the previous cases that led to the Court's decision. The articles met with critical acclaim and won Rowan further recognition and awards.

That same year, 1954, Rowan was invited by the U.S. State Department to go to India to discuss the role of the free press. In addition to his talks, Rowan wrote a series for the *Tribune* on India and on Southeast Asia, where he traveled after finishing his tour of India. These articles earned Rowan additional awards and formed the basis of his book, *The Pitiful and the Proud* (1956).

The civil rights movement was gaining ground in America, and Rowan already had reported on civil rights abuses in the South. He wanted to write about the turbulent events of the 1950s and early 1960s. He also became actively involved as a member of the Committee of 100, which raised money for the NAACP Legal Defense Fund. Rowan's writing began appearing in a variety of magazines and newspapers throughout the country. He was respected for his views and reporting and was in demand as a reporter. Rowan expressed his opinions of the government's role in the search for black equality in his 1957 book *Go South to Sorrow*, which, as he later said, lashed "out at President Eisenhower, Hodding Carter, and other gradualists who, in my view, were compromising away the freedom of America's black people" (LaBlanc 210).

In 1956, Rowan was assigned to cover events at the United Nations in New York. He became particularly incensed at the Soviet Union's reprisal against Hungary after the Hungarian uprising in 1956 and at the United States for tip-toeing around the situation. The United States, rather than condemning either Hungary or the Soviet Union, took a "moderate approach" (Smith 583).

In 1960, he interviewed the two presidential candidates, Richard M. Nixon and John F. Kennedy. Kennedy was very impressed with Rowan and, in 1961, asked him to accept the position of deputy assistant secretary of state for public affairs. For Rowan, this was one of the most difficult positions he had ever held because of the sensitive nature of much of the information he was handling. He was torn between the necessity of keeping some information from the press and his journalistic impulse toward fully informing the public. During this time, the United States was becoming involved in Vietnam and was negotiating for the exchange of pilot Francis Gary Powers, who was being held on spy charges in the Soviet Union.

In 1963, President Lyndon Johnson appointed Rowan ambassador to Finland. The following year, President Johnson named him director of the United States Information Agency, which was the highest federal position ever held by an African American up to that time. Rowan and his agency were asked to develop a psychological warfare program to help the war effort.

Rowan resigned from the agency in 1965 to return to journalism and accepted an offer from the Field Newspaper Syndicate to write a national column. At the same time, he began broadcasting commentaries on national and foreign events for the Westinghouse Broadcasting Company and later for the Post-Newsweek Broadcasting Company. As a columnist and commentator, Rowan has, over the years, become known for his unblinking views on both public policies and public personalities. He became known as "one of the most respected and admired journalists on the Washington scene," as correspondent Helen Thomas said in her comments on his book *Breaking Barriers*, and "has held the liberal banner high for the disadvantaged and the afflicted" (LaBlanc 211).

In 1997, Rowan was presented with the NAACP's Spingarn Award at the NAACP convention in Pittsburgh, Pennsylvania. In presenting the award, NAACP chairperson, Myrlie Evers-Williams, said, "Carl Rowan has been repeatedly recognized by military, civic, and governmental groups ... His achievements and merit make him someone we are proud to recognize" ("Carl Rowan Wins NAACP Medal"). All his life, Rowan has been a proponent of self-help, believing that you can improve yourself and your situation if you only work at it. His life and achievements stand as prime examples of the results of that belief.

Sources

"Carl Rowan Wins NAACP Medal." *NAACP Online*. 9 July 1997. <http://www.naacp.org/president/releases/archives/1997/rowan.htm>

LaBlanc, Michael L., ed. *Contemporary Black Biography: Profiles from the International Black Community*, Vol. 1. Detroit, MI: Gale Research, 1992.

Rowan, Carl Thomas. *Breaking Barriers*. New York: Little, Brown and Co., 1991.

Smith, Jessie Carney, ed. *Black Heroes of the 20th Century*. Detroit, MI: Visible Ink Press, 1998.

S

Gustavus "Gus" Savage

Reproduced from AP/Wide World Photos, by Doug Mills

Born: October 30, 1925, in Detroit, Michigan

Status: Retired from public office

Education: Graduate, 1943, Wendell Phillips High School, Chicago, Illinois; B.A. in philosophy, 1951, Roosevelt University, Chicago, Illinois; attended Chicago-Kent College of Law, Chicago, Illinois, 1952–1953

Position: U.S. Army, 1943–1946; organizer, Progressive Party, Chicago, Illinois, late 1940s; journalist, Chicago, Illinois, 1954; chairman, South End Voters' Conference, Chicago, Illinois, 1960s; publisher and editor, *Citizen Newspapers*, Chicago, Illinois, 1965–1998; U.S. representative from the Second Congressional District of Illinois, Chicago, 1981–1992

Early Years

Gus Savage was born in Detroit, Michigan, on October 30, 1925, and grew up in Chicago, Illinois, where he learned firsthand about racism and segregation during the 1930s and the Great Depression. These lessons were to color the rest of his life and influence his unceasing battle for civil rights.

After graduating from Chicago's Wendell Phillips High School in 1943, Savage entered the U.S. Army.

Higher Education

When Savage was discharged from the army in 1946, he returned to Chicago and began studies in philosophy at Roosevelt University, from which he graduated in 1951. In addition to studying, Savage worked full time as an organizer for the Progressive Party in Chicago. Planning to pursue a career in law, Savage entered the Chicago-Kent College of Law in 1952, but left in 1953 to begin a career in journalism.

Career Highlights

The late 1950s and early 1960s were turbulent times in America. The civil rights movement was gaining strength. The images of Rosa Parks and Martin Luther King, Jr., had come to represent a new kind of freedom for African Americans across the country. Many joined wholeheartedly in the marches and protests for equality. Gus Savage was one of those many; in addition to reporting on the events that were occurring daily, he also promoted the programs of Dr. King and of Elijah Muhammad and became actively involved in Chicago politics. During the 1960s, Savage held the position of chairman of Chicago's South End Voters Conference, as well as campaign manager for the Midwest League of Negro Voters.

Savage realized the power of the written word and, in 1965, became the editor and publisher of *Citizen Newspapers*, which published a group of independent community news weeklies. In his papers, Savage continued his battle for civil rights, with rhetoric that was often militant.

In 1968, Savage involved himself directly in the political process when he challenged incumbent congressman William T. Murphy for his seat in Congress. But Murphy had the support of Chicago's "political machine," an entity Savage had loudly and publicly denounced, and easily overcame Savage's challenge in the primary election.

Savage again unsuccessfully challenged Murphy in 1970. In December, 1979, Murphy announced his upcoming retirement from Congress and Savage was at last victorious. Entering the race against a machine-backed candidate and two others, Savage was able to win the favor of the predominantly black neighborhoods of the Second District. He easily defeated the primary challenge and walked away with 88 percent of the vote in the general election.

When Savage became a member of Congress on January 3, 1981, he was appointed to the Committee on Public Works and Transportation and to the Subcommittee on Economic Development. He sought to promote minority interests and, in 1986, successfully sponsored an amendment that provided funds for minority-owned businesses, institutions, and black colleges.

Although he continued his work for civil rights in Congress, increasingly his militant views and speech were alienating people. As he had done in print in his newspapers, Savage vocally attacked anyone he felt hindered minority interests. Until 1990, this was a popular tactic with his constituents, who were primarily black. In 1990, however, as is required every 10 years, Illinois underwent redistricting. The new district was not entirely African American. Its boundaries extended southward, "away from Savage's inner-city base and into areas that [were] more affluent and more white suburban, including several largely Jewish communities" ("Congressional Elections").

Two years later, Savage was challenged for his seat in Congress by Mel Reynolds. Unlike Savage, whose verbal attacks were becoming more vitriolic, Reynolds presented a moderate image. A college instructor and Rhodes scholar, Reynolds was more acceptable to the white suburban constituents than was Savage. Reynolds had challenged Savage earlier, in 1988, but Savage had managed to hang on, relying on his popularity with his predominantly black constituents. In 1992, however, the circumstances were entirely new.

Savage had attacked Jewish interests while in Congress, and he carried this into his 1992 campaign. He proclaimed himself a "warrior" for black causes and attacked white racism, the "white racist media," "Jewish money," and "racist Jewish reactionaries" ("Congressional Elections"). Reynolds, who maintained strong support in the suburbs, worked on building support in the inner-city neighborhoods and gained popularity by campaigning in the black churches and other gathering places.

The contest seemed close, but on March 12, 1992, it swung in favor of Reynolds. That day, drive-by shooters fired at Reynolds's car, and he was slightly injured by flying glass. "Although Reynolds said he believed there was no connection between the incident and Savage's campaign, he blamed Savage for using overheated rhetoric that had the potential to incite violence" ("Congressional Elections"). Following this incident, Reynolds became the favored candidate, and Savage lost, receiving only 36.9 percent of the vote to Reynolds's 63.1 percent ("Congressional Elections"). Savage was unrepentant in his loss, proclaiming in his concession speech that, "We have lost to the white racist press and to the racist reactionary Jewish misleaders" ("A Bigot Gets the Boot" 33).

Sources

"A Bigot Gets the Boot." *Time Magazine*, 30 March 1992, 33.

Clay, William L. *Just Permanent Interests: Black Americans in Congress, 1870–1991*. New York: Amistad Press, 1992.

"Congressional Elections: Incumbent Tremors in Illinois." *Congressional Quarterly Weekly Report*, 21 March 1992, 739–44.

"Former Black Members of Congress." *Congressional Times Journal*. <http://www.usbol.com/ctjournal/FrBlkCongMemList.html>. Accessed: 2/21/98.

Robert Smalls

Reproduced from the Collections of the Library of Congress

Born: April 5, 1839, in Beaufort, South Carolina

Status: Died February 22, 1915, in Beaufort, South Carolina; buried in the Tabernacle Baptist Church Cemetery, Beaufort, South Carolina

Education: Self-educated

Position: Slave, hired out as a stevedore, foreman of stevedores, and sailmaker, 1850s; deckhand, "wheelman," C.S.S. *Planter*, 1855–1862; "wheelman," U.S.S. *Planter*, U.S.S. *Keokuk*, 1862–1863; captain, U.S.S. *Planter*, 1863–1866; storekeeper, Beaufort, South Carolina, 1866–c. 1875; delegate, South Carolina State Constitutional Convention, 1868; representative, South Carolina State Legislature, 1868–1870; senator, South Carolina State Senate, 1870–1874; delegate for South Carolina, Republican National Convention, Philadelphia, Pennsylvania, 1872; U.S. representative from the Third Congressional District of South Carolina,

1875–1879, 1882–1883, 1884–1887; member, South Carolina State Constitutional Convention, 1895; customs collector, Beaufort, South Carolina, 1889–1913

Early Years

Robert Smalls was born into slavery on April 5, 1939, in Beaufort, South Carolina, the son of Lydia Small, a slave, and a white man whose name is unknown. At the early age of 12, Smalls was taken by his master, Henry McKee, to Charleston, South Carolina, and hired out to earn money for his owner.

Smalls worked first on the docks of the city as a stevedore, foreman, and then sailmaker. As he grew older, however, he became more knowledgeable about the ships and was hired out to work on the various steamboats sailing out of Charleston's harbor, first as a deckhand, and finally as a "wheelman." Smalls and other black steamer pilots were called "wheelmen" because the "title of 'pilot' was reserved for whites" (Asante and Mattson 81).

During these years, Smalls grew up quickly, not only working hard, but marrying and beginning a family. He married Hannah Jones, a hotel maid who also was a slave, and their first child, Elizabeth Lydia Smalls, was born on February 12, 1858.

Although Smalls had no formal education, he was intelligent and eager to learn at every opportunity. He quickly mastered the skills and knowledge necessary to be an expert pilot and, later in his life, he sought further education. During the Civil War, while his ship underwent repairs in Philadelphia, Pennsylvania, Smalls spent the time studying with hired tutors. Similarly, after the war, when Smalls settled again in Beaufort, he hired a teacher to come to his home and give him lessons. Although his education was haphazard at the best of times, his natural intelligence allowed him to profit from what he had learned.

Career Highlights

Soon after his first daughter was born in 1858, Smalls made arrangements with his wife's owner to pay for her freedom and the freedom of his child. He hoped that they all, himself included, would be free eventually. With the outbreak of the Civil War, however, Smalls was impressed into service as a wheelman on the Confederate steamship *Planter* and, on May 13, 1862, seized freedom for himself and his family.

The previous day, May 12, had been busy. Guns and other supplies were loaded onto the *Planter* for the Confederate troops, and the ship was to sail the next day. In the evening, the white officers went ashore, leaving Smalls and seven other black men to guard the *Planter*. Early on the morning of May 13, Smalls took the wheel of the ship and slipped out of Charleston harbor, stopping briefly only at the North Atlantic wharf where Smalls's wife, children, and eight other blacks awaited the ship. Smalls then steered the *Planter* northward, right under the very noses of the Confederates, hauling up a white flag of surrender as the ship neared a Union stronghold. In addition to gaining his own freedom and that of his family and friends, Smalls was able to turn over to the Union a valuable prize of war, a ship with its entire cargo. At that time, the value of the ship was approximately $60,000. Later, Smalls received a reward from the federal government for the capture of the *Planter*, but his share (the $1,500 award was divided among the crew) was only a pittance. The navy had set the value of the *Planter* at $9,000, vastly underestimating its actual worth; Congress later criticized the navy for this fact.

A hero and famous in both the North and the South, Smalls was appointed pilot by Abraham Lincoln and spent the remainder of the Civil War on a number of Union ships, finishing as he had begun, on the *Planter*, which was being used to transport troops. But this time Smalls commanded the ship as its captain, and it was Smalls who, in 1866, steered it to Baltimore where it was decommissioned at last.

After the war, Smalls and his wife and children returned to his birthplace, Beaufort, South Carolina. Ironically, Smalls was able to purchase the property at 511 Prince Street that had belonged to his former owner, Henry McKee. (On May 30, 1973, Smalls's home was designated a national historic landmark.) Smalls settled into Beaufort life as a storekeeper and as an active participant in both local and state politics. In 1868, he attended the South Carolina State Constitutional Convention as a delegate and, in April of that same year, was elected to the state house of representatives, a position he held until 1870. From 1870 to 1874, he served in the South Carolina State Senate.

Smalls worked hard in the Reconstruction government to provide for the newly freed black citizens of South Carolina. He promoted suffrage and unsuccessfully urged the state to support free public education. At the same time, Smalls was indefatigable in supporting the Republicans both nationally and within his state. In 1874, he was elected to Congress.

Smalls joined the 44th Congress on March 4, 1875, and was appointed to the Agricultural Committee. Even though he was a freshman representative, Smalls joined actively in the debates before Congress. During his first term in office, he was successful in having Port Royale, South Carolina, designated a naval port and in eliciting funds for its improvement. He also pushed for progressive legislation aimed at promoting black equality and the protection of newly freed African Americans. One bill before Congress that Smalls adamantly campaigned against proposed transferring federal troops from the South to the Texas frontier. This, he pointed out, would give groups such as the Ku Klux Klan free license to further terrorize black citizens, who were already being harassed in the South.

During his first campaign for Congress, Smalls met with enthusiasm and support from voters. His record in state government spoke positively for him. By the time he campaigned for reelection in 1876, South Carolina, like most southern states, was in the midst of change. White conservative groups were intimidating voters of every race and driving blacks from public office by every means. Smalls's run for reelection was filled with such turmoil, and the results were challenged by his Democratic opponent, George D. Tillman. Although Congress upheld Smalls's victory, the Democrats, who had regained control of the South Carolina State Legislature in 1877, charged Smalls with accepting a bribe of $5,000 while he was in the state senate. A jury convicted and sentenced him to three years of hard labor despite a lack of evidence. Fortunately—and surprisingly—while Smalls awaited the decision of an appeal to the U.S. Supreme Court, Governor William D. Simpson, a Democrat, issued him a pardon.

Although pardoned, the charges brought against Smalls, coupled with the continued pressure by white groups on black voters, doomed Smalls's bid for reelection in 1878. Undeterred, Smalls ran again in 1880, and, although defeated, he successfully contested the election results and regained his seat in Congress in 1882.

Smalls was again appointed to the Committee on Agriculture and was newly appointed to the Committee on the Militia. However, Smalls's time in Congress was brief. The deliberations on the election results were lengthy, and Smalls was not seated until July 19, 1882, just in time to run for reelection. In September of that same year, he was defeated for the Republican nomination by Edmund W.M. Mackey. But, when Mackey died in January, 1884, Smalls was elected to finish his term of office, and later that year he was reelected to a full term.

Again Smalls tried to promote racial equality in the resolutions he proposed. With other black members of Congress, he proposed that restaurants in Washington, D.C., be required to serve everyone, regardless of color. Discrimination in restaurants was a hardship for black legislators; even the dining room at the Capitol refused to serve them. Smalls also supported legislation to provide equal accommodations for all people, regardless of race.

In 1886, Smalls again ran for reelection to Congress, but by this time, conservative Democrats were fully in charge in South Carolina. Smalls was the one remaining Republican in office, and the Democrats were determined to be rid of him. He ran against William Elliott, a staunch Democrat and former Confederate. When Elliott was declared the victor, Smalls once again challenged the election results, but this time without the support of the House. Congress refused to unseat Elliott, and Robert Smalls's political career was finished.

In 1883, Smalls's wife, Hannah, died. After his defeat in Congress, Smalls returned to Beaufort and, in 1891, married Annie Wigg. In 1889, President Harrison appointed him collector of revenues for the port of Beaufort. Although he was no longer in office, Smalls remained active in politics and attended South Carolina's constitutional convention of 1895 and the Republican National Conventions. Robert Smalls died in his sleep at his Beaufort home on February 22, 1915. He was remembered as a Civil War hero, an outstanding member of Congress, and a champion of black rights.

Sources

Asante, Molefi K., and Mark T. Mattson, eds.. *The Historical and Cultural Atlas of African Americans*. New York: Macmillan, 1991.

Christopher, Maurine. *America's Black Congressmen*. New York: Thomas Y. Crowell, 1971.

Clay, William L. *Just Permanent Interests: Black Americans in Congress, 1870–1991*. New York: Amistad Press, 1992.

"Former Black Members of Congress." *Congressional Times Journal*. <http://www.usbol.com/ctjournal/FrBlkCongMemList.html>. Accessed: 2/13/98.

Carl Burton Stokes

Reproduced from the Cleveland Public Library Photograph Collection

Born: June 21, 1927, in Cleveland, Ohio

Status: Died April 3, 1996, in Cleveland, Ohio

Education: Attended West Virginia State College, Institute, West Virginia, 1947–1948; attended Case Western Reserve University, Cleveland, Ohio, 1948–1950; B.S., 1954, University of Minnesota, Minneapolis-St. Paul, Minnesota; J.D., 1956, Cleveland-Marshall Law School, Cleveland, Ohio

Position: Valve inspector, Thompson Products Company, Cleveland, Ohio, 1944–1945; private, corporal, U.S. Army, 1945–1946; driver for John Holly, Cleveland, Ohio, 1949–1950; enforcement agent, Ohio Department of Liquor Control, 1950–1952; attorney and partner, Stokes and Stokes (later, Minor, McCurdy, Stokes and Stokes), 1956–1958; assistant city prosecutor, Cleveland, Ohio, 1958–1962; state representative, Ohio State Assembly, 1962–1967; mayor, Cleveland, Ohio, 1967–1972; news correspondent, anchorman, WNBC-TV, New York, New York, 1972–1980; senior law partner, Green, Schiavoni, Murphy, Haines, and

Sgambati, Cleveland, Ohio, 1980–1983; law partner, Stokes, Character, Terry, Perry, Whitehead, Young and Davidson, Cleveland, Ohio, 1982–1983; presiding administrative judge, Cleveland Municipal Court, Cleveland, Ohio, 1983–1986; chief judge, Cleveland Municipal Court, Cleveland, Ohio, 1986–1994; ambassador, Republic of the Seychelles, 1994–1996

Early Years

Carl Burton Stokes was born in Cleveland, Ohio, on June 21, 1927, the younger son of Charles Stokes, who worked at a laundry, and Louise Stokes. Shortly after Carl's second birthday, his father died, leaving his mother alone to provide for her two sons.

In 1929, the stock market crash heralded the Great Depression. Jobs were scarce for everyone, but especially for a poor, black woman with no skills. Louise and her sons moved in with her parents, who lived in a housing project in Cleveland, and Louise set out to earn a living. After trying time and again, she finally found a job as a domestic in the home of a wealthy white family in the city. Carl and his older brother, Louis, were left in the care of Louise's parents while she worked. Looking back, Stokes found similarities between his childhood and those of Eastern European immigrants' children who had come to the United States earlier. Louise, according to Stokes, "raised me and my brother with the argument that, if you study hard, you've got to become somebody. I know every European immigrant parent told his children the same thing" (Stokes 18).

Carl and Louis attended the racially segregated schools of Cleveland and encountered few whites during their childhood. Stokes and his brother grew up with little hatred for whites, mainly, he felt, because he and his brother were avid readers. When she could, Louise bought books for the boys and encouraged their reading. Stokes read widely on the history of blacks in America, as well as about other ethnic groups. He developed a pride in his race and a sense of community with other people who had struggled to succeed in America. But reading was not valued in the neighborhood where Stokes lived. When he borrowed library books, he usually had to smuggle them home under his jacket, otherwise boys on the street would beat him up and destroy the books.

Although Stokes enjoyed learning, he was bored in school and dropped out of high school at age 17. Louise was very upset about his decision, but Stokes felt there were plenty of new opportunities in the factories because of the increased production of goods needed for the Second World War. If he worked, he could support himself and help the family with expenses. So, despite Louise's disapproval, in 1944 Stokes got a job inspecting valves at the Thompson Products Company.

During the day he worked, but at night, Stokes trained to become a boxer. Sports was an avenue out of poverty, out of the ghetto. Stokes saw the successes of such men as Sugar Ray Robinson and Joe Louis and felt that, perhaps, success for him also lay in boxing. In high school, he competed in Golden Gloves contests, and many felt he had talent. But his great career in boxing never materialized; he was drafted into the army in 1945 and shipped to Europe.

While in the army, Stokes came to realize the value of an education. Although blacks were segregated from whites in the army, the officers overseeing the black units were white men. Stokes envisioned that, following the war, the white men would not return to the projects of Cleveland, but that they would return to good jobs not only because they were white but also because they were educated. He decided that when he was discharged, he would go back and get the education he had earlier rejected.

Stokes received his army discharge in 1946. Returning to Cleveland, he reenrolled in East Technical High School, the school he had left in 1944, and in 1947, at the age of 20, he graduated.

Higher Education

The G.I. Bill opened avenues to him that had been closed in 1944, and after his high school graduation, Stokes enrolled at West Virginia State College in Institute, West Virginia. In 1948, he transferred to Case Western Reserve University in Cleveland, where he studied for two years. There he became involved in local politics and, once again, dropped out of school.

In 1949, Democrat Frank J. Lausche ran for governor of Ohio and recruited a black politician, John Holly, to help rally the black vote. Stokes had become acquainted with Holly and asked him for a job to help with college expenses. Holly hired him as his driver, and Stokes drove him around the state as Holly campaigned for Lausche. Watching and listening to Holly fascinated Stokes; he was enthralled with politics. In 1950, after the successful election of Lausche, Holly helped Stokes obtain a job as a state liquor enforcement agent, which seemed a glamorous job to Stokes. Stokes dropped out of school to work at this job for the next two years.

During this time, he married Shirley Edwards, whose family had moved to Dayton, Ohio, from Mississippi. Shirley did not like Stokes's job as an enforcement agent because, at times, it was dangerous. Following his involvement in a gunfight with two men who shot another liquor agent, Stokes decided his wife was right. Stokes's brother, Louis, was enrolled in law school at the time, and Stokes decided that he, too, would become a lawyer.

In 1950, Stokes enrolled at the University of Minnesota. To support himself and his family, he worked weekends as a dining-car waiter on the Northern Pacific Railroad. He also became involved in local Minnesota politics, managing the campaign of a black policeman who decided to run for Minneapolis City Council. Between his studies, work, and political activities, Stokes had little time for anything else, and his marriage suffered; Stokes and his wife divorced in 1973.

In 1954, Stokes graduated from the University of Minnesota and returned to Cleveland, where he followed in his brother's footsteps. He enrolled in the Cleveland-Marshall Law School and received his law degree in 1956. Although 12 years had passed from the time he dropped out of high school, Stokes now was an educated man, just like the white officers he had seen during his stint in the army.

Career Highlights

Louis Stokes graduated with his law degree in 1953 and set up a private law practice. When Carl Stokes graduated, he went into partnership with his brother but, unlike his brother at that time, Carl was keenly interested in local politics. In 1958, he was appointed assistant city prosecutor in Cleveland, but he was looking for a higher office, one with more political influence. He spurned the notion of running for city council. Although there were a number of African Americans on the Cleveland City Council, and it was relatively easy to be elected, few councilmen had influence outside their own districts. Citywide, blacks made up less than 30 percent of the population, and there was little chance of a black man being elected to an office higher than city councilman. Countywide, however, blacks had a stronger vote, and Stokes thought that it would be easier for him to gain a seat in the state legislature.

In 1958 and in 1960, Stokes filed nominating petitions for the Democratic primary for the state legislature. Because he was not known in 1958, however, he finished far down in the list of candidates and again was unsuccessful in 1960. Never one to give up, and having tested the political waters, Stokes was ready to run again. In 1962, he mounted a campaign overseen by his brother Louis, and this time the results were in his favor. The past four years of campaig n experience paid off, and Stokes was elected to the Ohio house of representatives, becoming the first black Democrat ever to be elected to this body.

Almost as soon as he took his seat in the Ohio house, Stokes established a name for himself as an activist. He began a fight for congressional redistricting and worked unceasingly on civil rights and welfare legislation. Reelected to his seat twice more, Stokes began to lose interest in state politics. He wanted to be mayor of Cleveland, to help with the problems he had known so well during his formative years. In 1965, he entered the mayoral race as an independent against incumbent mayor Ralph Locher and his Republican challenger. Because of the three-way split, Stokes came in second to Locher, but he immediately began planning his next campaign against the mayor.

In 1966, events occurred that helped Stokes's candidacy. That summer, the Hough neighborhood of Cleveland erupted in riot. Cleveland was a racially polarized, tension-filled city. Locher and his councilmen were against the wall, and called in the Ohio National Guard to quell the arson, looting, and shootings. Black leaders accused Locher of pandering to the city's whites and ignoring the black community. Leaders of the black community had earlier supported Stokes's challenge to Locher and now wholeheartedly threw themselves behind him. Stokes campaigned tirelessly in both the black and white communities and was able to beat Locher in the primary by nearly 20,000 votes. In the general election, Stokes faced Seth Taft, a Republican with deep political connections. Cleveland, however, was a staunchly Democratic town, and despite Taft's political clout, Stokes was able to squeak by, winning by 1,644 votes, just 0.6 percent of the vote.

Stokes became the first African American elected mayor of a major U.S. city without a majority black population and the first black mayor of Cleveland. However, as he said on election night, "This is not a Carl Stokes victory, not a vote for a man but a vote for a program, for a visionary dream of what our city can become" (Mabunda 233). In 1968, Stokes's brother Louis was elected to Congress from the 11th District of Ohio, putting both brothers in positions to effect change.

Over the next few years, as mayor of Cleveland, Stokes guided the city through some of its most turbulent times. He steadfastly worked to improve Cleveland, winning urban renewal money from the federal government, pushing for laws to help minorities, creating job opportunities, and generally improving the quality of life in the city. But many of the changes he enacted also made enemies. He was in conflict with the chief of police, the city council president, and city workers who were laid off from their jobs. Although Stokes won reelection in 1969, in 1971 he announced he would not run again.

Having lost much of his political support in the city, Stokes moved to New York, where he accepted a position as a television anchorman and news commentator. In 1980, he returned to Cleveland and to the practice of law. In 1983, he was elected to a judgeship in the Cleveland Municipal Court and became chief judge in 1986. In 1994, he was appointed by President Bill Clinton to the post of ambassador to the Republic of the Seychelles, a job he held until his death in 1996.

When Stokes died on April 3, 1996, the loss was felt by many. As his brother, U.S. Representative Louis Stokes, said, "I have lost a brother and the nation has lost one of its most famous sons" (Mabunda 23.). The mayor of Cleveland, Michael White, said of him that, "As mayor, Stokes inspired 14-year-old Mike White's dream of becoming the mayor of Cleveland" ("Obituary . . .").

Sources

Haskins, James. *A Piece of the Power: Four Black Mayors.* New York: Dial, 1972.

Joint Center for Political Studies. *Profiles of Black Mayors in America.* Washington, DC/Chicago, IL: The Joint Center for Political Studies/Johnson Publishing, 1977.

Mabunda, L. Mpho, ed. *Contemporary Black Biography: Profiles from the International Black Community,* Vol. 10. Detroit, MI: Gale Research, 1996.

"Obituary: Carl B. Stokes, 68, First Black Elected Mayor of a Major American City." *The Detroit News,* 1996.

<http://www.detnews.com/menu/stories/42613.htm>. Accessed: 3/12/98.

Weinberg, Kenneth. *Black Victory: Carl Stokes and the Winning of Cleveland.* Chicago, IL: Quadrangle Books, 1968.

Louis Stokes

Reproduced from the Cleveland Public Library Photograph Collection

Born: February 23, 1925, in Cleveland, Ohio

Status: Retired

Education: Graduate, East Technical High School, Cleveland, Ohio; graduate, 1948, Case Western Reserve University, Cleveland, Ohio; J.D., 1953, Marshall Law School, Cleveland State University, Cleveland, Ohio; recipient of more than 20 honorary doctorates from various colleges and universities

Position: U.S. Army, 1943–1946; employee, Department of the Treasury, Cleveland, Ohio, 1946–1948; lawyer, Stokes and Stokes (later, Stokes, Character, Terry, Perry, Whitehead, Young and Davidson), Cleveland, Ohio, 1954–1968; U.S. representative from the 11th Congressional District of Ohio, 1969–1998

Awards and honors: Distinguished service award, NAACP, Cleveland, Ohio; certificate of appreciation, U.S. Commission on Civil Rights; William L. Dawson Award, Congressional Black Caucus; named to the Public Housing Hall of Fame by the Department of Housing and Urban Development, 1995

Early Years

Louis Stokes was born February 23, 1925, in Cleveland, Ohio, the elder son of Charles and Louise (Stone) Stokes. When Louis was four years old and his younger brother, Carl, was two, Louis's father died, leaving his mother penniless. Louise did not have a job but was determined to keep her family together. After being on welfare for a short time, she found a job as a domestic. Louise wanted her boys to do well. She encouraged both Louis and Carl to read as much as possible. **Carl Burton Stokes** would later say, however, that "reading was against the mores of the neighborhood," and both he and his brother had to sneak books into the house for fear of being beaten up by neighborhood bullies (Weinberg 20).

Both Louis and Carl attended public schools in the east-side Cleveland neighborhood where they lived, which was entirely African American. Louis graduated from Cleveland's East Technical High School and then joined the army.

Higher Education

Louis served in the army until after the end of World War II and was discharged in 1946. The G.I. Bill gave him the opportunity to continue his education. Stokes enrolled at Case Western Reserve University, attending at night while working during the day at the Cleveland branch of the Treasury Department. He graduated in 1948 and continued on at Cleveland State University's Marshall Law School, where he received his law degree in 1953.

Career Highlights

After graduating from law school, Stokes began practicing law. In 1958, after his brother Carl earned his own law degree, together they set up the law firm of Stokes and Stokes (later Stokes, Character, Terry, Perry, Whitehead, Young and Davidson) in Cleveland. While Louis worked successfully on civil rights cases in the law firm, Carl was becoming increasingly involved in Cleveland's local politics. Louis began to get a taste of politics while working on his brother's campaign for mayor. When his brother was elected the first black mayor of Cleveland in 1967, Louis himself shared the glory as he had worked long and hard on his brother's campaign.

That same year, Louis entered politics. The Ohio Supreme Court had ordered a redistricting of the state, and with the redistricting, Louis had a good chance to win a congressional seat. Prior to redistricting, the black vote in the 21st District had only been 40 percent black; with redistricting, it became 65 percent black. Carl's popularity as mayor helped his brother's campaign as well, and with the black vote concentrated, Louis Stokes easily won nomination in the Democratic primary in 1968.

Stokes's victory in the election in the fall of 1968 was decisive, and he became the first black member of Congress from the state of Ohio. He realized that his district was one of the poorest in the state and that strong leadership and support were essential. When he took his seat in the 91st Congress, he faced a new wave of conservatism under the leadership of the newly elected president, Richard Nixon. Stokes was assigned to the House Internal Security Committee and to the Education and Labor Committee, but most of his battles took place on the floor of the House. One of his first involved the administration's attempt to weaken the Voting Rights Act of 1965. Stokes argued that by weakening the act the country would be taking a step backward. In Mississippi in 1969, he said, "Many did not register because of bombing threats. Others could not because of intentionally shortened registration hours or deceptive practices which gave the voters the impression they were registering when they were not" (Bigelow 238). If the Voting Rights Act is weakened, he argued, such incidents would become commonplace throughout the country.

One of Stokes's most visible assignments in the House was his appointment in 1977 to chair the Select Committee on Assassinations, which was formed to investigate the assassinations of President John F. Kennedy and Martin Luther King, Jr. Stokes heavily criticized the Warren Commission Report on Kennedy's assassination for dismissing claims of a conspiracy and the fact that most government documents surrounding both cases had not yet been released to the public.

In 1987 and 1988, Stokes was involved in investigation again, this time with the House Intelligence Committee. He was on the Iran-Contra Investigating Committee that was looking into the government's—and particularly, President Ronald Reagan's—involvement in selling arms to Iran to obtain money for the Nicaraguan Contras. During the committee's hearing, Stokes strongly urged Reagan not to pardon Colonel Oliver North.

In 1991, Stokes was appointed the chair of the House Ethics Committee. As he said, "My whole career has been one of fighting for the underdog. I'm sure that's reflected in my votes. But I think that even more than that, my record for being fair is what makes people respect me" (Bigelow 239). The 1990s were fraught with ethics cases, and Stokes maintained his record of fairness, weighing each statement and decision.

By the mid-1990s, Stokes had served for nearly 30 years without losing an election. Although his most visible actions took place while he was chairing various investigative committees, or on the powerful House Appropriations Committee as the committee's first black member, Stokes also worked quietly and steadily to improve the lot of his constituents and of all minorities in America. He never forgot his first goals; as he said in a message to his constituents in the 1990s,

> Our country is in need of meaningful reform to address the challenges we face. We must be able to provide families with decent and affordable housing; health care that is effective and affordable; educational and job training opportunities; and crime free and drug free neighborhoods. ("Congressman Stokes' Newsletter")

In 1998, however, Stokes announced his decision to retire; he was 73 years old. His brother Carl had died of cancer in 1996. While his career in Congress had been filled with tough decisions, he said in his retirement announcement, retiring "is probably the most difficult decision I have had to make in the last 30 years" ("Ohio's Stokes ..."). Louis Stokes long served as the voice of the minority, the disenfranchised, and the poor and will be remembered and revered for his accomplishments.

Sources

Bigelow, Barbara Carlisle, ed. *Contemporary Black Biography: Profiles from the International Black Community*, Vol. 3. Detroit, MI: Gale Research, 1993.

"Biographical Data: The Honorable Louis Stokes." *U.S. House of Representatives*. <http://www.house.gov/stokes/bio.htm>. Accessed: 3/6/98.

Christopher, Maurine. *America's Black Congressmen*. New York: Thomas Y. Crowell, 1971.

Clay, William L. *Just Permanent Interests: Black Americans in Congress, 1870–1991*. New York: Amistad Press, 1992.

"Congressman Stokes' Newsletter." *Cleveland State University*. <http://www.csuohio.edu/cmha/stokesnl.html>. Accessed: 4/9/98.

Estell, Kenneth. *African America: Celebrating 400 Years of Achievement*. Detroit, MI: Visible Ink Press, 1994.

"Ohio's Stokes to End 30 Years in D.C." *Hartford Courant*, 3 March 1998, A18.

"Representative Louis Stokes." Member Profile. <http://www.hrcusa.org/actncntr/profiles/OH11.html>. Accessed: 4/28/98.

Weinberg, Kenneth. *Black Victory: Carl Stokes and the Winning of Cleveland*. Chicago, IL: Quadrangle Books, 1968.

Louis Wade Sullivan

Reproduced from AP/Wide World Photos, by John Duricka

Born: November 3, 1933, in Atlanta, Georgia

Status: President, Morehouse School of Medicine, Atlanta, Georgia

Education: B.S. magna cum laude, 1954, Morehouse College, Atlanta, Georgia; M.D. cum laude, 1958, Boston University Medical School, Boston, Massachusetts; member, Phi Beta Kappa; recipient of more than 40 honorary degrees from various colleges and universities

Position: Fellow in pathology, Massachusetts General Hospital, Boston, Massachusetts, 1960– 1961; fellow in hematology, Thorndike Memorial Research Laboratories, Harvard Medical School at Boston City Hospital, Boston, Massachusetts, 1961–1964; instructor, Harvard Medical School, Cambridge, Massachusetts, 1963–1964; assistant professor of medicine, Seton Hall College of Medicine (later, New Jersey College of Medicine), 1964–1966; codirector of hematology, Boston University Medical Center, Boston, Massachusetts, 1966–1968; assistant professor of medicine (1966–1968), associate professor of medicine (1968–

1974), professor of medicine (1974–1975), Boston University School of Medicine, Boston, Massachusetts; project codirector (1972–1973), project director (1973–1975), Boston Sickle Cell Center, Boston, Massachusetts; director of hematology, Boston City Hospital, Boston, Massachusetts, 1973–1975; professor of biology and medicine, founding dean, Medical Education Program, Morehouse College, Atlanta, Georgia, 1975–1981; dean, president, Morehouse School of Medicine, Atlanta, Georgia, 1981–1989, 1993– ; vice chairman, Commission on Health and Human Services, Southern Regional Education Board, 1985–1987; secretary, Department of Health and Human Services, 1989–1993

Early Years

Louis Wade Sullivan was born in Atlanta, Georgia, on November 3, 1933, to Walter Wade Sullivan, Sr., and Lubirda Priester Sullivan. When Sullivan was a small child, the family moved from Atlanta to Blakely, Georgia, where his father worked as an undertaker and his mother taught school. In an effort to combat the racism that was prevalent in the small town, Sullivan's parents founded a chapter of the National Association for the Advancement of Colored People (NAACP) in Blakely, a move that did not increase their popularity.

Sullivan's parents wanted a good education for him and his older brother, Walter, and knew that the segregated school in Blakely would not provide the quality of education they desired for their sons. So Sullivan and his brother were sent to Atlanta to live with family friends and attend public school. Both boys graduated from high school and went on to college.

Higher Education

Sullivan attended Morehouse College as an undergraduate and graduated magna cum laude. He then attended Boston University Medical School on a scholarship. Again, Sullivan excelled in his class and graduated cum laude in 1958. After graduating, Sullivan did his internship and residency at New York Hospital-Cornell Medical Center in New York. He then accepted a fellowship in pathology at Massachusetts General Hospital in Boston, and the following year, one in hematology at the prestigious Thorndike Memorial Research Laboratories at Harvard Medical School at Boston City Hospital in Boston.

Career Highlights

Rather than establish a private practice, Sullivan turned to teaching and research in the area of hematology, specializing in blood disorders caused by vitamin deficiencies and in Sickle Cell Anemia. During the early 1970s, in addition to teaching at Boston University School of Medicine, he also was codirector, then director, of the Boston Sickle Cell Center, and director of hematology at Boston City Hospital. Throughout his career, Sullivan wanted to help other African Americans. As an article in *Emerge* stated, he was dedicated to "training more minorities to serve not only as health professionals in their communities, but to serve as leaders in their communities" (Mabunda 241). And when he was invited by Morehouse College to help create a two-year medical program there, he accepted.

In 1975, Sullivan moved to Atlanta where he had grown up and assumed the position of professor of biology and medicine. Over the course of the next few years, he worked on planning the new program at Morehouse, raising funds, and recruiting professors. In 1978, he became the founding dean of the Medical Education Program, which Sullivan dreamed of expanding to a full four-year program. Sullivan continued fundraising, and in 1981 his dream became reality when Morehouse School of Medicine was established with Sullivan as its dean and first president. The school was the first minority medical school founded in the United States in this century.

Sullivan's fund-raising experience brought him in contact with many people, including politicians. Among them were Vice President George Bush and his wife Barbara, with whom he became firm friends. Barbara Bush, in fact, was named to the medical school's board of trustees. In 1982, George Bush invited Sullivan to be a member of Bush's official 12-member delegation to seven African countries, and later, in 1988, Sullivan was asked to introduce Mrs. Bush at the Republican National Convention.

As president, George Bush nominated Sullivan as his secretary of health and human services in 1989. Sullivan certainly had the credentials as well as the experience for the position. From 1985 to 1987, he had served as vice chairman of the Commission on Health and Human Services, Southern Regional Board. The nomination, however, met with strong opposition.

The dissension to his nomination was not over Sullivan's qualifications or experience, but his stance on abortion. Although he opposed federal funding of abortions, he had stated in a newspaper article that he believed in a woman's right to choose. Sullivan rescued his nomination by issuing a statement in which he explained that he opposed abortion except in cases of rape, incest, or for the protection of the life of the mother. This modification seemed to be enough to satisfy his critics, and his nomination proceeded through Congress. Sullivan was sworn in in February of 1989, the only African American in the Bush cabinet.

Sullivan had strong views, which he expressed as secretary of health and human services—much to the dismay of many. He supported needle exchange programs for drug addicts to stem the spread of AIDS. Initially, he seemed to approve of fetal tissue research programs, but after consultations with Bush's officials, reversed his position. While he seemed to sway back and forth on some issues, he was solid and unwavering in running the department. Faced with budget cuts, he took care not to decrease services to those who needed them most—the poor and minorities. He came out strongly against the tobacco companies and against smoking, especially when R.J. Reynolds produced a brand of cigarette called "Uptown" that was targeted primarily at blacks. *Newsweek* commented that, "For a man who once seemed determined to avoid controversy at any cost, Dr. Louis Sullivan … has lately been displaying a notable zest for combat" (Mabunda 243).

When George Bush was defeated by Bill Clinton in his bid for reelection, Sullivan returned to his position as president of the Morehouse School of Medicine, which he holds at this writing. In addition to overseeing the medical program at Morehouse, Sullivan serves on the boards of a number of nonprofit corporations and foundations, and publishes extensively in his area of specialization.

Sources

"Louis W. Sullivan." <http://www.ssa.gov/history/sullivan.html>. Accessed: 3/18/98.

"Louis W. Sullivan, M.D.: Biographical Sketch." *The Black Health Net*. 1998. <http://www.blackhealthnet.com/doctors/cv/lsullivan.asp>. Accessed: 4/23/98.

Mabunda, L. Mpho, ed. *Contemporary Black Biography: Profiles from the International Black Community*, Vol. 8. Detroit, MI: Gale Research, 1995.

T

Clarence Thomas

Reproduced from Reuters/Corbis-Bettmann

Born: June 23, 1948, in Savannah, Georgia

Status: Associate justice of the United States Supreme Court

Education: Attended Immaculate Conception Seminary, Conception, Missouri, 1967–1968; B.A., 1971, Holy Cross College, Worcester, Massachusetts; J.D., 1974, Yale University Law School, New Haven, Connecticut; admitted to the bar of Missouri, 1974–

Position: Assistant attorney general for Missouri, 1974–1977; attorney, Monsanto Company, St. Louis, Missouri, 1977–1979; legislative assistant to Missouri senator John C. Danforth, 1979–1981; assistant secretary for civil rights, U.S. Department of Education, 1981–1982; chairman, U.S. Equal Employment Opportunity Commission, 1982–1990; judge, U.S. Court of Appeals for the District of Columbia, 1990–1991; associate justice of the United States Supreme Court, 1991–

Early Years

Newsweek magazine noted in 1991, when Clarence Thomas was nominated for a position on the United States Supreme Court, that "For every Clarence Thomas revealed ... there seems to be an equal and opposite Clarence Thomas somewhere else" (Kaplan et al. 20). On the one hand, there was the "black Horatio Alger" who had pulled himself up from poverty by his bootstraps; on the other, there was the "bitter, impulsive, hotheaded and opportunistic Thomas" (Kaplan et al. 20). Thomas has shown himself to be a complex man and, in many ways, an enigma to both his critics and admirers.

Born on June 23, 1948, in Savannah, Georgia, Clarence Thomas was the second child of Leola Thomas and M.C. Thomas; he had an older sister, Emma Mae. Soon after his birth the family moved to the community of Pinpoint, Georgia, a small town filled with poverty and want whose inhabitants eked out a living cleaning crabs, shucking oysters, and farming. The Thomas family moved into the home of an aunt, Annie Graham. Her house had only one room, dirt floors, and no plumbing or electricity.

When Thomas was two years old, his father abandoned the family. His mother, who was pregnant with a third child, tried her best to hold the family together, cleaning crabs and doing housework for a local white family. When Thomas was seven years old, however, the house they were living in burned down. The family moved back to Savannah and lived near Leola's parents, Myers Anderson and his wife.

Thomas's mother struggled to support the family. One day, her mother said, "They [the children] know you're their mother, but can I keep them all the time?" (Kaplan et al. 22). Leola had remarried and her new husband didn't want the burden of a family, so Leola agreed to leave the children with her mother. Thomas's sister returned to Pinpoint to live once again with Aunt Annie Graham, and Clarence and his younger brother, Myers, moved in with their grandparents. In many ways, this was a fortunate move for Thomas. Although having had little education himself, Thomas's grandfather was determined that his grandsons get the education he lacked. His grandfather told him, "Boy, you are going to school today. You goin' do better'n I'm doing" (Kaplan et al. 20). Thomas and his brother were enrolled in an all-black parochial elementary school, St. Benedict the Moor. Although Thomas did well in school, he endured the taunts of the other children because of the darkness of his skin. He was called "A.B.C.—short for America's Blackest Child" (Kaplan et al. 20). Thomas toed the line his grandfather had drawn, however. As he later said, in a speech to the Heritage Foundation, his grandfather promoted "School, discipline, hard work and 'right-from-wrong'" (Kaplan et al. 23).

For two years, Thomas attended the all-black St. Pius X High School in Savannah. Then, urged by his grandfather to become a priest, he was sent to a white Catholic boarding school, St. John Vianney Minor Seminary, just outside Savannah. As the only black youth in his class, Thomas was the subject of racial harassment by the other students. The taunts led to a period during which Thomas hated himself: "you hate yourself for being part of a group that's gotten the hell kicked out of them. I don't fit in with whites and I don't fit in with blacks" (Kaplan et al. 25). Despite this, Thomas did well academically and after graduation entered Immaculate Conception Seminary in Missouri.

Higher Education

At Immaculate Conception, Thomas continued to encounter the racism that had dogged him through high school. On April 4, 1968, however, Thomas decided to leave. That evening, he and a number of fellow students were watching television when the announcement came that Martin Luther King, Jr., had been shot in Memphis, Tennessee. One student cheered, "Good, I hope the s.o.b. dies." With that, Thomas later said, "I knew I couldn't stay in this so-called Christian environment" (Kaplan et al. 25). Shortly after this incident, Thomas left the seminary and enrolled at Holy Cross College in Worcester, Massachusetts.

While at Holy Cross, Thomas and a number of other black students founded the Black Student Union. The group demanded a room in which to meet and more classes on African American subjects. The year after Thomas came to Holy Cross, the black students all decided to live together and were given a section of one dormitory. Thomas was the only one to vote against the "segregation" the other black students wanted to create by living together. He felt they should learn from living with students of other races. Overruled, he went along with the other students and moved into an all-black section of one dormitory. Despite all the turmoil, Thomas, as always, excelled in his classes and graduated with a major in English literature in June, 1971. He entered law school at Yale University the following fall. The day after he graduated from Holy Cross, Thomas married Kathy Ambush, a student at a nearby Catholic women's college.

Thomas was accepted for admittance by three graduate schools and decided on Yale because of the financial aid it offered. The fact that Yale had an aggressive affirmative action program irritated Thomas. He felt that, although his academic record as an undergraduate was good, he was chosen in part because of his color. This made him feel that he constantly had to prove himself to other students and to the school.

When Thomas graduated from Yale in 1974, he had few job offers. The firms he interviewed with stressed pro bono (free) work over corporate work. Thomas, angered, said, "I went to school to be a lawyer, not a social worker" (Kaplan et al. 26). He finally accepted a position with Missouri's Republican attorney general, John Danforth, as assistant attorney general.

Career Highlights

The attorney general's office was overburdened with cases and the offices were old and deteriorating, but Thomas threw himself into his work. He enjoyed the challenge of courtroom work and was conscientious about preparing his cases. In 1977, John Danforth was elected to the Senate. When Danforth left for Washington, as a friend of Thomas's said, "Once Jack left, he didn't see any reason for being there" (Kaplan et al. 26). Thomas became an attorney with Monsanto Company in St. Louis, a job that paid him a great deal more than he had earned in the attorney general's office.

While in Missouri, Thomas had discovered the writing of conservative black economists Thomas Sowell and Walter Williams. Before, Thomas had felt somewhat alienated from most African Americans who were, in the main, liberal. Sowell and Williams, though, seemed to be saying the same things that Thomas believed: "that affirmative action hurt blacks more than it helped ... Individual enterprise, not government handouts, would liberate blacks" (Kaplan et al. 26). Thomas had found a basis for the views that would shape his decisions in later life.

In 1979, John Danforth invited Thomas to join his staff in Washington and Thomas, seeing it as a step upward, accepted. In 1981, he was offered a position in Ronald Reagan's White House dealing with energy and environmental issues, the same issues he had worked on for Danforth. Thomas refused the White House job, however, feeling he was offered the position only because he was black. Four months later, he accepted the job of assistant secretary for civil rights with the U.S. Department of Education.

Thomas had strong views on education, partially shaped by the philosophies of Sowell and Williams, and he was often in conflict with others at the Department of Education. In 1982, after 10 months in the department, Reagan offered him the chairmanship of the U.S. Equal Employment Opportunity Commission (EEOC). As *Newsweek* reported, "In eight years at EEOC, Thomas was a model of inconsistency" (Kaplan et al. 30). Conservative in outlook, he fought against affirmative action, the very program his department was conceived to enforce, then changed his mind, supporting such programs for a while; later, he spoke out against preferences. He also argued with employees, capriciously transferred them, and fell behind in the department's work.

In addition, he was having difficulties in his personal life. Thomas and his wife, Kathy, separated in 1981 and divorced in 1983, and Thomas received custody of their son, Jamal. After dating a number of women, in April, 1987, he met Virginia Bess Lamp, a white woman who worked in the U.S. Chamber of Commerce; five months later they were married.

Despite his problems with the EEOC, Thomas labored to maintain his contacts in government, often joking to friends that he wanted a place on the Supreme Court. In 1990, President George Bush appointed him to the appeals court for the District of Columbia. While in the court, Thomas wrote 20 decisions, most of them conservative—one generating national attention. He threw out a previous decision awarding more than $10 million in a case against Ralston-Purina (the company was founded and owned in part by his friend, John Danforth). In 1991, Thomas's dream came true: he was nominated for the U.S. Supreme Court to replace **Thurgood Marshall** after the Senate turned down the nomination of Robert Bork.

Many felt that Thomas's nomination was an attempt by President George Bush to satisfy both the liberals and the conservatives. Thomas was black, but he was conservative. In the days preceding the Senate confirmation hearings on his nomination, the national press made much of his rags-to-riches background. Many black groups, however, were sharply divided on Thomas's nomination because of his conservatism and his anti-abortion stance. Despite the controversy surrounding Thomas, the hearings progressed without much difficulty until a witness appeared who raised questions about Thomas's qualifications.

During October, 1991, Anita Hill, a black law professor at the University of Oklahoma, testified that while she was working for the EEOC Thomas had sexually harassed her, pressuring her to date him, discussing the plots of pornographic movies, and bragging about his sexual exploits. Thomas, in turn, accused Hill of lying. "This is a circus," Thomas said before the Senate. "It's a national disgrace. From my standpoint as a black American, it is a high-tech lynching for uppity blacks who in any way deign to think for themselves, to do for themselves" (Berke L9). Furious, Thomas denounced Hill and accused the Judiciary Committee of besmirching his reputation. During the following days, the accusations were the only topic of conversation in the Senate and around the country. Women's groups soundly denounced Thomas and his nomination to the Court. Was Hill fabricating her accusations, or was Thomas lying in his denunciation of them? Although the accusations lingered, the Senate came down on the side of Clarence Thomas, confirming his nomination. On October 23, 1991, Thomas was sworn in as an associate justice of the United States Supreme Court.

During the time Thomas has been in the highest court of the United States, he has remained in the background, speaking very rarely and generally voting with the majority on the cases that have come before the Court. When he has voiced an opinion, he has taken a moderate or conservative position. It remains to be seen whether his presence on the Supreme Court will have any significant impact on the nation.

Sources

"Associate Justice Clarence Thomas." Clarence Thomas Links, rev. 11/1/97. <http://www2.cybernex.net/~vanalst/clarence.html>. Accessed: 3/18/98.

"Associate Justice Clarence Thomas." *Court TV Online*. 1998. <http://www.courttv.com/library/supreme/justices/thomas.html>. Accessed: 3/18/98.

Berke, Richard L. "Thomas Accuser Tells Hearing of Obscene Talk and Advances: Judge Complains of 'Lynching'." *The New York Times*, 12 October 1991, 1, L9.

"Clarence Thomas." *Cornell University*. <http://supct.law.cornell.edu/supct/justices/thomas.bio.html>. Accessed: 3/18/98.

Estell, Kenneth. *African America: Celebrating 400 Years of Achievement*. Detroit, MI: Visible Ink Press, 1994.

Kane, Joseph J., and Staci D. Kramer. "Marching to a Different Drummer." *Time Magazine*, 15 July 1991, 18–22.

Kaplan, David A., et al. "Supreme Mystery." *Newsweek*, 16 September 1991, 18–31.

"Thomas, Clarence." *Biography Online Database*. <http://www.biography.com/find/bioengine.cgi?cmd=1&rec =13876>. Accessed: 4/11/98.

Thomas, Evan, et al. "Where Does He Stand?" *Newsweek*, 15 July 1991, 16–17.

Edolphus Towns

Courtesy of the Office of Congressman Edolphus Towns

Born: July 21, 1934, in Chadbourn, North Carolina

Status: U.S. representative from the 10th Congressional District of New York

Education: B.A., 1956, North Carolina A and T State University, Greensboro, North Carolina; M.S. in social work, 1973; Adelphi University, Garden City, New York; ordained as a Baptist minister; recipient of honorary degrees from Adelphi University, Long Island University, New York College of Podiatric Medicine, North Carolina A and T State University, Shaw University, and Virginia Seminary

Position: Officer, U.S. Army, 1956–1958; teacher, New York, New York; professor, Medgar Evers College, New York, New York; assistant administrator, Beth Israel Medical Center, New York, New York; professor, Fordham University, New York, New York; Brooklyn deputy borough president; Democratic state committeeman, 40th Assembly District of New York; U.S. representative from the 11th (later, the 10th) Congressional District of New York, 1982–

Early Years

Edolphus Towns was born in Chadbourn, North Carolina, on July 21, 1934.

Higher Education

Towns received a bachelor's degree from North Carolina A and T State University in Greensboro, North Carolina. After graduation, he attended Adelphi University in Garden City, New York, where he earned a master's degree in social work.

Career Highlights

Upon graduating from Adelphi, Towns initially got a job teaching in the New York City school system. He also became involved in politics in Brooklyn, where he lived. Over the next 20 years, Towns held a number of positions within his borough, culminating in his election as the first African American to serve as Brooklyn deputy borough president. He also held a variety of jobs: assistant administrator at Beth Israel Medical Center; professor at New York's Medgar Evers College and at Fordham University; and social worker. His work in the latter field gave him keen insight into the many problems that faced urban areas of the United States. During this time, he additionally worked to facilitate the development of new neighborhood housing projects.

As a result of the 1980 census, congressional district boundaries had been redrawn. The 11th Congressional District seat had been held by Frederick W. Richmond, but Richmond, a wealthy white businessman, resigned after facing charges of income tax evasion. This left the seat vacant, and Towns decided to run for it.

With the redistricting, the 11th District was now primarily black and Hispanic. In addition to Towns, two Hispanics, John Jack Olivero and Louis Hernandez, entered the race. Because the Hispanic vote in the Democratic primary was split between these two candidates, Towns was able to win with less than 50 percent of the vote. He then went on to win the regular election and was seated in Congress in 1982.

Towns was backed in his run for the House by Brooklyn Democratic Party leader Meade Esposito, and by a reform group headed by New York assemblyman Al Vann. Because of this backing, Towns faced charges that he was controlled by these groups, but he proved them false as he began his work in Congress.

During the 1980s, the administration of President Ronald Reagan was cutting back on social, jobs, educational, and other programs that particularly benefited the poor and minorities. Towns was one of many who adamantly fought against these cuts. Over the years, he became known for his efforts on behalf of minority farmers, bilingual education, and national health care reform. Towns received acclaim for his successful efforts to dramatize the health care needs of women, the disadvantaged, the elderly, and other groups. He also supported the "Brady Bill" gun control measure.

Time and again, Towns was reelected to his seat in Congress with little opposition. During the 102nd Congress, he was elected chairman of the Congressional Black Caucus, and over the years he has served on the Public Works Committee, the Government Operations Committee, the Select Committee on Narcotics Abuse and Control, the Committee on Energy and Commerce, and the House Government Reform and Oversight Committee.

In 1990, again the result of the 10-year census, Towns's district became the 10th Congressional District, although the profile of voters changed little. In 1992, he was reelected and seated, and because of his long tenure in the House he became the ranking minority on the Subcommittee for Human Resources and Intergovernmental Relations.

In recent years, Towns has added a concern to his agenda: the nation's food supply. He chaired hearings on the implications of eating raw seafood and on the effectiveness of the inspection system of the USDA, among other topics.

At present, Towns lives with his wife, Gwendolyn Forbes, in the Cypress Hills section of Brooklyn. They have two grown children, one of whom, Darryl Towns, made history when he was elected to the New York State Assembly. With his election, he and his father became the first African American father and son to be elected to public office in New York State at the same time.

Sources

Clay, William L. *Just Permanent Interests: Black Americans in Congress, 1870–1991.* New York: Amistad Press, 1992.

Congressional Black Caucus '93–'94 Guide. <http://www.sas.upenn.edu/African_ Studies/Govern_Political/CBC_Guide.html>. Accessed: 3/10/98.

"Congressman Edolphus Towns." *U.S. House of Representatives.* <http://www.house.gov/towns/welcome.htm>. Accessed: 3/6/98.

"Congressman Edolphus Towns, 10th Congressional District." *New York State Democratic Committee Home Page.* <http://www.nydems.org/elected/towns.html>. Accessed: 4/9/98.

Benjamin Sterling Turner

Reproduced from the Collections of the Library of Congress

Born: March 17, 1825, in Weldon, North Carolina

Status: Died March 21, 1894, in Selma, Alabama; buried at Live Oak Cemetery, Selma, Alabama

Education: Self-educated

Position: Merchant, livery stable owner, 1860s; elected tax collector, Dallas County, Alabama, 1867; councilman, Selma City Council, Selma, Alabama, 1869; U.S. representative from the First Congressional District of Alabama, 1871–1873; farmer, Selma, Alabama, 1874–1894; delegate, Republican National Convention, Chicago, Illinois, 1880

Early Years

Benjamin Sterling Turner was born into slavery on March 17, 1825, in Weldon, North Carolina. When he was five years old, he was taken to Alabama; whether he was sold or transported there as part of his owner's property is unknown.

Growing up a slave in Alabama, Sterling was forbidden a formal education, but he managed to become educated and could read and write. In 1865, when the Civil War ended, Sterling was finally freed. He decided to settle in Selma, Alabama, an area with which he was familiar.

Career Highlights

There is some confusion about what, exactly, Turner did after the Civil War before he entered public office. The *New National Era*, edited by Frederick Douglass, described Turner at the time he entered Congress as a schoolteacher, but other accounts indicate that he was a livery stable owner "of scanty education who could write his name and nothing more" (Lamson 118). Regardless of what profession Turner had pursued, in 1867 he began his career in public office when he was elected tax collector of Dallas County.

Like so many African American men during the Reconstruction period, Turner saw an opportunity to fight for equality by serving in the new governments being formed in the southern states. In 1869, he was elected a city councilman in Selma, Alabama, and the following year won election as a Republican to the House of Representatives, becoming Alabama's first black member of Congress.

Turner was sworn into the 42nd Congress in 1871 and assigned to the Committee on Invalid Pensions. One of his first acts upon taking his seat in Congress was to introduce a bill that would have removed penalties imposed upon former Confederates. Like **Hiram Rhodes Revels,** Turner felt a move such as this would lessen hostilities between blacks and former Confederates in the southern states. The House, however, failed even to consider his measure, and the bill died of inaction. Turner also attempted to obtain $200,000 for the construction of a federal building in his hometown of Selma, and he introduced legislation for relief for St. Paul's Episcopal Church in Selma, which had suffered during the war.

Turner was able to gain passage of two private pension bills through his membership on the Committee on Invalid Pensions. One provided full pensions of $8 a month for a black regiment that had fought in the Civil War.

On May 31, 1872, Turner addressed the full House on the matter of rebating the cotton tax that had been collected from the Mobile, Alabama, board of trade from 1866 to 1868. He charged the tax was unconstitutional and spoke of the hardship such a tax laid upon both the workers and buyers of cotton in Mobile. At the same time, he proposed that the government buy tracts of land to be distributed to landless freedmen in the South. The House did not act on either proposal; matters proposed by the black members of Congress were frequently ignored by the white members at this time.

In 1872, Turner won the Republican nomination to run again for his seat in Congress. Another black candidate, however, Philip Joseph, ran against him as an Independent. Because the vote was split, the victory went to Frederick G. Bromberg, the Democratic candidate.

After stepping down from office, Turner returned to Alabama, bought land, and became a farmer. Although active politically on the local level, his only other venture into national politics came when he was elected as a delegate to the 1880 Republican National Convention held in Chicago, Illinois. Turner spent the remainder of his life farming. He died on March 21, 1894, in Selma.

Sources

"Former Black Members of Congress." *Congressional Times Journal*. <http://www.usbol.com/ctjournal/FrBlkCongMemList.html>. Accessed: 4/2/98.

Lamson, Peggy. *The Glorious Failure: Black Congressman Robert Brown Elliott and the Reconstruction of South Carolina*. New York: W.W. Norton and Co., 1973.

W

Josiah Thomas Walls

Reproduced from the Collections of the Library of Congress

Born: December 30, 1842, in or near Winchester, Virginia

Status: Died May 15, 1905, in Tallahassee, Florida; buried at Negro Cemetery, Tallahassee, Florida

Education: Briefly attended normal school, Harrisburg, Pennsylvania, 1850s

Position: Impressed into the Confederate army, 1860s; enlisted in the Third Infantry Regiment, United States Colored Troops, Philadelphia, Pennsylvania, July, 1863; sawmill worker, Florida, 1865; teacher, Archer, Florida, 1866; delegate, Florida State Constitutional Convention, 1868; state representative, Florida State Assembly, 1868; state senator, Florida State Senate, 1868–1870, 1876–1879; U.S. representative from Florida, 1871–1875; farmer, Alachua County, Florida, 1879–1895; farm supervisor, Florida Normal College (later, Florida A and M University), Tallahassee, Florida, 1895–1905

Early Years

Josiah Thomas Walls was born a slave in or near Winchester, Virginia, on December 30, 1842. When he was a child, Walls moved to Darkesville, West Virginia. It is not known whether he went to West Virginia of his own free will or was sold by his owner.

Higher Education

At some time, he briefly attended a normal school in Harrisburg, Pennsylvania, and may have obtained more schooling on his own.

Career Highlights

At the outbreak of the Civil War, like **Robert Smalls,** who was to be his fellow congressman, Walls was impressed into the Confederate army. During a siege of Yorktown, Virginia, in May of 1862, however, he was captured by Northern forces and freed. A year later, in July of 1863, Walls enlisted with the Third Infantry Regiment of the United States Colored Troops in Philadelphia, Pennsylvania. By October, he had been promoted to the rank of corporal, and in February, 1864, his regiment was sent to Florida.

Walls liked what he saw of Florida, and when he was discharged from the army in October of 1865, he decided to stay. He obtained a job as a sawmill worker, and later was hired as a teacher in the town of Archer in Alachua County, Florida. He also became involved in state politics.

The Florida constitutional convention was held in 1868, and Walls attended as a delegate from Alachua County, which had also nominated him for a seat in the state assembly. At the convention, Walls was elected to the assembly and took his seat in June of 1868. Later that year, he was nominated for and elected to a seat in the state senate; he then resigned from his assembly seat and took his place in the state senate in January of 1868. While serving in the state senate, Walls also attended several conventions held by black voters. He made a proposal at the 1871 Southern States Convention of Colored Men that called upon Republicans to support **John Mercer Langston** for vice president in 1872.

At that time, Florida had only one seat in Congress, and in 1870 Walls was nominated as the Republican candidate. Though the race was a tough one, Walls managed to win a narrow victory, which was challenged by his opponent Silas L. Niblack. The House, however, initially accepted Walls's credentials, seating him and assigning him to the Committee on Militia, the Committee on Mileage, and the Committee on Expenditures in the Navy Department. Niblack pursued his challenge, saying that election officials had thrown out some of his ballots while keeping illegal votes for Walls. Walls countered by saying that the totals had been fraudulent, and that many voters had been harassed and threatened at the polls. On January 29, 1873, the House Committee on Elections ruled in favor of Niblack, unseating Walls. However, Walls had already defeated him in the November, 1872, election for one of Florida's two new congressional seats.

Although his first tenure in Congress had been brief, Walls managed to propose legislation he felt was important. He supported a bill that would have provided a national educational fund for public education from the sale of public lands. Walls also supported bills that promoted internal improvements in the state of Florida.

In 1874, Walls ran for reelection and won and, again, was challenged. He had defeated his opponent, Jesse J. Finley, by only 371 votes. The House Committee on Elections was split this time. The Democrats and one Independent Republican contended that Walls's ballots in one county precinct had been tampered with and did not count, making Finley the winner. The Republicans on the committee, however, declared that the ballots, which had mysteriously burned in a fire, did count and that Walls was entitled to the seat. Finally, the decision was reached in favor of Finley on the floor of the Democrat-controlled House; Walls was unseated.

Although Walls again tried for Congress in 1876, he was defeated in the nominating process by Republican Horatio Bisbee. He again ran, successfully, for the Florida State Senate, where he fought for mandatory public education. In 1879, however, Walls took an indefinite leave of absence from the state senate; he was frustrated that none of the measures he proposed were adopted. He returned to Alachua County and to farming. In 1884, he tried once again for Congress and was defeated.

Walls's health was poor, and a disastrous freeze had wiped out both his crops and money in 1895. During the last years of his life, he accepted a position running the farm at Florida Normal College (now Florida A and M University), in Tallahassee, Florida. It was there, on May 15, 1905, that he died.

Sources

Christopher, Maurine. *America's Black Congressmen*. New York: Thomas Y. Crowell, 1971

Clay, William L. *Just Permanent Interests: Black Americans in Congress, 1870–1991*. New York: Amistad Press, 1992.

"Former Black Members of Congress." *Congressional Times Journal*. <http://www.Usbol.com/ctjournal/FrBlkCongMemList.html>. Accessed: 4/2/98.

Harold Washington

Reproduced from AP/Wide World Photos, by Charlie Bennett

Born: April 15, 1922, in Chicago, Illinois

Status: Died November 25, 1987, in Chicago, Illinois; buried in Oakwoods Cemetery, Chicago, Illinois

Education: B.A., 1949, Roosevelt University, Chicago, Illinois; J.D., 1952, Northwestern University School of Law, Evanston, Illinois; admitted to the Illinois bar, 1953

Position: U.S. Air Force Engineers, 1943–1946; lawyer, 1952–1954; elected precinct captain, Third Ward Democrats, Chicago, Illinois, 1954; assistant city prosecutor, City of Chicago, 1954–1958; arbitrator, Illinois State Industrial Commission, 1960–1964; representative, Illinois State Legislature, 1965–1977; senator, Illinois State Senate, 1977–1981; U.S. representative from the First Congressional District of Illinois, 1981–1983; mayor, City of Chicago, 1983–1987

Early Years

Harold Washington was born on April 15, 1922, on Chicago's South Side. His father, Roy Washington, Sr., worked in a meatpacking house, and at the time of Washington's birth was attending law school at night. One of the few Democrats at that time in the South Side, Roy served as the Democratic precinct captain, registering voters and working on various candidates' campaigns. When Washington was just a baby, his father finished law school and went to work as an assistant prosecutor out of a South Side police station.

Washington attended Forrestville School as a child, and then DuSable High School. In high school, he excelled in track and was a bright student, but he dropped out of school the summer after his junior year because he was bored. He went to work in a meatpacking plant, as his father had before him; but then his father got Washington a job at the local U.S. Treasury office. On July 22, 1942, Washington married Nancy Dorothy Finch, who lived near his family (they divorced in 1950). In 1943, Washington was drafted into the U.S. Air Force Engineers and served in the South Pacific as a first sergeant. It was during his stint in the U.S. Air Force that he earned his high school equivalency degree.

Higher Education

When the war ended, Washington returned to Chicago, and since the G.I. Bill provided educational funds he decided to continue his schooling. He entered Roosevelt University in Chicago. Unlike high school, college challenged Washington, and he did well. The school was predominately white, but Washington was intelligent and likable; he was elected senior class president in 1949.

Upon graduation, Washington enrolled at Northwestern University's school of law. When he graduated in 1952, he went into practice with his father and passed the Illinois bar exam in 1953.

Career Highlights

Roy Washington, Sr., died in 1954, and Washington was offered a job by his father's friend, **Ralph Harold Metcalfe**, who at that time was a ward committeeman and member of the Chicago City Council (Metcalfe would go on to be elected congressman from the First District, the same district that would send Washington to Congress in 1980). Metcalfe offered Washington the job of assistant city prosecutor, a position Washington would hold until 1958. At the same time, Washington succeeded his late father in the position of precinct captain of the Third Ward of Chicago.

Growing up in a political milieu, Washington was drawn to politics in his adult life. Mayor Richard J. Daley ran the Democratic political machine and rewarded those who delivered Democratic votes. Washington was a tireless worker in the Third Ward, building up the organization and fighting to get people to vote Democratic in each election. From 1960 to 1964, Washington, having left the prosecutor's office, was working as an arbitrator for the Illinois State Industrial Commission; this job provided him with additional contacts in both the political and labor communities.

In 1964, Washington decided to throw his own hat into the political arena, running for state representative. With all the connections he had made over the years, he easily won election. Once in the state house of representatives, however, he began to show that he was not just another cog in Daley's political machine. He worked to organize the first black caucus of the legislature, and frequently voted against legislation the Chicago machine promoted. He fought for fair housing and equal employment opportunities, and worked against police brutality in his district. In 1976, Mayor Richard Daley died, and a special primary was called to fill his position. Washington ran in the primary against three other Democrats, but finished third with only 11 percent of the vote. That same year, Washington ran for the Illinois State Senate and defeated his opponent. At least on the state level, Washington had support.

Washington had been in the state senate three years when he decided to run for Congress. Despite the fact that his opponent in the Democratic primary, Congressman Bennett Stewart, had the support of the Chicago political machine, Washington easily beat him and the Republican candidate, garnering 92 percent of the vote.

When Washington was sworn into the House of Representatives on January 3, 1981, he was in the minority in more ways than one. Not only was he African American, but he was a liberal in the conservative era of President Ronald Reagan. He was assigned to the Education and Labor, Government Operations, and Judiciary Committees. As a member of these committees, and as a congressman, he waged a battle against Reagan conservatism.

At the time, Reagan was cutting social spending left and right. He had proposed his "trickle down" theory of economics, saying that the public would voluntarily close the gap between what the government was providing and what the various social services in the country needed. Washington knew this was not true and fought long and hard against the cuts in social services, and against Reagan's proposed increases in military spending. He refused to support cuts to student aid, job training programs, and child nutrition programs. As a member of the Judiciary Committee, he also negotiated an agreement to extend the Voting Rights Act of 1965, "which guaranteed that jurisdictions with a history of voting rights abuses would be unable to take advantage of the measure's 'bailout' provisions and escape coverage under the act" (Clay 392). Washington, with his determination to help not only his own constituents in Illinois but those around the country, was a popular figure with liberal Democrats; in 1982, he easily won reelection to Congress with nearly 100 percent of the vote.

In 1983, however, the people of Chicago called upon Washington to serve in a different capacity. There had never been a black mayor of Chicago, and under Mayor Jane Byrne city jobs going to African Americans fell from 47 percent in 1980 to 28 percent in 1982 (Bigelow 282). Black Democrats approached Washington to ask if he would challenge Byrne in the upcoming election, and Washington agreed, as long as they increased black voter registration in the city. When they delivered, Washington announced his candidacy.

In the Democratic primary, Washington ran against Jane Byrne and Richard M. Daley, son of the late Mayor Richard J. Daley. He pledged to destroy the Chicago political machine, which doled out city jobs to political cronies. As he had done when in the state legislature, he vowed to work for better housing and against police brutality. Before the primary, Democratic Party Chairman Edward Vrdolyak was overheard saying, "It's a racial thing. Don't kid yourself ... We're fighting to keep the city the way it is" (Bigelow 283). When news of this statement was reported in the press, the reaction was overwhelming. Black voters were determined to vote—and to vote for Washington. Although the race was close, Washington won with 36 percent of the vote and would go on to defeat his Republican opponent, Bernard Epton.

Although Epton had initially sworn that the campaign was not to be a racial one, his supporters wore "Whites for Epton" and "Epton—Before It's Too Late" campaign buttons. Epton revealed that Washington had had his law license suspended for a year in 1970 because he had failed to do work for a number of his clients, and that the IRS had fined him and sentenced him to 40 days in jail for failing to file income tax returns for four years. The campaign was an ugly one, but black and Hispanic voters turned out in record numbers; Washington walked away the clear winner, becoming the first black mayor of Chicago.

Washington vowed to do away with Chicago's political machine, which was an uphill battle. The Democrats had packed the Chicago City Council with their allies, who opposed or voted down every proposal sent to them by Washington. But the council "machine" members did not have the votes to override his veto, so despite the fact that many measures were permanently stalled, Washington did manage to get a few things enacted. He set out to cut the grossly inflated city budget, laying off 700 city employees and cutting his own salary as mayor by 20 percent. He also—and perhaps most significantly—managed to enact the Shakman decree, which outlawed patronage in the hiring and firing of city employees. He worked on getting more minorities hired and improving the neighborhoods of Chicago. By the time Washington's term of office was up, Chicago had changed in a number of significant ways.

The reelection campaign of 1987 was just as harsh as the earlier one had been, with a great deal of mudslinging. In the primary, Washington was challenged by Jane Byrne again. He defeated her, and in the general election, he faced Democratic Party Chairman Vrdolyak and Thomas Hynes, who was the assessor for Cook County (both were running as independents) and the Republican candidate Donald Haider. Washington triumphed and began his second term.

Washington worked with a cooperative city council and looked forward to a second term in office that promised to be much less taxing than his first term; but on November 25, 1987, while working in his office at city hall, Washington collapsed from a heart attack and died.

With his death, many of the gains he had made in the city also perished; political fighting reared its head again in the scramble to fill the vacant office of mayor.

Sources

Bigelow, Barbara Carlisle, ed. *Contemporary Black Biography: Profiles from the International Black Community*, Vol. 6. Detroit, MI: Gale Research, 1994.

Clay, William L. *Just Permanent Interests: Black Americans in Congress, 1870–1991*. New York: Amistad Press, 1992.

Estell, Kenneth. *African America: Celebrating 400 Years of Achievement*. Detroit, MI: Visible Ink Press, 1994.

"Former Black Members of Congress." *Congressional Times Journal*. <http://www.usbol.com/ctjournal/FrBlkCongMemList.html>. Accessed: 2/21/98.

New Grolier Multimedia Encyclopedia. Novato, CA: The Software Toolworks, Inc./Grolier, Inc., 1993.

Walter Edward Washington

Copyright Washington Post, *reprinted by permission of D.C. Public Library, by Rosemary Martufi*

Born: April 15, 1915, in Dawson, Georgia

Status: Retired

Education: Graduate in public administration and sociology, 1938, Howard University, Washington, D.C.; graduate, c. 1948, Howard University Law School, Washington, D.C.

Position: Employee, National Capital Housing Administration, Washington, D.C., 1938–1960; appointed executive director, National Capital Housing Administration, Washington, D.C., 1961; chairman, New York Public Housing Authority, New York, New York, 1966–1967; appointed mayor, Washington, D.C., 1967–1973; elective mayor, Washington, D.C., 1974–1978

Early Years

Walter Washington was born on April 15, 1915, in Dawson, Georgia. He was the only child of William L. Washington and Willie Mae Thornton Washington. While he was still a child, his parents moved the family to Jamestown, New York, where Washington grew up and attended public school, graduating from high school in 1933. His parents wanted the best for their only child so, despite the fact that the Depression had limited jobs and money, Washington was sent to Howard University in Washington, D.C.

Higher Education

Even as a young man, Washington was interested in the politics of rule and, in college, majored in public administration and sociology. He graduated from Howard in 1938 and began working, hoping to earn enough money to continue his studies. Over the next 10 years, Washington worked in Washington, D.C., in a variety of jobs, also taking classes at Howard University's school of law. He was an administrative intern and then junior housing assistant with the National Capital Housing Authority. In 1948, he received his law degree from Howard, but he continued to work with the Housing Authority, becoming its executive director in 1961. During this time, he married Bennetta Bullock, with whom he had one daughter. Bennetta, who went on to obtain a Ph.D. in sociology, would become as involved in politics as her husband, working as associate director of women's programs for education in the U.S. Department of Labor.

Career Highlights

Washington, D.C., home of the federal government and hub of the nation, is also one of the largest cities in the United States and has one of the largest African American populations. Despite the need for local direction, until 1974 the city was governed by the federal government, and its highest offices were appointed. Ironically, the citizens of the nation's capital had no direct say in how they were governed.

Walter Washington was intimately familiar with the problems of the city. As director of the National Capital Housing Authority, he confronted the poverty and want of its citizens on a daily basis. His familiarity with such situations garnered him the appointment in 1966 as chairman of the New York Public Housing Authority, a body that faced problems similar to those in the capital; but in 1967, Washington was offered the appointed position of mayor of Washington, D.C., by President Lyndon Johnson. Since the capital had been his home for so long, he resigned the New York chairmanship to accept Johnson's offer. With his acceptance, Washington became the first black mayor of Washington, D.C.

The city of Washington during the late 1960s and early 1970s was in a state of turmoil. When Walter Washington assumed the office of mayor, the Vietnam War was at its height, as were protests against it. Racial inequities were being protested on the streets. "Through the administrations of three presidents, his [Washington's] administration ... had to put down riots, handle anti-war and welfare demonstrations and battle the whims of a sometimes unsympathetic Congress and White House" (Joint Center For Political Studies 47).

Washington steadfastly worked for self-rule for the city. Although this endeavor could have put him out of a job, he felt that the city needed local rule, with citizen elections and input. In 1972, the first of a number of national black political conventions were held by the major African American political leaders in the country. "A major purpose of the conclave was to bring black people together to develop a national black agenda that set forth priorities as well as to develop plans for unified black action at the summer conventions of the Democratic and Republican parties" (Smythe 591). A second convention was held on March 15, 1974. At this meeting, one of the resolutions passed called for self-rule in the District of Columbia. This was one resolution that was successful in Congress, and that same year a referendum on the issue was passed. In 1974, Washington, D.C., called for its first mayoral election in more than 100 years.

Walter Washington, having been in office for seven years, decided to run for election. The campaign was a heated one. Washington's challenger was Clifford Alexander, former chairman of the U.S. Equal Employment Opportunity Commission. Alexander had strong political support, but it was Washington's past record with the city that helped him ultimately defeat his opponent and, in 1974, Walter Washington became the first elected black mayor of Washington, D.C.

Walter Washington's two terms as mayor of the District of Columbia were spent reorganizing its government. It had been dependent upon the federal government for so long that a total reorganization was necessary. He also worked to make the local government more responsive to its citizens, and to address the problems plaguing the city: housing, unemployment, and poverty. By the end of his second term of office in 1978, when **Marion S. Barry, Jr.**, was elected mayor of the city, Walter Washington had given Washington, D.C., a strong, responsive central government.

Sources

Joint Center for Political Studies. *Profiles of Black Mayors in America*. Washington, DC/Chicago, IL: The Joint Center for Political Studies/Johnson Publishing, 1977.

Smith, Jessie Carney, ed. *Black Firsts: 2,000 Years of Extraordinary Achievement*. Detroit, MI: Visible Ink Press, 1994.

Smythe, Mabel M., ed. *The Black American Reference Book*. Englewood Cliffs, NJ: Prentice-Hall, Inc., 1976.

Maxine Waters

Reproduced from AP/Wide World Photos, by Greg Gibson

Born: August 15, 1938, in St. Louis, Missouri

Status: U.S. representative from the 35th Congressional District of California

Education: B.A. in sociology, 1972, California State University, Los Angeles; recipient of numerous honorary degrees from various colleges and universities

Position: Factory worker, telephone operator, 1956–1965; assistant teacher, Head Start program, Los Angeles, California, 1965–c. 1972; chief deputy to David Cunningham, Los Angeles City Council, Los Angeles, California, 1973–1976; representative, California State Assembly, 1976–1990; U.S. representative from the 29th Congressional District of California, 1990–1992; U.S. representative from the 35th Congressional District of California, 1993–

Early Years

"Most people say I'm too pushy, I'm too aggressive, I'm too assertive, I'm too confrontational. That I ask for too much. I've never been considered patient, or even conciliatory in most instances" (Smith 639). Maxine Waters was the product of a childhood in which hard work was a necessity, which carried her to one of the most important offices in the United States.

Waters was born Maxine Moore on August 15, 1938, in St. Louis, Missouri. When she was only two years old, her parents, Remus Moore and Velma Lee Carr Moore, divorced. Her mother remarried soon after the divorce, and Waters grew up in a household that consisted eventually of 13 children. With all those children competing for their parents' attention, it is no wonder that Waters grew to be assertive.

Waters attended school in St. Louis and, as a teenager, worked to earn spending money and help with family finances; but she also had time for some school activities, doing well in music, track, and swimming. In 1956, she graduated from high school and that same year married Edward Waters, her high school sweetheart. To support themselves and their two children, Edward and Karen, both Waters and her husband went to work in factories in St. Louis.

In 1961, the Waterses decided to move to Los Angeles, feeling there was more opportunity there for them. After settling in the city, they again found jobs in city factories. Waters worked in a garment factory and at a telephone company, but she resigned from her telephone job after suffering a miscarriage.

In many ways, the civil rights movement of the 1960s passed by Waters without much notice; she was working too hard caring for a family. She could not ignore, however, the Watts riots of 1965, which took place around her. In many ways, the riots, although tragic, proved fortuitous for Waters. The federal government had begun the Head Start program to help areas such as Watts, and Waters obtained a job as an assistant teacher in the program. Through the program, Waters became convinced of the value of education, particularly for the disenfranchised, and in 1968, while continuing to work with Head Start, she began college at California State University in Los Angeles.

Higher Education

In 1972, Waters graduated with a bachelor's degree in sociology. Unfortunately, the pressures of working, caring for a family, and attending school had taken its toll on her marriage, and she and Edward Waters divorced that same year.

Career Highlights

While working with the Head Start program, Waters often found herself in the position of spokesperson for both the enrolled children and their parents. She urged the parents to contact their governmental representatives for more funding for the program and for improvements to it that would best suit their community. Her work on behalf of the program led her to become involved in local politics, campaigning for candidates who held views similar to her own. In 1972, she was chosen as a delegate to the Democratic National Convention, which whetted her interest in politics even more. After she graduated from college, she was offered the position of chief deputy to David Cunningham, a council member on the Los Angeles City Council. In 1976, after three years with Cunningham, Waters herself decided to run for public office.

Waters ran for a seat in the California State Assembly. By now a familiar figure in her district of Los Angeles, she had strong support from those who admired her fearlessness in speaking out about issues of importance. She was supported in her campaign by Sidney Williams, a Los Angeles car salesman and former Cleveland Browns football player, whom she had been dating for a number of years. Waters easily won the election, took her seat in 1976, and, the following year, married Williams.

During her 14 years in the California State Assembly, Waters became the first woman to serve on a number of legislative committees, such as the Joint Legislative Budget Committee and the Natural Resources Committee. She also became the first woman in California to be elected chair of the Democratic caucus.

Waters quickly got a reputation as a fearless and vocal advocate for women, children, African Americans, Hispanics, and the poor. The fact that the assembly was dominated by men did not cow her in the least, and she worked tirelessly on issues she felt were of importance. She created the nation's first Child Abuse Prevention Training Program, and sponsored legislation that prohibited strip searches of people arrested for misdemeanors. She also pushed a bill that required California to divest its state pension funds of investments in firms doing business with South Africa. As Jessie Carney Smith points out, over the years, Waters became known as "the conscience of the California legislature" (Smith 636).

Waters also worked for the Democrats on the national level. In 1980, she became a member of the Democratic National Committee and that same year seconded the nomination of Senator Edward Kennedy for president at the National Democratic Convention. In 1984, she cochaired the national presidential campaign of **Jesse Louis Jackson**, supporting him again in 1988. And in 1992, after she had entered Congress, she seconded President Bill Clinton's nomination at the National Democratic Convention and served as national cochair of his campaign.

In an effort to promote women's rights, Waters joined with Ethel Bradley, the wife of Los Angeles mayor, **Thomas Bradley**, and Ruth Washington, a publisher, to form the Black Women's Forum. In 1984, on the national level, she joined with others in organizing the National Political Congress of Black Women. Both organizations aim "to promote and encourage the participation of Black women in the political process" to promote equality and empowerment (Smith 637).

In 1990, Congressman **Augustus Freeman Hawkins** of the 29th Congressional District of California announced his retirement from office. Waters decided to run for the vacant seat despite strong opposition. Although her opponent was endorsed by the local Democrats,

Waters won 88 percent of the vote in the primary and easily beat her Republican opponent in the general election. In the years to come, despite congressional redistricting that expanded the area of Waters's district, which became the 35th, she continued to win reelection.

As she had in the California assembly, Waters had no hesitation about speaking out in the House of Representatives, continually supporting women, children, and minorities. And over the years, her participation in key congressional committees has helped her generate legislation that has aided people nationwide. In the fall of 1992, her Emergency Development Loan Guarantee Program was signed into law. This authorizes $2 billion per year in Section 108 loan guarantees to cities for the development of housing, small businesses, and economic and infrastructure development. On July 2, 1993, President Clinton signed into law Waters's "Youth Fair Chance" program that provides job and life skills training for unskilled and unemployed people from 17 to 30 years old. After riots in Los Angeles following the verdict in the Rodney King trial in 1992, Waters helped raise $3 million in Labor Department funds to provide relief in South Central Los Angeles.

The riots also brought Waters national attention, defining on television the hopelessness and despair that is so prevalent in the poorer sections of cities across the country. "World News Tonight" on ABC-TV profiled her as "Person of the Week," and Peter Jennings called her "a woman who simply will not go unheard" ("Congresswoman Maxine Waters"). In 1996, Waters again came to national attention when she was chosen to chair the Congressional Black Caucus for the 105th congressional term.

Waters continues to be vocal in Congress and nationally, and to be popular with her constituents. Her performance in office over the years has proven the statement she made when first elected to national office: "The women of this country, the Black women, ... have wanted very much to increase their numbers. So I think our voices are going to be extremely important, not only to articulate the aspirations of Black women, but to add our voices to the voices of Black men" (Smith 638). Waters's voice has become one that is important—and she makes sure it is heard.

Sources

Congressional Black Caucus '93–'94 Guide. <http://www.sas.upenn.edu/African_Studies/Govern_Political/CBC_Guide.html>. Accessed: 3/10/98.

"Congresswoman Maxine Waters." *U.S. House of Representatives*. <http://www.house.gov/waters/bio.htm>. Accessed: 3/13/98.

Estell, Kenneth. *African America: Celebrating 400 Years of Achievement*. Detroit, MI: Visible Ink Press, 1994.

"Maxine Waters." *Congressional Times Journal*. <http://www.usbol.com/ctjournal/Bios/mwaters.html>. Accessed: 2/26/98.

Smith, Jessie Carney, ed. *Black Heroes of the 20th Century*. Detroit, MI: Visible Ink Press, 1998.

Melvin L. Watt

Courtesy of the Office of Congressman Melvin L. Watt

Born: August 26, 1945, in Steele Creek, Mecklenburg County, North Carolina

Status: U.S. representative from the 12th Congressional District of North Carolina; part owner, East Towne Manor, Charlotte, North Carolina

Education: B.S. in business administration, 1967, University of North Carolina, Chapel Hill; J.D., 1970, Yale University Law School, New Haven, Connecticut; recipient of honorary degrees from North Carolina A and T State University and Johnson C. Smith University

Position: Attorney, Chambers, Stein, Ferguson and Becton (later Ferguson, Stein, Watt, Wallas, Adkins and Gresham), Charlotte, North Carolina, 1971–1992; campaign manager for Harvey Gantt's campaigns for city council, mayor (1980s), and U.S. Senate (1990), Charlotte, North Carolina; state senator, North Carolina State Senate, 1985–1986; part owner, East Towne Manor, Charlotte, North Carolina, 1989– ; U.S. representative from the 12th Congressional District of North Carolina, 1993–

Early Years

Melvin "Mel" L. Watt was born in rural Mecklenburg County, North Carolina, and raised solely by his mother. The family lived at first in stark poverty in a tin-roofed shack with no running water or electricity. Watt attended the segregated schools of North Carolina and was a bright student.

Higher Education

When Watt graduated from York Road High School in Charlotte, he entered the University of North Carolina at Chapel Hill, where he did well, majoring in business administration. In 1967, he graduated Phi Beta Kappa, and entered Yale University in New Haven, Connecticut, to work on a degree in law. While at Yale, Watt again did well, receiving a spot on the *Yale Law Review*.

Career Highlights

After graduating from Yale in 1970, Watt returned to North Carolina, where he joined the law firm of Chambers, Stein, Ferguson and Becton (later Ferguson, Stein, Watt, Wallas, Adkins and Gresham) in Charlotte. He married Eulada Paysour; the couple would have two sons, Brian and Jason, who would follow in their father's footsteps by going to Yale University.

Over the ensuing years, Watt became involved in local politics, serving as campaign manager for local politician Harvey Gantt as Gantt ran successfully for Charlotte City Council and mayor, and unsuccessfully for the U.S. Senate. Gantt needed someone who was organized and who could organize others. As Gantt later said of Watt, "Mel has the ability to be very organized, to know what he wants to do. There is an element of stubbornness in him. After doing his reading and research, being very focused, he'll stick with his decision" (Sonyakay 4).

Although Watt had helped with another's campaign, he himself did not consider entering public office until 1985. That year, he reluctantly accepted the offer by local Democrats to serve in the North Carolina senate after their chosen candidate died at the end of the campaign.

While in the North Carolina senate, Watt was highly regarded as "the most effective freshman legislator," and was nicknamed "the conscience of the Senate." In 1986, however, he declared that he would not run for reelection as he wished to remain out of public office until his two sons graduated from high school. After stepping down from the senate, Watt returned to his law practice and, in 1989, became a part-owner of East Towne Manor, a care facility for the elderly and disabled.

In 1992, North Carolina underwent redistricting based on the 1990 census. The newly created 12th Congressional District was an odd shape, described by the *Congressional Quarterly Weekly Report* as "a snake-like ink blot" ("Melvin Watt" 119). The district is 52 percent black and 48 percent white and is primarily urban in makeup. Watt decided to run for a seat in the House from this new district, running on the idea of "What's good for one of us is good for all of us" (Sonyakay 3), and on his concern for the urban poor.

The election was a tough one, and Watt came under some criticism for accepting nearly $204,000 in PAC money to finance his campaign; but he was able to convince the voters that he was an independent thinker, not liable to special interests. In the primary, Watt won 47 percent of the vote and went on to win the general election. When he took his seat in Congress in January of 1993, he and **Eva M. Clayton** from North Carolina's First Congressional District, who had also been elected, became the first black North Carolinians in Congress since Republican George White had resigned his seat in protest of state lawmakers' decision to strip blacks of their voting rights in 1901 ("Melvin Watt" 119). Watt was assigned to the Banking, Finance and Urban Affairs Committee and the Judiciary Committee; his fellow freshman Democrats also elected him to one of three seats on the Steering and Policy Committee, which makes committee assignments.

Regarding his position on the Banking Committee, Watt said, "Where there's a direct conflict between the bank's interest and the consumer's, I'll be on the consumer's side" ("Melvin Watt" 119). And indeed, in 1995, Floyd Stoner, director of legislative operations for the American Bankers Association, said of Watt that he "has been supportive on powers issues and geography but on issues that are characterized as consumer issues, he has frequently voted against positions we (the ABA) have taken" (Sonyakay 4).

Watt again demonstrated his independent thinking when he voted against President Clinton's North American Free Trade Agreement (NAFTA). He opposed the agreement because he felt it would lead to a "loss of jobs, lower wages, company relocations to Mexico, and devaluation of the peso" (Sonyakay 3). And, as he later said, "It's almost scary to look back a year later and see how accurate my projections were" (Sonyakay 3).

In 1995, Watt weathered a storm when the redistricting of 1992 was challenged in the courts. It was argued that his district, the 12th District, had been created to get a black voter majority; and the United States Supreme Court had ruled that it may be illegal to draw a congressional district with an odd shape merely to redistribute voters. As Watt pointed out, however, the district was created as an urban district, and race was not a dominating factor in its creation. With a nearly 50 to 50 split between black and white voters, Watt said that the 12th was "the most integrated congressional district North Carolina has" (Sonyakay 4).

In 1998, Watt won reelection a fourth time. He continues today to promote the things he feels are important: gun control, abortion rights, doing away with the death penalty, and full funding for Head Start programs. As he has said, "I don't have to equivocate on where I stand" ("Melvin Watt" 119).

Sources

Congressional Black Caucus '93–'94 Guide. <http://www.sas.upenn.edu/African_ Studies/Govern_Political/CBC_Guide.html>. Accessed: 3/10/98.

"Melvin Watt." *Congressional Quarterly Weekly Report*, 16 January 1993, 119.

"Melvin Watt Biography." *U.S. House of Representatives*. <http://www.house.gov/watt/bio_mel.htm>. Accessed: 3/6/98.

"National Elections '98." The Washington Post, 4 November 1998. <http://elections98.washingtonpost.com/wp-srv/results98/national/>. Accessed: 11/19/98.

Sonyakay, Arati. "Giving 'Em Mel." *Business Journal of Charlotte*, 11 September 1995, 3–5.

Robert Clifton Weaver

Reproduced from UPI/Corbis-Bettmann

Born: December 29, 1907, in Washington, D.C.

Status: Died July 17, 1997, in New York, New York

Education: Graduate, 1925, Dunbar High School, Washington, D.C.; B.S. cum laude, 1929, Harvard University, Cambridge, Massachusetts; M.S., 1931, Harvard University, Cambridge, Massachusetts; Ph.D., 1934, Harvard University, Cambridge, Massachusetts; recipient of more than 30 honorary degrees from various colleges and universities

Position: Professor of economics, North Carolina Agricultural and Technical State College, Greensboro, North Carolina, 1931–1932; advisor on racial problems, Department of the Interior, Washington, D.C., 1934–1938; special assistant to the head of the National Housing Authority, 1938–1940; assistant to Sidney Hillman, National Defense Advisory Committee, 1940–1941; appointed to the National Production Board, and the Negro Manpower Commission, 1941–1944; executive director, Mayor's Commission on Race Relations, Chicago, Illinois, 1944–1945; director, community services, American Council on Race Relations, 1945–1948; United Nations Relief and Rehabilitation Administration, 1946–1947; lecturer, Northwestern University, Evanston, Illinois, 1947–1948; professor, Teachers College, Columbia University, New York, New York, summers, 1947 and 1949; professor, New York University, 1948–1951; director, Opportunity Fellowships Program, John Hay Whitney Foundation, New York, New York, 1949–1955; appointed deputy state rent commissioner, New York State, 1955; state rent commissioner, New York State, 1955–c. 1959; chairman of the board, National Association for the Advancement of Colored People (NAACP), 1960–1961; vice chairman, New York City Housing and Redevelopment Board, New York, New York, 1960–1961; appointed director of the Federal Housing and Home Finance Agency, 1960; secretary of housing and urban development, 1966–1969; president, Bernard M. Baruch College, New York, New York, 1969–1970; distinguished professor, Department of Urban Affairs, Hunter College, New York, New York, 1971–1978

Awards and honors: Spingarn Medal, 1962; Russwurm Award, 1963; Albert Einstein Commemorative Award, 1968; Frederick Douglass Award from the New York City Urban League,1977; M. Justin Herman Award, 1986

Early Years

Robert Clifton Weaver was born in Washington, D.C., on December 29, 1907. His father, Mortimer Grover, was a postal clerk. His mother, Florence Freeman Weaver, valued education; her father, Robert Mortimer Freeman, had been the first black man to earn a dental degree in the United States as a member of the first graduating class of Harvard University's dental school.

Weaver grew up in a suburb of Washington, D.C., attending Dunbar High School and working as an electrician after school. When he applied to join the electricians' union, he was denied membership because of his race. It is quite likely that, had he been accepted, he would have continued in this field after graduating from high school in 1925. Since he could not, he decided to follow in his grandfather's footsteps and attend college, majoring in economics.

Higher Education

Upon graduating from high school, Weaver entered Harvard University in Cambridge, Massachusetts. He was an outstanding student, graduating cum laude in 1929 and immediately continuing to graduate school. In 1931, he received his master of science degree, and in 1934 his doctorate, both at Harvard. After graduation, on July 18, 1935, he married Ella V. Haith; they adopted a son, Robert C. Weaver, Jr., who died in the 1960s.

Career Highlights

When Weaver graduated from college, he intended to become a college professor, and he began his career teaching economics at North Carolina Agricultural and Technical State College in Greensboro, North Carolina, in 1931. The Depression, however, affected his life just as it affected the life of every other American.

Since the stock market crash of 1929, the economy had been in a decline. President Herbert Hoover assumed, as did most Americans, that the decline would be temporary and that the economy would soon revive. Hoover felt that government intervention was not necessary to check the downturn; but, by 1931, it was clear that the country was in an economic crisis. Of the many suffering from the Depression, few were as hard-hit as African Americans, but when the federal government began instituting programs to help alleviate unemployment and starvation, blacks were often overlooked.

Weaver had the training and ambition to help other African Americans during the Depression. In 1934, he became an employee of the Department of the Interior in Washington, D.C., advising on race relations; and throughout the Depression he worked in various capacities, such as participating in Franklin Delano Roosevelt's "Black Cabinet." From 1938 to 1940 he served as a special assistant to the head of the National Housing Authority and, until the start of World War II in 1941, as assistant to Sidney Hillman, who was then head of the National Defense Advisory Committee.

According to Jessie Carney Smith, in her *Black Heroes of the Twentieth Century* (1998), Weaver had an important role to play in the presidential election of 1940. Smith writes that,

> ... Roosevelt's press secretary jostled a black policeman to the ground ... in New York's Madison Square Garden. White House aides contacted Weaver at midnight about how to repair the damage this incident might cause among black voters. Weaver suggested that more than a speech was necessary ... Within forty-eight hours, the nation had its first black general, Benjamin O. Davis, Sr. (644)

When World War II began for the United States, it effectively ended the Depression, but Weaver continued his service to the government during the war, working with the War Production Board and the Negro Manpower Commission until 1944. Again, his jobs involved bettering race relations and promoting greater African American involvement in the war. Like others who were working for the same goals, however, Weaver was fast becoming disillusioned with the federal government's snail-like progress in achieving racial equality. In 1944, he decided to shift to a smaller arena and accepted a position as executive director of the Mayor's Commission on Race Relations in Chicago, Illinois.

Weaver did not completely sever his ties with the federal government. At the same time he was working in Chicago, he was also serving as the director of community services for the American Council of Race Relations, a position he held until 1948. In 1946, Weaver traveled to the Ukraine as part of the United Nations Relief and Rehabilitation Administration. Also during these years, Weaver authored the first two of his four books, *Negro Labor, A National Problem* (1946), and *The Negro Ghetto* (1948).

Weaver enjoyed teaching as well as actively working to better conditions for blacks. From 1947 to 1948, he taught at Northwestern University in Evanston, Illinois, and, in 1948, took a position as professor at New York University. His move to New York was occasioned by his acceptance of the position of director of the Opportunity Fellowships Program of the John Hay Whitney Foundation. He also became involved with the Democratic Party in New York, bringing him to the attention of those in power.

In 1955, Weaver stepped down from his directorship of the John Hay Whitney Foundation to accept an appointment as deputy state rent commissioner for New York State. Soon after, Weaver assumed the position of commissioner for the same agency. With this appointment, Weaver became the first African American to hold a cabinet position in state government.

As an important member of government in New York and as chairman of the board of the National Association for the Advancement of Colored People (NAACP) from 1960 to 1961, Weaver was noticed by those on the national level. In 1960, President John F. Kennedy appointed Weaver head of the federal Housing and Home Finance Agency, which oversaw the activities of five smaller agencies. The following year, Kennedy attempted to have this agency made part of the cabinet, but Congress blocked the move. Five years later, in 1966, after President Lyndon B. Johnson created the Department of Housing and Urban Development in 1965, this department was included in the president's cabinet, and Weaver at last achieved a cabinet position as secretary, the first African American to do so.

Weaver believed strongly in the work of his department; while in Washington, D.C., he chose to live in an apartment in an urban redevelopment area of the city. During his work with urban development and housing over the years, Weaver had seen benign neglect at work. He realized that to fight slums within the country's cities, the government had to take an active role. During his term as secretary of housing and urban development, Weaver built a strong and involved department, creating many of the federal housing programs that are in existence today. His opinions and ideas are discussed in his two books written during the 1960s: *The Urban Complex* (1964) and *Dilemmas of Urban America* (1965).

With the election of Republican Richard Nixon to the presidency, Weaver stepped down from his cabinet position to assume the presidency of Bernard M. Baruch College in New York City from 1969 to 1970. He then accepted a position as distinguished professor in the Department of Urban Affairs at Hunter College in New York City, a position he held until his retirement in 1978. While teaching, Weaver also served on the boards of many companies and organizations, one of which was the National Committee against Discrimination in Housing. Weaver served as president of this association from 1973 until 1987.

Until his death of lung cancer on July 17, 1997, Robert Weaver worked tirelessly to improve conditions for African Americans and for all people. He was the recipient of numerous awards, including the Spingarn Medal in 1962, New York City Urban League's Frederick Douglass Award in 1977, and the M. Justin Herman Award in 1986.

Sources

Estell, Kenneth. *African America: Celebrating 400 Years of Achievement*. Detroit, MI: Visible Ink Press, 1994.

Smith, Jessie Carney, ed. *Black Heroes of the 20th Century*. Detroit, MI: Visible Ink Press, 1998.

"Weaver, Robert C(lifton)." *Encyclopedia Britannica*. 1996. <http://www.eb.com/cgi-bin/g?keywords=Robert+Weaver>. Accessed: 4/11/98.

Verda Freeman Welcome

Born: 1907, in Uree (later, Lake Lure), North Carolina

Status: Died April 24, 1990

Education: Graduate, 1932, Coppin State Teachers College, Baltimore, Maryland; graduate, 1939, Morgan State University, Baltimore, Maryland; M.A., 1943, New York University, New York; awarded honorary degrees from: the University of Maryland, College Park, 1970; Howard University, Washington, D.C., 1972; and Morgan State University, Baltimore, Maryland, 1976

Position: Teacher; president, North West Improvement Association, Baltimore, Maryland, 1950s; elected to the Maryland house of delegates from the Fourth Legislative District of Baltimore, 1958; elected to the Maryland State Senate, 1962

Early Years

Verda Freeman Welcome was born in 1907 in Uree (later renamed Lake Lure), North Carolina, the third of 16 children born to James and Docia Freeman. When Welcome was still a child, her mother died and she had to assume the responsibility of caring for the family. It was difficult for her to do well at school and to take care of 15 other children, but Welcome met the challenge. She was a strong, determined young woman, a born leader.

Higher Education

In 1929, Welcome moved to Baltimore, Maryland, where she enrolled in Coppin State Teachers College, and studied for a teaching certificate. After graduating from Coppin in 1932, she began teaching in the Baltimore public school system while continuing her education at Morgan State University in Baltimore, where she graduated in 1939. In 1943, she received her master's degree from New York University. These years were busy ones for Welcome; she was teaching, going to school, and also caring for her baby daughter, Mary Sue, who had been born shortly after her marriage in 1935 to Dr. Henry C. Welcome.

Career Highlights

Welcome devoted most of her time to her family and her teaching, but in the 1950s, with civil rights issues becoming more and more prominent, she began to get involved politically. She was elected president of the North West Improvement Association of Baltimore, an activist organization that worked to integrate public facilities in the city. By 1958, Welcome had assumed a leadership role in the civil rights movement in Baltimore and, backed by a group called the Valiant Women, mounted a challenge to Jack Pollack for his seat in the Maryland House of Delegates from the Fourth District in Baltimore.

Pollack's political backing was strong, and he had held his seat for a number of years. But Welcome had the advantage of race, because the Fourth Legislative District was predominantly black and she represented the kind of political involvement African Americans were increasingly claiming for themselves in the late 1950s. It was no surprise that she was able to sweep into office, or that she would hold a seat in the Maryland senate for almost 20 years.

Welcome continued to advocate for civil rights in the legislature throughout the turbulent 1960s, fulfilling a vow she had made as a young woman when she had seen her father abused while trying to exercise his rights: "One day I am going to vote and pay back the insult to my father" (Hine 1241).

Welcome stepped down from her seat in the House of Delegates in 1962 to run for a seat in the Maryland State Senate. Again, she swept the election. When she assumed her seat in 1962, Welcome became the first black woman to be elected to a state senate in the United States.

In the state senate, Welcome continued legislating for civil rights, supporting bills to open public accommodations to blacks, providing for equality in pay, and repealing Maryland's law against miscegenation. She also worked for gun control. As a member of the Finance Committee encouraging voter registration, she was perhaps one of the most influential legislators in the state outside the legislature.

Because of her influence, an assassin attempted to end her life in April of 1964. Welcome, shaken but undaunted, continued the civil rights and other legislative work she had begun upon first entering political life.

After nearly 20 years in office, Welcome stepped down from her seat in the 1980s. Upon her death on April 24, 1990, Welcome was mourned by all who had known her and was remembered by newspapers across the country for her strength in facing opposition.

Sources

Hine, Darlene Clark, ed. *Black Women in America: An Historical Encyclopedia*, Vol. II, M–Z. Brooklyn, NY: Carlson Publishing Co., 1993.

Smith, Jessie Carney, ed. *Black Firsts: 2,000 Years of Extraordinary Achievement*. Detroit, MI: Visible Ink Press, 1994.

Lawrence Douglas Wilder

Reproduced from AP/Wide World Photos

Born: January 17, 1931, in Richmond, Virginia

Status: Attorney; radio talk show host, "The Doug Wilder Show," Richmond, Virginia

Education: B.S. in chemistry, 1952, Virginia Union University, Richmond, Virginia; J.S., 1959, Howard University School of Law, Washington, D.C.

Position: U.S. Army, 1952–1953; attorney, Richmond, Virginia, 1959– ; state senator, Virginia State Senate, 1969–1986; lieutenant governor of Virginia, 1986–1990; governor of Virginia, 1990–1994; Democratic candidate for the presidential nomination, 1992

Awards and honors: Bronze Star; Spingarn Medal, NAACP, 1990; Anna Eleanor Roosevelt Medallion of Honor; Citation of Honor for Contributions to American Politics

Early Years

Lawrence Douglas Wilder was born in Richmond, Virginia, on January 17, 1931, the son of Robert Judson Wilder, Sr., and Beulah Wilder. Wilder was the seventh of eight children. He described his childhood in an interview with the *Atlanta Constitution* as "gentle poverty" (Bigelow 256). Their situation was much better than that of Wilder's grandparents. Robert Wilder's parents had been slaves and had been separated and sold to different owners, able to visit each other only on Sundays.

Robert Wilder was a salesman for Southern Aid Insurance and Beulah raised the children, but providing for so many children and withstanding the Depression made life difficult. However, as Wilder said in a *Washington Post* interview, "It was stressed that however things are, they can be better if you make them better. We were never told there were limitations. Our parents acted as if we had great opportunities compared to what they had. We were never afraid of challenge" (Bigelow 256).

Wilder grew up not fully aware of racism as he encountered few white people in the area of Richmond where the family lived. He saw that whites and blacks were treated differently—he went to one school, and white children went to others—but it wasn't until he graduated from high school that segregation was gradually brought home to him. His first major encounter with it was when he was unable to gain admission to most of the universities in Virginia, as they did not admit blacks.

Higher Education

Wilder began his higher education at Virginia Union University, an all-black college in Richmond. While going to school, he waited on tables. At that time, also, he was reading Ralph Ellison's *Invisible Man*. Later, he said,

> ... I didn't understand it at first. But then I realized, I'm experiencing this. I'm invisible. Here I am serving the coffee, pouring the tea, and guys are telling all these kinds of [racial] jokes around me. (Bigelow 256)

When Wilder graduated from Virginia Union in 1952, he entered the army, seeing combat in the Korean War. He entered as a private and had achieved the rank of sergeant by the time of his discharge. In 1953, Wilder was awarded the Bronze Star for his part in the battle of Pork Chop Hill. Life in the army further opened his eyes about black-white relations. He noticed that the black soldiers were frequently passed over for promotion, and he spoke out against this. As a result, blacks in his company began being promoted.

When Wilder was discharged from the army in 1953, he returned to Richmond and held a number of jobs. Then in 1954, the United States Supreme Court handed down its decision in *Brown v. Board of Education, Topeka, Kansas*. According to Wilder, "It restored my faith. It had a very startling effect on me because nine white men wrote the decision ... it was something that was cathartic to me" (Bigelow 256). The decision spurred Wilder to enter law school at Howard University in 1956. While studying at Howard, Wilder met Eunice Montgomery from Philadelphia. They were married on October 11, 1958 (the couple divorced in 1978).

Career Highlights

When Wilder graduated with his degree in law in 1959, he and his wife moved to his hometown of Richmond; their first child was born on May 19, 1959, the same month both Wilder and Eunice graduated from Howard. After he passed the bar, Wilder set up his own law office in Richmond, specializing in personal injury law.

Wilder's life was all he could wish for: his law firm was making money, and he and his wife bought a home and had two more children, Lawrence Douglas, Jr., and Loren Deane. As a prosperous member of the community, Wilder began to make political contacts and to think about running for office himself. In 1969, he entered the race for a seat in the Virginia State Senate. No African American had ever been elected to that body, but Wilder felt he had a good chance because times were changing. Although Wilder faced opposition from two other candidates, he was successful, garnering 50 percent of the vote. When he took his seat in the state senate, Wilder became the first black person to be elected to that body.

Wilder immediately proved that he was not one to keep quiet. His first speech before the Virginia senate in February, 1970, called upon that body to drop the state song, "Carry Me Back to Old Virginia"; the song was offensive to blacks, particularly in the line, "that's where this old darkie's heart am longin' to go." Wilder proclaimed that it glorified slavery and denigrated blacks. His protest upset his white colleagues, but it established him as spokesperson for black Virginians (Bigelow 256).

Margaret Edds, in her biography of Wilder, *Claiming the Dream*, writes of him at this time:

> Throughout the 1970s Wilder pursued a liberal, civil rights-oriented legislative agenda. He pushed for fair housing laws and a holiday honoring Martin Luther King Jr. He backed proposals to strip the sales tax from food and nonprescription drugs ... He opposed the death penalty and fought tough crime legislation including bills creating a sentence of life in prison without parole and prescribing a

> separate offense for the use of a gun in committing a felony. (Smith 665–66)

Wilder was a champion on civil rights issues to his fellow black Virginians. As he became more powerful on the state level, however, he began to think of higher office. In 1985, Wilder ran for lieutenant governor and, although many predicted he would never win, was able to defeat his Republican opponent, garnering 52 percent of the vote. But his ambitions did not stop there. "When Wilder was the only black in the state senate...," a 1990 *Time* article reported, "he gave voice to his overarching aspirations, a notion of empowerment far beyond what seemed plausible amid the genteel conservatism of the Old Dominion. 'If people will elect you Lieutenant Governor,' Wilder predicted with startling prescience, 'they'll elect you Governor'" (Shapiro). By 1989, Wilder's prediction was coming true; he entered the race for governor of Virginia.

During the race, the media often compared Wilder with **Jesse Louis Jackson**, but Wilder lacked Jackson's militancy and rhetoric. As *Time* reported, "Wilder had consciously shaped his persona to make his blackness and groundbreaking achievements seem almost boring and quietly inevitable. He did not disown his racial identity ... His style, rather, was to envelop the historic implications of his campaign in a protective cloak of Bill Cosbyesque banalities" (Shapiro). Wilder sagaciously courted the white voters of Virginia, careful not to frighten them away with the idea of an African American as governor. Wilder's Republican opponent, J. Marshall Coleman, allied himself with conservative Virginia tradition, and Wilder countered by campaigning on the idea that Virginia should not be dragged backward into the past. Although the media reported Wilder had a comfortable lead on election day, he won by only a slim margin. Wilder was sworn in in January of 1990, becoming the first black governor since **Pinckney Benton Stewart Pinchback** was governor of Louisiana from 1872 to 1873.

Wilder's term as governor was characterized by fiscal responsibility. During the recession of the early 1990s, Wilder kept firm control of Virginia's budget, laying off state employees only when necessary to keep the budget in line. As he said, "We should spend for needed services, not for nonsense" (Bigelow 258). In 1991, Wilder announced that he would seek the 1992 presidential nomination, but he withdrew from the race in January, 1992, saying, "I said that if it became too difficult for me to govern the Commonwealth and conduct a presidential campaign, I would terminate one endeavor" (Bigelow 258). Wilder's campaign had been underfinanced and vague in its platform, drawing few supporters.

In 1994, after Wilder stepped down from the post of governor (governors are not permitted to serve consecutive terms in Virginia), he announced he would challenge incumbent Charles Robb for his seat in the U.S. Senate. Running as an Independent, Wilder faced not only Robb, but Republican candidate Oliver North and Marshall Coleman, who had run against Wilder for governor. The media, however, focused on Wilder and Robb, calling their opposition a "feud." Wilder charged the conservative Robb with phone tapping and called for an investigation. When it became evident that Robb was leading in the polls, Wilder abandoned his challenge and gave his support to Robb, strengthening Robb's battle against North.

Although Wilder has not entered another political race, he continues to be active in Virginia politics and hosts a morning talk show, "The Doug Wilder Show," which covers discussions of various political and social issues.

Sources

Bigelow, Barbara Carlisle, ed. *Contemporary Black Biography: Profiles from the International Black Community*, Vol. 3. Detroit, MI: Gale Research, 1993.

Estell, Kenneth. *African America: Celebrating 400 years of Achievement*. Detroit, MI: Visible Ink Press, 1994.

Shapiro, Walter. "Breakthrough in Virginia." *Time Magazine*, 20 November 1989. *Time Almanac*, Reference Edition. Fort Lauderdale, FL: Compact Publishing, 1994.

Smith, Jessie Carney, ed. *Black Heroes of the 20th Century*. Detroit, MI: Visible Ink Press, 1998.

Y

Andrew Jackson Young, Jr.

Reproduced from AP/Wide World Photos

Born: March 12, 1932, in New Orleans, Louisiana

Status: Head, Young Ideas, Atlanta, Georgia, and GoodWork, International, LLC, Atlanta, Georgia

Education: Attended Dillard University, New Orleans, Louisiana, 1947; B.S., 1951, Howard University, Washington, D.C.; B.Div., 1955, Hartford Theological Seminary, Hartford, Connecticut; ordained as a minister, 1955, United Church of Christ; recipient of numerous honorary degrees from various colleges and universities

Position: Pastor, Marion, Alabama, Thomasville, Georgia, and Beachton, Georgia, 1955–1957; associate director for youth work, National Council of Churches, New York, New York, 1957–1961; administrative assistant, Southern Christian Leadership Conference (SCLC), 1962–1964; executive director, SCLC, 1964–1968; executive vice president, SCLC, 1968–1970; chairman, Atlanta Community Relations Commission, Atlanta, Georgia, 1970–1972; U.S. representative from the Fifth Congressional District of Georgia, 1973–1977; U.S. ambassador to the United Nations, 1977–1979; mayor, Atlanta, Georgia, 1982–1990; chairman, Atlanta Committee for the Olympic Games, Atlanta, Georgia, 1990–1996; founder and head, Young Ideas, Atlanta, Georgia, and GoodWork, International, LLC, Atlanta, Georgia

Awards and honors: Pax-Christi Award, St. Johns University, 1970; Spingarn Medal, NAACP, 1978; Presidential Medal of Freedom, presented by President Jimmy Carter, 1980

Early Years

Andrew Young was born on March 12, 1932, in New Orleans, Louisiana. He was luckier than most black children born in the South at that time. His grandfather had been a successful businessman in the town of Franklin, Louisiana, operating a drugstore, pool hall, and saloon, and sponsoring boat trips up the bayous. He had been able to send his son, Andrew Young, Sr., to college to become a dentist, and Young's parents became a part of the upper middle class of New Orleans's black society.

Despite their position of privilege within the African American community, the Youngs suffered from the same discrimination all blacks faced during the 1930s and 1940s, when Andrew and his younger brother, Walter, were growing up. As Young said in his autobiography, *An Easy Burden*, however,

> Daddy taught me that racism was a sickness, and to have compassion for racist whites as I would have compassion for a polio victim. Racism wasn't a problem with me, he told me, it was a problem they had. Daddy had a genuine, turn-the-other-cheek attitude, although he didn't believe in becoming a victim. (Young)

The Youngs were a religious family. Young's mother, who had been born in New Orleans, was superintendent of the Sunday school at the Central Congregational Church. As a boy, Young attended Sunday school and sang in the choir. He also began school in the church's Hill School, which offered kindergarten and first grade. Being bright, Young learned quickly and was placed in the third grade when it was time to enter the Valena C. Jones Public School.

Once Young had learned to read, he read everything he could get his hands on. His father encouraged both Young and his brother Walter in their reading, getting them library cards and taking them regularly to the local Negro library. Young was also active in sports from the time he was a young child. He learned to swim at a summer camp run by the local black YMCA. His mother reported, "He never feared anything. He just went right into the water and started swimming. And as he grew older, he played ball with the other boys, and got into fights like a normal boy does" (Haskins 18).

Andrew Young, Sr., taught Young to box, because he felt his sons should know how to defend themselves. Young's father also opened up the world to his sons, taking them on trips to New York City. As Dr. Young recalled, "We wanted them to be able to experience the things that they were denied at home—like going into the nice restaurants and hotels" (Haskins 19).

When Young was 14, the family moved across the city to a predominantly white neighborhood near Dillard University, a black college. Young was enrolled at Gilbert Academy, a private high school, and, although he was not enthusiastic about studying, he did well, graduating at the age of 15.

Higher Education

Young wanted to attend a college in Iowa, but his parents felt he was too young to be that far from home, so he enrolled in Dillard University for his freshman year and lived at home. He joined the freshman swimming team, but was not very interested in class work. He studied only enough to get grades that would enable him to transfer to another school. He wanted to remain at Dillard, but when the time came, his parents preferred that he go to Howard University in Washington, D.C., as his father had. His mother said, "we knew some people there who would sort of keep an eye on Andrew. He was only sixteen years old" (Haskins 26).

When Young arrived at Howard, he had trouble adjusting to the school and the other students. He was a sophomore and 16 years old, two years younger than most freshman students. And with the end of World War II and the G.I. Bill, many of his classmates were much older than Young.

Young's father intended for him to follow in his footsteps eventually and become a dentist, so, as an undergraduate, Young studied biology. But he did not spend much time studying. "I was always reading," he said. "I was always curious. But I was never studying the assignments" (Haskins 26). By his senior year, Young knew that he didn't want to go into dentistry; he did not send out applications to graduate schools. His mother dissuaded him from joining the army, and both his parents traveled to Washington, D.C., to see him graduate and to take him home to New Orleans until he could decide what he wanted.

On the trip back from Washington, the family stopped in King's Mountain, North Carolina, to spend the night in a religious camp that operated there each summer. Young was assigned a room with a young white minister who was going to Africa as a missionary. The minister told Young of his plans and of how he had prepared himself for the mission ahead. As Young said,

> In all my growing up, through college, nobody ever said to me, "You've got a responsibility to do something for somebody else." And I thought to myself, "Now here's a young white guy going off to Africa to work with my people. This is something I should be doing. It was a judgment on me. If you want to put it in southern language, which I didn't at the time, it was around that experience that I was "born again." (Haskins 29)

Young returned to New Orleans, but the seeds of an idea were planted in his head. Over the next several months, he became more active in his church and with the United Christian Youth Movement, traveling to various states to recruit young people into the movement. The movement sent him to Indiana for a training course and then assigned him to Rhode Island and Connecticut. His headquarters were in the Hartford Seminary in Hartford, Connecticut. Finally, he decided he wanted to enter the ministry.

When Young announced his plans to his parents, they were surprised and disappointed. His father declared that he would not help pay for Young's education at the Hartford Seminary. "I requested and received a partial scholarship from Hartford," Young said. "I also took on three part-time jobs: washing dishes in the school cafeteria, working in the library, and cleaning and tending the furnace of an apartment building" (Young).

For the first time in his life, Young was excited about studying and was doing well at the seminary. He also was dating a young woman, Jean Childs, who was attending Manchester College in Indiana. He had met her while doing an internship at a small church in her hometown in Marion, Alabama. On June 7, 1954, after Jean had graduated from Manchester, the two were married. Young graduated from the Hartford Seminary in 1955 and was ordained a minister in the United Church of Christ.

Career Highlights

After serving as pastor in the towns of Thomasville and Beachton, Georgia, Young decided that he needed to become more involved with the budding civil rights movement. Locally, he began organizing voter registration drives and action groups, but, by 1957, Young was feeling restless. Change was difficult to institute in a small town, and he was drawn by the larger things that were happening in the country at the time. Thus, when the National Council of Churches (NCC) approached him about going to work at their headquarters in New York City as associate director for youth work, Young was receptive.

Young's wife, Jean, was not happy about the move to New York. They had two young daughters, Andrea and Lisa, and Jean had a good job teaching. But after a great deal of prayer, Young accepted the job, moving his family to the borough of Queens. The Youngs' third daughter, Paula, was born there.

The job Young undertook for the National Council of Churches prepared him for many of the things he would face later in his life. For the first time, he was the only non-white person in an organization; because he was black, the council also assigned him to oversee race relations. Working with young people was rewarding for him, and he sought to reach more of them. He began an NCC-sponsored television program called "Look Up and Live." "It introduced me to the area of mass media," Young said, "and gave me an appreciation of the methods and the values of modern communication. That experience was tremendously helpful when I got to the civil rights movement" (Haskins 50).

In 1961, the United Church of Christ instituted a voter education program aimed at southern blacks and asked Young to lead it. Moving to Atlanta, Young also became involved with the Southern Christian Leadership Conference (SCLC), founded in 1957 with Martin Luther King, Jr., as its president, and, in 1962, became King's administrative assistant. The SCLC was fraught with political infighting and, at times, was a difficult place for Young to work, particularly when he was appointed its executive director in 1964. Many who were intimately involved in the movement considered him an outsider, and they felt he was too calm and rational.

Young was thoroughly involved with the civil rights movement in the 1960s, traveling with Martin Luther King, Jr., and helping to organize the various marches and campaigns. Like most of the SCLC leadership at that time, Young opposed King's decision to go to Memphis in 1968. The sanitation workers were on strike in Memphis, and the strike had erupted into violence. King felt he had to go to show the world that the violence was an aberration, that nonviolence was the more effective way in which to seek justice.

Once in Memphis, all seemed to go smoothly. On April 4, 1968, King and other SCLC members met with the leaders of the black strikers. The SCLC leaders had been invited to dinner at the home of a local minister and were planning on attending a mass meeting afterward. Young and a number of other SCLC leaders were waiting for King in the parking lot of the Lorraine Motel. As they stood there, Martin Luther King, Jr., came out on the balcony and shouted a few instructions to his aides. He turned to go inside once again, a shot rang out, and King fell. Young and the others ran up the steps to the balcony and found King dead.

Although King's followers carried on after King's death, April 4, 1968, marked not only his death but, in many ways, the death of the civil rights movement. As Young said of the movement, "It was probably the happiest time of my life. It was rough, but the issues were very clear-cut. We knew what we had to do and we had a group of people pretty much committed to doing it" (Haskins 96). Without King, the movement lost its momentum, and in 1970 Young decided to leave the SCLC and run for Congress.

Although many things had changed in the South, Young still faced a tough race for Congress, facing one black and two white candidates in the Democratic primary. He managed to win that race, but lost to the Republican candidate, Fletcher Thompson, in the general election because of low black voter turnout.

Young then accepted the position of chairman of the Atlanta Community Relations Commission, which allowed him to build recognition and a political base for a new campaign in 1972. In the congressional election that year, Young defeated Republican Rodney M. Cook, garnering 53 percent of the vote and becoming the first black representative to be elected from the South since Reconstruction.

When Young entered the 93rd Congress, he was appointed to the Committee on Banking and Currency and, after a year, was appointed to the House Rules Committee. Young worked hard in Congress and became known for his leadership and negotiating skills. During his first and second terms, he worked to strengthen the Voting Rights Act, and supported legislation to stop South Africa's sugar quota. He pushed civil rights issues and publicly criticized President Nixon's halting measures in those areas.

In January 1977, during his second term in Congress, Young stepped down from his post when President Jimmy Carter offered him the appointment as United States representative to the United Nations. In many ways, Young saw the appointment as an opportunity to battle racism around the world.

Young established an informal style in the United Nations, which had a reputation of being very formal. He again utilized his leadership and negotiating skills, working to communicate with others. He met with African delegates to work out resolutions before they came before the Security Council. As he said, "Nobody had ever done that before ... nobody had ever sat down with them and said, 'Look, this is what we're thinking about. What do you think of it?'" (Haskins 154).

During his time at the United Nations, Young often made comments that were controversial; statements, according to the United States government, that were Young's own and not representative of the government. His penchant for being outspoken, as well as his informality, finally caused problems for Young. In August of 1979, in direct violation of State Department rules, Young met with the UN observer from the Palestine Liberation Organization. When news of the meeting reached the press, Young could do little but resign, although, as he said, "I really don't feel a bit sorry for anything that I have done" (Bigelow 266).

Young returned to Atlanta and began his consulting firm, Young Ideas, and with Hamilton Jordan, GoodWork International, LLC. In 1981, at the urging of his friends, among whom was Coretta Scott King, widow of Martin Luther King, Jr., Young decided to run for mayor of Atlanta. Although the election was filled with overtones of racism, Young managed to win with 55 percent of the vote.

As mayor, Young again was in the negotiating business, balancing white and black interests in a city filled with racial divisions. As he told *Esquire* magazine, "My job is to see that whites get some of the power and blacks get some of the money" (Bigelow 266). Young worked at building business in the city and improving public housing and job opportunities. While many had doubted his capabilities when he was first elected, by the time he ran for a second term, he had the majority of Atlantans behind him.

Barred from running a third time for mayor, Young tried for the office of governor in 1990 but was unsuccessful. Instead, he accepted the appointment of chairman of the Atlanta Committee for the Olympic Games, which were held in 1996. Since that time, he has worked with his consulting firms, and in 1997 published his autobiography, *An Easy Burden: The Civil Rights Movement and the Transformation of America.*

Sources

Bigelow, Barbara Carlisle, ed. *Contemporary Black Biography: Profiles from the International Black Community*, Vol. 3. Detroit, MI: Gale Research, 1993.

"Former Black Members of Congress." *Congressional Times Journal*. <http:www.usbol.com/ctjournal/FrBlkCongMemList.html>. Accessed: 2/26/98.

Haskins, James. *Andrew Young: Man with a Mission*. New York: Lothrop, Lee and Shepard Co., 1979.

Smith, Jessie Carney, ed. *Black Heroes of the 20th Century*. Detroit, MI: Visible Ink Press, 1998.

Young, Andrew. "An Easy Burden." *African-American Pioneers*. <http://www.kaiwan.com/~mcivr/andyoung.html>. Accessed: 4/23/98.

Coleman Alexander Young

Born: May 24, 1918, in Tuscaloosa, Alabama

Status: Died November 29, 1997, in Detroit, Michigan; buried in Elmwood Cemetery, Detroit, Michigan

Education: Graduate (with honors), 1936, Eastern High School, Detroit, Michigan; completed electricans' apprentice school, c. 1939, Ford Motor Company, Detroit, Michigan

Position: Assembly-line worker, Ford Motor Company, Detroit, Michigan, c. 1939–40; worker, U.S. Postal Service, Detroit, Michigan, 1940–42; second lieutenant and bombardier-navigator, Army Air Corps, c. 1942–46; worker, U.S. Postal Service, Detroit, Michigan, 1947–50; director of organization, Wayne County AFL-CIO, 1947; manager, dry-cleaning plant,

Detroit, Michigan, c. 1950–51; founder and director, National Negro Labor Council, Detroit, Michigan, 1951–56; insurance salesman, Detroit, Michigan, c. 1957–64; delegate, Michigan Constitutional Convention, 1961; senator, Michigan State Senate, 1965–73; mayor, Detroit, Michigan, 1974–94; member, Democratic National Committee, 1977–81; faculty member, Wayne State University, Detroit, Michigan, 1995–97.

Awards and Honors: Recipient of the Spingarn Medal, 1981

Early Years

Coleman Alexander Young was born in Tuscaloosa, Alabama, on May 24, 1918, the son of Coleman Young, a tailor, and Ida Reese Jones Young. Although Young's father worked hard, opportunities were few for blacks in the south at that time, and the neighborhood in which Young lived was often terrorized by the Ku Klux Klan. In 1926, when Young was eight years old, his father moved the family north to Detroit, Michigan, hoping for greater opportunity and seeking to escape the terrifying shadow of the Klan that seemed to hang over Tuscaloosa.

In Detroit, Young's father opened a dry-cleaning business, and the family found a home in the Black Bottom area of East Detroit that was, according to Young, "a cohesive community, a mixture of working- [and] middle-class people. In many ways it was more secure and comfortable than today's communities" (LaBlanc 252). Although secure in the neighborhood in which they lived, the family, consisting of Young, his four brothers and sisters, and his parents, keenly felt the effects of the Depression as the 1930s progressed. Young, as he admits in his autobiography, *Hard Stuff*, frequently turned to petty thievery to get some of the things he wanted.

Higher Education

After elementary school, Young attended Catholic Central High School, and then Eastern High School, graduating from the latter in 1936. He did well in school, earning honors upon graduation, and was offered a scholarship to the University of Michigan in Ann Arbor. He was forced to turn down the scholarship, however, when the Eastern High School Association, which usually assisted lower-income students with college costs not covered by scholarships, refused to help him because of his race.

Instead of going to college, Young entered the electricians' apprentice school at the Ford Motor Company. Although he finished first in the program, once again Young encountered racism. When he applied for a job as an electrician at Ford, he was passed over, the job going to a white electrician. Blocked from pursuing the career for which he had trained, Young accepted a job on the Ford assembly line.

Career Highlights

Angry at being passed over for a job for which he was qualified, Young was soon involved in underground union and civil rights activities while working on the Ford assembly line. He was a constant target for racial slurs by white assembly-line workers, harassment that eventually led to Young's dismissal. One day, he was physically attacked by a white worker. In defending himself, Young hit the worker on the head with a steel bar; he was immediately fired ("Coleman A. Young").

Young was fortunate enough to find a job with the U.S. Postal Service in Detroit, but he did not give up his union activities, still championing equal employment opportunities and equal treatment for African Americans. Even in 1942, when he was drafted into the army, Young continued speaking out on these issues.

Young was chosen for training with the Tuskegee Airmen, an elite black unit of the Army Air Corps. During World War II, he flew on missions in Europe as a bombardier-navigator, with the rank of second lieutenant. Toward the end of the war, Young was stationed at Freeman Field, Indiana, and once again began protesting unequal treatment. He organized nearly 100 other black airmen, including his fellow officers **Thurgood Marshall** and Percy Sutton, in a demonstration against the officers' clubs, which excluded blacks. Young and a number of others were arrested and endured three days in jail before being released, but they had triumphed. The publicity generated by the incident forced the army to reconsider its policies and to integrate its officers' clubs.

After his discharge from the Army, Young returned to Detroit, to his job with the postal service, and to his union activities. In 1947, he was named director of organization of the Wayne County AFL-CIO, but he was fired from that position in 1948 when he supported Henry Wallace, the Progressive Party candidate in the race for U.S. president.

Young became manager of a dry-cleaning plant in Detroit after leaving the U.S. Postal Service in 1950. He was devoting more and more of his time to union activities, however, and in 1951 founded and assumed the directorship of the National Negro Labor Council. The Council soon became a vocal advocate for equal employment, persuading Sears, Roebuck and Company and the San Francisco Transit Authority to hire blacks ("Coleman Young"). But the success of the Council brought it to the attention of the House Un-American Activities Committee, headed by Senator Joseph McCarthy, which was engaged in discovering alleged communists in the United States. "Their method was to hold hearings at which defendants were required to produce names of people purportedly associated with the [Communist] Party" ("Coleman Young").

When Coleman Young was called before the committee, he did not flinch, nor did he reveal names. "Called to account by Georgia Congressman John Wood for his connection with 'the National Niggra Labor Council,' Young replied: 'The word is *Negro*'. . ." ("Mayor on the Line"). Young then spoke out against the discrimination against blacks and the past record of lynchings in Georgia, all of which went into the record. While he was lauded as a hero, Young's National Negro Labor Council was placed on the subversive list by the United States attorney general, Herbert Brownell. Rather than reveal its membership list to Brownell, Young dissolved the Council in 1956.

For the next seven years, Young worked as an insurance salesman in Detroit and started involving himself in politics. In 1961, he was elected a delegate to the Michigan Constitution Convention. In 1964, he won a seat in the Michigan State Senate, where he became a vocal supporter of equal rights. As senator, Young spoke up for civil rights, low-income housing, urban reform, and an end to employment discrimination.

In 1973, Young declared his candidacy for mayor of the city of Detroit, a move that was met with great approval by the black population, but with disapprobation by much of Detroit's white citizenry. He was up against John F. Nichols, a white police commissioner, who was running on a "law and order" platform. Young ran on an urban reform platform, and against crime in all segments of society. As he said at a prayer breakfast while campaigning, "I issue a warning now to all dope pushers, to all rip-off artists, to all muggers: It's time to leave Detroit. And I don't give a damn if they are black or white or if they wear Superfly suits or blue uniforms with silver badges. Hit the road!" (Wilkie 1). When the votes were counted, Young had received 92 percent of the black vote, while Nichols had 91 percent of the white vote (LaBlanc 253). Because Detroit had a predominately black population, Young was the winner, becoming one of the first African Americans to be elected mayor of a large American city. He had won the position that he would hold for nearly the rest of his life, and as *Detroit Free Press* columnist Cliff Russell was to remark in 1997, "For 20 years, there was no question as to who was the boss in Detroit" (Russell 1).

Young was described by his admirers as an intellectual, a charmer, a humorist. His critics, however, saw him as crude, as riding rough-shod over Detroit, and disdained the fact that he often resorted to profanity. When he took office in 1974, Detroit was in an economic slump, and was billed as "Murder City" because of its high homicide rate. Young immediately worked to rehabilitate the city: "We are going to turn this city around," he stated in his inaugural address (LaBlanc 253). He set out to attract new business to the city, fought for federal funds, and convinced Henry Ford II to complete the Renaissance Center, a huge hotel-shopping-entertainment complex on the Detroit River. He also reformed Detroit's police department, forcing the hiring of more black officers, and requiring that officers live in the city they patrolled.

Over the next 20 years, however, Young often faced sharp criticism and scandal. He was blamed for the "white flight" from Detroit to the suburbs, attacked when it was discovered that girders used for the tracks of a commuter train had come from South Africa, and taken to task for his personal life and his political liaisons. In 1976, he supported Jimmy Carter, who, after his election to the presidency, offered him a cabinet position. In the 1980s, he vociferously attacked the Reagan and Bush administrations for their cutbacks in federal aid to urban areas. In 1984, Young earned the scorn of many Detroit blacks because of his support of Walter F. Mondale for president against Jesse Jackson, as he did in 1988 with his support of Michael Dukakis. Through it all, Young persisted, driven by a dream of a revitalized Detroit in which equality was the norm, not the exception. In 1993, Young announced that he would step down. He was suffering from chronic emphysema, and he felt the time had come to retire from public office. He said of his tenure as mayor, "I certainly had an interesting time, and I will always look back with a warm feeling to the experience . . . There will be no regrets" (Wilkie 3). After his retirement from office, Young worked with writer Lonnie Wheeler on his autobiography, *Hard Stuff: The Autobiography of Coleman Young*, and assumed a faculty position at Wayne State University in Detroit. On July 24, 1997, Young was hospitalized at Detroit's Sinai Hospital because of his emphysema, and on November 12, he suffered a heart attack that put him into a coma. On November 29, 1997, he died of respiratory failure.

Thousands mourned Young's passing. Congresswoman **Maxine Waters** of California articulated the thoughts of many when she said of Young, "He took over the reins of a city in 1974 that was steeped in racism and discord. During his tenure, he attempted to open up economic opportunities for all people in the city. He provided a special sense of pride and empowerment to Detroit's black community and a special place in all of our hearts."

Sources

"Black Politicians in Michigan." *The Political Graveyard*. <http://www.potifos.com/tpg/ group/black/MI.html>. Accessed: 3/12/98.

"Coleman A. Young." *The African American Almanac*, 7th ed. Detroit, MI: Gale Research, 1997. <http://www.gale.com/gale/bhm/youngcol.html>. Accessed: 3/3/99.

Estleman, Loren. "Mayor on the Line." *Washingtonpost.com*, 13 March 1994. <http://www.washingtonpost.com/wp-srv/digest/daily/nov/30/bio30.htm>. Accessed: 3/4/99.

Heinlein, Gary, and George Weeks. "Breaking Barriers: Ex-Mayor Built for Archer, Others." *The Detroit News*, 1 December 1997. <http://www.detnews.com/1997/ young/971205/12010167.htm>. Accessed: 4/16/98.

LaBlanc, Michael L., ed. *Contemporary Black Biography: Profiles from the International Black Community*, Vol. 1. Detroit, MI: Gale Research, 1992.

Russell, Cliff. "He Was So Many Men—and, Above All, the People's Champion."

Detroit Free Press, 1 December 1997. <http://www.freep.com/voices/columnists/qruss1.htm>. Accessed: 4/16/98.

Waters, Maxine. *Press Release*. 1 December 1997. <http://www.house. gov/waters/12197pr.htm>. Accessed: 3/4/99.

Wilkie, Curtis. "Ex-Detroit Mayor Coleman Young, 79, Dies." *Boston Globe*, 30 November 1997. <http://www.virtuallynw.com/stories/1997/Nov/30/S313001.asp>. Accessed: 4/16/98.

Bibliography

"About Congresswoman Cynthia McKinney." *U.S. House of Representatives*. <http://www.house.gov./mckinney>. Accessed: 3/13/98.

Adams, Russell L. *Great Negroes Past and Present*, 3rd ed. Chicago, IL: Afro-Am Publishing, 1984.

Alvarez, Lizette. "House Member Describes Snub at White House." *The New York Times on the Web*. <http://archives.nytimes.com>. 9 May 1998.

Asante, Molefi K., and Mark T. Mattson, eds. *The Historical and Cultural Atlas of African Americans*. New York: Macmillan, 1991.

"Associate Justice Clarence Thomas." Clarence Thomas Links. 1997. <http://www2.cyber nex.net/~vanalst/clarence.html>. Accessed: 3/18/98.

"Associate Justice Clarence Thomas." *Court TV Online*. 1998. <http://www.courttv.com/library/supreme/justices/thomas.html>. Accessed: 3/18/98.

Ayres, B. Drummond, Jr. "Political Briefing; 3 Rare Battles Loom in the South." *The New York Times on the Web*. <http://archives.nytimes.com>. 17 April 1998.

"Barbara Jordan." Legislative Biographies. <http://www.glue.umd.edu/~cliswp/Politicians/Leg/Bios/legbioj.htm>. Accessed: 2/27/98.

"Barbara-Rose Collins." <http://www.inform.umd.e...se/collins-barbara-rose>. Accessed: 2/26/98.

Benenson, Bob. "Incumbent Tremors in Illinois." *Congressional Quarterly Weekly Report*, 21 March 1992, 739–44.

Berke, Richard L. "Thomas Accuser Tells Hearing of Obscene Talk and Advances: Judge Complains of 'Lynching'." *The New York Times*, 12 October 1991, 1, L9.

Bigelow, Barbara Carlisle, ed. *Contemporary Black Biography: Profiles from the International Black Community*, Vol. 2, 3, 4, 5, 6, 7. Detroit, MI: Gale Research, 1992, 1993, 1994.

"Biographical Data: The Honorable Louis Stokes." *U.S. House of Representatives*. <http://www.house.gov/stokes/ bio.htm>. Accessed: 3/6/98.

"Biographical Sketch of Congressman Alcee L. Hastings." *U.S. House of Representatives*. <http://www.house.gov/alceehastings/bio.htm>. Accessed: 3/6/98.

"Biographical Sketch of Congresswoman Eva M. Clayton." *U.S. House of Representatives*. <http://www.house.gov/clayton/bio.htm>. Accessed: 4/28/98.

"Biography: Honorable William L. Clay." *U.S. House of Representatives*. <http://www.house.gov/clay/bio.htm>. Accessed: 3/6/98.

"Biography of Congressman James E. Clyburn." *U.S. House of Representatives*. <http://www.house.gov/clyburn/bio.html>. Accessed: 3/11/98.

"Biography of Congressman John Conyers, Jr." *U.S. House of Representatives*. 1995. <http://www.house.gov/conyers/bio_john_conyers.html>. Accessed: 3/6/98.

"Biography of Congressman John Lewis." *U.S. House of Representatives*. <http://www.house.gov/johnlewis/bio.html>. Accessed: 3/6/98.

"Biography of Congresswoman Cardiss Collins." <http://www.inform.umd.e...s/House/collins-cardiss> Accessed: 2/27/98.

"Biography of Congresswoman Eddie Bernice Johnson." *U.S. House of Representatives*. <http://www.house.gov/ebjohnson/bio.htm>. Accessed: 3/6/98.

"Biography of Congresswoman Eva Clayton." *U.S. House of Representatives*. <http://www.house.gov/democrats/bio_eva_clayton.html>. Accessed: 4/28/98.

"Biography of Marion Barry, Jr." Mayor's Page. <http://www.ci.washington.dc.us/MAYOR/mayorbio.htm> Accessed: 3/13/98.

"A Biography." *U.S. House of Representatives*. <http://www.house.gov/dellums/dellums_bio.html>. Accessed: 3/6/98.

"Biography: Willie L. Brown, Jr." Mayoral Candidates. <http://sf95.election.digital.com/ CVF2/BROWN/bio.html>. Accessed: 3/12/98.

"Black Game." *Time Magazine*, 17 August 1936. *Time Almanac*, Reference Edition. Fort Lauderdale, FL: Compact Publishing, 1994.

"Black Involvement in Politics: Grace Towns Hamilton." <http://www.lib.gsu.edu/spcoll/ggdp/hamilton.htm>. Accessed: 3/11/98.

"Blanche Kelso Bruce." *Notable Kansans of African Descent*. Kansas State Historical Society. <http://www.ukans.edu/heritage/kshs/people/afampeop.htm>. Accessed: 3/18/98.

Bond, Julian. "Remembering Another Atlanta: Gate City." Southern Changes. *Southern Regional Council*. <http://www.src.w1.com/bond182nf.htm#Bond>. Accessed: 3/11/98.

"Bradley, Thomas." *Encyclopedia.com*. Electric Library. <http://www.eneyclopedia.com/printable/01782-a.html>. Accessed: 2/20/98.

"Breakthrough in Virginia." *Time Almanac*, Reference Edition. Fort Lauderdale, FL: Compact Publishing, 1994.

"Brown, Ron." *Biography Online Database*. <http://www.biography.com/find/bioengine.cgi?cmd=1&rec=15916>. Accessed: 4/11/98.

"Campaign Notes: Marion Barry Wins D.C. Nomination." *Congressional Quarterly Report*, 17 September 1994, 2603.

"Cardiss Collins." Legislative Biographies. <http://www.glue.umd.edu/~cliswp/Politicians/Leg/Bios/legbioc.htm> Accessed: 2/27/98.

"Carl B. Stokes, 68, First Black Elected Mayor of a Major American City." *The Detroit News*. 4 April 1996. <http://detnews.com/menu/stories/42613.htm>. Accessed: 3/12/98.

"Carl Rowan Wins NAACP Medal." *NAACP Online*. 9 July 1997. <http://www.naacp. org/president/releases/rowan.htm>. Accessed: 4/24/98.

Carlson, Margaret, Ann Blackman, and Richard Woodbury. "Prognosis: Controversy." *Time Magazine*, 19 July 1993. *Time Almanac*, Reference Edition. Fort Lauderdale, FL: Compact Publishing, 1994.

Carman, Harry J., Harold C. Syrett, and Bernard W. Wishy. *A History of the American People, Volume II—Since 1865*, 3rd ed. New York: Alfred A. Knopf, 1952.

Chapelle, Tony. "Adam Clayton Powell, Jr.: Black Power between Heaven and Hell." *The Black Collegian Online*. The Black Collegian Services, Inc., 1997. <http://www.black-collegian.com/adam.html>. Accessed: 3/31/98.

Chisholm, Shirley. *Unbought and Unbossed*. New York: Avon, 1970.

Christopher, Maurine. *America's Black Congressmen*. New York: Thomas Y. Crowell, 1971.

"Civil Rights Activist Julian Bond to Deliver Keynote Address during Emory's Martin Luther King Jr. Week." News and Information. *Emory University*. 23 December 1997. <http://www.emory.edu/WELCOME/journcontents/releases/mklweek.html>. Accessed: 4/20/98.

"Civil Rights March in Frankfort, 1964." Kentucky Department of Public Information Collection, rev. 2/17/98. <http://www.kdla.state.ky.us/arch/king.htm>. Accessed: 4/14/98.

"Clarence Thomas." *Cornell University*. <http://supct.law.cornell.edu/supct/justices /thomas.bio.html>. Accessed: 3/18/98.

Clay, William L. *Just Permanent Interests: Black Americans in Congress, 1870–1991*. New York: Amistad Press, 1992.

"Collins' Backers Stay Loyal Despite Allegations." *The Detroit News*, 3 April 1996. <http://www.detnews.com/menu/stories/42365.htm>. Accessed: 5/12/98.

Commager, Henry Steele, ed. *Documents of American History, Volume II: Since 1898*. New York: Appleton-Century-Crofts, 1963.

"Conference of Black Mayors Honors Negro Fund President." *Amsterdam News*, 17 May 1997, 8.

Congressional Black Caucus '93–'94 Guide. <http://www.sas.upenn.edu/African_Studies/Govern_Political/CBC_Guide.html>.

"Congressional Elections: Incumbent Tremors in Illinois." *Congressional Quarterly Weekly Report*, 21 March 1992, 739–44.

"Congressman Charles B. Rangel." *New York State Democratic Committee Home Page*. <http://www.nydems.org/elected/rangel. html>. Accessed: 4/9/98.

"Congressman Dellums' Biography." *U.S. House of Representatives*. <http://www.house.gov/dellums/dellums_bio.html>. Accessed: 3/6/98.

"Congressman Edolphus Towns." *U.S. House of Representatives*. <http://www.house.gov./towns/welcome.htm>. Accessed: 3/6/98.

"Congressman Edolphus Towns, 10th Congressional District." *New York State Democratic Committee Home Page*. <http://www.nydems.org/elected/towns. html>. Accessed: 4/9/98.

"Congressman Stokes' Newsletter." *Cleveland State University*. <http://www.csuohio.edu/cmha/stokesnl.html>. Accessed: 4/9/98.

"Congresswoman Eleanor Holmes Norton." *U.S. House of Representatives*. <http://www.house.gov/norton/bio.htm>. Accessed: 3/11/98.

"Congresswoman Maxine Waters." *U.S. House of Representatives*. <http://www.house.gov/waters/bio.htm>. Accessed: 3/13/98.

Cromwell, John W. *The Negro in American History*. Washington, DC: American Negro Academy, 1914.

"David Dinkins Returns to the Classroom." *Columbia University Record*, 29 September 1995. <http://www.columbia. edu/cu/record21/record2104.32.html>. Accessed: 5/5/98.

"David Norman Dinkins." SIPA Faculty Bio. *Columbia University*. <http:// www.columbia.edu/cu/sipa/RESEARCH/DDinkins.html>. Accessed: 3/11/98.

Dobnik, Verena. "Bond Elected Chairman of NAACP." *The Hartford Courant*, 22 February 1998, A18.

"Donald McHenry." Background Information. *Columbia University*. <http://www.cc.columbia.edu/cu/secretary /trustees/bios/McHenry.html>. Accessed: 5/4/98.

"Donald F. McHenry." *United Nations Association of the United States of America*. 1997. <http://www.unausa.org/about_UNAUSA/mchenry.htm>. Accessed: 3/18/98.

"Douglas Wilder to Speak on Campus." Rev. 23 December 1996. *Furman University*. <http://www.furman.edu/admin/univrel/press/PR1996/p96_142.html>. Accessed: 3/10/98.

"'An Easy Burden' by Andrew Young." Voice of America. 24 February 1997. <http:// www.kaiwan.com/~mcivr/andyoung.html>. Accessed: 4/23/98.

"Elders, M. (Minnie) Joycelyn." *Biography Online Database*. 1995. <http://www.biography.com/find/bioengine.cgi?cmd=1&rec=17292>. Accessed: 4/11/98.

"Eleanor Holmes Norton." *Georgetown Law School*. 1997. <http://www.law.georgetown.edu/faculty/vitas/norton.html>. Accessed: 5/7/98.

Esparza, Santiago. "Collins' Backers Stay Loyal Despite Allegations." *The Detroit News*. 3 April 1996. <http://www.detnews.com/menu/stories/42365.htm>. Accessed: 5/12/98.

"Espy Acquitted in Gifts Case." *The Washington Post*, 3 December 1998, A01. <http://www.washingtonpost.com/wp-srv/politics/special/counsels/stories/espy120398.htm>. Accessed: 12/3/98.

Estell, Kenneth. *African America: Celebrating 400 Years of Achievement*. Detroit, MI: Visible Ink Press, 1994.

Evers, Charles, and Andrew Szanton. *Have No Fear: The Charles Evers Story*. New York: John Wiley and Sons, 1997.

Family Encyclopedia of American History. Pleasantville, NY: The Reader's Digest Assoc., Inc., 1975.

"Former Black Members of Congress." *Congressional Times Journal*. <http://www. usbol.com/ctjournal/FrBlkCongMemList.html>.

"Former Representative Running for Senate." *Nando.net/Associated Press*. 1998. 20 January 1998. <http://www.nando.net/newsroom/ntn/politics/012098/politics2 _29787_noframes.html>. Accessed: 4/9/98.

"Former Sen. Carol Moseley-Braun to Become Education Advisor." *AP News Service*, 1999. <http://abcnews.go.com/wire/US/AP19990106_174.html>. Accessed: 1/8/99.

Foxworth, Sharon W. "Mary McLeod Bethune." *Black History Is No Mystery*. 1996. <http://www.bkh.com/bkhallhtmlfolder/bethune.html>. Accessed: 3/10/98.

"Franks Formally Runs for Dodd's Senate Seat." Channel 8 News Online. *WTNH-TV News*. 1998. <http://www.wtnh.com/news/012098b.html>. Accessed: 3/3/98.

"George Thomas (Mickey) Leland." *U.S. House of Representatives*. <http://www.house.gov/leland.htm> Accessed: 5/21/98.

"Goode Named Deputy Assistant Secretary at Ed." *U.S. Department of Education*. 1997. <http://www.ed.gov/PressReleases/04-1997/goode.html>. Accessed: 3/13/98.

"Grace Towns Hamilton." Black Involvement in Politics. 1997. <http://www.lib.gsu. edu/spcoll/ggdp/hamilton.htm>. Accessed: 3/11/98.

Gunzburger, Ron. "Politics 1: The Last Hurrah (Deaths, Scandals and Other Milestones." *Politics 1*. <http://www.politics1.com/hurrah.htm>. Accessed: 1/7/99.

Haskins, James. *A Piece of the Power: Four Black Mayors*. New York: Dial, 1972.

———. *Adam Clayton Powell, Jr.: A Portrait of a Marching Black*. Trenton, NJ: African World Press, 1993.

———. *African American Entrepreneurs*. New York: John Wiley and Sons, 1998.

———. *Andrew Young: Man with a Mission*. New York: Lothrop, Lee and Shepard Co., 1979.

———. *The First Black Governor: Pinckney Benton Stewart Pinchback*. Trenton, NJ: African World Press, 1973.

———. *Thurgood Marshall: A Life for Justice*. New York: Henry Holt and Co., 1992.

Hine, Darlene Clark, ed. *Black Women in America: An Historical Encyclopedia*, Vol. I,II. Brooklyn, NY: Carlson Publishing Co., 1993.

"Hiram Rhoades Revels." <http://www.ils.unc.edu/nc/HiramRevels.html>. Accessed: 1/21/98.

"Hiram Rhodes Revels." *North Carolina Encyclopedia*. State Library of North Carolina. <http://www.cler.state.nc.us/nc/bio/afro/revels.html>. Accessed: 1/21/98.

"Honorary Degree Recipients: Unita Z. Blackwell, '83G." *University of Massachusetts*.1995. <http://www.umass.edu/pubaffs/commencement/95/honord.html>. Accessed: 4/21/98.

"The House: A Bigot Gets the Boot." *Time Magazine*, 30 March 1992, 33.

"Incumbent Tremors in Illinois." *Congressional Quarterly Weekly Report*, 21 March 1992, 739–44.

"Jefferson, William J." *Encarta Online*. Microsoft Corp. 1998. <http://encarta.msn.com/ index/concise/0vol49/oB0B7000.asp>. Accessed: 4/21/98.

"John Conyers, Jr." Michigan Democratic Party. <http://www.hven.org/info/mdp/Congress/Conyers.htm>. Accessed: 2/26/98.

"John Mercer Langston (1829–1897)." *Oberlin College Archives*. <http://www.oberlin.edu/~EOG/OYTT-images/JMLangston.html>. Accessed: 1/21/98.

Joint Center for Political Studies. *Profiles of Black Mayors in America*. Washington, DC/Chicago, IL: The Joint Center for Political Studies/Johnson Publishing, 1977.

Jordan, Barbara, and Shelby Hearon. *Barbara Jordan: A Self-Portrait*. Garden City, NY: Doubleday and Co., 1979.

Kane, Joseph J., and Staci D. Kramer. "Marching to a Different Drummer." *Time Magazine*, 15 July 1991, 18–22.

Kaplan, David A., Bob Cohn, Vern E. Smith, Howard Manly, Carolyn Friday, Karen Springen, Todd Barrett, Lydia Denworth, Elizabeth Ann Leonard and Alden Cohen. "Supreme Mystery." *Newsweek*, 16 September 1991, 18–31.

Kestenbaum, Lawrence. *Political Graveyard: A Database of Historical Cemeteries*, rev. 1/13/98. <http://www.potifos.com/tpg.html>. Accessed: 1/17/98.

"Kweisi Mfume, President and CEO of the NAACP." *NAACP Online*. <http://www.naacp.org/president/kbio.html>. Accessed: 5/12/98.

LaBlanc, Michael L., ed. *Contemporary Black Biography: Profiles from the International Black Community*, Vol. 1. Detroit, MI: Gale Research, 1992.

Lamson, Peggy. *The Glorious Failure: Black Congressman Robert Brown Elliott and the Reconstruction of South Carolina*. New York: W.W. Norton and Co., 1973.

"Law Alumna Motley Given Allen Award." *Columbia University Record*, 9 June 1995. <http://www.columbia.edu/cu/rcord/record2031.22html>. Accessed: 3/11/98.

Logan, Rayford W., and Michael R. Winston, eds. *Dictionary of American Negro Biography*. New York: W.W. Norton, and Co., 1982.

"Louis W. Sullivan." <http://www.ssa.gov/history/sullivan.html>. Accessed: 3/18/98.

"Louis W. Sullivan, M.D. *The Black Health Net*. 1998. <http://www.blackhealthnet. com/doctors/cv/lsullivan.asp>. Accessed: 4/23/98.

Mabunda, L. Mpho, ed. *Contemporary Black Biography: Profiles from the International Black Community*, Vol. 8, 10. Detroit, MI: Gale Research, 1995, 1996.

Mabunda, L. Mpho, and Shirelle Phelps, eds. *Contemporary Black Biography: Profiles from the International Black Community*, Vol. 11, 14. Detroit, MI: Gale Research, 1996.

"Marion Barry Wins D.C. Nomination." *Congressional Quarterly Weekly Report*, 17 September 1994, 2603.

"Marshall, Thurgood." *Encyclopedia Britannica*. <http:/ /blackhistory.eb.com/micro/378/26.html>. Accessed: 3/18/98.

"Marshall, Thurgood." *Biography Online Database*. <http://www.biography.com/find /bioengine.cgi/cmd=1&rec=7132. Accessed: 4/11/98.

"Mary McLeod Bethune." *Mary McLeod Bethune Papers: The Bethune Foundation Collection. University Publications of America. <http://www.upapubs.com/newtitle/bethune.htm#bethune>. Accessed: 2/18/98.*

"Mary McLeod Bethune." *The African American Almanac*, 7th ed. Detroit, MI: Gale Research, 1997. <http://www.gale.com/gale/bhm/bethune.html>. Accessed: 2/17/98.

"Mary McLeod Bethune." *Women in History*. <http://www.lkwdpl.org/wihohio/beth-mar htm>. Accessed: 2/18/98.

"Mary McLeod Bethune, Political Leader, Educator, Organizer." *Mary McLeod Bethune Home Page*. <http://www.fas.harvard.edu/-felder/bethune.html>. Accessed: 2/18/98.

"Maxine Waters." *Congressional Times Journal*. <http://www.usbol.com/ctjournal/Bios/mwaters.html>. Accessed: 2/26/98.

"Mayor Marion S. Barry, Jr." *Congressional Times Journal*. <http://www.usbol.com/ctjournal/>. Accessed: 3/10/98.

"Mayor Who Shaped L. A. Dies." *Los Angeles Times*, 30 September 1998, obituary. <http://www.latimes.com>. Access: 9/30/98.

McCoy, Frank. "Freshman on the Hill." *Black Enterprise*, April 1991, 25.

"Meet Mrs. Bethune." *National Park Service*. <http://www. nps.gov/mamc/bethune/meet/main.htm>. Accessed: 2/18/98.

Meltzer, Milton. *The Black Americans: A History in Their Own Words 1619–1987*. New York: Thomas Y. Crowell, 1984.

"Melvin Watt." *Congressional Quarterly Weekly Report*, 16 January 1993, 119.

"Melvin Watt Biography." *U.S. House of Representatives*. <http://www.house.gov/watt/bio_mel.htm>. Accessed: 3/6/98.

Mfume, Kweisi, and Ron Stodgill II. *No Free Ride: From the Mean Streets to the Mainstream*. New York: Ballantine, 1996.

"Mike Espy." *Congressional Times Journal*. <http://www.usbol.com/ctjournal/MEspybio.html>. Accessed: 2/26/98.

"Mike Espy Joins Mississippi Law Firm." *Jet*, 29 January 1996, 40.

"Mike Espy Trial Is Postponed." *Nation's Restaurant News*, 30 March 1998, 68.

"Milestones: Indicted. Marion S. Barry . . ." *Time Magazine*, 21 May 1990. *Time Almanac*, Reference Edition. Fort Lauderdale, FL: Compact Publishing, 1994.

"Milestones: Sentenced. Marion Barry . . ." *Time Magazine*, 5 November 1990. *Time Almanac*, Reference Edition. Fort Lauderdale, FL: Compact Publishing, 1994.

"Mitchell Suffers Stroke." *Congressional Times Journal*, 8 March 1996. <http://www. usbol.com/ctjournal/ctj2.html>. Accessed: 4/14/98.

Myers, Walter Dean. *Now Is Your Time! The African-American Struggle for Freedom*. New York: HarpersCollins, 1991.

"National Elections '98." *The Washington Post*, 4 November 1998. <http://elections98.washingtonpost.com/wp-sev/results98/national/>. Accessed: 11/19/98.

"The Negro Vote." *Time Magazine*, 22 October 1956. *Time Almanac*, Reference Edition. Fort Lauderdale, FL: Compact Publishing, 1994.

New Grolier Multimedia Encyclopedia. Novato, CA: The Software Toolworks, Inc./Grolier, Inc., 1993.

Neyer, Constance. "Black Governors Buried in History." *Hartford Courant*, 1 February 1998, A1, A12.

Novak, Viveca. "Chasing Good-Time Charlie." *Time Magazine*, 8 September 1997. <http:www.pathfinder.com/time/magazine/1997/dom/970908/nation.chasing_god tim.html>. Accessed: 3/10/98.

"Obituary: Carl B. Stokes, 68, First Black Elected Mayor of a Major American City." *The Detroit News*, 1996. <http://www.detnews.com/menu/stories/42613.htm>. Accessed: 3/12/98.

O'Brien, Catherine. "Millions Await Conyers, Other Long-Serving Pols in Retirement." *The Detroit News*, 12 May 1996. <http://www.detnews.com/menu/stories, 47505.htm>. Accessed: 5/7/98.

"Ohio's Stokes to End 30 Years in D.C." *Hartford Courant*, 3 March 1998, A18.

"The Old Magic." *Time Magazine*, 2 October 1944. *Time Almanac*, Reference Edition. Fort Lauderdale, FL: Compact Publishing, 1994.

Phelps, Shirelle, ed. *Contemporary Black Biography: Profiles from the International Black Community*, Vol. 16, 17. Detroit, MI: Gale Research, 1998.

Phillips, Andrew. "A Blight at the Centre of Power." *Maclean's*, 13 October 1997, 32–33.

Ploski, Harry A., and James Williams, eds. *The Negro Almanac: A Reference Work on the African American*. Detroit, MI: Gale Research, 1989.

Powers, Georgia Davis. *I Shared the Dream: The Pride, Passion and Politics of the First Black Woman Senator from Kentucky*. Far Hill, NJ: New Horizona Press,1995.

"Quantrill, William C." *New Grolier Multimedia Encyclopedia*. Novato, CA: The Software Toolworks, Inc./Grolier, Inc., 1993.

"Rangel Is Longtime Advocate of U.S.-Africa Trade." *Africa News Online*. 2 December 1997. <http://www.africanews.org/usaf/stories/19971202_feat4.html>. Accessed: 4/2/98.

"Rep. Clyburn of S. Carolina Will Chair Black Caucus." *The Washington Post*, 18 November 1998, A04. <http://search.washingtonpost.com/wp-srv/Wplate/1998-11/18/0471-111898-idx.html>. Accessed: 11/19/98.

"Representative Barbara-Rose Collins." *Project Vote Smart*. <http://www.vote-smart .org/congress/104/mi/mi-15-a/mi-15-ab.html>. Accessed: 2/26/98.

"Representative Carrie Meek: Biography." *U.S. House of Representatives*. <http://www.house.gov/meek/bio.html>. Accessed: 3/6/98.

"Representative Kweisi Mfume." *Project Vote Smart*. <http://www.vote-smart.org/congress/104/md/md-rs-a/md-07-ab.html>. Accessed: 5/21/98.

"Representative Louis Stokes." Member Profile. <http://www.hrcusa.org/actncntr/profiles/OH11.html>. Accessed: 4/28/98.

Review of *The New Deal's Black Congressman: A Life of Arthur Wergs Mitchell*, by Dennis S. Nordin. <http://www.system.missouri.edu/upress/spring 1997/nordin.htm>. Accessed: 2/13/98.

Riley, Michael. "A Bright, Broken Promise." *Time Magazine*, 26 June 1990. *Time Almanac*, Reference Edition. Fort Lauderdale, FL: Compact Publishing, 1994.

———. "'You Set Me Up!'" *Time Magazine*, 29 January 1990. *Time Almanac*, Reference Edition. Fort Lauderdale, FL: Compact Publishing, 1994.

Robinson, Melissa B. "Former Representative Running for Senate." *Nando.net/Associated Press*, 1998. <http://www.nando.net/newsroom/ntn/politics/012098/politics2_29787_noframes.html>. Accessed: 4/9/98.

"Ronald H. Brown, 30th U.S. Secretary of Commerce." <http://www.tnp.com/brown/BrownBio.html>. Accessed: 3/18/98.

Rowan, Carl Thomas. *Breaking Barriers*. New York: Little, Brown and Co., 1991.

Shapiro, Walter. "Breakthrough in Virginia." *Time Magazine*, 20 November 1989. *Time Almanac*, Reference Edition. Fort Lauderdale, FL: Compact Publishing, 1994.

"Sharon Pratt Kelly." *Washington City Paper*. Washington Free Weekly, Inc. 1996. <http://www.washingtoncitynewspaper.com/lips/bios/kellybio.html.>. Accessed: 3/13/98.

Shepard, Paul. "NAACP Leader's Decisions Stir Up Controversy." *Willimantic Chronicle*, 3 April 1998, 7.

"Shirley Anita Chisholm." Legislative Biographies. <http://www.glue.umed.edu/ ~cliswp/Politicians/Leg/Bios/legbioc.htm>. Accessed: 2/27/98.

"Shirley Chisholm." *African-American Pioneers*. <http://www.kaiwan.com/~mcivr/chis holm.html>. Accessed: 2/20/98.

"A Short Biography: From the Good Hope Memorial Service." *Armadillo*, 22 January 1996. <http://www.rice.edu/armadillo/Texas/Jordan/goodhopebio.html>. Accessed: 3/31/98.

Smith, Jessie Carney, ed. *Black Firsts: 2,000 Years of Extraordinary Achievement*. Detroit, MI: Visible Ink Press, 1994.

———, ed. *Black Heroes of the 20th Century*. Detroit, MI: Visible Ink Press, 1998.

———, ed. *Notable Black American Women*, Vol. I, II. Detroit, MI: Gale Research, 1992.

Smythe, Mabel M., ed. *The Black American Reference Book*. Englewood Cliffs, NJ: Prentice-Hall, Inc., 1976.

Sonyakay, Arati. "Giving 'Em Mel." *Business Journal of Charlotte*, 11 September 1995, 3–5.

"Special Envoy Jesse Jackson Travels Again to Africa." *Africa News Online*. Washington, DC: U.S. Department of State. 1998. <http://www.africanews.org/usafri ca/stories/19980206_feat3.html>. Accessed: 5/4/98.

Stewart, Jeffrey C. *1001 Things Everyone Should Know about African American History*. New York: Doubleday and Co., 1996.

Telephone interview with staff at Congressman Dixon's Washington, D.C., office, 26 May 1998.

Telephone interview with staff at Mount Holyoke College, Department of Sociology, 4 January 1999.

Telephone interview with staff at U.S. Embassy of Jamaica, 4 January 1999.

"Thomas, Clarence." *Biography Online Database*. <http://www.biography.com/find/bioengine.cgi?cmd=1&rec=13876>. Accessed: 4/11/98.

Thomas, Evan, Howard Fineman, Ann McDaniel, and Eleanor Clift. "Where Does He Stand?" *Newsweek*, 15 July 1991, 16–17.

"Thurgood Marshall." <http://tqd.advanced.org/337/tmarsh.html>. Accessed: 4/23/98.

"Thurgood Marshall, Supreme Court Justice." <http://provost.ucsd.edu/marshall/ advising/acad4.htm>. Accessed: 3/18/98.

"Thurgood Marshall." This Person in Black History. <http://www.ai.mit.edu/~isbell/HFh /black/e...nd_people/html/001.thurgood_marshall.html>. Accessed: 4/23/98.

"Thurgood Marshall." Voice of America. <http://www.kaiwan.com/~mcivr/thurgood.html>. Accessed: 4/23/98.

Townsel, Lisa Jones, Kevin Chappel, and Muriel L. Whetstone. "Sharon Pratt Kelly: Teaching and Writing a Book." *Ebony*, May 1996, 92.

Travano, Noel. "Jocelyn Elders." *University of Maryland*. <http://www.glue.umd.edu/~cliswp/Bios/jebio.html>. Accessed: 2/26/98.

"United Negro College Fund President to Speak at WSU." *Washington State University*. 11 September 1997. <http://www.wsu.edu/NIS/releases/mg111.htm>. Accessed: 3/12/98.

"US Representative James Clyburn." South Carolina Politics. 1997. <http://www.ricommunit y.com/scenic/politics/clyburn.htm>. Accessed: 2/26/98.

"Weaver, Robert C(lifton)." *Encyclopedia Britannica*. 1996. <http://www.eb.com/cgi-bin/g?keywords=Robert+Weaver>. Accessed: 4/11/98.

Weinberg, Kenneth. *Black Victory: Carl Stokes and the Winning of Cleveland*. Chicago, IL: Quadrangle Books, 1968.

"Will Women Vote for Women?" <http://www.glue.umed.edu/~cliswp/Politicians/Issue s/womvote.html>. Accessed: 2/27/98.

Young, Andrew. "An Easy Burden." *African-American Pioneers*. <http://www.kaiwan.com/~mcivr/andyoung.html>. Accessed: 4/23/98.

"Yvonne Braithwaite Burke." Legislative Biographies. <http://www.glue.umd.edu/~cliswp/Politicians/Leg/Bios/legbiob.htm#burke>. Accessed: 2/27/98.

Appendix 1

African American Political and Governmental Leaders by Birth Date

1810–1848 William Alexander Leidesdorff
1822 or 1827–1901 Hiram Rhodes Revels
1825–1887 Richard Harvey Cain
1825–1894 Benjamin Sterling Turner
1829–1897 John Mercer Langston
1829–1912 Charles Lewis Mitchell
1832–1887 Joseph Hayne Rainey
1836–1901 Jefferson Franklin Long
1837–1883 James Thomas Rapier
1837–1921 Pinckney Benton Stewart Pinchback
1838–1906 Benjamin William Arnett
1839–1915 Robert Smalls
1841–1898 Blanche Kelso Bruce
1842–1874 Robert Carlos DeLarge
1842–1884 Robert Brown Elliott
1842–1905 Josiah Thomas Walls
1844–1905 James Edward O'Hara
1846–c. 1916 Jeremiah Haralson
1847–1939 John Roy Lynch
1857–1935 Henry Plummer Cheatham
1871–1951 Oscar Stanton De Priest
1875–1955 Mary McLeod Bethune
1883–1968 Arthur Wergs Mitchell
1886–1971 William Levi Dawson
1893–1965 Crystal Dreda Bird Fauset
1905–1987 Robert Nelson Cornelius Nix, Sr.
1907–1990 Verda Freeman Welcome
1907–1992 Grace Towns Hamilton
1907–1997 Robert Clifton Weaver
1907– Augustus Freeman Hawkins
1908–1972 Adam Clayton Powell, Jr.
1908–1993 Thurgood Marshall
1910–1978 Ralph Harold Metcalfe
1915– Walter Edward Washington
1917–1984 Melvin Herbert Evans
1917–1998 Thomas Bradley
1918–1997 Charles Arthur Hayes
1919– Edward William Brooke III
1921– Constance Baker Motley
1922–1987 Harold Washington
1922– James Charles Evers
1922–1998 Charles Coles Diggs, Jr.
1922– Parren James Mitchell
1923– Hannah Diggs Atkins
1923– Georgia Montgomery Davis Powers
1924– Shirley Anita St. Hill Chisholm
1924–1985 Patricia Roberts Harris
1925–1972 George Washington Collins
1925– Gustavus "Gus" Savage
1925– Carl Thomas Rowan
1925– Louis Stokes
1926– Mervyn Malcolm Dymally
1926– Carrie Pittman Meek
1927–1996 Carl Burton Stokes
1927– David Norman Dinkins
1929– John Conyers, Jr.
1930– Charles Bernard Rangel

1931–	Lucien E. Blackwell
1931–	William Lacy Clay, Sr.
1931–	Cardiss Robertson Collins
1931–	Carrie Saxon Perry
1931–	Lawrence Douglas Wilder
1932–	Yvonne Braithwaite Burke
1932–	Kenneth Allen Gibson
1932–	Andrew Jackson Young, Jr.
1933–	Unita Z. Blackwell
1933–	Joycelyn Elders
1933–	Walter Edward Fauntroy
1933–	Richard Gordon Hatcher
1933–	Louis Wade Sullivan
1934–	Willie L. Brown, Jr.
1934–	Eva M. Clayton
1934–	Julian Carey Dixon
1934–	Edolphus Towns
1935–	Ronald Vernie Dellums
1935–	Eddie Bernice Johnson
1936–1996	Barbara Charline Jordan
1936–	Marion S. Barry, Jr.
1936–	Alcee Lamar Hastings
1936–	Donald F. McHenry
1936–	Major Robert Odell Owens
1937–	Eleanor Holmes Norton
1938–	Maynard Holbrook Jackson, Jr.
1938–	Woodrow Wilson Goode
1938–	Maxine Waters
1939–	Barbara-Rose Collins
1940–	Julian Bond
1940–	James Enos Clyburn
1940–	John Lewis
1941–1996	Ronald Harmon Brown
1941–	William Herbert Gray III
1941–	Jesse Louis Jackson
1944–1989	George Thomas "Mickey" Leland
1944–	Sharon Pratt Dixon Kelly
1945–	Floyd H. Flake
1945–	Melvin L. Watt
1947–	Carol Moseley-Braun
1947–	William Jennings Jefferson
1948–	Kweisi Mfume
1948–	Clarence Thomas
1953–	A. Michael "Mike" Espy
1953–	Gary A. Franks
1955–	Cynthia Ann McKinney

Appendix 2
African American Political and Governmental Leaders by Position

City Government Officials

Marion S. Barry, Washington, D.C.
Lucien E. Blackwell, Philadelphia, Pa.
Thomas Bradley, Los Angeles, Calif.
William Lacy Clay, Sr., St. Louis, Mo.
Barbara-Rose Collins, Detroit, Mich.
Cardiss Robertson Collins, Chicago, Ill.
George Washington Collins, Chicago, Ill.
William Levi Dawson, Chicago, Ill.
Robert Carlos DeLarge, Charleston, S.C.
Ronald Vernie Dellums, Berkeley, Calif.
David Norman Dinkins, New York, N.Y.
Walter Edward Fauntroy, Washington, D.C.
Gary A. Franks, Waterbury, Conn.
Richard Gordon Hatcher, Gary, Ind.
Maynard Holbrook Jackson, Jr., Atlanta, Ga.
William Alexander Leidesdorff, San Francisco, Calif.
John Lewis, Atlanta, Ga.
Ralph Harold Metcalfe, Chicago, Ill.
Kweisi Mfume, Baltimore, Md.
Carol Moseley-Braun, Chicago, Ill.
Constance Baker Motley, New York, N.Y.
Robert Nelson Cornelius Nix, Sr., Philadelphia, Pa.
Major Robert Odell Owens, New York, N.Y.
Adam Clayton Powell, Jr., New York, N.Y.
Benjamin Sterling Turner, Selma, Ala.
Walter Edward Washington, New York, N.Y.
Robert Clifton Weaver, New York, N.Y., and Chicago, Ill.
Andrew Jackson Young, Jr., Atlanta, Ga.

County Government Officials

Blanche Kelso Bruce, Bolivar Co., Miss.
Yvonne Braithwaite Burke, Los Angeles Co., Calif.
Henry Plummer Cheatham, Vance Co., N.C.
Eva M. Clayton, Warren Co., N.C.
George Washington Collins, Cook Co., Ill.
Oscar Stanton De Priest, Cook Co., Ill.
Georgia Montgomery Davis Powers, Jefferson Co., Ky.
Benjamin Sterling Turner, Dallas Co., Ala.

Governors

Melvin Herbert Evans, Virgin Islands
Pinckney Benton Stewart Pinchback, Louisiana
Lawrence Douglas Wilder, Virginia

Justices

Alcee Lamar Hastings
Thurgood Marshall
Constance Baker Motley
Carl Burton Stokes
Clarence Thomas

Lieutenant Governors

Mervyn Malcolm Dymally, California
Pinckney Benton Stewart Pinchback, Louisiana
Lawrence Douglas Wilder, Virginia

Mayors

Marion S. Barry, Jr., Washington, D.C.
Unita Z. Blackwell, Mayersville, Miss.
Thomas Bradley, Los Angeles, Calif.
Willie L. Brown, Jr., San Francisco, Calif.
David Norman Dinkins, New York, N.Y.
James Charles Evers, Fayette, Miss.
Kenneth Allen Gibson, Newark, N.J.
Woodrow Wilson Goode, Philadelphia, Pa.
Richard Gordon Hatcher, Gary, Ind.
Maynard Holbrook Jackson, Jr., Atlanta, Ga.
Sharon Pratt Dixon Kelly, Washington, D.C.
Carrie Saxon Perry, Hartford, Conn.
Carl Burton Stokes, Cleveland, Ohio
Harold Washington, Chicago, Ill.
Walter Edward Washington, Washington, D.C.
Andrew Jackson Young, Jr., Atlanta, Ga.

National Government Officials

Hannah Diggs Atkins
Mary McLeod Bethune
Lucien E. Blackwell
Unita Z. Blackwell
Edward William Brooke III
Ronald Harmon Brown
Blanche Kelso Bruce
Yvonne Braithwaite Burke
Richard Harvey Cain
Henry Plummer Cheatham
Shirley Anita St. Hill Chisholm
William Lacy Clay, Sr.
Eva M. Clayton
James Enos Clyburn
Barbara-Rose Collins
Cardiss Robertson Collins
George Washington Collins
John Conyers, Jr.
William Levi Dawson
Robert Carlos DeLarge
Ronald Vernie Dellums
Oscar Stanton De Priest
Charles Coles Diggs, Jr.
Julian Carey Dixon
Mervyn Malcolm Dymally
Joycelyn Elders
Robert Brown Elliott
A. Michael "Mike" Espy
Melvin Herbert Evans
Walter Edward Fauntroy
Crystal Dreda Bird Fauset
Floyd H. Flake
Gary A. Franks
Woodrow Wilson Goode
William Herbert Gray III
Jeremiah Haralson
Patricia Roberts Harris
Alcee Lamar Hastings
Augustus Freeman Hawkins
Charles Arthur Hayes
Jesse Louis Jackson
Maynard Holbrook Jackson, Jr.
William Jennings Jefferson
Eddie Bernice Johnson
Barbara Charline Jordan
John Mercer Langston
William Alexander Leidesdorff
George Thomas "Mickey" Leland
John Lewis
Jefferson Franklin Long
John Roy Lynch
Thurgood Marshall
Donald F. McHenry
Cynthia Ann McKinney
Carrie Pittman Meek
Ralph Harold Metcalfe
Kweisi Mfume
Arthur Wergs Mitchell
Charles Lewis Mitchell
Parren James Mitchell
Carol Moseley-Braun
Constance Baker Motley
Robert Nelson Cornelius Nix, Sr.
Eleanor Holmes Norton
James Edward O'Hara
Major Robert Odell Owens
Pinckney Benton Steward Pinchback
Adam Clayton Powell, Jr.
Joseph Hayne Rainey
Charles Bernard Rangel
James Thomas Rapier

Hiram Rhodes Revels
Carl Thomas Rowan
Gustavus "Gus" Savage
Robert Smalls
Carl Burton Stokes
Louis Stokes
Louis Wade Sullivan
Clarence Thomas
Edolphus Towns
Benjamin Sterling Turner
Josiah Thomas Walls
Harold Washington
Maxine Waters
Melvin L. Watt
Robert Clifton Weaver
Andrew Jackson Young, Jr.

State Government Officials (including the District of Columbia)

Benjamin William Arnett, Ohio
Hannah Diggs Atkins, Oklahoma
Lucien E. Blackwell, Pennsylvania
Julian Bond, Georgia
Edward William Brooke III, Massachusetts
Willie L. Brown, Jr., California
Blanche Kelso Bruce, Mississippi and District of Columbia
Yvonne Braithwaite Burke, California
Richard Harvey Cain, South Carolina
Henry Plummer Cheatham, District of Columbia
Shirley Anita St. Hill Chisholm, New York
James Enos Clyburn, South Carolina
Barbara-Rose Collins, Michigan
Cardiss Robertson Collins, Illinois
William Levi Dawson, Illinois
Robert Carlos DeLarge, South Carolina
Charles Coles Diggs, Jr., Michigan
David Norman Dinkins, New York
Julian Carey Dixon, California
Mervyn Malcolm Dymally, California
Joycelyn Elders, Arkansas
Robert Brown Elliott, South Carolina
Crystal Dreda Bird Fauset, Pennsylvania
Grace Towns Hamilton, Georgia
Jeremiah Haralson, Alabama
Augustus Freeman Hawkins, California
Jesse Louis Jackson, District of Columbia
William Jennings Jefferson, Louisiana
Eddie Bernice Johnson, Texas
Barbara Charline Jordan, Texas
John Mercer Langston, District of Columbia
George Thomas "Mickey" Leland, Texas
John Roy Lynch, Mississippi
Cynthia Ann McKinney, Georgia
Carrie Pittman Meek, Florida
Charles Lewis Mitchell, Massachusetts
Carol Moseley-Braun, Illinois
Constance Baker Motley, New York
Robert Nelson Cornelius Nix, Sr., Pennsylvania
James Edward O'Hara, North Carolina
Major Robert Odell Owens, New York
Carrie Saxon Perry, Connecticut
Pinckney Benton Stewart Pinchback, Louisiana
Georgia Montgomery Davis Powers, Kentucky
Joseph Hayne Rainey, South Carolina
Charles Bernard Rangel, New York
James Thomas Rapier, Alabama
Hiram Rhodes Revels, Mississippi
Robert Smalls, South Carolina
Carl Burton Stokes, Ohio
Clarence Thomas, Missouri
Edolphus Towns, New York
Josiah Thomas Walls, Florida
Harold Washington, Illinois
Maxine Waters, California
Melvin L. Watt, North Carolina
Robert Clifton Weaver, New York
Verda Freeman Welcome, Maryland
Lawrence Douglas Wilder, Virginia

U.S. Advisors and Consultants

Mary McLeod Bethune
Crystal Dreda Bird Fauset
William Herbert Gray III
Carol Moseley-Braun
Robert Clifton Weaver

U.S. Ambassadors and Diplomats

Melvin Herbert Evans, ambassador, Trinidad and Tobago
Patricia Roberts Harris, ambassador, Luxembourg
Jesse Louis Jackson, special envoy, Africa
John Mercer Langston, minister, Haiti, and chargé d'affaires, Santo Domingo

William Alexander Leidesdorff, vice consul, Mexico
Donald F. McHenry, ambassador, United Nations
Carl Thomas Rowan, ambassador, Finland
Carl Burton Stokes, ambassador, Republic of the Seychelles
Andrew Jackson Young, Jr., ambassador, United Nations

U.S. Cabinet Members

Ronald Harmon Brown, secretary, U.S. Department of Commerce
A. Michael "Mike" Espy, secretary, U.S. Department of Agriculture
Patricia Roberts Harris, secretary, U.S. Department of Health and Human Services
Louis Wade Sullivan, secretary, U.S. Department of Health and Human Services
Robert Clifton Weaver, secretary, U.S. Department of Housing and Urban Development

U.S. Congressmen/Congresswomen

Lucien E. Blackwell, Pennsylvania
Yvonne Braithwaite Burke, California
Richard Harvey Cain, South Carolina
Henry Plummer Cheatham, North Carolina
Shirley Anita St. Hill Chisholm, New York
William Lacy Clay, Sr., Missouri
Eva M. Clayton, North Carolina
James Enos Clyburn, South Carolina
Barbara-Rose Collins, Michigan
Cardiss Robertson Collins, Illinois
George Washington Collins, Illinois
John Conyers, Jr., Michigan
William Levi Dawson, Illinois
Robert Carlos DeLarge, South Carolina
Ronald Vernie Dellums, California
Oscar Stanton De Priest, Illinois
Charles Coles Diggs, Jr., Michigan
Julian Carey Dixon, California
Mervyn Malcolm Dymally, California
Robert Brown Elliott, South Carolina
A. Michael "Mike" Espy, Mississippi
Melvin Herbert Evans, Virgin Islands
Walter Edward Fauntroy, District of Columbia
Floyd H. Flake, New York
Gary A. Franks, Connecticut
William Herbert Gray III, Pennsylvania
Jeremiah Haralson, Alabama
Alcee Lamar Hastings, Florida
Augustus Freeman Hawkins, California
Charles Arthur Hayes, Illinois
William Jennings Jefferson, Louisiana
Eddie Bernice Johnson, Texas
Barbara Charline Jordan, Texas
John Mercer Langston, Virginia
George Thomas "Mickey" Leland, Texas
John Lewis, Georgia
Jefferson Franklin Long, Georgia
John Roy Lynch, Mississippi
Cynthia Ann McKinney, Georgia
Carrie Pittman Meek, Florida
Ralph Harold Metcalfe, Illinois
Kweisi Mfume, Maryland
Arthur Wergs Mitchell, Illinois
Parren James Mitchell, Maryland
Robert Nelson Cornelius Nix, Sr., Pennsylvania
Eleanor Holmes Norton, District of Columbia
James Edward O'Hara, North Carolina
Major Robert Odell Owens, New York
Adam Clayton Powell, Jr., New York
Joseph Hayne Rainey, South Carolina
Charles Bernard Rangel, New York
James Thomas Rapier, Alabama
Gustavus "Gus" Savage, Illinois
Robert Smalls, South Carolina
Louis Stokes, Ohio
Edolphus Towns, New York
Benjamin Sterling Turner, Alabama
Josiah Thomas Walls, Florida
Harold Washington, Illinois
Maxine Waters, California
Melvin L. Watt, North Carolina
Andrew Jackson Young, Jr., Georgia

U.S. Senators

Edward William Brooke III, Massachusetts
Blanche Kelso Bruce, Mississippi
Carol Moseley-Braun, Illinois
Hiram Rhodes Revels, Mississippi

U.S. Surgeon General

Joycelyn Elders

Appendix 3

African American Political and Governmental Leaders by State

(including the District of Columbia and Virgin Islands)

Alabama

Jeremiah Haralson
James Thomas Rapier
Benjamin Sterling Turner

Arkansas

Joycelyn Elders

California

Thomas Bradley
Willie L. Brown, Jr.
Yvonne Braithwaite Burke
Ronald Vernie Dellums
Julian Carey Dixon
Mervyn Malcolm Dymally
Augustus Freeman Hawkins
William Alexander Leidesdorff
Maxine Waters

Connecticut

Gary A. Franks
Carrie Saxon Perry

District of Columbia

Marion S. Barry, Jr.
Ronald Harmon Brown
Walter Edward Fauntroy
Patricia Roberts Harris
Sharon Pratt Dixon Kelly
Donald F. McHenry
Eleanor Holmes Norton
Walter Edward Washington

Florida

Mary McLeod Bethune
Alcee Lamar Hastings
Carrie Pittman Meek
Josiah Thomas Walls

Georgia

Julian Bond
Grace Towns Hamilton
Maynard Holbrook Jackson, Jr.
John Lewis
Jefferson Franklin Long
Cynthia Ann McKinney
Andrew Jackson Young, Jr.

Illinois

Cardiss Robertson Collins
George Washington Collins
William Levi Dawson
Oscar Stanton De Priest
Charles Arthur Hayes
Jesse Louis Jackson
Ralph Harold Metcalfe
Arthur Wergs Mitchell
Carol Moseley-Braun
Gustavus "Gus" Savage

Harold Washington
Robert Clifton Weaver

Indiana

Richard Gordon Hatcher

Kentucky

Georgia Montgomery Davis Powers

Louisiana

William Jennings Jefferson
Pinckney Benton Stewart Pinchback

Maryland

Kweisi Mfume
Parren James Mitchell
Verda Freeman Welcome

Massachusetts

Edward William Brooke III
Charles Lewis Mitchell

Michigan

Barbara-Rose Collins
John Conyers, Jr.
Charles Coles Diggs, Jr.

Mississippi

Unita Z. Blackwell
Blanche Kelso Bruce
A. Michael "Mike" Espy
James Charles Evers
John Roy Lynch
Hiram Rhodes Revels

Missouri

William Lacy Clay, Sr.

New Jersey

Kenneth Allen Gibson

New York

Shirley Anita St. Hill Chisholm
David Norman Dinkins
Floyd H. Flake
Constance Baker Motley
Major Robert Odell Owens
Adam Clayton Powell, Jr.
Charles Bernard Rangel
Edolphus Towns
Walter Edward Washington
Robert Clifton Weaver

North Carolina

Henry Plummer Cheatham
Eva M. Clayton
James Edward O'Hara
Melvin L. Watt

Ohio

Benjamin William Arnett
Carl Burton Stokes
Louis Stokes

Oklahoma

Hannah Diggs Atkins

Pennsylvania

Lucien E. Blackwell
Crystal Dreda Bird Fauset
Woodrow Wilson Goode
William Herbert Gray III
Robert Nelson Cornelius Nix, Sr.

South Carolina

Richard Harvey Cain
James Enos Clyburn
Robert Carlos DeLarge
Robert Brown Elliott
Joseph Hayne Rainey
Robert Smalls

Texas

Eddie Bernice Johnson
Barbara Charline Jordan
George Thomas "Mickey" Leland

Virginia

John Mercer Langston
Lawrence Douglas Wilder

Virgin Islands

Melvin Herbert Evans

Appendix 4

Selected African American Political and Governmental Leaders by Party Affiliation

Mayors

Name	Party Affiliation	City and State	Term of Office
Barry, Marion S., Jr.	D	Washington, D.C.	1978–90, 1994
Blackwell, Unita Z.	D	Mayersville, Miss.	1976–92, 1996–
Bradley, Thomas	D	Los Angeles, Calif.	1973–93
Brown, Willie L., Jr.	D	San Francisco, Calif.	1995–
Dinkins, David Norman	D	New York, N.Y.	1990–93
Evers, James Charles	D	Fayette, Miss.	1969–89
Gibson, Kenneth Allen	D	Newark, N.J.	1970–86
Goode, Woodrow Wilson	D	Philadelphia, Pa.	1984–92
Hatcher, Richard Gordon	D	Gary, Ind.	1967–75
Jackson, Maynard Holbrook, Jr.		Atlanta, Ga.	1973–81, 1989–97
Kelly, Sharon Pratt Dixon	D	Washington, D.C.	1991–95
Perry, Carrie Saxon	D	Hartford, Conn.	1987–91
Stokes, Carl Burton	D	Cleveland, Ohio	1967–72
Washington, Harold	D	Chicago, Ill.	1983–87
Washington, Walter Edward	D	Washington, D.C.	1967–78
Young, Andrew Jackson, Jr.	D	Atlanta, Ga.	1982–90

Governors

Name	Party Affiliation	State or Territory	Term of Office
Evans, Melvin Herbert	R	U.S. Virgin Islands	1969–75
Pinchback, Pinckney Benton Stewart	R	Louisiana	Dec. 1872–Jan. 1873
Wilder, Lawrence Douglas	D	Virginia	1990–94

U.S. Congressional Representatives

Name	Party Affiliation	State	Term of Office
Blackwell, Lucien E.	D	Pennsylvania	1991–94
Burke, Yvonne Braithwaite	D	California	1973–78
Cain, Richard Harvey	R	South Carolina	1872–74, 1877–79
Cheatham, Henry Plummer	R	North Carolina	1889–93
Chisholm, Shirley Anita St. Hill	D	New York	1969–82
Clay, William Lacy, Sr.	D	Missouri	1969–
Clayton, Eva M.	D	North Carolina	1993–
Clyburn, James Enos	D	South Carolina	1993–
Collins, Barbara-Rose	D	Michigan	1991, 1992–97
Collins, Cardiss Robertson	D	Illinois	1973–96
Collins, George Washington	D	Illinois	1970–72
Conyers, John, Jr.	D	Michigan	1965–
Dawson, William Levi	D	Illinois	1943–70
DeLarge, Robert Carlos	R	South Carolina	1871–73
Dellums, Ronald Vernie	D	California	1970–98
De Priest, Oscar Stanton	R	Illinois	1929–35
Diggs, Charles Coles, Jr.	D	Michigan	1955–80
Dixon, Julian Carey	D	California	1979–
Dymally, Mervyn Malcolm	D	California	1981–92
Elliott, Robert Brown	R	South Carolina	1871–72, 1873–74
Espy, A. Michael	D	Mississippi	1987–93
Evans, Melvin Herbert	R	U.S. Virgin Islands	1979–80
Fauntroy, Walter Edward	D	District of Columbia	1971–90
Flake, Floyd H.	D	New York	1986–97
Franks, Gary A.	R	Connecticut	1990–97
Gray, William Herbert, III	D	Pennsylvania	1979–91
Haralson, Jeremiah	R	Alabama	1875–77
Hastings, Alcee Lamar	D	Florida	1993–
Hawkins, Augustus Freeman	D	California	1963–90
Hayes, Charles Arthur	D	Illinois	1983–92
Jefferson, William Jennings	D	Louisiana	1991–
Johnson, Eddie Bernice	D	Texas	1993–
Jordan, Barbara Charline	D	Texas	1973–79

Langston, John Mercer	R	Virginia	1890–91
Leland, George Thomas	D	Texas	1979–89
Lewis, John	D	Georgia	1987–
Long, Jefferson Franklin	R	Georgia	1871
Lynch, John Roy	R	Mississippi	1873–77, 1882–83
McKinney, Cynthia Ann	D	Georgia	1993–
Meek, Carrie Pittman	D	Florida	1993–
Metcalfe, Ralph Harold	D	Illinois	1971–78
Mfume, Kweisi	D	Maryland	1987–96
Mitchell, Arthur Wergs	D	Illinois	1935–43
Mitchell, Parren James	D	Maryland	1971–87
Nix, Robert Nelson Cornelius, Sr.	D	Pennsylvania	1958–79
Norton, Eleanor Holmes	D	District of Columbia	1991–
O'Hara, James Edward	R	North Carolina	1883–87
Owens, Major Robert Odell	D	New York	1983–
Powell, Adam Clayton, Jr.	D	New York	1945–67, 1969–70
Rainey, Joseph Hayne	R	South Carolina	1870–79
Rangel, Charles Bernard	D	New York	1970–
Rapier, James Thomas	R	Alabama	1873–75
Savage, Gustavus	D	Illinois	1981–92
Smalls, Robert	R	South Carolina	1875–79, 1882–83, 1884–87
Stokes, Louis	D	Ohio	1969–98
Towns, Edolphus	D	New York	1982–
Turner, Benjamin Sterling	R	Alabama	1871–73
Walls, Josiah Thomas	R	Florida	1871–75
Washington, Harold	D	Illinois	1981–83
Waters, Maxine	D	California	1990–
Watt, Melvin L.	D	North Carolina	1993–
Young, Andrew Jackson, Jr.	D	Georgia	1973–77

U.S. Senators

Name	Party Affiliation	State	Term of Office
Brooke, Edward William, III	R	Massachusetts	1967–79
Bruce, Blanche Kelso	R	Mississippi	1875–81
Moseley-Braun, Carol	D	Illinois	1993–98
Revels, Hiram Rhodes	R	Mississippi	1870–71

Index

by Linda Webster

Boldface page numbers refer to photographs.